On the Edge of the Abyss

On the Edge of the Abyss

THE JEWISH UNCONSCIOUS
BEFORE FREUD

Clémence Boulouque

The University of Chicago Press   CHICAGO AND LONDON

The University of Chicago Press, Chicago 60637
The University of Chicago Press, Ltd., London
© 2025 by The University of Chicago
All rights reserved. No part of this book may be used or reproduced in any manner whatsoever without written permission, except in the case of brief quotations in critical articles and reviews. For more information, contact the University of Chicago Press, 1427 E. 60th St., Chicago, IL 60637.
Published 2025

34 33 32 31 30 29 28 27 26 25   1 2 3 4 5

ISBN-13: 978-0-226-83820-5 (cloth)
ISBN-13: 978-0-226-83821-2 (paper)
ISBN-13: 978-0-226-83822-9 (e-book)
DOI: https://doi.org/10.7208/chicago/9780226838229.001.0001

Library of Congress Cataloging-in-Publication Data

Names: Boulouque, Clémence, author.
Title: On the edge of the abyss : the Jewish unconscious before Freud / Clémence Boulouque.
Description: Chicago : The University of Chicago Press, 2025. | Includes bibliographical references and index.
Identifiers: LCCN 2024026541 | ISBN 9780226838205 (cloth) | ISBN 9780226838212 (paperback) | ISBN 9780226838229 (ebook)
Subjects: LCSH: Subconsciousness—Philosophy. | Jewish philosophy—19th century. | Psychology—Religious aspects—Judaism. | Cabala—Psychological aspects. | Wissenschaft des Judentums (Movement)
Classification: LCC BF315 .B665 2025 | DDC 154.2—dc23/eng/20240807
LC record available at https://lccn.loc.gov/2024026541

Contents

Introduction * 1

PART I: BEYOND REASON: *The Unconscious as a Bond for Humanity* * 17

1. The Kabbalistic Genesis of the Unconscious: Schelling's Legacy * 21
2. Schelling's Jewish Receptions: Kabbalah and/as the Unconscious * 37
3. The Margins of Reason: The *Wissenschaft des Judentums*, Kabbalah Studies, and the Emerging Science of the Mind * 63
4. Emerson's Oversoul, "American Religion," and Kabbalistic Motives * 87

PART II: THE MIND AS BATTLEGROUND: *The Collective Psyche in Jewish Thought and the Many Claims to the Unconscious* * 105

5. Jewish Spirit, National Spirit, and Absolute Spirit: Building Blocks of the Collective Unconscious and the Defense of Judaism * 109
6. *Völkerpsychologie*: A Psychology of Culture against a Race-Based Spirit * 119
7. The Unconscious as Mystique? Hartmann's *Philosophy of the Unconscious* and Its Jewish Critics * 145
8. The "Retrospective Unconscious": Reading the Jewish Tradition as Psychology * 165

Coda * 197

Acknowledgments * 201
Notes * 203
Bibliography * 253
Index * 305

Introduction

The Freudian unconscious ushered in the twentieth century. Published on the cusp of 1900, Sigmund Freud's *Die Traumdeutung* (*The Interpretation of Dreams*) set out to illuminate the workings of the unconscious by analyzing dreams—which, he argued, represent conflicts, wish fulfillment, and unconscious desires. In his theory of dreamwork, the mechanisms of condensation and displacement cipher latent contents into manifest ones, and it is incumbent on the analyst to facilitate the exploration of the repressed contents embedded within the dream through the technique of free association.

By Freud's time, the idea of the unconscious had in fact been developing for a full century. Throughout that period, however, the unconscious was understood in a philosophical, rather than a scientific, light. Before Freud's work, as he himself pointed out, it was "philosophy, and not the exact sciences" that had "dominated the mind."[1] Indeed, it was the philosopher Friedrich Wilhelm Joseph von Schelling who first used the noun "the Unconscious" (*das Unbewusste*), in his *System des transcendentalen Idealismus* (*System of Transcendental Idealism*), published in 1800.[2] In the wake of Schelling and throughout the nineteenth century, several generations of philosophers developed the concept in great depth.

The pre-Freudian unconscious was a porous notion, a border concept inflected with tropes derived from Jewish mysticism. It operated at the intersection of philosophy, theology, and the nascent science of the mind. While Freud's own Jewishness and his Jewish sources and influences have been analyzed in many publications, the Jewishness of the pre-Freudian philosophical unconscious has only been dimly perceived.[3] Precisely because of the fluidity of the concept and its seeming affinities with their own tradition, the new notion was embraced by a range of Jewish thinkers, from proponents of the Reform movement to advocates of Orthodoxy.

This book is the first extensive study of the pre-Freudian unconscious in Jewish thought, but it also demonstrates the intercultural origins of the concept and the deep intertwining of Jewish and non-Jewish thought in its emergence.[4] Engaging in conversation with current scholarship at the confluence of religion, psychoanalysis, and intellectual and cultural history, I examine how the notion of an unconscious became part of public discourse in the long nineteenth century.[5] Drawing on previous studies of the pre-Freudian unconscious as a narrative of cultural history, I explore the contexts and motivations for the embrace of the budding concept specifically among Jewish thinkers.[6] I find that they turned the notion into a defense against perceptions of Judaism as a source of alienation, materialism, and dry rationalism by showing its perceptiveness regarding the human psyche and its adequacy to the modern age. They also grounded it in the conversations of the specific national ethoses and societies to which they aspired to belong. In fact, the history of the Jewish reception of the unconscious before Freud provides a lens through which to tell a novel and multilayered intellectual and cultural history of Jewish emancipation: that of a minority reappropriating its own tradition in an early instance of self-affirmation. Such a gesture should shed light on similar attempts by other minority groups to reposition themselves as full participants, if not originators, of a paradigm shift as well as provide a new narrative of either their contribution to mainstream culture or the indebtedness of a dominant culture toward them.

In these pages, I attempt to decipher the rationale that pushed a range of Jewish intellectuals to recognize the unconscious as a usable and reclaimable tool and to build on it to defend their own tradition as having made a key contribution to modernity. Indeed, through the unconscious they sought to promote their theological and ideological agendas by showing how Judaism—understood expansively and as a worldview comprising the biblical, rabbinical, and kabbalistic traditions—had anticipated the most recent discoveries about the workings of the mind. Thus, by demonstrating the validity of Judaism's conceptual apparatus and by reappropriating the motifs drawn from Judaism that permeated the philosophical and the public discourses of the time, these thinkers aimed to deliver its universal and timeless truths and to inscribe Judaism in modernity.

The Early Discourse of the Unconscious and Its Jewish Reception

The principal exponents of the idea of the unconscious in the nineteenth century—Friedrich Wilhelm von Schelling, Carl Gustav Carus, and Eduard von Hartmann—couched the notion in metaphysical, even mystical language. But that century was also defined by another strand of thought, positivism, which saw itself as bringing philosophy and science together. Positivism was averse to metaphysical speculations; a metaphysical unconscious was thus at odds with that part of the ethos.[7] A handful of Jewish thinkers, however, strove to break these dichotomies through religiously inflected concepts, such as progressive revelation, according to which nothing is outside the realm of the divine, not least scientific discoveries that are part of a supernatural design.[8]

The initial proximity of the concept of the unconscious to religious language explains the resistance to this notion in the later part of the nineteenth century. One of the pioneers of clinical psychology, Gustav Theodor Fechner (1801–1887), called the unconscious a "survival from psychological mysticism."[9] The influential psychologist Paul Janet (1823–1899) later advocated abandoning the term altogether, judging it too fraught with metaphysical overtones, and coined the term *subconscious* as a replacement.[10] In 1933, reminiscing about the beginnings of his endeavor in his *Vorlesungen zur Einführung in die Psychoanalyse* (*New Introductory Lectures on Psycho-Analysis*), Freud pointed out the parallel between "mystical practices" and psychoanalysis and explained how he had had to disentangle the new field of knowledge he had created from religious belief systems.[11] Taking an opposing stance, Theodor Lipps (1851–1914), who built a bridge between philosophy and psychology and in 1883 published a comprehensive survey of psychology, *Grundtatsachen des Seelenlebens* (*The Fundamental Facts of the Inner Life*), gave specific attention to the unconscious.[12] His talk on the topic at the Third International Congress of Psychology in 1896 defended the unconscious against the lingering suspicion of covert metaphysics.[13]

Building on the scholarship that explores the tensions and affinities between religion (specifically mysticism) and psychology, this study probes these porosities and the reception of the new theories of the psyche in the nineteenth century.[14] While the history of this reception by other religious communities remains to be written,[15] I find that Jewish thinkers were uniquely attuned to the unconscious because they could identify the recognizably Jewish genealogy of the discourse on the unconscious in the writings of its first exponent, Schelling, and in German idealism in general.

In his seminal 1961 essay, "The German Idealism of Jewish Philosophers," Jürgen Habermas vindicates the position of these nineteenth-century Jewish thinkers, who were eager to reclaim this relationship between their tradition and German thought[16] and to reclaim more generally the previously subterranean influence of Kabbalah.

> It remains astonishing how productively central motifs of the philosophy of German Idealism shaped so essentially by Protestantism can be developed in terms of the experience of the Jewish tradition. Because the legacy of the Kabbalah already flowed into and was absorbed by Idealism, its light seems to refract all the more richly in the spectrum of a spirit in which something of the spirit of Jewish mysticism lives on, in however hidden a way.[17]

Yet, already in the nineteenth century, a handful of Jewish thinkers had taken notice of how the legacy of Kabbalah had enriched idealism. The fact that Schelling's philosophy was based in part on veiled kabbalistic elements, especially the mythopoetic dimension of Kabbalah, appeared to indicate the worthiness of Judaism, and it behooved Jewish thinkers to label explicitly as Kabbalah that which had hitherto gone unattributed.

I will argue that the Jewish gesture of reclaiming the theories of the unconscious was an instance of self-assertion—a proclamation by Jews that Judaism offers a cultural and religious tradition valuable to all, a form of universalism validated by scientific discoveries. Such a stance of self-affirmation signals, and belongs to, a shift that characterizes the discourse of modernity.[18] Indeed, Jewish thinkers sought to marshal scientific findings, principles, and methods in order to affirm the validity and relevance of Judaism writ large in contemporary debates.

Paul Ricœur explores the relationship of psychology to modern culture in his book *Freud and Philosophy*: "By interpreting culture, it modifies it; by giving it an instrument of reflection it stamps it with a lasting mark."[19] The same can be said of the pre-Freudian unconscious and of the Jewish interpreters of that unconscious, who were eager to make the dominant culture aware of its indebtedness to Judaism as well as to modify that ethos. By interpreting the unconscious in a Jewish key or by showing how Schelling's depiction of the unconscious, described as a dissociation of the self and a repository of myths, was actually a transposition of Jewish motifs, they advanced the idea that Judaism could be seen "more as an interpretative and mythical tradition than a mystical one," in the words of Harold Bloom.[20]

Between Assimilation and Accommodation

The appropriation or rejection of science or of emerging scientific concepts is a significant marker of religious or political identity. When Jewish thinkers invoked the figures of myths or of the unconscious, it was an act of *re*appropriation and thus of assertive repossession. This is because Schelling's image of the unconscious (the *Ungrund*—the "unground," abyss, depth, or groundless ground), created by divine contraction, draws on concepts immediately identifiable as belonging to the Jewish tradition, especially *tsimtsum*, the divine contraction or retraction. This kind of appropriation goes against Ricœur's argument, in *Hermeneutics and the Human Sciences*, that appropriation—absorbing an alien concept from a different culture—is more akin to a dispossession than a possession.[21]

More broadly, probing the Ricœurian categories of the cultural appropriation of notions at the intersection of science, philosophy, and the arts can raise the question of the strategy of religious groups facing new concepts and aligning their positions with the cultural conversations of their time. In order to refine the narrative of assimilation—generally understood as the erasure of differences—the Jewish-German existentialist philosopher and theologian Franz Rosenzweig (1886–1929) coined the term *dis*similation in 1922. ("In every age, alongside the obvious phenomenon of assimilation, we can notice the dissimilation that always accompanies it.")[22] His philosophy sought to explore the articulations between the individual and revelation, specifically the consciousness of the "I" in relation to God, as well as the relation between Judaism and Christianity and between Germans and Jews. To be sure, a narrative of subversion has rightly drawn attention to the dissenting voices of Jewish thinkers in modernity.[23] But the search by Jewish intellectuals for a common stock of concepts in German philosophy—as part of their efforts to testify to the affinity between Judaism and Germanness and as a strategy for occupying a position in the polity—should not be ignored.[24]

Specifically, reframing as Jewish the mythopoetic roots of the concept of the unconscious essentially meant revisiting the original way of grasping a spiritual truth, coupled with an urge to create a sense of unity by narrowing the gap between the self and the world.²⁵ Emphasizing the mystical unconscious also amounted to a reappropriation of a stock of ostensibly German references that were duly returned to the Jewish tradition, whether undertaken as affirmative apologetics for Hasidism or as an instance of the Jewish contribution to civilization and culture by advocates of emancipation. Apologetics, in this case, need not be an exercise in justification. I am calling their endeavor "affirmative apologetics" to differentiate it from a more traditional defense of one's faith "in the face of critical challenge."²⁶ Here is a broader world and system-building proclamation of the value of Judaism, and an illustration of its worth for society as a whole.

The impact of such apologetics, and the new articulation of the unconscious within the Jewish tradition that it provided, went beyond Germany. My study expands to aspects of the intellectual history of Italy, France, Russia, and the United States in the analysis of its reception. Beyond the German model of civic emancipation through education or *Bildung* (a multifaceted concept routinely translated as "culture"), the choice of whether to accommodate or reject the unconscious illuminates a range of national mentalities and cultural proclivities, as we will see in the cases of France and the United States.²⁷ At stake is not simply a convergence of values between Judaism and the host country's dominant narrative—a positivist one in France, for instance—but the claim that Judaism had actually carried these values first, and thus the potential to make a case for the inseparability of Judaism from the various national fabrics and narratives.

The theories of the unconscious advanced by nineteenth-century Jewish thinkers in Germany destabilized the assumption of the primacy of reason as a quintessential social bond, but they also eschewed an increasingly dominant discourse in nationalist circles that hailed the irrational as a marker of German identity. The realm of the unconscious is beyond reason, but exploring it—and theorizing it—does not imply devolving into the irrational.

From Schelling to Hartmann, the emphasis on the mystical roots of the unconscious nuances the claim that a narrative of emancipation had been—and could be—based exclusively on reason and that modernity had dispensed with the mystical.²⁸ The fact that the construction of the unconscious as a discourse accompanied a rediscovery of the Kabbalah, and of mysticism writ large, in a cross-fertilization complicates the claim made by Gershom Scholem, the pioneer of the scholarly study of Jewish mysticism, that the study of mysticism could only be established once the necessity of an emancipation discourse based on Jewish worthiness and reason had been abandoned as futile and ineffective and had been supplanted by an anarchist and, later, Zionist agenda.[29]

Since the early modern period, kabbalistic narratives ceased to be solely understood as a retelling of a primordial historical event—that of the creation of the universe—and became a receptacle of philosophical tools, addressing for instance notions of sovereignty, evil, and language.[30] Expanding on these interpretations, Scholem specifically focused on the writings of the sixteenth-century kabbalist Isaac Luria and his doctrine of the Creation, in which God contracted to make space for a universe that was thus devoid of divine presence. Scholem read this cosmogony as the kabbalists' response to the expulsion from Spain and the exile. God's contraction, the *tsimtsum*, explained his absence later, at critical junctures of history. It was not that the Jews had been abandoned by God, but that God was not present for them because he had exiled himself from this world. This is how Scholem's reading of that cosmogony became, in Bloom's words, "a doctrine of Exile, a theory of influence made to explain Exile."[31] But it is more than a doctrine of exile.

Adding new perspectives to the argument about the link between Kabbalah and exile, I contend that the kabbalistic cosmogony (above all, the tropes about God's retraction) also became, a few centuries later, a discourse about otherness and interdependence, especially when read in the light of Emmanuel Levinas's philosophy of the Other.[32] According to Levinas, the discourse of Western philosophy valorizes sameness or unity as the Good.[33] However, in this narrative of creation ex nihilo, with this generative contraction as a central theme, what is set in motion is a dialectics or dynamics between sameness and otherness. God's contraction creates a space for what is not him; and in this dissociation of God from his own omnipresence, he creates otherness and duality out of his desire for them. This narrative is a stark departure from the traditional Western metaphysics, in which separation, cessation of unity, is seen as a stigma instantiated by, and culminating in, human fallenness. Contraction, on the other hand, is the limitation of an omnipotent and omnipresent power (what Levinas calls totality) that is necessary for the universe to exist (he designates its existence as *infinity*). This contraction actually fosters the Good, because it breaks with an oppressive sameness. Levinas then transposes it to a collective level: "what is at issue is society."[34] And for these thinkers, society—and their place in it—was indeed at stake.

The Schellingian unconscious, the unground or abyss, is also born out of a contraction; it proceeds from this self-limitation. The process is one of differentiation: God wills to extract himself from the totality that he created in a primordial division, in order to make space for what is not him, out of a desire (*Sehnsucht*) for difference.[35] That which is not him is still part of his creation, and from that dissociation the Other emerges. The unconscious thus manifests the presence of the Other as part of oneself that is not one's self but is not completely alien. This unconscious proves that otherness is a necessary part of the individual's psyche. It is on this construct that Jacques Lacan went on to ground his understanding of the unconscious as a way to identify with the Other, *l'Autre*.[36]

In this book, I make a claim that the understanding of the unconscious developed in the nineteenth century set the stage for new understandings of otherness. The idea of *tsimtsum* involves the divine retracting from the universe that it had fully occupied, thereby creating a void where otherness can manifest. Beginning with Friedrich von Schelling, this idea is transposed into the psychological realm, where it becomes the unconscious—a place of emptiness, a void that makes space for otherness even within oneself. The reception of the pre-Freudian unconscious in Jewish thought, shaped by a Schellingian reinterpretation of Kabbalah, also needs to be understood that way. Centered less on the individual (which will be a feature of the Freudian concept) than on the collective psyche, the very concept of the unconscious establishes the presence of, and need for, alterity in social, political, and theological perspectives. The narrative could be geared toward a non-Jewish audience (as an invitation to make space for this specific minority group) as well as a Jewish one. Jews could not ignore the fact that they constituted the Other in national narratives and in the body politic, but the kabbalistic and Schellingian paradigm of *tsimtsum* (the subject of part 1), predicated on the necessity of making space for Jews as the Other, gave them a philosophical template by which to assert that they belonged.

Jewish thinkers turned to this protopsychology as a response to an increasingly oppressive nationalism coupled with the advent of racialization—and the newly coined anti-Semitism—meant to expel them from national communities. Their emphasis on a collective psyche, which served as a veiled discourse about the value of plurality, and the harmony between one's self and the Other in a polity took on a new significance at the turn of the twentieth century. After having devoted their careers to the notion of a collective spirit in an effort to dispel the race-based idea of Spirit (*Geist*), and after having been defeated by the ethos of the time and its scientific racism, the key exponents, notably Moritz Lazarus and Heymann Steinthal, would later write treatises on ethics in which they emphasized the place of the Other in society as a moral imperative. This anticipated one of Lacan's conclusions, that "the status of the unconscious is ethical and not ontic"—that is, rather than mere fact, it entails a duty: the obligation to recognize what is other in oneself, from one's psyche to a capacious national identity enriched by multiple minorities.[37] This metaphysically inflected, ethical, and collective understanding of the unconscious in nineteenth-century Germany would soon be toppled and replaced by an a-religious and individual-focused twentieth-century version, theorized in Vienna: Sigmund Freud's. Indeed, the death drive of the Freudian unconscious wrecked the hopes of universalism and of coexistence that were at the core of its precursor, developed in Berlin.

The Roads Not Taken: Avoiding a Freudian Teleology

In thinking through the Jewishness of the pre-Freudian unconscious, it is imperative to avoid a teleology, a predetermined, inevitable path to the Freudian unconscious. One should not misread the thinking of the prior century as "unconceptualized psychoanalysis."[38] All the more so because Freud himself, a few years after *The Interpretation of Dreams* (1900), acknowledged the differences and further staked out his territory, claiming, "Our unconscious is not quite the same as that of the philosophers and what is more, most philosophers wish to know nothing of the 'psychical unconscious.'"[39] When probing Freud's contribution, and acrimoniously distancing himself from his past mentor, Carl Gustav Jung notably played down the Viennese physician's role, writing, "I had these thoughts long before I came to Freud. *Unconscious* is an *epistemological* term deriving from Von Hartmann. Freud was not much of a philosopher; he was strictly a medical man. I had read these philosophers long before I ever saw Freud."[40]

The use of novel philosophical and scientific concepts to bolster the legitimacy of one's religious tradition was definitely part of the ethos of the time, a time when thinkers shaped the pre-Freudian unconscious by projecting the Schellingian unconscious back onto images or myths that predated his construct.[41] To describe such attempts, I coined the term "retrospective unconscious" (in chapter 8).[42] Kabbalistic insights such as *qadmut ha-sekhel* ("the beginnings of consciousness"), which has been taken to mean the unconscious, were presented in the nineteenth century as intuitions of the pre-Freudian concept itself and were thought to demonstrate the perceptiveness of the communities from which the construct was derived. This was especially true in the case of Hasidism, though advocates of emancipation, including Jews themselves, stigmatized such practices and beliefs as alien to modernity.

The effort to map this Hasidic concept onto the newly dominant psychological version of the unconscious in the late nineteenth century matters more than their exact commensurability, insofar as the retrospective unconscious indicates the stakes of reinscribing the cultural and religious production of a marginal community onto the mainstream scientific discourse. In retracing these efforts and attempting to conjure up and understand the mental and cultural landscape in which they emerged, I disentangle the ways Jewish thinkers came to use certain philosophical and scientific constructs as a validation of Judaism, and then I explore the logic that led them to do so.

Despite the ubiquity of the Freudian concept of the unconscious, even (and especially) in its simplified version, it is important to treat earlier concepts, though seemingly cognates of their Freudian successors, on their own terms and in their own time. Take the term *condensation* (*Verdichtung*), which appeared in the work of the thinker and educator Moritz Lazarus in the 1860s as well as in the writings of his close associate Heymann Steinthal. It is impossible to ignore that Freud himself employed this rare term, and indeed its centrality in *The Interpretation of Dreams*. It is a key part of Freud's dreamwork—the transformation process that articulates the latent and the manifest contents of the dream and its symbolization system. Yet the earlier proponents of condensation used it to designate a different process of the aggregation of memories. This understanding of the unconscious in terms of condensation resembles Henri Bergson's notion of the unconscious as mnemonic layers, which cannot be conflated with its psychoanalytical meaning.[43] While the Freudian terminology and concepts are now the dominant references we use to talk about the unconscious, nineteenth-century conceptions also give us insights into the roads not taken, such as the concept of the unthought, which might have inspired psychoanalysis but fell into oblivion—and could now be mobilized for a novel critique of psychoanalysis.

Examining the concept without a Freudian teleology is all the more important because, as I have noted, this study spans the long nineteenth century, ending with the First World War. Between 1869—when Eduard von Hartmann's *Philosophy of the Unconscious* came out—and the 1920s, most theories of the unconscious in general circulation were arguably predicated almost exclusively on Hartmann's terms, which were brimming with a metaphysical but somewhat abstract pessimism and lacking any therapeutic ambition or value. It was the shell-shocked generation of the 1920s, requiring new remedies for coping with the trauma of the war, that would draw the Freudian unconscious into the public discourse, attempting to make sense of a traumatized civilization and its discontents.

Freud arguably had no significant impact on Jewish theological leaders until the 1920s at the earliest[44]—and in the United States, it was the subsequent influx of refugees from Nazi Germany that brought his ideas into the mainstream.[45] The first phase of the popularization of Freudianism was contentious or at least complex. A young rabbi, Joshua Loth Liebman, challenged the argument contained in Freud's *Future of an Illusion* (1927), that religion is a neurosis. Liebman, the first prominent public figure to admit that he had undergone psychotherapy, saw Freud as an ally in self-help and essentially a way to cope with postwar grief. However, he toned down the text's curative aspect and presented the Jewish tradition to non-Jewish audiences as a better therapeutic tool.[46] But in effect, Freudianism had won out. The lingering presence of Hartmann is only discreetly mentioned in Jungian psychology, even if he heavily relies on its concepts. In France, his legacy, by way of a Bergsonian unconscious, can mostly be identified in philosophy—namely, in the writings of Maurice Merleau-Ponty and Gilles Deleuze.[47]

The study of the pre-Freudian unconscious spans multiple countries and traditions; and while Schelling may have coined the term, its roots go back even further and in multiple directions that exceed a Schellingian origin. There is a rhizomic or nonlinear quality to the nascent conception of the unconscious, characterized by its subterranean nodes, or hidden webs of influences, and a rupture with the model of arborescence—that is, a vertical and hierarchical understanding of knowledge and Western philosophy.[48] Seeking to unveil some of the subterranean nodes, this study illuminates the multifaceted nature of the nascent concept of both the unconscious and its reappropriations.

My contention is that a generation of Jewish thinkers availed themselves of the notion in order to refute the idea of a disharmony between Judaism and the world—and even to affirm that it belongs in the world—by proposing a Jewish-inflected philosophy or psychology of religion. In doing so, they sought to remedy the seemingly inherent alienation in the modern world and to highlight the Jewish contribution to society.

A novel narrative of emancipation thus emerges. The roots of a cultural or scientific concept are reclaimed by a specific ethnic group in an attempt to find a place in society. That group's relationship to philosophy, and to canonical texts or mainstream concepts in general, charts a new model of a minority's interaction with the majority culture.

The Itinerary of the Book

The first part of the book deals with the paradigm shift brought about by the nineteenth-century unconscious, before Freud developed his own conception of it. Relying on Schelling's work and its kabbalistic inclinations was a way for Jewish thinkers to move past a narrative of reason as the exclusive basis for mutual understanding across communities and for coexistence, which they called a shared humanity. They conceived of the unconscious not as the irrational but as the not-yet-thought: an aspect of the mind that could eventually be illuminated but should at least be accounted for in individual and collective representations, which the Jewish tradition had captured in the form of myths.

Chapter 1 describes Schelling's reliance on the work of Jacob Boehme, the sixteenth-century mystic known as the father of esoteric psychology. Using a stock of tropes and narratives drawn from Jewish mysticism—especially the image of the abyss (*Ungrund*), created by divine contraction (*tsimtsum*) in order for God to make space for what is not God and, by extension, the *I* making space for the *not-I* in order for creation to happen—Boehme turned metaphysics into psychology. Schelling then updated Boehme's innovation by identifying the unconscious with the *Ungrund* and the abyss from which creation can spring forth, thereby reappropriating a cosmogony linking the psyche and the universe.

Chapter 2 recounts how Schelling's Jewish followers perceived a unique potential in his work. His recourse to kabbalistic tropes, the role of myth, and the psychologization of metaphysics seemed to vindicate Jewish thought, to offer a continuity between tradition and modernity, and to remedy the dissonance between them through a mysticism *built* on reason, no longer pitted against it. Schelling's pronouncements also offered a pathway toward understanding and proclaiming the need for otherness, which aptly described the place of the Jews in the national fabric at the time the nation-state emerged.

Chapter 3 tells the story of how the early theories of the unconscious coincided with the nascent Jewish scholarship on Judaism, the *Wissenschaft des Judentums*. The group's proponents initially advocated a study of Judaism based on reason to undergird the credo of Jewish universalism—the idea that the precepts of Judaism are valid for, and beneficial to, all humanity, unrestricted by ethnicity. But their embrace of Schelling's thought encouraged them to seek, in Kabbalah and Jewish thought more generally, universal elements that would transcend reason without being irrational, and would constitute a real basis for the possibility of mutual understanding based on shared mental images and processes that could foster a sense of common humanity.

Chapter 4 shows how the history of the unconscious and its Jewish reception and dissemination spans multiple countries and was particularly important in the United States. Ralph Waldo Emerson channeled Friedrich von Schelling's mystical views and turned kabbalistic tropes into what the literary critic Harold Bloom called "the American religion." But another vehicle for the quiet penetration of Schelling's ideas emerged with the emigration of his Jewish students, whose careers in Germany had been made precarious by the reactionary turn of the mid-1800s. Settling in the United States, they brought Schelling's conceptual apparatus with them, using it to decipher the importance of myth in the Jewish tradition and in religion in general. Sorting out what corresponded to deep universal human needs from the more contingent and dispensable parts of the tradition was a way to reform Judaism: such a solution would enable both an enduring faithfulness to a trimmed-down faith and a better integration of Jews. These thinkers would go on to become key figures of the Jewish Reform movement in the United States, contributing to the making of "the American religion."

The second part of the book details the politicization of the unconscious before Freud, more specifically the transformation of the unconscious into a battleground between conflicting narratives of belonging. The idea of the unconscious seemed to call reason into question as the exclusive path toward greater insights into the workings of the mind or as a way to foster bonds for coexistence. The role of psychology, and of the unconscious, understood as *collective* unconscious and a form of intervention in the public discourse, would become more prevalent as the nineteenth century unfolded.

Chapter 5 examines the philosophical building blocks of the collective unconscious, starting with the Italian philosopher Giovanni Battista Vico's concept of poetic universals, Johann Gottfried von Herder's "spirit of humanity," and the "absolute spirit" in Georg Wilhelm Friedrich Hegel. I argue that Jewish thinkers such as Nachman Krochmal seized on the notion to promote what they saw as evidence of the specific bond between the Jews and the absolute spirit, and to thereby dismiss accusations of Jewish alienation present in the writings of Immanuel Kant and Hegel.

Chapter 6 examines the founders of *Völkerpsychologie*, Moritz Lazarus and Heymann Steinthal. They framed the workings of the psyche as evidence of a universal human connectedness, capable of fending off an increased nationalization of the notion of *Geist*, Spirit, which was being instrumentalized against "rootless" Jews in novel tropes of anti-Semitic discourse. Unable to find a place at a German university in the face of this hostile environment, Lazarus and Steinthal increasingly gravitated back to the Jewish tradition, grounding their understanding of psychology in ethics and later writing treatises on Jewish ethics. Their worldview remains obliquely present in the work of some of their students on alienation, most important the sociologist Georg Simmel.

Chapter 7 probes Jewish thinkers' reception of *Philosophy of the Unconscious*, the major work by the foremost figure of the popularization of the unconscious in the nineteenth century, Eduard von Hartmann; they saw in it a unifying principle needed to mend the fractures of modernity. Hartmann established the concept as a worldview, a monistic principle encompassing the relationship between the individual and the universal, a reconciliation between micro- and macrocosm, in which he saw a regenerative principle—a key to the future of Christianity and of religions in general as well as a usable system of ethics. His praise of mysticism and the metaphysical undertones of the concept drew the criticism of a generation of German Jewish thinkers, including Lazarus and Steinthal, who favored a reason-based understanding of religion and the psyche. At the same time, it attracted a younger generation of thinkers, such as Ernst Bloch, who saw there the potential to describe a messianic force. It drew criticism from French Jewish thinkers such as Adolphe Franck, who saw the concept as an instance of the German attraction to the irrational, thus at odds with the mysticism of reason and progress that defined Franco-Judaism. The Jewish reception of the unconscious had become a fault line between generations and nations.

The final chapter describes the "retrospective unconscious," a projection of the contemporary concept on older traditions. It explores how the concept was co-opted by a generation of Jewish Orthodox thinkers in multiple countries. They include Ahron Marcus in Germany, who sought to show how Hasidism had anticipated the latest scientific discoveries, and the Italian thinker Elia Benamozegh, who used Hartmann to validate the concept of progressive revelation, through which science and religion would be reconciled. At the cusp of the twentieth century, the figure of Hartmann also appears in the trajectory of Ernst Bloch's and Martin Buber's return to, or reinterpretation of, Judaism: for Bloch, this was found in the understanding of the rationalism of the irrational, and for Buber, in a turn to mysticism as a form of ethics. Their interpretations of the unconscious showed how key concepts of the secular world could be enriched by introducing aspects of religious traditions, thus demonstrating how they had always been a subterranean cultural presence and could be used to neutralize the dichotomy between religion and secularism.[49]

❉ PART I ❉
Beyond Reason
The Unconscious as a Bond for Humanity

Understanding the place of the nascent concept of the unconscious within the context of broader cultural debates of the nineteenth century requires assessing its articulation with reason, the construct that arguably defined the self-understanding of modernity. Friedrich Wilhelm Joseph von Schelling (1775–1854) posited the existence of the unconscious in his *System of Transcendental Idealism* in 1800. Ten years later, he argued that the origins of the natural world—and of the individual psyche—are opaque. They are buried in what he called "the deepest night of the past": "Darkness and concealment are the character of the primordial age. All life first forms itself and comes into being in the night," he professed.[1] Such a tragic, anxiety-ridden relation to the past, entailing the impossibility of knowledge and self-knowledge and the limitation of reason, inscribes him in a Romantic tradition, possibly an antimodern one.

Because he equated nature with history, and because both lie hidden, Schelling held that "it is precisely this past that is borne by the present creation, and that still remains fundamentally concealed."[2] It has been hypothesized that Schelling's equation of nature and history might have been inspired by his contemporary, the poet Friedrich Schiller (1759–1805), whose ballad, "Das verschleierte Bild zu Sais" (The Veiled Image to Sais), invokes the mysteries around the cult of Isis, with the goddess proclaiming, "I am what then was, what is, and what will be: no mortal has lifted my veil."[3] The goddess's striking pronouncement echoes the words of the biblical God in the theophany of the burning bush (Exod. 3:1–4:23): "I am who I am" (Eyeh asher eyeh), but more accurately translated as "I will be who I will be." Since the Hebrew language has no present tense for "to be," the phrase denotes both past and future and has been interpreted as God's eternity.

The framing of history and nature as mysteries also implies that only initiates can understand them, a trope common to the Jewish and Greek traditions. This stands in contrast to Ludwig Feuerbach's assumption that the driving force of history is the act of lifting the veil, of pushing the boundaries of what is accessible to human intelligence, and that this would be the imperative of an Enlightened humanity.[4] The claim that a significant part of the Enlightenment project was about humankind illuminating its own past puts it at odds with the Romantic tradition, in which the source of life is dark and unknowable. This is a tradition to which Schelling belongs and with which he shared a penchant for the esoteric.[5] The symbolism of Isis contained in Heraclitus's enigmatic aphorism, "Nature loves to hide," as well as the meaning of its inscrutability, has led to a variety of interpretations. Schelling and other commentators seem to have oscillated between a Promethean reading, eager to unveil the meaning of both nature and history, and an Orphic contemplation of the awe and sacrality of nature.

Reflecting on these approaches, Pierre Hadot has perceived a third avenue, the sublime, which has been explored in art and is couched in myths. Myths are "imagistic modes of expression, adapted for simple people while providing sages with matter for thought," thus telling the truth hiding behind fiction.[6] These foundational myths represent principles that will unfold in history or in the human spirit. In his view, these principles, or "potencies," ought to be deciphered, and pondered.[7] This approach resonates with Schelling's dictum in *Die Weltalter* (*The Ages of the World*), that "all development presupposed envelopment."[8] The primordial envelopment, in Schelling's view, is the contraction from which the creation of the universe can unfold—an image closely resembling kabbalistic cosmogony.

In this invocation of the dark and obscure nature of beginnings and the unknowable, Schelling appears to belong to the legacy of the anti-Enlightenment. A more nuanced picture emerges, however, if one examines him from the standpoint of Jewish thinkers. For Schelling, because the soul emanates from the same source as the universe, it has a "co-knowledge" (*Mitwissenschaft*) of its origin.[9] This can also be translated as "shared science," literally a "con-science" (*mit* signifying "with," and *Wissenschaft*, "science"). Myths, he proposed, are a place of revelation through the telling of a story (he used the model of Platonic myths to sustain his argument), concretizing abstractions and enabling this deeper understanding, this shared science, of the world. They are means through which the mind accesses self-consciousness, and they are a pivotal stage of religious consciousness, because they allow the mind to contact its transcendent dimension. They make the finite emanations of the infinite, which he called "potencies," intelligible so that they should lead back to the Absolute.[10]

Although Schelling's understanding of the Absolute evolved, and despite the instability of the Romantic notion, suffice it to say here that the Absolute is not an object that contains all things but a whole in which individuals partake—and it is often understood as God, or the All.[11] This idea resonated with Jewish thinkers who saw it as akin to the Jewish doctrine of emanation in Kabbalah; identifying and tracing these potencies back to their infinite source was a form of participatory knowledge, of con-science. It is along these lines that the concept of progressive revelation operates: the divine makes itself known through human interpretation.[12] And these can still operate within a religious framework, as Schelling's *Philosophy of Revelation* professes: "The principles of mythology are necessarily the principles of the revealed religion if only for the very reason that both are religions."[13]

As we will see, the unconscious, couched in metaphysical terms, is presumed to be a narrative of a primordial stage of creation; thus, it can be subjected to the same rules of interpretation as mythology. This task of interpretation also entails an ethical dimension: it should lead human beings to pursue knowledge if they want to be coparticipants in an expanded understanding of the Absolute.[14] Indeed, the ultimate stage of this *Philosophy of Revelation* should lead to an emancipation of human consciousness from myths, which Schelling constructed both as a historical moment and an ahistorical, experiential instance of the surrender of selfhood, the encounter with the Other, and the necessity of that encounter.[15]

In probing his image of the abyss of origins, Schelling fostered a new interpretation—a human production of sense comparable to a mythmaking activity. The Schellingian narrative of the "deepest night" thus enabled a fluid reading, both conservative and radical, of the unconscious as a progressive unveiling or revelation.

In this first part of the book, I probe the dual movement by which, on one hand, the psyche was read through a metaphysical lens, and on the other, the Jewish tradition, especially its mysticism, seemingly provided psychological insights into the makeup of the human mind. In their constructs, and in opposition to future understandings of the notion, the unconscious cannot be reduced to the irrational. Rather, it is a realm beyond reason that challenges the received notion of rationality as modernity and as the only aspect of human psyche that can foster coexistence. If reason no longer needed to be used as a centerpiece, as the prevailing narrative of modernity and of the role that Jews could play in it, then Jews no longer needed to interpret Judaism as a religion of reason to show themselves worthy of assimilation. And they could highlight the significance of the mythical dimension of their tradition: Kabbalah.

❋ 1 ❋
The Kabbalistic Genesis of the Unconscious
Schelling's Legacy

To situate the writings of Friedrich Wilhelm von Schelling in the emerging conceptions of the unconscious and to gauge his impact on Jewish thought, I will look at three historical-philosophical perspectives: cognitive, Romantic, and instinctive-irrational, which are the key approaches to the unconscious before Sigmund Freud. I will also probe the influence of the sixteenth-century mystic Jacob Boehme, who is credited with being the father of "esoteric psychology."[1]

Before Schelling: From the Cognitive to the Romantic Unconscious

The genealogies and approaches that paved the way to the concept of the unconscious before Freud can be convoluted. The typologies traced by the psychoanalyst and scholar Günter Gödde in his voluminous study *Traditionslinien des Unbewussten* (*Lineages of the Unconscious*) help map out the concept's provenances.[2]

The first approach to the unconscious was cognitive in orientation. Stemming from the Enlightenment era, its main representatives were the German philosophers Gottfried Wilhelm Leibniz, Immanuel Kant, and Christian Wolff. Departing from Cartesianism, which nullified the possibility of the existence of perceptions without an awareness of them, Leibniz (1646–1716) was the first to establish a theoretical framework for the unconscious and to affirm its importance. "Insensible perceptions are as important to pneumatology [the science of minds and souls] as insensible corpuscles are to natural science, and it is just as unreasonable to reject the one as the other on the pretext that they are beyond the reach of our senses," he professes in *New Essays on Human Understanding* (1704).[3] The volume, a methodical rebuttal of John Locke's *Essay concerning Human Understanding*, criticizes Locke's refusal to consider that "anything should think, and not be conscious of it."[4] Leibniz describes the myriad insensible "petites perceptions"—small perceptions that stay below the threshold of our consciousness—not as *unbewusst* (unconscious) but as *unterbewusst* (below what is conscious).[5] He also claims that these natural properties are gradual and not sudden; hence his famous adage, "Nature never makes leaps." Leibniz's *Principles of Nature and Grace* (1714), a popular introduction to his philosophy of nature, also posits that "our confused perceptions are the result of the impressions which the whole universe makes on us."[6] It is here that Leibniz first articulates the distinction between *perception*, which is immediate and spontaneous but cannot be consciously apprehended, and *apperception*, which is retrospective, intellectual, and based on "consciousness, or the reflective knowledge of this internal state."[7] He also ponders the difference between *volition*—apperceived desires—and *appetition*, that which is unperceived. This foreshadowed the idea of the will as the force behind the unconscious in Schelling, Arthur Schopenhauer, and Eduard von Hartmann's constructs.[8]

The Leibnizian taxonomy that categorizes every concept as either obscure or clear, and every clear concept as either confused or distinct, was taken up by Christian Wolff (1679–1754). It pertains to the concept of the unconscious in that the latter was first understood as the dark or confused perceptions of the inner experience. Indeed, Wolff distinguished between rational and empirical psychology. He defined the *empirical* as what actually occurs and belongs to the inner experience, whereas rational psychology aims to lay out the laws governing the mind and body along with the immortality of the soul.[9]

Using the terms *dark* and *obscure* to designate thoughts below the threshold of consciousness, Immanuel Kant (1724–1804) applies notions of physics in one of his early writings, "Attempt to Introduce the Concept of Negative Magnitudes into Philosophy," theorizing a mental process in which certain thoughts could cancel each other out, as opposing forces of various intensities would do in physics, and formulating their intensity in terms of clarity and obscurity.[10] He further elaborates on obscure representations in his *Anthropology from a Pragmatic Point of View* (1798), famously proposing a topography of consciousness in which "only a few places on the vast map of our minds are illuminated."[11]

In suggesting a contrast between consciousness and what is not conscious, Kant departs from the principle of continuity evoked by Leibniz for whom changes in natural things and properties happen gradually. Perception, for Kant, could thus happen without notice. He even compares the phenomenon of these suddenly illuminated fields to the biblical injunction of God ordaining "let there be light"—and thus consciousness. He also allows for the possibility of a consciousness of the unconscious as a disruptive and unpredictable phenomenon. Adding to the characterization of obscurity, Kant ponders the question of the measurability of "the field of sensuous intuitions and sensations of which we are not conscious, even though we can undoubtedly conclude that we have them."[12]

Sometimes seen as a minor work, geared to a broader audience, and empirical in nature, *Anthropology from a Pragmatic Point of View*, a volume of lectures Kant gave between 1772 and 1796, raises the question of the increasing importance of psychology over metaphysics in his time, even in the realm of morals. Psychology should not supplement or replace metaphysics, Kant admonishes. A hundred and fifty years later, his warnings against the fallacy of a metaphysical treatment of epistemology informed the work of Michel Foucault. In his dissertation on this work by Kant, Foucault demonstrates that the unconscious is de facto an epistemological concept and that Kant focused his anthropology on the reality and limitations of cognitive powers when confronting concrete existence.[13] That the shadow cast by the unconscious on representations should not be turned into metaphysics was a stance at odds with the Romantic and Schellingian turn in the understanding of the unconscious.

The second, Romantic or vitalist approach to the unconscious arose from the fear that the Enlightenment would stagnate into a superficial rationalism if the emotional, natural, and artistic dimensions of human experience were not taken into account. Both Johann Gottfried von Herder (1744–1803), in his naturalist reading of Baruch Spinoza (1632–1677), and Johann Wolfgang von Goethe (1749–1832), who was also indebted to the Dutch Jewish philosopher, highlighted the importance of the identity that exists between nature and the divine, in which the mind resides.[14] In the twentieth century, Ludwig Klages (1872–1956), the philosopher and proponent of vitalism, hailed Goethe retrospectively as the true discoverer of the unconscious. Goethe saw the unconscious as our natural habitat.[15] "The human," he wrote, "cannot remain in a conscious state or in consciousness for long; he must flee once again into unconsciousness, as therein live his roots."[16] Not everyone, however, could access those roots: enter the quasi-prophetic figure of the artist. Goethe asserted that a divinely inspired genius—which he characterized as the "daemonic"—can channel the forces of nature. "There is always something daemonic," he insisted, "in poetry, especially in that which is unconscious, before which reason and understanding fall short, and which therefore produces effects so far surpassing all conception."[17] The unconscious is thus a human in-between, an obscure region that still defines humanity as it connects us to an immanent divine in nature, with Spinozistic overtones.

This tradition was deepened in Schelling's *Naturphilosophie*, a reassessment of Johann Gottlieb Fichte's philosophy of the subject that made the empirical self the basis of all experience, with consciousness, which determines the nature of reality, being determined by the self. Against Spinoza, who posited consciousness as a product of nature, Fichte viewed nature as produced by consciousness. In Schelling's view, however—especially in his later period—if the identity of humanity and nature could not be absolute, it was at least a cocreation: "Poured from the source of things and the same as the source, the human soul has a co-knowledge/conscience [*Mitwissenschaft*] of creation."[18] This view promoted organicism, in which elements are naturally ordered and part of a whole: in the late nineteenth century, theories of holism would stem from and draw on this tradition.[19]

The third approach, the "instinctive-irrational" (*Triebhaft-irrationale*), set itself up in opposition to the main streams of German idealism: against the transcendental idealism associated with Kant, against Fichte's omnipotent individual self, and against Georg Wilhelm Friedrich Hegel's "panlogicism," in which everything thinkable is resolvable through reason—even contradictions. Concepts of will as well as sexual and destructive drives are central to this construct; Arthur Schopenhauer, Friedrich Nietzsche, and Eduard von Hartmann are its key figures. This is what the philosopher Georg Lukács described as the driving force behind bourgeois society and the path to Nazism, prompting him to pen his famous scathing critique of irrationalism, *The Destruction of Reason* (1954). In this Marxist-inflected indictment of the work of Schelling, Schopenhauer, and Nietzsche, he goes so far as to trace a direct path from Schelling to Hitler.[20]

These last two approaches can be seen as overlapping, thus underscoring the limitations of typologies. The irrational approach emerged because Schelling's recognition of potentially dangerous and destructive urges within human nature led him to define the will as impulse (*Drang*), drive (*Trieb*), and desire (*Begierde*). His source for these concepts can be located in the work of the German mystic Jacob Boehme.[21]

Metaphysics as Psychology: Reading Boehme in the Nineteenth Century

In his *Forty Questions of the Soul*, written in 1620, the Rhenish thinker, writer, mystic, and cobbler Jacob Boehme (1575–1624) asks, "Where, from the beginning of the world, does the soul originate?"[22] He goes on to locate it in the *Ungrund*, often translated as "abyss" or "depth," the "groundless ground" from which the divine will emerged into self-awareness and proceeded to create the world.

The text, published in Amsterdam in 1632, eight years after the author's death, was given the subtitle *Psychologia Vera (True Psychology)*.[23] It would be an exaggeration to say that this editorial decision reveals how Boehme's work lent itself instantly to a psychological reading, but the fate of the text does show that this is indeed the perception that quickly prevailed, and increasingly so over the course of the nineteenth century.[24] In addition to Hegel, who called him "the first German philosopher," Boehme drew the attention of a number of writers, including Friedrich von Schelling and Ludwig Feuerbach.[25] These thinkers set out to demonstrate the relevance of his intuitions regarding the human psyche: Boehme's reception shows a path by which religion becomes a source of self-knowledge. In 1612, in *Aurora (Dawn Ascending)*, Boehme's first and best-known text and the retelling of a vision he had had twelve years earlier, the author claims to have glimpsed the foundation of the world and asserts, "In His depth [*Ungrund*], God Himself does not know what He is."[26]

The word *Ungrund* appears in earlier mystical writings between the twelfth and sixteenth centuries, most notably those of the early fourteenth-century Rhenish mystic Meister Eckhart (1260–1328). His "mysticism of the ground" describes the identity of the soul and the divine or a reciprocity between them.[27] "God's ground," Eckhart declares, "is the soul's ground and the soul's ground is God's ground."[28] His disciple, the Dominican Johannes Tauler (1300–1341), similarly invokes Psalms 41:8—"the abyss draws the abyss into itself"—to show the indeterminacy of the relationship between God and creation, or their possible confluence.[29]

If the word *Grund* conveys what is determined and engendered, *Ungrund* is the groundless ground, free of all determination: the prefix *un-* is privative (marking absence) but also works as an intensifier, emphasizing its ontological dimension. In contrast, the term *abyss*, the usual translation of *Ungrund*, does not render this negation.[30] It has been remarked that Boehme used *Ungrund* to convey "the purging of reason"[31] and a principle of uncertainty, thus paving the way for a negative, or apophatic, theology in which the only possible knowledge of the divine is its unknowability. To speak truthfully about God, one must avoid positive assertions about the essence or the attributes of the divine. But since there is an equivalence between the *Ungrund* and the psyche, if the *Ungrund* is a principle of uncertainty, what can be said about the psyche positively? How can a motif lending itself to negative theology become an epistemological tool in psychology? How can it avoid veering into Gnosticism—a theological approach in which God has abandoned the world, leaving his creation under the domination of an evil deity known as the demiurge ("craftsman" in Greek)? Human perceptions of the world are an illusion shaped by this artisan god.[32] These are questions that the notion of *Ungrund* raises. Answering them without falling into a pit of nihilism is the task that Boehme's successors, especially Schelling, would need to wrestle with.

In addition to *Ungrund*, Boehme uses another cognate term, *Abgrunt* (the Middle High German spelling of *Abgrund*), or *pit*, in earlier texts and continued using it alongside *Ungrund* in his *Forty Questions*. *Abgrunt* is also found in the writings of Meister Eckhart.[33] These two terms are not synonymous, however. *Abgrund* is a nothingness that threatens to engulf humanity in its darkness and can even be an internal inferno, whereas the "unground" is a source from which qualities (*Qualitäten* or *Quellgeister*) spring.[34] In Boehme's words, "Seeing then there is an abyss [*Ungrund*] which in regard of the impression of the darkness is called ground, wherein the source is a cause of the life (for the wrathful flash is the awakening of the life although it is nothing there but in itself); therefore it is also a desiring and that desiring is a seeking and yet it can find nothing but a glass, and a similitude of the dark wrathful source, wherein nothing is."[35]

This "source" is ambiguous: what emerges from it is called *Qualität*, whose root, *quaal*, also means "torture"—it is characterized by wrath. The internal life of God is characterized by a painful process, a simultaneous creativeness and destruction within the *Ungrund*. There is a sense of chaos, also known as *turba*, and of anguish present in Boehme's understanding of this source of life—an aspect central to Schelling's understanding of *Ungrund* as abyss. If the unconscious can be mapped on this unground, it conveys a sense of the unconscious as a tumultuous source of creation.

The *Ungrund* becomes untranquil once it leaves its self-sufficiency and enters the realm of otherness and time, as Boehme asserts.

> In eternity, that is, in the abyss outside of nature, there is nothing but quiet without being; nor does it have anything that could yield something; it is an eternal calm and not like [anything], an abyss without beginning or end. . . . This abyss is like an eye; for it is its own mirror; nor does it have light or darkness.[36]

Nothingness, Boehme contends, is essential for fostering the creation process. The eye conveys the desire of the abyss, of this quiet absence of being, to mirror itself; it conceives a desire for substance. In order to create this substance, however, the limitless has to limit itself: the *Ungrund* must concentrate in order to make space and create the substance, the ground. It must withdraw into itself, thereby creating the self. What Boehme describes here—the self-limitation of the *Ungrund*'s limitlessness—is the kabbalistic doctrine of *tsimtsum*, God's contraction before, and necessary for, the creation of the universe.[37]

Many scholars have tried to account for Boehme's exposure to Kabbalah. In addition to sources drawn from Christian Kabbalah, his biography might explain the new directions his writing took in 1617 after his encounter with Balthasar Walter, the head of an alchemical laboratory in Dresden who was versed in Johannes Reuchlin's *Arte Cabbalistica*.[38] In fact, Boehme wrote, the book *Forty Questions* (1620) was "framed by a Lover of the Great Mysteries, Doctor Balthasar Walter." A few years later, he invokes Kabbalah overtly in his *Theosophical Questions or Considerations on the Divine Revelation* (1624).[39] That same year, he links Jews and an apophatic understanding of the *Grund* in the introduction to his treatise *Clavis* (*The Key*): "Also the wise Heathens and Jews have hid the deep Ground of Nature under such Words, as having well understood that the Knowledge of Nature is not for everyone, but it belongs to those only, whom God by Nature has chosen for it."[40]

Gershom Scholem was the first to bring attention to the influence of the kabbalistic teachings on Boehme's writings.[41] He also explored the notion of the *tsimtsum* first found in the work of Isaac Luria, known as the Ari (meaning "Lion"), a rabbi and kabbalist from Safed, Galilee, and one of the most influential figures in Jewish thought and history. His teachings were collected and organized by his foremost student, Haim Vital (1542–1620), as well as by Israel Sarug. Sarug's relationship with Luria is less clear, but he introduced Lurianic Kabbalah into Italy, and its impact on Italian and European Kabbalah runs deep.[42] Since then, the importance of the motif of *tsimtsum* in cultural and religious history has been probed further.[43] In addition to Luria's influence on Boehme, the impact of a Sarugian model of the divine, in which God's contraction happens out of anger rather than generosity, has come to the fore—an aspect to which I will return when addressing the dark side of the divine in Schelling and its implications.[44]

In Lurianic Kabbalah, God, as the *Ein Sof*, the limitless, is portrayed as the source in which all things are contained; and because it contains everything, it needs to contract itself to make space for that which is not God. The act of creation is preceded by a separation, the *tsimtsum* (contraction): by contracting himself, God created the space for otherness, or for something else to emerge. This reconciles the notions of creation *ex nihilo* and *ex materia*, since God had to create that nothing in order to create anything—but that nothing only came about because God can negate himself. The description is not of creation but of *proto*creation, an earlier creation from which this world ultimately emerged (in the wake of previous failed attempts), and the glaring absence of the language of creation of Genesis 1 and 2 in Luria's account of the *tsimtsum* signals that this is not the reference that Luria wanted to conjure up. The *tsimtsum* is a prehistory and a prefiguration: it corresponds to what the unconscious will come to represent—a liminality.

In Boehme, what causes the contraction to happen is a desire and a will. Only through this manifested will can the *Ungrund* be the source of the Creation. Likewise, in Lurianic Kabbalah, the limitless God, the *Ein Sof*, is the Will that wills itself (*razon ha-elyon*) and becomes the divine Will (*razon Elohim*). This is what fosters the bifurcated divinity before the Creation: thus, creation can only come about after the creation within God of what is not God—that is, of an Other within God.[45]

The *Ungrund* is that which contains and precedes the divine will, arousing itself to self-awareness. Boehme's cosmology makes differentiation and desire paramount to God's creation and thus to the soul that emerges from that *Ungrund* contemplating itself, with the abyss being "like an eye."[46]

Boehme often emphasized the possibility of an isomorphism between the divine and the human psyche: "All our doctrine," he wrote, "is nothing but the way in which man must light up in himself the divine world of light."[47] While the greater goal is to achieve the stillness that preceded creation—the "mysterium magnum"[48]—every soul aspires first to self-awareness and self-knowledge.[49] It is by giving existence to things, by opposing things to oneself, that the divine gains consciousness: the abyss is thus active, and it is moved by desires or urges (*Trieb*) for self-knowledge. Boehme thus went beyond a mysticism of contemplation and introduced a form of self-knowledge. Let us return to the opening interrogation of the *Forty Questions*: immediately after the interpellation "Where does the soul originate?," Boehme claims that readers should know by way of reason (*Vernunft*) that all things have their origin in eternity. The use of the term *Vernunft* here denotes *intuitive* reasoning, a capacity to grasp reality without concepts, and the possession of the highest form of knowledge—the language of the Absolute, and the initial indifferentiation, in opposition to *Verstand*, the process of achieving knowledge.

Despite this recourse to reasoning, understanding the place of the *Ungrund* in the universe as a reflection of God does not make his will comprehensible in Boehme's mind: "This abyss . . . has a will, after which we must not strive or search, for this would throw us into confusion."[50] While God's will is partly identified with the abyss because it is his creation, and while this will is unknowable, Boehme nevertheless offers a glimpse into God's internal structure, which is defined by its dynamism and the gesture of going beyond its initial unity, which he calls the *Aufthun der Einheit* (the opening of unity). This creation process is predicated on a will that is incomprehensible. It can, however, be approached obliquely: the reflection of the abyss in *sofia* (wisdom) is what makes the will real—the will might not be intelligible, but it is generative and shapes the universe. As Boehme proposes, "For a transparent and quiet will is as nothing, and generateth nothing: but if a will must generate, then it must be in *somewhat*, wherein it may form and may generate in that thing."[51] Indeed, the Boehmian will can be identified with the nothingness—that is, the divine—in Kabbalah before the creation of the universe. It must condense itself into this "somewhat"—this barely fathomable, obscure place that the term *abyss* also conveys—from which creation can spring forth.

From Cocreation to Conscience

Boehme established that the soul originates from the *Ungrund* and that there is a resemblance, even an isomorphy, between the soul and the ground that the *Ungrund* creates by concentrating. The opening of unity of the Ungrund must therefore be applied to the human psyche. Just as the will needs that which it is not, so the I creates a not-I that is still within the self. I refer to this, as Elliot Wolfson does, as the "not-I I." From the bifurcation in the divine between the will and a contrary principle ensues the bifurcation in the human psyche between the self and a not-self. In addition, the soul must grow aware of its origins. The world is thus not solely a cocreation but a *con-science* in which human cooperation is required.

Based on this metaphysical proposition, theology pervaded the realm of psychology and, in many ways, *became* psychology: it ceased to provide an understanding of God and instead offered an understanding of man. Ludwig Feuerbach (1804–1872) famously claims, in *Essence of Christianity* (1841), that God is merely a reflection of either human characteristics or the deepest wishes of human nature.[52] But even before this conclusion, he had already started to develop an anthropology and psychology of religion by way of Boehme. In his *Geschichte der neueren Philosophie* (*History of Modern Philosophy*, 1833–37), Feuerbach asserts, "Jacob Boehme is the most profoundly unconscious and uneducated psychologist ... [which is] the most instructive and at the same time interesting proof that the mysteries of theology and the metaphysics within psychology find their explanation in that metaphysics are nothing but esoteric psychology."[53]

These interpretations converged with one of the claims about Kabbalah made by Salomon Maimon (1753–1800), Immanuel Kant's disciple and inspiration, which portrayed psychology as part of a secret knowledge: "Originally the Cabbalah was nothing but psychology, physics, ethics, politics and such sciences, presented by means of symbols and hieroglyphs in fables and allegories the hidden meaning of which was disclosed only to those who were capable of grasping it."[54]

Friedrich von Schelling further constructed this arc between mind and metaphysics and coined a word by which he shows his awareness of what evades the mind. The term *the unconscious* (*das Unbewusste*) appears in his *System of Transcendental Idealism* (1800). This book is usually considered the "later Schelling," written after he had distanced himself from his years in Jena, where he had been close with Johann Gottlieb Fichte and Johann Wolfgang von Goethe and had extensively formulated his *Naturphilosophie*, in *Ideas concerning a Philosophy of Nature* in 1797 and *On the World Soul* the following year. In the *System*, Schelling posits that the main problem of philosophy is to shed light on self-consciousness and its emergence from a place where it did not exist, and to reflect on the conditions in which the subject becomes able to understand this, thus effectively turning philosophy into a "the progressive history of self-consciousness"—and of what came before.⁵⁵ The "before" is a moment of the Absolute's identity with itself: "The absolutely identical . . . already separates itself in the first act of consciousness, and produces the whole system of finitude by this separation."⁵⁶ The language of the Absolute, and the initial indifferentiation (seen in the phrase "absolutely identical") it conveys, is imbued with Romantic overtones but also reminiscent of Boehme.

Thinking of the soul as being modeled on the *Ungrund* leads to thinking of the unconscious as a veiled yet active principle whose act of dissociation is the condition for fostering consciousness, for the process of dissociation that characterizes the Schellingian unconscious, the I / not I necessary for the self to grasp itself. Because it does not create a predicate, however, a subject/object binary does not apply: the Other that is created is not an absolute Other. It is not an opposition between an I and a not-I but the creation of a not-I within the I: the I/not-I necessary for the self to grasp itself. And it is because the self longs for this self-understanding by way of the Other that Schelling uses a language of affect and desire, *Sehnsucht* (longing), to describe the impulse that prompts the infinite to break into the finite.

> This eternal unconscious [*dieses ewig Unbewusste*],⁵⁷ which, like the everlasting sun in the realm of spirits, conceals itself behind its own unclouded light, and though never becoming an object, impresses its identity upon all free actions, is simultaneously the same for all intelligences, the invisible root of which all intelligences are but powers.⁵⁸

If the *Ungrund* is the matrix, the unconscious is a reflection of this Absolute. History is thus the gradual self-disclosing of the Absolute in an existential manner, in which the bifurcation of the subjective and the objective can only be an absolute, distinct from Georg Wilhelm Friedrich Hegel's Idea, which reveals itself. It is a thinking of the Absolute rather than a path toward it.

After publishing the *System*, Schelling moved to Munich in 1806 and published his *Philosophical Investigations into the Essence of Human Freedom* shortly before the death of his wife Caroline in 1809. The latter year is usually held as a turning point, with a somber tone and darkness as the mark of the later Schelling.⁵⁹

The ruptures and continuities in Schelling's work and his inability to create a philosophical system both obfuscated his legacy and attracted readers who chose one facet of Schelling over others, as will become clear in subsequent chapters in which I trace his legacy. These circumstances were accentuated by Schelling's silence during the final thirty years of his life, when he worked on unpublished manuscripts and gave lectures at the University of Munich until 1841 and then in Berlin, after his appointment as Prussian privy counselor and member of the Berlin Academy. His lectures (the private lectures in Munich in 1810 and the public address of October 1815) as well as "The Philosophy of Mythology" and "The Philosophy of Revelation" were posthumously published by his son a few years after his death in 1854.[60]

The later part of Schelling's work is characterized by a foray into mysticism, which became perceptible in his essay on freedom. A necessary self-limitation is the basis for creation, and the same rules seem to apply for the self and the divine, as suggested in the Munich lectures of 1810.

> To limit oneself, to concentrate oneself in One point, yet also to hold onto the latter with all one's might and not to let go until it has been expanded into a world, constitutes the greatest power and perfection. . . . Contraction, then, is the beginning of all reality. . . . It is indeed God's descent that is the greatest, even in Christianity.[61]

This mystical turn then became central in Schelling's *The Ages of the World*, written between 1811 and 1819. In addition to the biographical elements, the concept of a dark side of God and of the psyche has been ascribed to a broader, politically conservative turn in the early years of the nineteenth century. This turn was represented by the Munich-based theologian Franz Xaver von Baader (1765–1841). It was von Baader who got Schelling interested in Boehme and reinjected Boehme's thought into the cultural conversation at the beginning of the century, in an effort to shield Catholicism from an increasingly rationalist and dogmatic turn and to reject Hegel's speculative philosophy.[62] Von Baader's affinity with reactionary figures such as the French Catholic thinkers Félicité Lamennais and Joseph de Maistre (1753–1821) might have also influenced, or further resonated with, his views on the limits of reason.[63]

In such an atmosphere, thinkers were attracted to mysticism and engaged with it because they were critical of Enlightenment rationalism. Thus, Schelling's philosophical depiction of the divine was no longer dictated by a science of reason. God now functioned as a model of existence.

Hegel's *Phenomenology of Spirit* (1807) marked the culmination of negative philosophy, one that emphasized the unknowability of reality or truth, which Schelling deemed an unsuccessful attempt at a science of existence. In response to Hegel, he turned his negative theology into a positive one. The German-Swiss philosopher and psychiatrist Karl Jaspers (1883–1969) explains the philosophical consequences: "In negative philosophy God is treated as the end, while in positive philosophy He is treated as a beginning."[64] Unlike humans, God is not chained to logical necessity. God's abyss, the differentiation from himself, is a manifestation of his own freedom, but it is his freedom that dictates the contingency of being and of the mind. Positive philosophy also treated God as a beginning for the understanding of the human psyche. In 1810, regarding the formation of human personalities, Schelling stated that "a state of unconsciousness in which everything still exists without separation" becomes "two principles, an unconscious, dark one and a conscious one."[65] The divine also has these two principles in it; there is thus an equivalence between the divine and the human.[66]

Schelling articulated this equivalence further, writing of a "primordial deed" by which the human soul comes into being: "That primordial deed which makes a man genuinely himself precedes all individual actions; but immediately after it is put into exuberant freedom, this deed sinks into the night of unconsciousness."[67] Since the dissociation within God is a precondition for creation, or a protocreation, the primordial deed for human beings is a comparable separation: this initial individuality is first forced on them (being "put into ... freedom"), and that which separates them from the world is subsequently relegated to the realm of the unthought. The unconscious is the *unthought*, not the *repressed*. This would be where future constructs of the unconscious would bifurcate, between a Schellingian-Bergsonian model of oblivion, on one side, and repression as an essential tenet of Freudian psychoanalysis, on the other.

This "primordial deed" should be read as myth-like; it becomes a template of principle, both in time and in nature. This deed, the act of creating a separation within oneself, a dissociation, is where the unconscious and Kabbalah meet: every human personality rests on a dark ground.[68] This dark principle is precisely what Franz Rosenzweig identified in 1917 as Schelling's kabbalistic language.

> Just as there "is" a God before all relation, whether to the world or to Himself, and this being of God which is wholly unhypothetical, is the see-point of the actuality of God, which Schelling ... calls the "dark ground"

[*dunkeln Grund*], etc., an interiorization of God that precedes not merely His self-externalization, but rather even His self.[69]

The *Ungrund*, or unground, is pivotal in Schelling's positive philosophy and his theory of consciousness and of the Absolute.[70] In his essay on freedom, he mentions a ground that is an unground, and a nonground that precedes all ground ("vor allem Grund vorhergehenden Ungrund").[71] There is an isomorphy between the Kabbalah-inflected *Ungrund* and the unconscious—and the Absolute is set between these two "relativities." The abyss, the *Ungrund*, like the unconscious, is not just a pit; it is a dynamic locus from which creation or individuation happens, born out of desiring or longing (*Sehnsucht*), as we have seen before in the works of Boehme. And it can only be accessed and fathomed indirectly and existentially—when applied to man, it is what makes humans transcend themselves and participate in creation through their shared consciousness of it and of the soul.

> Man must be granted an essence outside and above the world; for how could he alone, of all creatures, retrace the long path of developments from the present back into the deepest night of the past, how could he alone rise up to the beginning of things unless there were in him an essence from the beginning of times? Drawn from the source of things and akin to it, what is eternal of the soul has a co-science/con-sciousness [*Mitwissenschaft*] of creation.[72]

It is because of the *Ungrund*—which is constitutive of humanity and is the mnemonic trace of being part of the creation of the universe—that man can have access to the "con-science" of the world—but a conscience that reveals itself progressively.

Much has been written on how Kabbalah may have influenced Schelling. Although his writing is brimming with mystical references, including musings on Kabbalah, he rarely made direct reference to Jewish mysticism.[73] His main discussion of it appeared in the short pamphlet *Über die Gottheiten von Samothrake* (*On the Deities of Samothrace*, 1815). In it, he echoes Salomon Maimon's characterization of Kabbalah as an outdated belief system containing "fragments and remnants, very disfigured if one wills, but nevertheless remnants of that primordial system which is the key of all religious systems." He adds that "the Jews do not speak entirely untruly when they present the Kabbalah as the transmission of a doctrine which, apart from the system of the revealed, manifested (and therefore open) scriptural documents, was more comprehensible but secret, neither universally communicated nor communicable."[74]

In spite of his denigration of Kabbalah as "disfigured," if not "entirely untru[e]," Schelling betrays, in the rest of the passage, a knowledge of the most up-to-date developments in the study of Kabbalah, notably *Ben Jochai*, the controversial work of the Hungarian scholar Moses Kunitz (1774–1837) about the presumed author of the Zohar (the Book of Splendor, central to Kabbalah).[75] This volume professes the importance of *aggada*, the narrative part of the oral law, often deemed to be of lesser value than the *halakha*, its legislative body, which parallels the need for narration that Schelling develops in the *System of Transcendental Idealism*. In this text, he turns philosophy into a history of self-consciousness, enabling myth to be reassessed as a matter of truth.[76]

Non-Jewish thinkers commonly claimed that Jews had been unable to grasp the philosophy behind Kabbalah. This allegation was spread by the likes of Henry More, the seventeenth-century English philosopher who argued that Jews lacked this capacity because of what he held to be their literalism, their inability to grasp the spirit of their own tradition (a characterization based on the dichotomy drawn by Paul in 2 Cor. 3:6 between the letter and the spirit of the law, in which he berates the Corinthians for their narrow legalism).[77] References to Schelling enabled a handful of Jewish thinkers to affirm the opposite and seize on the affinity between philosophy and Kabbalah as well as between Kabbalah and myth, thereby demonstrating their capacity to see the symbolism of Judaism and its potentialities as mythopoesis—that is, as a capacity to foster mythology. Schelling's writings and their invitation to examine religious myths as potencies and as a foray into consciousness, and even creation, use a language of potencies reminiscent of the notion of emanations in Kabbalah. As the philosopher wrote, "The mythological process does not have to do with natural objects, but rather with the pure creating potencies whose original product is consciousness itself. . . . The same potencies, which in their collective effectivity and in their unity make consciousness into what posits God, become in their divergence the causes of the process by which gods are posited."[78]

The stakes are high: an incorrect understanding of the forces at work could lead to fragmentation—as represented by the split between polytheism and monotheism. Schelling's references enabled the Jewish corpus to be examined in a way that could shed new light onto its mythopoetic force—and on the foundations of both consciousness and the unconscious. His philosophy could thus become a testament to the relevance of Judaism to modern times, in which Jewish affirmative apologetics become a minority reappropriating their own tradition, eager and ready to enter mainstream cultural conversations and to show how their faith had the potential to unify a fractured world.

✳ 2 ✳
Schelling's Jewish Receptions
Kabbalah and/as the Unconscious

Probing the logic of the derivation of Jewish thought from Schellingian philosophy is essential to grasp the pre-Freudian Jewish understanding of the unconscious.

A whole generation of Jewish thinkers was influenced by Schelling and found in him an ally in its defense of Kabbalah. Not only did Jewish mysticism, with its creation narrative and *Ungrund*, serve as the basis of Schellingian philosophy, but these thinkers also increasingly saw in Kabbalah a mythmaking force within Judaism.[1] This aspect further accorded with the philosophical ethos of the time. As we have seen, for Schelling, mythologies were but refractions of an original revelation: by way of narratives, they offered the means to access a spiritual understanding of God, and it behooved human beings to understand divine unity under the multiplicity found in myth. In addition, Schelling saw in myths the mechanisms at work in the psyche: they capture a prehistory of consciousness and, once correctly comprehended, they can be turned into an instrument for self-understanding and transcendence.

While the echoes of Kabbalah in Schelling have received significant attention, the systematic analysis of his impact on Jewish thought has been far more modest. Indeed, only a couple of scholars, Werner Cahnman and Paul Franks, have investigated the question.

Cahnman focuses on two intellectuals, Isaac Bernays and Hirsch Maier Löwengard, both of whom will be important in this chapter. He argues that the kabbalistic motives found in Schelling's work on mythology explain their attraction. In contrast, Franks's picture is more granular. In his view, Schelling had a twofold impact on Jewish thought. While the defense of Kabbalah did bespeak an increased importance of myth among German Jews, this remained a tangential phenomenon, he claims. In addition, beyond the German circles, he shows that the philosophy of Schelling was used in the fight against antinomianism—the rejection of the law, and in this case of the Jewish law—among eastern European Jews. He specifically examines the work of the well-known Galician *maskil* (a proponent of the Jewish Enlightenment) Nachman Krochmal and the lesser-known scholars Isaac Mieses and his nephew Fabius. What drew these thinkers to Schelling, Franks argues, is their finding in him "a middle way, both conservative and progressive, between self-enclosed traditionalism and a radicalism."[2]

Both of these approaches—the embrace of myth and the rejection of antinomianism—are indeed pivotal. This chapter suggests, however, that it is worth expanding the cast of figures who engaged with Schelling's thought and probing its reception to get a more detailed picture. Among the other thinkers who drew on Schelling, most saw this confluence between the kabbalistic and Schellingian systems as a way to advance their own understanding of Judaism in their time and place, as well as to foster greater acceptance. Meyer Landauer, David Einhorn, and Joseph Judah Löb Sossnitz, for instance, broaden the narrative that Schelling helped them construct: they posit myth as a prehistory of consciousness and an instrument for self-reformation.

South of Reason? Schellingian Myth in the Works of Bernays, Löwengard, and Landauer
ISAAC BERNAYS: THE ETHICAL CORE OF MYTH

One of the most influential intellectuals to espouse Schelling's worldview and introduce it into Jewish thought was Isaac Bernays (1792–1849), a student of Rabbi Abraham Naftali Hertz Scheuer (1751–1822) in Mainz. Scheuer's opposition to secular studies led Bernays to leave the rabbi and study in Würzburg under Abraham Bing (1752–1841), himself a student of Nathan Adler (1741–1800), who has been called Germany's last kabbalist.[3] Bing's yeshiva allowed his students to complete a university degree, and a number of them attended Schelling's lectures at the University of Würzburg, where he taught until he moved to Munich in 1806—prompting certain students to follow him.

Bernays was among them. This future chief rabbi of Hamburg left no writings in his own name, though he is the putative author of the short-lived periodical that offers the best account of a Schellingian view of myth: *Der*

Bibel'sche Orient (*The Biblical Orient*). Published in two issues in 1821, its title squarely situates it within the ambit of German thought by alluding to the Orient that Johann Gottfried von Herder, a key figure of the German Enlightenment and precursor of Romanticism, had evoked in his famous *Vom Geist der hebräischen Poesie* (*The Spirit of Hebrew Poetry*), published almost forty years earlier.[4]

The Biblical Orient emphasizes the importance of the pagan milieu in shaping the Jewish tradition. It asserts, for instance, that the Egyptians had a mystery religion that was kept hidden until it was revealed in the Ptolemaic period (between the fourth and first centuries BCE) by the Neoplatonists. This religion strikingly resembles Kabbalah. The journal thus draws parallels between ancient religions and Judaism. It even professes that the tradition of mysteries was handed down across generations of initiates and that polytheism as the external form of paganism actually concealed a primordial monotheism, in which the power of myth was paramount.

Outrage erupted shortly after the first issue of *The Biblical Orient* was published anonymously in 1821. Riddled with contradictions, the text seems to feature two different approaches.[5] It is based on sources betraying an intimate knowledge of both Christian and Jewish traditions, ultimately creating a dissonant text that might mirror the inevitable frictions of comparative approaches by authors from different backgrounds, probably a Jew and a Christian.[6] The role Bernays played in the journal continues to be disputed, but not the fact that he did have a hand in it.

Regardless of the question of dual authorship, I would also argue that *The Biblical Orient* seems to exhibit contradictions that need not be elevated or resolved and that, in showing the various layers and possibilities of interpretations, it establishes the dynamic tension of a thought process that is of a kabbalistic/Schellingian nature. The eventual coherence of the text, along with its identity, suggests a silently acknowledged coincidence of opposites—a kabbalistic concept positing that different views can eventually be reconciled, because nothing is mutually exclusive in God's creation.

For the author(s) of *The Biblical Orient*, the ethical component of the monotheistic traditions was essential and was best understood when couched in the mythical stories found in Kabbalah. This is why Kabbalah is of particular relevance, because of its capacity to harness inwardness, spirituality, and the power of myth to address audiences on their own terms and convey key ideas in a form accessible to laypeople. Among these ideas, the journal highlights the psychological dramas that beset the patriarchs when facing trials or temptations, torn between their faithfulness to God and their human inclinations. These dramas are meant to illustrate the moral weaknesses of humankind. *The Biblical Orient* describes them as "dramas that describe the entry of mankind into history, and are authenticated, concrete monuments of the emergence of mankind from the original nearness with God."[7] The journal professes that "every religion is brought back to its central idea"[8]—in the case of Judaism, it emphasizes the ethical core from which this religious tradition unfolded.

The development of this argument to its logical conclusion implicitly pitted the ethical core of biblical and kabbalistic universalism found in Judaism against a narrow-minded observance focused on commandments (the 613 *mitsvot* found in the Torah, as listed by the Talmud in tractate Makkot 23b) or on Talmudic law. This indictment—effectively reminiscent of anti-Jewish rhetoric, according to which legalistic-minded Jews were incapable of comprehending and espousing the universalism of Christianity and its moral message—is partly what caused the uproar, although a straightforward condemnation of the observance of Jewish law is nowhere to be found in the work. This may also reflect the text's plural authorship as well as Bernays's personal proclivities. In his subsequent positions, Bernays opposed a strict Orthodoxy, though stopping short of fully embracing the Reform movement.[9] Advocates of a liberal Judaism, such as Isidore Singer (1859–1939), the progressive editor of the *Jewish Encyclopedia*, praised *Der Bibel'sche Orient* as an attempt to bring Kabbalah into the mainstream conversation, an effort directed at enlightened Jews, to convince them to reconsider their own tradition.

That effort to recuperate one's tradition was not lost on Heinrich Graetz (1817–1891), a pioneering historian of the Jewish people, who called Bernays "the man who intelligently opposed the prevailing flaccidity of semi-enlightened reform and thought." While generally harsh toward mystical fervor, Graetz praised the nature of Bernays's mysticism. He perceived it as a reflection of a more inspired German South, which enabled him to draw geographically based intellectual distinctions in German Jewish intellectual and spiritual life.

> In South Germany, in contradistinction to North Germany (where formal tendencies did not rise above the narrow spheres of simple minds), a mystic and philosophical school had been established, which promoted

visionary notions. In all things, both the smallest and the greatest objects, in nature and history, in groups of things, numbers, colours and names, in a simple series of thoughts, mere germs of ideas, this philosophy beheld the shattered ruins of a gigantic mirror, reflecting the original thoughts in a magnified form. Isaac Bernays belonged to this school. To his vision Judaism in its literature and historical progress revealed itself half unveiled.[10]

This favorable appreciation comes from what Graetz perceived as Bernays's distinctive capacity to intertwine mysticism and philosophy in the service of Judaism as a religion of progress. In this depiction, and despite the language of ruins, this form of philosophical mysticism returns Judaism to its core without obfuscating it altogether.

It is no coincidence that South Germany is where Schelling held his lectures, in Würzburg and Munich. Kauffman Kohler (1843–1926), a German-born American rabbi and key figure of the Reform movement, retrospectively (in the early twentieth century) described the region's culture: "The spirit fostered there, and particularly under the influence of the romantic King Ludwig I, was thoroughly conservative. The chilling blasts of historical criticism which obtained dominion elsewhere in Germany through the Hegelian school, were not allowed to affect the philosophical or theological studies in Bavaria. Schelling was the leader and the idol of the schools, and he stopped neither at Kant's criticism nor at Fichte's subjectivism."[11]

It is worth noting that while conservatism is associated with a Schellingian ethos, in the rest of this essay Kohler makes a case for how the philosopher influenced a novel and expansive reading of religion, whose paradigms could be found in myth and the workings of the mind. He describes historicism as stifling the creative potential of religion as a mythopoetic force, whereas this dimension is precisely what could best answer the needs of the time.

It might appear somewhat surprising that echoes of Isaac Bernays's thought appear in Sigmund Freud's early writings. Freud's interest in Bernays's work was nurtured by what might otherwise have amounted to a mere biographical accident: his wife Martha was Bernays's granddaughter. In the abundant epistolary exchanges during the courtship, Freud mentions meeting a former student of Bernays and asserts that for the man, now an older Jewish engraver,

> religion was no longer treated as a rigid dogma; it became an object of reflection for the satisfaction of cultivated artistic taste and of

intensified logical efforts, and [Bernays] recommended it finally not because it happened to exist and had been declared holy, but because he was pleased by the deeper meaning that he found in it or that he projected into it.[12]

This language, in which religion rejects dogma and uses terms related to *depth* and *projection*, is arresting. So is Freud's understanding of religion here, as a vessel of deeper meaning, which is at odds with the view of religion as infantile and neurotic that he would later advance in *The Future of an Illusion* (1927) and *Civilization and Its Discontents* (1929). Rather, his assessment echoes the tenets of the positive philosophy that runs through the later Schelling, traces of which can be found in *Der Bibel'sche Orient*. Regardless of the extent of Bernays's authorship, the very stance of the journal indicates the porosity of the line between religious discourses and Schelling's worldview, and the importance of Kabbalah as mythopoesis. Bernays's students, Samson Raphael Hirsch and Ahron Marcus, would carry the teachings of *Der Bibel'sche Orient* forward, professing that every religion contains a central idea and drawing attention to the ethical and psychological depth of Judaism couched in myths (see chapter 8). Marcus in particular gave special importance to the intertwining of Kabbalah and myth and Kabbalah and the unconscious, but so did one of his predecessors, Hirsch Maier Löwengard.

HIRSCH MAIER LÖWENGARD: MYTH AS A PREHISTORY OF RELIGIOUS CONSCIOUSNESS

Myth also traverses the work of a relatively obscure figure, Rabbi Hirsch Maier Löwengard (1813–1886), whom Schelling held in such esteem that he recommended the young rabbi to the king of Bavaria, Max II, for a prestigious scholarly position to accompany Jewish emancipation in Bavaria. The position was never instituted, and Schelling blamed Löwengard's lack of professional success on the political circumstances.[13] After a short rabbinical career in Württemberg and a brief stint at *Der Israelit*, an Orthodox publication founded in 1860, Löwengard immigrated to Switzerland and sank into oblivion.

The first of Löwengard's three contributions, *Beiträge zur Kritik der Reformbestrebungen in der Synagoge* (*Contribution to a Critique of the Reform Movement in the Synagogue*), was published in 1841 under the pseudonym Juda Leon.[14] The following year, this time under his own name, he penned *Auch einige Worte über das neue Gebetbuch im Hamburger Tempel* (*A Few*

Words about the New Prayerbook in the Hamburg Temple).[15] His final book, *Jehova, nicht Moloch, war der Gott der alten Hebräer* (*Jehovah, not Moloch, Was the God of the Ancient Hebrews*), is a rebuttal of accusations of Jewish human sacrifices.[16] The book was published in 1843, the same year as Bruno Bauer's *Die Judenfrage* (*The Jewish Problem*), in which the historian and theologian argues that Judaism is impossible to reform.[17]

Löwengard's sparse writings explicitly celebrate Friedrich von Schelling and express his view of the significance of Schelling's philosophy of mythology, which he held to be an answer to the conundrums of his time.[18] A key argument, most salient in his last published book, is that pagan mythology constitutes a prehistory of the religious consciousness. This mythology, he contends, is not properly acknowledged because of the pusillanimity and the desire for respectability of Jewish leaders who sought to distance themselves from any historical research likely to fuel anti-Jewish tropes and misleading characterizations of Judaism's past and present.

Löwengard's work captures the anxiety of his time: he feared that Judaism would devolve into petty bourgeois ideals, notably by being too focused on the individual, even in the liturgy. He warned that this would result in a spiritual void and that his coreligionists would face "an empty abyss." He lamented the religion's direction all the more so because he felt that Jews believed themselves to be emancipated when they weren't yet—a view he adamantly expressed at a rabbinical conference in 1845 to the "disapproval of all sides."[19] At the same time, he tried to articulate Judaism's monotheism, its ancient Near Eastern roots—while refuting the attacks against Judaism unleashed by accusations of Jewish sacrifices—and the importance of comparative myth. His diagnosis was sharp and bleak. Moreover, like Joseph Roth's response eighty years later when staring down the nascent Nazi Party, he sensed that the accusations leveled at Judaism revealed a more destructive appetite of the soul that would soon engulf other faiths and the broader world.[20] In the concluding words of *Jehovah, not Moloch*, he poses a question: "The old darkness has been stirring mightily in these last years. All evil passions, all superannuated errors, all mean insinuations are awakened to a life of terrible reality and set upon the Jews. Or is the aim only against the Jews? Is this possibly the beginning of a widely extended historical tragedy?"[21]

From there, he exhorts Jews, and especially learned scholars, to revive their own tradition. Far from suspecting Schelling to be an agent of the destruction, as Georg Lukács would, he lays the blame on the political myopia of his contemporaries: their own blindness, he claims, will precipitate their world into the abyss.

MEYER LANDAUER: MYTH AS WORLD SOUL

Meyer Heinrich Hirsch Landauer (1808–1841) is regarded by scholars today as the pioneer of Kabbalah studies. Born into a religious family, the son of a Württemberg cantor, he studied under Schelling in Munich, completed a doctorate in Bible studies at Tübingen, and was ordained as a rabbi shortly before his death at age thirty-three. His two books, *Jehova und Elohim, oder Die althebräische Gotteslehre als Grundlage der Geschichte, der Symbolik und der Gesetzgebung der Bücher Mosis* (*Jehovah and Elohim—or, The Ancient Hebrew Teaching on God as Foundation of the History, Symbolism, and Law-Giving of the Books of Moses*, 1836) and *Wesen und Form des Pentateuchs* (*Essence and Form of the Pentateuch*, 1838), strongly bear the influence of Schelling.[22] This is clear from his central reference to "essence and form," pivotal concepts in Schellingian philosophy. Abraham Geiger (1810–1874), the leading figure of the Reform movement, accordingly lamented him as being part of "the symbolical-philosophical school of Schelling."[23]

Yet, in contrast to Löwengard's feverish invocation of Schelling, Landauer never refers to the philosopher directly. Instead, he pushes against Geiger's accusation in the preface to *Essence and Form of the Pentateuch* by asking why such symbolism should be shunned, even advocating for its relevance in biblical analysis.[24] Landauer compared the Bible, more than Kabbalah, with Hinduism, because he sought to highlight the archetypal nature of its figures, including Adam, and also the link between the two cultures. According to certain traditions, Abraham's father, Terah, had come from India. Landauer thus strove to identify a shared origin and the mythical core of religious narratives, just as Schelling had in his *Philosophy of Mythology*.[25] Most important, in *Essence and Form of the Pentateuch* Landauer pivots to a study of Kabbalah in which he examines the various ways the notion of a "world soul," to which Schelling had dedicated his 1797 essay, might emerge from both mystical traditions and effectively shed light on the psyche's mechanisms across time and space.[26] The world soul, as an underlying premise of both faiths, would later build into a collective representation and a collective unconscious, as we will see in the work of Ralph Waldo Emerson. Landauer pioneered this comparative study of world mysticisms and of spiritual connections across traditions.

Mysticism and the Mind: Centralization and Condensation

The significance of Schelling's afterlife lies in the reassessment of mysticism as mythical by those whom he influenced as well as in their understanding of myth as a narrative both reflecting something primordial in the human psyche and giving valuable insights into the realities of the mind—especially in its condensation mechanisms.

Samuel Abraham Hirsch (1843–1923) was an Amsterdam-born rabbi trained in Berlin and Heidelberg; he received a doctorate at Heidelberg in 1869 before moving to London.[27] Steeped in German philosophy, he was pessimistic about the contemporary reception of mysticism. Yet in 1907, Hirsch published "Jewish Mystics: An Appreciation," in which he claims that mysticism is "a natural continuation of certain modes of thought and feeling which had never been absent . . . and the actual rise of which may be said . . . from a psychological point of view . . . to be rooted in the construction of that eternally inscrutable enigma which is called the human soul."[28]

By connecting mysticism and investigations into the human psyche, Hirsch shows how German philosophy, starting with Immanuel Kant and continuing with Johann Gottlieb Fichte, had demolished every preexisting thought system. He concludes that Schelling had gone "boldly forwards, discovered fresh insufficiencies" and that his inquiry had yielded new findings as he "ended by surrendering himself, hand and foot, to mysticism. The philosophical chrysalis had become metamorphosed into a mystical butterfly."[29] This both restates the influence of Jewish mystical thought on Schelling and captures the efforts at unveiling it that had started almost a century earlier with David Einhorn.

DAVID EINHORN: CENTRALIZATION, MYTHS, AND THE PSYCHE OF JEWISH UNIVERSALISM

The question of center and margins, in theology as well as in the politics and psychology of religion—a question very much influenced by Schelling—permeates the work of David Einhorn (1809–1879). Einhorn played a significant role in Germany and, even more important, transported his Reform worldview to the United States and significantly shaped Judaism in America, a development I return to in the fourth chapter.[30]

Born into a traditional milieu from which he grew estranged, Einhorn attended university in Munich in 1832, studied under Schelling, and earned a doctorate in 1834. He belongs to the generation whose radical vision prompted him to leave Europe in the wake of the post-1848 conservative turn: after holding a few rabbinical positions in Europe, he immigrated to the United States in 1855. Kauffman Kohler, a prominent Reform rabbi and one of his sons-in-law, penned a biographical sketch in which he confirms the impact of Schelling and his mysticism of the mind in Einhorn's intellectual development.

> Schelling . . . entwined philosophy and religion, unifying the ideal and the real, so as to make seer and sage, seeker after the One God. To him all heathen mythologies were but refractions of an original revelation; and the startling discoveries and decipherments of the time which brought buried civilizations of a hoary antiquity with their modes of worship and of thought to the light of day, seemed to confirm this view. Here seemed to be offered the key wherewith to unlock the mysteries of old India and Egypt. The symbolism of Kreuzer [sic] and the mysticism of Goerres, both admired for their comprehensive grasp of the religions of the East and their mysteries, were taken as corroborative proofs of Schelling's system. Nature and the human soul were studied from this new point of view, and the Mosaic cult, too, appeared in a new light because of the symbolic meaning lent thereto.[31]

Kohler compares Judaism—which he refers to as "the Mosaic cult," a common term in the nineteenth century—with world mythologies, only to show how it encompasses them all and offers the original narrative of revelation. Thus, it can be seen as a truly universal religion because it constitutes the core of all faiths and myths.

It is worth pondering the two figures Kohler mentions in this passage, Görres and Creuzer, who exerted a major influence on Einhorn as they validated the Schellingian worldview. All partook in a similar understanding of religious symbolism predicated on the unity and centralizing nature of religion.

Joseph von Görres (1774–1848) was a German writer, philosopher, theologian, and pamphleteer. Initially an admirer of the French Revolution, he then became a staunch critic of it, having grown suspicious of rationalism. This trajectory resembles the path trod by many a German Romantic of the Heidelberg group influenced by Schelling. After arguing, in *Mythengeschichte der asiatischen Welt* (*History of the Myths of the Asiatic World*, 1810), that all Oriental myths descend from a common source, Görres then produced a study on Christian mysticism.³² The impact of the latter work on the intellectual education of both Richard Wagner and Carl Gustav Jung was so powerful that each mention him in their respective memoirs, highlighting the common origin of t human myths.³³

The other figure Kohler mentions is Friedrich Creuzer (1771–1858), a linguist and professor at the University of Heidelberg. His *Symbolik und Mythologie der alten Völker, besonders der Griechen* (*Symbolism and Mythology of the Ancients, Particularly the Greeks*), first published in 1810–12, sought to demonstrate that the Homeric tradition and Greek religion came from the Orient through the Pelasgians (pre-Greek indigenous inhabitants of the Greek Isles), share much with the Jewish tradition, and contain the seeds of the concept of revelation.³⁴ He thus affirmed the religious nature of myths instead of drawing a line between the ancient Near East and the Greek civilization. Creuzer describes his ambition as investigating "the cohesion and the spirit of ancient faith, poetry, and the arts and to show in the works of Antiquity the religious center in which they come together."³⁵ His thesis made an impression on Schelling and his followers, as it contributed to collapsing the dichotomy between religion and mythology, thus following Schelling's conclusions in his *Philosophy of Revelation*.³⁶

A final aspect of Creuzer's thought that made its way into or resonated with Einhorn's approach concerns the nature of the divine itself as a centralizing principle. Creuzer expressed this in terms of a centrifugal/centripetal dynamic and, probing the Brahmanic tradition, affirmed that it was a centrifugal force that presided over Brahma's constriction from infinitude to finitude and restored back into infinitude through Vishnu.³⁷ Einhorn puts forth a similar principle in his *Das Prinzip des Mosaismus und dessen Verhältnis zum Heidenthum und Rabbinischen Judenthum* (*The Principle of Mosaism and Its Relationship to Paganism and to Rabbinical Judaism*), which he published in 1854 shortly before leaving Europe for the United States. In it, he professes that "the law of centralization is the basis of all natural formations in the physical and spiritual world."³⁸

Einhorn sought to establish a positive theology of Judaism as a faith from which all other monotheisms had emerged—or could emerge, and of a principle of plurality out of a central core.

> Our task is to determine precisely the essence of Mosaic doctrine. It is to establish a principle which endures as the innermost soul of, and the primary source for, all formations of Mosaism without exception. This

principle reads: Centralization of different existences without willful impairment of any individual existence.[39]

This principle of the innermost soul, here expressed in a theology of plurality and unity within Judaism, would also become a heuristic tool for both the individual and the collective psyche as well as the basis of a collective unconscious.

FRANZ JOSEPH MOLITOR: EXOTERIC ESOTERICISM

To the list of this first generation of Jewish thinkers influenced by Friedrich von Schelling, it is worth adding Franz Molitor (1779–1860), a non-Jewish figure whose writings had an outsize impact, decades later, on a handful of young men who changed the course of Jewish thought. A student of Franz Xaver von Baader and Schelling, he had penned a first attempt in 1805, but it took an additional twenty years for him to finish the *Philosophie der Geschichte, oder Über die Tradition* (*Philosophy of History, or On Tradition*), a two-thousand-page book that came out in 1827. It was meant to be the introduction to a volume entirely dedicated to Kabbalah that Molitor did not live to complete.[40]

This book was transformative for a later generation that turned to Kabbalah and sought to elevate it to a system of thought. Its chief representatives were Gershom Scholem, Walter Benjamin, and Ernst Bloch.[41] Scholem rejected Molitor's efforts "to give the Kabbalah a Christological turn" but recognized that despite this flaw, "the book is still noteworthy."[42] What Scholem (rightly) faulted Molitor for was to have explained the Jewish tradition in light of Christianity, as conveyed in the book's full subtitle, *On Tradition in the Old Covenant and Its Relation to the Church of the New Covenant*. He offered grounds for a Judeo-Christian tradition, which effectively meant collapsing Judaism into Christianity. The coexistence is expressed in centrifugal and centripetal terms that also convey a hierarchy whereby the core is more valuable than the outer part of a faith. Judaism is centrifugal, as its law is the outward form of the inwardness of Christianity—whereas Christianity is centripetal in essence, since it rests on inwardness. In this depiction of the dynamism toward inwardness, Molitor was the first to explicitly avail himself of the kabbalistic concept of *tsimtsum* as a hermeneutical tool and a way to describe a centralization process that could pertain to religious attitudes.

Molitor also saw the philosophy of Jacob Boehme as the heir to the mystical tradition and the German people—and even literally the tribe, *germanische Völkerstamm*—as its natural custodian. Despite this assertion—and a few others—that were vexing for Jewish readers, the thoroughness of his work made it a reference for many scholars.

The confluence of mysticism and notions of the soul that would evolve into studies within Schellingian circles of the psyche and its dark corners is attested by the relationship between Molitor and the influential physician and academic Gotthilf Heinrich von Schubert (1780–1860)—the author of *Die Geschichte der Seele* (*History of the Soul*).[43] In this synthesis of religion, medicine, and Schellingian philosophy, Schubert praises Molitor, and his kabbalistic motifs probably bespeak Molitor's influence.[44] His *Symbolism of Dreams*, published in 1814, is cited as influence by Freud and Jung, and in his time it had previously garnered him the admiration of writers like E. T. A. Hoffmann, whose 1817 story "The Sandman" inspired Freud's concept of the uncanny (*unheimlich*).[45]

A pivotal aspect of Molitor's thought is his refutation of the separation between mysticism and the law, between the rational and the irrational. He held the binary to be a construct of the Enlightenment and of apologetics on the part of Jewish thinkers who wanted to present Judaism as a religion of reason. It was thus wrongly characterized as alien to any theosophy or esotericism, whereas the long history of Judaism shows that the distinction between esoteric and exoteric realms, or religion and myth, has never been so clear-cut.

A non-Jewish figure in this cast of characters, Molitor nevertheless showed how Jewish motifs started influencing non-Jewish scholarship on the philosophy and psychology of religion, thereby penetrating the dominant discourse and demonstrating to all the power of the Jewish tradition to illuminate contemporary issues.

Schelling and the Mending of Eastern European Jewish Fractures

If the importance of myth in Schelling that was upheld by his scholarly followers has been established, another aspect of Schelling resonated with Jewish writers in eastern Europe: his early writings offered a defense against the dual peril of antinomianism and materialism, as Paul Franks has perceptively noted.

In a Jewish world still reeling from the false messiah Sabbatai Zevi, who claimed to have abolished the law and rabbinical authority, and from the Emden-Eibeschütz controversy, the fractured religious landscape that emerged became increasingly traversed and defined by opposition. The Hasidim were followers of a new charismatic Judaism (Hasidism), while the Mitnaggedim opposed it.[46] Because it seemed to de-emphasize the commandments and an experiential service of God characterized by the immanence of the divine, Hasidism seemed to be a new force of antinomianism—and thus not just a theological menace but a threat to societal norms.

Isaac Mieses (1802–1883)[47] and his nephew Fabius Mieses (1824–1898) mobilized Schelling's thought as they sought to both reconcile philosophy and Habad (the Hasidic sect founded in the eighteenth century by Rabbi Schneur Zalman of Liadi) and make the case for Hasidism's affinity with his philosophy of nature. Thus, they displayed a remarkable intellectual sophistication, at odds with the depiction of backward superstition or shamanism that prevailed among German enlightened circles.[48] They advanced a different rationale for invoking Schelling than his use of mythology: "Anyone who is expert in the books of the kabbalists, both early and late, and especially in the approach of the masters of Habad ... will be astonished to see how most of their content as well as the style of their form and language agrees with the scholarship of Schelling!"[49]

Their argument was forceful enough to be taken up by a contemporary, the polymath Joseph Judah Löb Sossnitz (1837–1910), a Russian-born American Talmudic scholar, scientist, and proponent of Darwinism. Sossnitz moved to the United States in 1891 and for two years tutored Mordecai Kaplan, who in 1922 founded the Reconstructionist movement, one of the key movements of American Judaism.[50]

Sossnitz turned to Schelling to specifically demonstrate how the Hasidic notion of the "leap," which characterizes God's unique freedom to fall from the Absolute in order to grasp itself in its selfhood, illuminates and enriches Schelling's understanding of dissociation (here called differentiation). This freedom is best understood, he claimed, in light of a theory of the leap (*Sprung*, or sometimes *dillug*), a one-time, sudden, supernatural occurrence.[51]

The notion at stake here is articulated in Schelling's *Philosophy and Religion* (1804), in which he addresses and questions the very possibility of a transition from the Absolute (infinitude) into finitude: "There is no continuous transition from the Absolute to the actual; the origin [*Ursprung*] of the phenomenal world is conceivable only as a complete breaking-away [*Abbrechen*] from absoluteness by means of a leap [*Sprung*].... There is no positive effect coming out of the Absolute that creates a conduit or bridge between the infinite and the finite."[52]

The leap is a cornerstone of the key text of Habad Hasidism, the *Liqqutei Amarim* (*Collection of Statements*), also known as *Tanya*, written by the founder of Habad, Rabbi Zalman, and first published in 1797.[53] If the unconscious is modeled on the universe and is of God's creation or protocreation in the act of self-contraction, what we see here is a process of dissociation that characterizes the Schellingian unconscious, the dissociation process (the not-I I) necessary for the self to grasp itself, as the rest of the passage indicates: "The Absolute is the only actual; the finite world, by contrast, is not real. Its cause, therefore, cannot lie in an impartation of reality from the Absolute to the finite world or its substrate; it can only lie in a remove [*Entfernung*], in a falling-away [*Abfall*] from the Absolute." The "real" is the reality that cannot be expressed and that surpasses our understanding, a state of absolute being or being-in-itself, which anticipates the Lacanian category.[54]

Rabbi Dovbaer Schneuri (1773–1827)—also known as Mitteler Rebbe, "middle rabbi," because he was the son of son of Zalman of Liadi, and thus the second of the first three generations of Habad rabbis—wrote in 1826 that "the generation of the created being from the divine nothing comes by way of the leap."[55] Here, the connection between the first stage of the condensation process (*tsimtsum*), which results from the "divine nothing" (or divine nothingness), and the Creation is made clear: it happens through that leap.

Notably, the *leap* (*dillug/Sprung*) is a construction first found in the work of the early modern kabbalist Abraham Abulafia, alongside the concept of *kefitsa*, skipping from one thought to another, which he used to describe the associative process of moving from one idea to the next while meditating, and thus revealing the hidden similarities of seemingly opposite aspects. Meyer Landauer had just discovered Abulafia's work, and Scholem would write about his contribution as foreshadowing the findings of the workings of the psyche and, essentially, the field of psychology (and the Freudian unconscious). But for most of the nineteenth century, these earlier scholars could not have known the work of Abulafia.[56]

As I will discuss, finding the continuities between Schelling and Hasidism and showing how the theology of the movement could be coterminous with philosophy, as well as how it anticipated scientific discoveries, would become paramount for the defense of Hasidism in the second half of the nineteenth century. The first instances can be found here, however, with this reading of Schelling by Mieses, Mieses, and Sossnitz.

Sossnitz further marshals his arguments in a pamphlet entitled *Aken Yesh Adonai* (*Yes, There Is a God*)—an attack on modern materialism and particularly on one of its main proponents, Ludwig Büchner (1824–1899), and his book *Kraft und Stoff* (*Force and Matter*), which professes that there is no need for a transcendent and immaterial force to explain the universe and that the laws of physics and chemistry are sufficient.[57] Contra Büchner, he sought to explain the scientific unknown of the cosmos by way of Kabbalah and by using Schellingian categories, particularly the concept of *Sprung*, to account for a force outside matter. Schelling concluded that nature ought to be understood as dynamic and that this dynamism logically implies an evolutionary structure of nature. Sossnitz drew on the German physiologist Emil du Bois-Reymond's (1818–1896) theory of consciousness, which similarly links the creation of matter with the workings of the mind, not the other way around.[58] In this construct, the dynamism of knowledge merged with the notion of progressive revelation, whereby scientific inquiry would only affirm the validity and the unfolding of ancient knowledge contained in Kabbalah. This concept of progressive revelation also corresponds to the idea of *Nachträglichkeit* ("afterwardness") in Schelling—a deferred ascription of meaning to the past and its disclosure in time, which connects individuals—at all times, even in modernity—back to the transcendent ground from which they arose.[59] History for the Schellingians is an exercise in deciphering symbolic forms in nature and in the mind, and this effort can only unfold progressively, implying latency or belatedness. For Jewish thinkers, the stakes are even higher: the notion of progressive revelation—because it shows the compatibility between science and religion—has been called an Orthodox strategy of modernization, as it strives to uphold the tradition in its fullness while embracing the latest scientific developments.[60]

This possibility of Kabbalah as science of the mind was a continuation of the modern kabbalistic apologetics seen in the best-selling *Sefer ha-Brit* (*The Book of the Covenant*).[61] First published anonymously in 1797, its author, Pinchas Hurwitz, aimed to familiarize Jewish readers with key concepts of modern science through Kabbalah (the first part of his book being a science encyclopedia and the second consisting of a kabbalistic piety manual). Expanding scientific knowledge should depend on increasing religious knowledge and vice versa, he professed.

Friedrich von Schelling's identity philosophy, in which he sought to demonstrate that the Absolute expresses itself directly in all beings as the unity of the subjective and the objective, reflects the protodivinity or the protocreation leading to God's leap. It is a dissociation of God's inner life and his division between his essential nature and the world he decided to create. Schelling's philosophy of creation was thus channeled as an apologetics of a specific type, a confirmation of the principles of Judaism through the reappropriation of a discourse grounded in Jewish references.

Tsimtsum, *the Unconscious, and Otherness: Centering and Decentering Judaism*

I will now interrogate the impetus for the gesture that turned a Jewish theosophical imaginary into a stock of philosophical concepts for gaining insights into the mind. What is the logic for such a derivation of Jewish thought out of Schellingian philosophy, itself inspired by Jewish theosophy? To be sure, the more fluid and multifaceted a thought, the easier it is to adapt, and this was certainly the case with Schelling. The mercurial quality of his thinking led the French philosopher Vladimir Jankélévitch (1903–1985) to a mocking assessment: "Schelling, as we know, spent his time changing his mind on everything."[62]

Schelling's reception among his Jewish disciples, however, consistently emphasized the void created by self-restriction (and seemingly overlooked a troublesome aspect of the depiction of a withdrawn God, a potentially Gnostic theme). The notion of void in Hebrew can be conveyed by several expressions. One is *chalal*, which means space, outer space, void, or cavity, and whose triliteral root also means "the profane." The withdrawal of the divine is the profane. This sense of *chalal* as the void created by the withdrawal of the divine appears in the mystical writings of the Lurianic school, to which I will turn momentarily. The famous biblical phrase of Genesis 1:2, "tohu-va-vohu," can also be translated as "void"; in this case, the void and formless are part of the same expression. In what follows, however, I will be using the notions of abyss and void interchangeably for referring to the space created by the divine withdrawal, thus accepting Gershom Scholem's identification: "The void is the abyss, the chasm or crack which opens up in all that exists."[63]

As we have seen, Schelling incorporated in his thinking the notion of *tsimtsum* found in Lurianic Kabbalah—a process marked by a contraction, or a void-creating intensification—having derived this from Jacob Boehme and other Christian kabbalists. What is at stake in this concept is the dynamic relationship between center and periphery, the nature of presence and absence, and the possibility of a wrathful god that was introduced by Boehme in probing the reasons for God's contraction and the creation of the unground.

But *tsimtsum* is not only a kabbalistic concept; it had already appeared at other junctures in the Jewish tradition. In the Talmud, it is the place of God's presence in the Holy of Holies—the earthly dwelling place of God in the Bible—and it points not to a mere absence but rather to a condensed presence in a point. The commentaries offer a slightly different approach that depicts layers of concealment. The fourth-century-CE translation of the Hebrew Bible into Aramaic, called the Targum Neofiti, features the term *tsimtsum* when translating Rebekah's self-concealment behind a veil, which doesn't efface her presence but only strategically dissimulates it.[64] Although Scholem characterized *tsimtsum* as a withdrawal of the divine, it is not just a retreat from the world but a veiled intensification of the presence that can be traced back to pre-Lurianic sources and even in certain lines of transmission of Luria's thought.

Indeed, Luria's legacy bifurcated into two different schools. They are represented on the one hand by Haim Vital (1543–1620), who is universally regarded as Luria's successor, and on the other by Israel Sarug (d. 1610), who saw no distinction between philosophy and Kabbalah, disseminated Kabbalah in Italy and influenced Pico della Mirandola and the Neoplatonists.[65] Two different models of *tsimtsum* emerged from these two different strands, promoting a centripetal and a centrifugal model, respectively.

In his *Ets Haim* (*Tree of Life*), which recapitulates the teachings of his teacher Luria, Vital depicts God's effacement for the sake of his creation, intentionally becoming a peripheral presence: "And when it arose in the Simple Will to create worlds . . . then the Infinite *tsimtsem* itself at the central point within itself, at the exact centre of its light, and *tsimtsem* that light, and withdrew to extremities surrounding the central point, and then a vacant place and environment, and an empty space remained."[66] In these teachings on *tsimtsum*, Luria describes a voluntary act of the Infinite One, who first contracted in himself and then created a vacuum in his midst by sending himself to the circumference. Scholem was adamant that for the school of Luria, as propagated by Vital, *tsimtsum* meant limitation and withdrawal: "One is tempted to interpret this withdrawal of God into his own Being in terms of Exile, of banishing Himself from His totality into profound seclusion."[67] This is why Scholem favored a Lurianic-focused narrative for establishing his interpretation of Kabbalah as a theology of exile, a response of Spanish exiles to the cataclysm of the expulsion after the Reconquista. Vital's model is *ki-feshuto* (literal): it purports to depict a historical event and even a God willing to suffer for his creation.[68] Due to the opposition of Vital's son, however, these writings did not circulate before 1660, and another narrative, the Sarugian one, became influential.[69]

In the Sarugian story, *tsimtsum* is *lo-ki-feshuto* (metaphorical): it is a centrifugal model, placing God in the center. It posits an emanation of the divine presence that is comparable to another mystical system: Rabbi Moses Cordovero's Kabbalah and its Neoplatonic models of emanations that describe a progressive unfolding of diversity out of the infinite unity of the divine, and consequently a notion of unity born out of plurality. However, in opposition to the Cordoverian model, and even if he accepted the possibility of a continual process of emanation, Sarug rejected the notion of an equivalence of the divine and its emanations in the world. His operating model is *panentheism*—a term describing the doctrine that God is an essence that contains the entire universe within itself but is not exhausted by it, a position eschewing pantheism.[70]

Because of Sarug's proximity to Neoplatonism, Gershom Scholem, in his sustained effort to avoid collapsing Kabbalah with philosophy, dismissed him, calling his contributions "alien" as well as guilty of fueling Christian Kabbalah and injecting philosophical concepts into a Lurianic system that didn't contain them in the first place.[71] In addition, in Sarug's narrative God's initial state is one of inner harmony, or even autoerotic rapture (*sha'hashua*).[72] For him, *tsimtsum* is an act of rupture: an act of will, the production of a "drop of semen," which he identifies with *din* (the *sefira* of judgment).[73] The meaning of *din* conveys a sense of necessary restriction in order to create something other than the divine, but it is also the possible root of evil: the space created by the divine restriction can now be occupied by the nondivine, hence evil.

For Sarug, *tsimtsum* is a contraction as intensification. The consequence of *tsimtsum* is thus not an absence of God but a tumultuous presence that increases the darkness of the world and requires coknowledge and cocreation.⁷⁴ What is the nature of this darkness? In Schelling, the contraction of the initial divine potency is not directly linked to the demonic, but it is what causes the "dark ground," borrowing from the Boehmian analysis of God's wrath and emphasizing the divine attribute of *din*—judgment—instead of its opposite, *hesed*, mercy or grace).⁷⁵ By all measures, Boehme and then Schelling embraced a Sarugian model, to which they obtained access indirectly: the Sarugian Kabbalah had been disseminated among Christian kabbalists through Naftali Bacharach's *Emeq ha-Melekh* (*Valley of the King*) and Abraham Cohen de Herrera's *Puerta del Cielo* (*The Gate of Heaven*), found in the influential *Kabbala Denudata* by the German Hebraist Christian Knorr von Rosenroth (1636–1689).⁷⁶ This is where, conflating judgment with wrath, the image of a pre-Christian angry God was conveniently shaped.

With this reading, Schelling gestures toward the concept of the jealous God of the Hebrews, whereas God's true will, which leads him to contract himself in order to create finitude, to abandon the infinite for the finite, can be symbolically depicted as *hesed*.⁷⁷

The Sarug-inflected reading, insisting on *din* as judgment or even wrath, opened up the potential for a Marcionite interpretation—operating on the teachings of the Christian Gnostic sect of the second-century theologian Marcion of Sinope, which claimed to detach the Christian teachings from their corrupt Jewish sources and professed a wholesale rejection of the God of the Hebrew Bible.⁷⁸ Indeed, this interpretation became one of reasons for the attacks on Schelling: in *Die christliche Gnosis* (*The Christian Gnosis*, 1835), the Protestant theologian and founder of the Tübingen school, Ferdinand Christian Baur, questions whether the philosophy of Boehme and Schelling was nothing but a revival of Gnosticism.⁷⁹

The interpretation of the abyss as wrath extended into the twentieth century: in *Logique du sens* (*Logic of Sense*), Gilles Deleuze characterizes Schelling's treatment of the *Ungrund* (*sans-fond*) as the mystical language of a formless and blind wrath. He, however, didn't identify any Jewish motifs in it but aligned it with Nietzschean thought, pitting a groundlessness of Dionysus against the individuation principle found in Apollo and Socrates.⁸⁰

So why did these philosophers read the outcome of the *tsimtsum* in such a wrathful way—and, as Deleuze later did, with an emphasis on anger as a source of creation? And why were Jewish thinkers willing to co-opt this thought, regardless of the dangerous legacies and political overtones of Gnosticism and particularly of Marcionism? Does all this presuppose that the early philosophies of the unconscious based on kabbalistic concepts were also tainted by Christian readings of Kabbalah that had long been weaponized against Judaism itself—the *Ungrund* based on *din* rather than mercy being only an instance among many others?[81] Did this raise the stakes of Jewish engagement with Schelling? And what other interpretations of the abyss can be mobilized?

THE CREATION AND THE ENDURING ABYSS

The traditional reference to the abyss in the world is found in Genesis 1:2: "Now the earth was unformed and void [*tohu va vohu*], and darkness was upon the face of the abyss [*tehom*/deep]." While the biblical Hebrew describes the primeval ocean and the postcreation waters of the earth, kabbalistic literature takes them to mean "the deep"—a bottomless pit synonymous with the abyss. That the abyss should have remained in existence even after the creation of an ordered cosmos has been subject to questioning. This is especially true in the work of Nathan of Gaza (1643–1680), the disciple of the false messiah Sabbatai Zevi (1626–1676). Nathan's literary activity and mystical justification for abolishing the commandments made him the decisive propagandist of the Sabbatean movement and an advocate for his messiah's heterodoxy. Exhibiting notoriously aberrant behavior, he proclaimed that Jewish law ought to be abolished and that redemption should come about through sin—an ascent by way of descent. In Nathan's writings, in addition to the word traditionally used for abyss, *tehom*, another word describes the void left by the *tsimtsum*: *tehiru*—a term found in the Zohar that, in another reversal typical of the tradition, originally evoked brightness as well as judgment.[82] Whether *tehom* or *tehiru*, the abyss is a narrative of protocreation but also an enduring presence.

Because of the verticality of Sabbatean theology, with its various images and narratives of ascent and descent, the motif of the abyss naturally exerted a strong attraction: "Why has the abyss [*tehom*] remained in his world?" Nathan of Gaza asks.[83] This interpellation is part of his *Derush ha Taninim* (*Treatise on the Dragons*, 1666), a commentary on the Zoharic *Discourse on the Dragons*. The discourse is based on the Parasha Bo, the passage about Exodus 10:1–13:6, in which the secret of the great serpent, understood to be the evil principle, is revealed to Moses.[84]

This formlessness and the possibility of evil illustrate Deleuze's point about the abyss being wrath: the shapelessness of creation in mysticism posits the wrath of the formless and creates its mythopoetic inarticulation. If God presided over the creation of heaven and earth in Genesis 1:1, what accounts for the persistence of the formlessness and of the abyss? And why this similitude?

The belief in the proximity between divine presence and abyss is manifested at multiple junctures in the commentary tradition. A Talmudic text specifically discloses the location of a concealed passage situated beneath the altar of the Temple in Jerusalem that connects it to the deep (*tehom*).[85] In the Zohar, these conduits are said to be sealed on the side of the altar by the *'even shetiyah*, which means "weaving stone" but is often translated as "foundation stone." Multiple commentaries have described this stone as the place where the world began and where the Holy of Holies once stood.[86] This is in keeping with the notion of *tsimtsum* as a condensation of the divine presence (*shekhina*) that dwelled in the Holy of Holies.

In Nathan of Gaza's cosmic theology, which draws on but departs from Lurianic Kabbalah, *tehiru* describes the space from which God is absent: it is the *space-after*, the space left by the withdrawal. And yet God himself needs to tap into the void he has created: "The reason is that each time the blessed Holy One works a great miracle, he sifts/selects/clarifies [*borer*] siftings/selections/clarifications [*berurin*] from the mystery of this *tehiru*."[87]

The descent into the abyss is undertaken to purify the lowermost parts of creation. It is thus a messianic task: "And this clear abyss is not refined and will not be refined by anyone, but by the King Messiah."[88] This descent for the purpose of purification mirrors, and is connected to, the Sabbatean theology of redemption through sin, an early modern Jewish version of Gnosticism that wreaked havoc in the Jewish world and is often associated with the collapse of traditional rabbinical authority and Jewish modernity.[89]

There is another reference to *tehiru* in Nathan of Gaza: his major *Sefer ha Beria* (*Book of Commandments*). In a convoluted passage, he explains that "the seed of the primordial thought descends into the light that has no thought, and the tree emerges in the place of the straight line [*qaw hašawe*]."[90] Elliot Wolfson perceptively analyzes the concept of *tehiru* as the light that has no thought—that is, the consciousness that is not conscious, or the unconscious—which demonstrates the porosity of cosmology and of the mind.[91]

Jacques Derrida has addressed the "drama of God" and the *tehiru* in which it takes place, where "God goes out of himself and determines himself."[92] This is precisely why and how *tsimtsum* becomes ethical in post-Lurianic theology.[93] The isomorphy between God and the unconscious and the need to be cognizant of both charts an invitation to self-knowledge in a Kabbalah-inspired theology. This self-knowledge is only mediated through the not-I, the Other, in an imitation of God's bifurcation between his essential nature (*Ein Sof*) and his relational or creative nature (based on his Torah-based emanation process, as we have seen in Sarug's theology), a mysticism-inflected philosophy of otherness that would culminate with Franz Rosenzweig's and Martin Buber's I and Thou, as we will see in the second part of the book.[94] This interpretation, far from suggesting a disconnect in Judaism between mysticism and ethics, emphasized the *confluence* between the realm of ethics and the unconscious.[95]

OTHERNESS: DIFFERENCE, NOT ALIENATION

The Lurianic conception of *tsimtsum* was, Gershom Scholem tells us, "intended to give an explanation for the existence of something other than God."[96] At stake is the accommodation of the Otherness within oneself, what Elliot Wolfson calls an "otherness of the **not**-other."[97] Schelling articulates this problem, and its ethical implications, as follows: "Just as in everything living, so already in that which is primordially living, there is a doubling that has come down, through many stages, to that which has determined itself as what appears to us as light and darkness, masculine and feminine, spiritual and corporeal. Therefore, the oldest teachings [*die ältesten Lehren*] straightforwardly represented the first nature as a being with two conflicting modes of activity."[98]

The mention of "oldest teachings" is a possible allusion to Kabbalah, also conveyed by mentions of a downward movement that mimics the mystical emanation process. The rhetorical pairs or binaries, as a refraction of the bifurcated essence of their source, are another possible allusion.

It is God's self-consciousness that calls for and explains the dividedness of consciousness from which consciousness of the Other can emerge. It is the revelation of this bifurcation that is presented in Kabbalah and that

Schelling seizes on while harmonizing it with a greater philosophical system. If, as Scholem argues, the model of *tsimtsum* corresponded to the framework needed by Jews for making cosmic sense of the expulsion from Spain and the diaspora, the Schellingian reading of *tsimtsum*, with all its shortcomings and problems, paved the way for a mythical incorporation of the Other into oneself. Since this is modeled after God, in a dissociation of God from the world in order to bring the world into existence as a separate entity, such a mythology of protocreation makes no space for alienation, defined as a separation between the self and an Other that is essential to their nature, and thus between two elements that belong together. If correctly understood, Otherness results from a differentiation within the self, where the Other is the result of one's desire for something apart from the identical to oneself, something that is not the self but not alien, and it does not carry the potential trauma of separation.

To be sure, the symbolic representation of an absent God, a withdrawn God after the *tsimtsum*, the moment of retraction, became part of the attraction of Kabbalah beyond a strictly Jewish audience. As a tradition that made space for a disappeared God, and perhaps a theology that organized its own supersession, Kabbalah became alluring. It turned kabbalistic hermeneutics into a discourse of modernity: one about the disappearance of God and the existential solitude of man thrown into the universe, even if this could not have been further from the ethos of the Lurianic circles and their hermeticism.[99] To account for the withdrawn God, however, this narrative also exhibited features of an increasingly attractive (and threatening) rereading of Gnosticism—the appeal of which would culminate in the twentieth century.[100]

The stakes surrounding Gnosticism and its rejection were high. To be accepted as a religion of reason, which was the goal of the proponents of the *Wissenschaft des Judentums* (the scholarly study of Judaism, the WdJ), Judaism had to be demonstrably preserved from external influences. Therefore, if Schelling could be shown to have exhibited Gnostic features, adopting his thinking would be harmful. This is why WdJ scholars, such as Heinrich Graetz, were bent on proving the impurity of mysticism, which was seen as the product of foreign and superstitious accretions onto Judaism. These thinkers would never accept Schelling—especially his later work—as we will see in the next chapter. But this is also why the philosophical and scholarly approaches to the study of Kabbalah converged in order for Jewish thinkers to reclaim the legacy on which the philosopher had built his system.

Indeed, the benefit of reading Schelling's mythopoetic account of the Creation is to offer a reflection on the origins of consciousness, along with the dissociation being fueled by a desire and need for Otherness in the protocreation process within the divine itself. The myth or motif of *tsimtsum*, as the contraction creating the abyss, reflects the unconscious and operates as a paradigm of the psyche. I would argue that the *tsimtsum* can also be applied to society as a paradigm of identity in which a preliminary retraction is necessary for existence because it makes space for Otherness—a *tsimtsum* that could be metaphorized or still read in a religious manner, as is demonstrated by the range of thinkers who availed themselves of it, from scholars to rabbis.

A construct in which Kabbalah would enable one to seek Otherness within oneself is a strong departure from most instances of Otherness depicted in premodern kabbalistic texts. Otherness had been mostly framed as the *siṭra aḥra* (the other side), the demonic aspect within the divine that was then ascribed to non-Jews.[101] The novel reading thus gave a new validity to Kabbalah among Jews because it demonstrated its foresight, but also because it showed that Kabbalah could be used in conversation with the non-Jewish world.

Slavoj Žižek has applied Friedrich von Schelling and Jacques Lacan in his model of psychoanalysis as a philosophy of freedom.[102] It is beyond the scope of this book to engage in a critique of Žižek's contribution, but one can add to his approach. Probing the Jewish reception of the contiguities between the unconscious and Kabbalah, especially in their Schellingian articulations, buttresses Lacan's dictum that "the status of the unconscious is ethical and not ontic."[103] The path to psychoanalysis, fashioned in these pre-Freudian theories of the unconscious and based on Jewish mysticism, is a philosophy of the inner-otherness within the self, which can be inverted as a not-otherness of any given Other. Just as God had to contract himself and create the unground in order for the world to exist, a human individual needs to restrict the self in order to make space for the Other, which is how the self can exist. Likewise, a national entity needs to contract itself in order for others to inhabit the space left vacant, which will in turn shape its own identity. Instead of the narrative of exile described by Scholem, this is a narrative of identity and of rapprochement, if not assimilation. This is exactly why David Einhorn, among other thinkers, focused his attention on the mechanisms of centralization, the dynamics of margins and center. Such study must come from a desire to undertake it, however, and it goes back to Jacob Boehme's desiring and Schelling's

Sehnsucht (longing), which constitute the impulse for the initial contraction and the creation of the unground. As Lacan professes, desire "is the movement by which the subject is de-centered."[104]

The later version of Schelling's *The Ages of the World* also features this push and pull of the center, couched in psychological terms.[105] Realizing his shortcoming in the face of the divine, man flees the center. In this way, Schelling notes, "the anxiety [*Angst*] of life itself drives man out of the center in which he was created."[106] It is in that conception of man's drifting away from and reuniting with the "center" that the indebtedness of Lacanian psychoanalysis (whose "lack" is that split from the center) to Schelling is most evident.[107] It also aptly describes the mechanism of a minority culture trying to engage a majority culture, of attraction to, and distance from, that center. And over course of the nineteenth century, the uses of Kabbalah and of the unconscious became a modality of that engagement.

A useful operative concept to describe the significant role played by Schelling among Jewish thinkers and theologians is the notion of appropriation that Paul Ricœur details in *Hermeneutics and the Human Sciences*. For Ricœur, appropriation consists of taking an alien concept from a different culture and assimilating it.[108] I contend, however, that in this instance, the recourse to a philosophical yet theosophical-inflected Schellingian unconscious is an important act not just of validation of one's tradition but of its *re*appropriation—reclaiming it from others.[109]

In their progressive work, the scholars of the WdJ, who were mostly averse to Kabbalah at the onset of the movement, would come to see it as an asset to embrace in their bid to establish the worthiness of Judaism and Jewish culture based on scholarship as a language of shared values. This is the subject of the next chapter.

✳ 3 ✳
The Margins of Reason
The *Wissenschaft des Judentums*, Kabbalah Studies, and the Emerging Science of the Mind

In a 1937 letter to his publisher, Gershom Scholem described his desire to overcome the barriers to the study of Kabbalah: "It is only the misty walls of history that surround it that need to be penetrated. To penetrate it—that is the task I have set for myself."[1] He portrayed himself as a field-builder who had responded to a calling and breathed new life into a scholarly study of Judaism long stifled by a narrow-minded and petty approach to its tradition.

The scholarly study of Judaism (the *Wissenschaft des Judentums*, hereafter the WdJ) that Scholem faulted can be described as the use of academic methods and the pursuit of scholarly ideals in the study of Judaism, Jews, and Jewish history, aiming to demonstrate its value through its production of a variety of publications, institutions, and networks.[2] The movement began in Germany in 1818 with the pamphlet of the young scholar Leopold Zunz (1794–1886) titled *Etwas über die rabbinische Literatur* (*On Rabbinical Literature*), followed by a more programmatic essay by Immanuel Wolf (1799–1829), "On the Concept of a Science of Judaism," in 1822.[3] Eager to prove that Judaism could be a fit subject for scholarly study, the WdJ saw its effort as part of a movement to shape Jewish emancipation. This identity-building project was thus predicated on history and historiography, and proponents of the WdJ, the *Wissenschaftler*, rejected the aspects of Judaism that strayed from reason. Yet for Scholem, "the removal of the pointedly irrational and of demonic enthusiasms from Jewish history" was the "original sin" of this study of Judaism and its demise. To support his views, he famously quoted a quip attributed to the bibliographer Moritz Steinschneider: "We have only one task left: to give the remains of Judaism a decent burial."[4] In Scholem's view, only Zionism and the study of the irrational in the Jewish tradition could revive Judaism, and the neglect of Kabbalah was seen as a symbol of this bankruptcy.[5]

This view goes against the professed goal of the *Wissenschaftler* themselves, who strove at multiple junctures to make their scholarly endeavors relevant to their times and to breathe new life into their scholarship.[6] Recent scholars, however, have revisited this "narrative of neglect," this tale of the study of Kabbalah left barren before Scholem.[7] Yet, rather than nonexistent, the reception was ambivalent.[8]

WdJ participants were diverse, and their priorities and circumstances changed over the course of the century. Such diversity suggests the need for a granular approach in studying this academic movement, in order to highlight the inflection points or changes in how the WdJ related to the subjects it explored. Its second generation, that of scholars who began writing in the 1840s—such thinkers as Meyer Landauer, Nachman Krochmal, Adolf Jellinek, and Ahron Marcus in Germany, Adolphe Franck in France, and Elia Benamozegh in Italy—has received greater attention in recent years. Current scholars of the WdJ are also casting a wider net that now decenters the *Haskalah* (Jewish Enlightenment): the movement's origin and geographic boundaries have been expanded beyond Berlin. These boundaries originally excluded Italian scholars (who often wrote in Hebrew and were mostly concerned with philology), such as Samuel David Luzzatto (1800–1865). Thinkers who initiated scholarly studies of Judaism—as Elyakim Hamilzahgi (1780–1854) did in Galicia (present-day Poland and Ukraine)—had been erased from the master narrative because they had lost battles with key WdJ figures and because most of their work only circulated in manuscripts. Such figures are slowly being reintegrated.[9]

In addition to taking a more granular approach, I will also employ an expanded definition of the *Wissenschaft*, not just in terms of geography but also in terms of scholarly endeavors that should be included in the movement's orbit. Essentially, my aim is to demonstrate that the WdJ was accompanied by greater attention given to the science of the mind.

In this multiplicity of approaches and topics, Kabbalah came to play a significant role in the WdJ's politics of identity, one in which reason, both in and for Judaism, played a pivotal role, but in a more nuanced way than the Scholemian narrative seems to indicate. Probing the dichotomy between reason and the irrational is thus part of the task of reassessing the legacy of the WdJ.

If reason was paramount, it is primarily because it is a tenet of ethical monotheism and because it testified to Judaism's convergence with the philosophies of its day, Kantianism and Hegelianism in particular.[10] Indeed, I would argue that reason is essential because it is relational.[11] This explains its centrality in the narrative of assimilation, including why eastern European Hasidic communities were judged harshly by most western European Jews—chief among them the *Wissenschaftler*—and even caricatured for their seemingly irrational practices. But once a new paradigm could be established, by which the bond uniting humanity did not have to be exclusively one of reason but of a deeper layer of the psyche—the unconscious, by definition beyond reason (though not necessarily irrational)—a new defense of Hasidism would be mounted, as I show in the second part of the book.

Despite a few early studies, mysticism was not a priority at the onset of the WdJ. The *Wissenschaftler* grew more interested in it, however, in the later 1800s, a period coinciding with the emergence of new conceptions of consciousness and the mind. This change could only happen once the proponents of the WdJ had distanced themselves from its initial, rationalist stance and from an identity-building project predicated on history and on the historiographical examination of the Jewish past, as defined by Leopold Zunz in his 1818 pamphlet. In it, he characterizes "our scholarship" (*unsere Wissenschaft*)[12] as a retrospective inventory of the riches of Jewish history.[13] A new reading of the tradition—driven by an imperative of self-assertion—had emerged. This development brings to mind another definition of modernity, in which the modern is that which seeks knowledge of itself without necessarily finding that knowledge in the past.[14]

Starting in the mid-nineteenth century, scholars or proponents of Jewish mysticism availed themselves of psychological notions for explaining the attraction of Kabbalah but also for establishing it as hermeneutics—an interpretative tool springing from religion but going beyond it. In particular, they proclaimed it a reflection of the human psyche. This move coincided with the foundation of a science of the mind: viewing the human mind as a fit subject for scientific study and bestowing on it the authority of a full-fledged discipline. In 1883, the German philosopher and historian Wilhelm Dilthey argued that neither psychology nor sociology (because it pertained to the behavior of groups and had a psychological element to it) can be subsumed under the rubric of natural science (*Naturwissenschaft*). He instead popularized the term *Geisteswissenschaft*, science of the mind.[15] If the scholarly study of Kabbalah could illuminate the mechanisms of the psyche, it could partake in the science of the mind and thus become a legitimate field of study.

In this chapter, I begin by examining how the *Wissenschaft* project, heir to the Enlightenment, rejected nonrational elements of the Jewish tradition—namely, Kabbalah—but still addressed mysticism, albeit with a great deal of caution. I then show that when the movement later came to accept Kabbalah, it revealed an expansion of the topical borders of the movement. The move contributed to a more nuanced understanding of Kabbalah as hermeneutics as well as to a reassessment of Kabbalah as a tool for the revitalization of Judaism altogether, sometimes blurring the lines between the theological and the scholarly realms.

The Bonds of Reason: Revisiting the Rationale against Kabbalah

The relative failure—or reluctance—of the WdJ to address the irrational, and thus mysticism, arguably constitutes an early stage in the history of the movement and an embrace of its Enlightenment roots. Placing reason as its centerpiece accorded with the movement's intent, which can be explained as a response to both external and internal opponents. As a result, the main possible avenue for reassessing mysticism was to either emphasize its rationality or disparage it based on its limited reliance on reason.

Proclaiming the importance of reason for Judaism constituted the fulcrum of the WdJ. It sought to place Jewish culture on par with European culture through a methodical and critical examination of its texts and traditions. By studying Judaism with the tools of modern scholarship, its adherents would establish Judaism's relevance and prove its worth to both the non-Jewish majority and Jews growing distant from Judaism. The philosophical project was also political—indeed, the lack of other avenues for Jews, who were barred from university teaching and public office, led them to imbue philosophy with politics and to turn their intellectual work into a political experiment.[16]

The backdrop to the nascent WdJ was widespread social unrest, promoted by antirationalist movements. The Jewish philosopher Saul Ascher (1767–1832) saw in this trend a "sickness" of the German soul, using a language of pathology increasingly applied to national and ethnic groups.[17] The journalist and satirist Ludwig Börne (1786–1837), founder of the Junges Deutschland (Young Germany) group, also excoriated this affliction.[18] The anti-Semitic "Hep" riots that erupted in Bavaria in 1819 and swept through the German territories prompted a response from young Jewish intellectuals. In 1822, the Verein für Kultur und Wissenschaft der Juden (Society for the Culture and Science of Judaism) was created; among its members was the novelist and poet Henrich Heine, a reluctant convert to Christianity.[19]

The Two Fronts of Reason

The WdJ's need to distinguish itself from two other forces—one external (nationalist and often anti-Semitic), the other internal to Judaism (both Hasidism and an estrangement from the tradition)—provided an additional impetus for the movement to emphasize the role of reason and spurn the irrational. In "On the Concept of a Science of Judaism," the movement's opening salvo, Immanuel Wolf sets out to define the scope, method, and purposes of the new discipline: "Scientific knowledge of Judaism must decide on the merits and demerits of the Jews, their fitness or unfitness to be given the same status and respect as other citizens."[20] It followed, he argues, that "this attitude must ban the relationship of strangeness in which Jews and Judaism have hitherto stood in relation to the outside world. And if one day a bond is to join the whole of humanity, then it is the bond of science, the bond of pure reason, the bond of truth."[21]

Reason, pivotal in the philosopher Moses Mendelssohn's *Jerusalem* (1783), in which he reflects on the affinity between the Enlightenment and Judaism, was now linked with assimilation. Reason is what makes any engagement with others possible, against the long shadow of alienation—which Wolf calls "strangeness." In the same essay, Wolf does assert that mainstream rabbinical literature is less relevant than Essenian, Sadducean (two minority sectarian movements in ancient Judaism), or kabbalistic material for developing an understanding of Judaism's religious dynamics over time.[22] He thus implies that marginal phenomena are more illuminating than what became the canon. But his inclusive interpretation seems not to have prevailed among the first generation of scholars.[23] The emphasis on reason among other members of the Society for the Culture and Science of Judaism, especially the Hegelian jurist and thinker Eduard Gans (1797–1839), precluded the inclusion of mysticism and esoteric lore in the modern academic study of Judaism.[24]

Writing a couple of decades before them, the philosopher Salomon Maimon (1753–1800), whom Immanuel Kant recognized as one of his sharpest critics, penned his autobiography as a journey in which his brief attraction to Kabbalah prompts his embrace of philosophy when he realizes that the gap between mysticism and reason was unbridgeable.[25] He wrote,

> By and by... perhaps as the result of many revolutions, this occult meaning was lost, and the signs were taken for the things signified. But as it was easy to perceive that these signs necessarily had meant something, it was left to the imagination to invent an occult meaning that had long been lost. The most remote analogies between signs and objects were seized, till at last the Cabbalah degenerated into an art of *madness according to method*, or a systematic science resting on conceits. The big promise of its design, to work effects on nature at pleasure, the lofty strain and the pomp with which it announces itself, have naturally an extraordinary influence on minds of a visionary type, that are unenlightened by the sciences and especially by a thorough philosophy.[26]

Maimon's indictment of Kabbalah captures the mood of his era but offers a nuanced appreciation of Jewish mysticism. His rebuttal only concerns the state of Kabbalah in his time; he aims the accusation of "madness" at the eastern European communities from which he hailed. Gravitating toward historicism, he emphasizes the stages of the disjunction between signifier and signified and what had rendered the very category of Kabbalah disreputable because it had not been filled by systematic knowledge. For the proponents of the Enlightenment, mystical practices and traditions could only endanger civic worthiness and had to be forcefully denounced. This is why they catalogued instances of deviant behaviors in Zoharic and Hasidic texts, emphasizing lewdness, idleness, and drunkenness.[27]

A prime instance of the negative depiction of Hasidism can be found in the work of Joseph Perl, whose epistolary novels—generally considered the first novels in Hebrew—are biting accounts of what he held to be Hasidic perversions. In *The Revealer of Secrets* (1819) and later in *The Test of the Righteous* (1838), he pretends to narrate the story from a Hasidic perspective and offers devastating insights into the sect's supposed moral bankruptcy, seen as reflected in its adherents' poor command of, and lack of respect for, grammar.[28] Grammar is about more than proper expression: Mendelssohn's translation of the Pentateuch and his commentary, the *Biur* (exegesis), had unambiguously stated that to think without grammar is to speak without logic.[29] Conversely, jargon only creates exclusion and denotes flawed values. Perl therefore sought to draw attention to what he considered a faulty use of language by the Jews from Eastern Europe as a way of denouncing the Hasidic drift away from reason and shared values.

For the *Wissenschaftler*, ignoring grammar was a first step toward dismantling a system of logic and commonly held principles, and intentionally so: "When we see one of our kinfolk who writes language we call 'pure,' we consider him to be an *apikoyres* [nonbeliever or heretic]. I am sure that soon everyone will forget that pure language just as, with the help of God, the real *tsadikkim* [the righteous], they totally forgot grammar," professes one of the Hasidim in Perl's first novel.[30] In the Hasidic mindset, as vilified by its opponents, abolishing grammar captures a world of possible transgressions.

Hasidism, with its emphasis on religion qua experience and its turn to mysticism, not surprisingly appeared to the *Wissenschaftler* as antiassimilationist and thus as a foe, an unpalatable, disruptive force. Hasidism, in that account, is a double alienation, both from society and from Judaism.[31] Reason, as the basis of ethics and thus the fabric of society, had to be depicted as a bedrock of Judaism, thus fostering and buttressing the notion and/or self-perception of Judaism as "ethical monotheism."[32]

Brushing off grammatical constraints and the civilization markers they represented indicated a broader antinomianism. As they drew parallels between Hasidism and the Sabbatean and Frankist heretical movements of previous centuries, the *Wissenschaftler* repeatedly denounced Hasidism as a perilous retreat from history and from society, alien to the very essence of Judaism and to the civic values on which it prided itself.[33] Passing the traditional blame of Jewish misanthropy onto the Jews from eastern Europe, they denounced the use of Kabbalah in Hasidism and dismissed both, insisting that both could only destroy social bonds.

The anxiety around the supposed destruction of social bonds was magnified by, but not limited to, the question of Kabbalah. One of the movement's major historians, the previously mentioned Heinrich Graetz, set his sights wider, beyond Kabbalah alone. Indeed, he also targeted a similar worldview of exclusion and isolation that, he claimed, is found in the Talmud as well.[34] Others, such as Abraham Geiger, the scholar and pioneer of Reform Judaism, followed suit.[35] In expanding their critical view of their own tradition, the *Wissenschaftler* adopted a language reminiscent of their non-Jewish contemporaries' critiques of Judaism, such as Johann Gottlieb Fichte's argument that "the Jewish nation excluded itself ... from us [the German nation] by the most binding element of humankind—religion."[36]

The WdJ was riven by tensions, and the varying attitudes toward Kabbalah among its proponents suggest the movement's manifold sensitivities. One of its currents set out to define mysticism as reason manifesting itself in history. At the same time, a growing interest in the obscure workings of the mind and in Kabbalah challenged the WdJ's proclaimed scope. The move toward the inclusion of mysticism and Kabbalah signaled that the scholarly study of Judaism was shifting away from its initial premises and its identity-building project strictly predicated on history and historiography. The science of the mind, a lens through which to examine Jewishness, was the first foray into psychology through an examination of Jewish pathologies and their potential therapies.

Judaism's Psychology and the Making of a Mysticism of Reason
LAZARUS BENDAVID: KANTIAN UNIVERSALISM

Like many of his contemporaries, the philosopher and mathematician Lazarus Bendavid (1762–1832), widely held to be the first Jewish Kantian, occupied positions at the margin of German intellectual institutions: trained in Berlin and Halle, he was denied an academic position because of his Jewishness. He is now less known, but his popular lectures in Vienna introduced Kant to the Austrian public. A passionate educator, he led the Jüdische Freischule (the Jewish Free School) from 1806 until 1827. The school's mission, stated in typical Enlightenment terms, was "the education of the human being," and in a spirit of universalism, Bendavid opened it to non-Jewish students.[37] Having become a member of the board of the Society for the Culture and Science of Judaism in 1822, he expressed the possibility of a reasonable mysticism in the first—and only—issue of the society's journal.[38]

Before this period, Bendavid had ventured into popular psychology as a contributor to the first German-language psychology publication, *Gnothi Sauton, oder Magazin zur Erfahrungsseelenkunde als ein Lesebuch für Gelehrte und Ungelehrte* (*Know Yourself, or Journal of Empirical Psychology: A Reader for Scholars and Laymen*), which appeared for ten years (1783–93) and whose previous editor was Salomon Maimon.[39] The journal was devoted primarily to psychological case studies and self-study, as its title indicated. In contributions that supported his advocacy of Kantian universalism, "Selbstmord aus Rechtschaffenheit und Lebensüberdruck" (Suicide out of Honesty and Life-Weariness) and "Sonderbare Art des Trübsinnes" (A Peculiar Type of Melancholy), Bendavid examines the story of two Jewish patients. From there, he offers a narrative of the pathologies of Jewish psyches torn between the private and the public realms and grappling with conflicting obligations—all constituting an indictment of an irreconcilable contradiction of the Jewish condition in modernity.

Both of these patients are cases of tragic alienation, and Bendavid transposes the traditional Christian theological accusations onto a psychological level. Christian Dohm, a Prussian civil servant, had published a pamphlet in 1781, *Über die bürgerliche Verbesserung der Juden* (*The Improvement of the Civil Status of the Jews*), in which he sought to fight anti-Jewish sentiment by showing that the conditions under which Jews lived explained their overrepresentations in certain fields.[40] In response to Dohm, Bendavid published *Etwas zur Charackteristick der Juden* (*A Word on the Characteristics of the Jews*), in which he diagnosed Jewish weakness as a collective malady.[41] The process he describes—with Jews internalizing their external powerlessness and reframing moral value as the true source of strength, thereby creating the delusional acceptance of a prolonged state of subjugation—foreshadows the Nietzschean critique of Jewish weakness in *The Genealogy of Morals*.[42]

Bendavid distanced himself from Moses Mendelssohn's *Jerusalem*, published ten years earlier. Mendelssohn had decoupled Judaism as a religion from its legislation and mounted a defense of the freedom of conscience, arguing that the state should not interfere with the faith of its citizens, which belonged to the private sphere. Bendavid called for a complete autonomization of the subject, in convergence with the Kantian rational religion. He held that his categorical imperative of universal moral principles, as a precondition for any action, could cure pathologies induced by the dissonance between Judaism and modernity.[43] Despite its harsh character, these measures were meant to save Jews from conversion: embracing Kantian universals would paradoxically enable them to maintain their Jewish identity instead of shedding it—a proposition earning him the applause of a famously vocal reluctant convert, Heinrich Heine. Kantian philosophy and universalism, Bendavid held, ought to cure psychological dissonance in a modern polity and enable Jews to find a place in it.

Other members of the WdJ movement who were eager to find a place for Judaism in the state and reconcile mysticism and reason looked to another thinker: Georg Wilhelm Friedrich Hegel. He published his *Philosophy of Right* and delivered his *Lectures on the Philosophy of Religion* in 1821, the year preceding the creation of the WdJ. In *The Phenomenology of the Spirit* (1807), Hegel defines religion as a self-consciousness of the spirit that has not attained absolute knowledge, though it constituted a path toward consciousness and thus represented a trajectory of progress.[44] A few years later, in *Wissenschaft der Logic* (*The Science of Logic*), published between 1812 and 1816, he characterizes this arduous path toward greater clarity with a ghostly metaphor: "The *System of Logic* is the Realm of Shadows [*das Reich der Schatten*]. To study this science, to dwell and work in the realm of shadows [*Schattenreich*], is the absolute training and discipline of consciousness."[45] In this system, religious experience arguably enriches or replaces logic. Hegel's influence was such that this reappraisal, inspired by the philosopher's esoteric influences—including Jacob Boehme—started modifying the prevailing perception of mysticism, or making its articulation with the Hegelian philosophical system conceivable.[46] Yet most defenses of Kabbalah continued to be built on rationality, and this would be the case for at least two more decades.

At his death in 1831, Hegel left behind a rich but ambiguous body of philosophical writings for German intellectuals to interpret according to their various agendas. In the following decade, a handful identified themselves as Young Hegelians, although the several loose groups that adopted this name by no means agreed on the philosopher's legacy. Among the best known were the Left Hegelians; a few individuals from that group posited mysticism as rational and intellectual, viewing it as a blueprint for advancing human freedom.[47]

Thirty years after announcing his Kantian credo, and despite his reservations about the openly Christian tenets of Hegelianism, Bendavid struck a Hegelian chord when he claimed that messianism as an idea is both mystical and rational. His argument is twofold. First, messianism is not a part of the revealed scriptures and thus not central to the Bible. And second, it is instead a later, human creation whose development came about in the King David era and can be chalked up to the kabbalistic ethos of that time. Probing Maimonides's writings on the Messiah, Bendavid distinguished between the two figures, the king and the savior—the former being a political, rationalistic concept in which a mortal messiah would not accomplish miracles but would instill the fear of God in humanity. Despite being the minority opinion, this strand of rationalist messianism deserved attention. The other strand, however, which he analyzed in detail using scholarly tools for his interpretation of Kabbalah, was consonant with Christian theology.[48]

In a missive to the scholar Antoine-Isaac Silvestre de Sacy (1758–1838), to whom he sent his study, Bendavid claims that his inclusion of unexpected kabbalistic materials is a token of intellectual integrity and evidence of the breadth of his research.[49] Silvestre de Sacy, whom Edward Said uses in *Orientalism* as a case study of knowledge as power, shows a certain haughtiness toward his subject matter. He dares anyone to point out to him instances in which Jews as a nation would be worthy of civic rights and emancipation. In his view, Jews' messianic expectations were nothing short of a promise of disruption in society.[50]

This brief correspondence is a testament to the intellectual exchanges occurring in Europe but demonstrates the flawed dialogue, highlighted by the scathing tone of the response in which the French scholar dismisses his correspondent's work while displaying contempt for Kabbalah and for the current state of Judaism.[51] Since Silvestre de Sacy was held as a standard of scholarship, Jewish scholars who rejected Kabbalah might have modeled their interests and approach after his, internalizing Orientalist biases against what was perceived as an Oriental form of mysticism.[52] Regardless of the exchange, Lazarus Bendavid's contribution is evidence that a language of a rational mysticism was not thoroughly alien to the stance of the WdJ, even at its onset, and that he saw connections between the working of the mind and the symbolism of the Jewish esoteric tradition.

NACHMAN KROCHMAL: RECONCILING MYSTICISM AND REASON

The language of pathology, intertwined with the language of reason, is also used by Nachman Krochmal (1785–1840) in his *Moreh Nevukhe ha-Zeman* (*Guide for the Perplexed of Our Time*). A *maskil*, or proponent of the Jewish Enlightenment, from the margins of Galicia, Krochmal was one of the earliest Jewish scholars to try to demonstrate the affinity between Kabbalah and reason, as well as the philosophical proximity between German idealism and Kabbalah.[53] Left unfinished at his death in 1840, his *Guide* was published in 1851 by two key WdJ figures, Leopold Zunz and Moritz Steinschneider, at the request of Krochmal's son. Although the defense of Kabbalah is not central to Krochmal's work, it certainly occupies a significant place: the editorial decision to release the book in its full, unexpurgated form with its tribute to Kabbalah suggests the need for a reconsideration of the idea that the *Wissenschaftler* were irreducibly hostile toward Kabbalah.

An important aspect of Krochmal's work is his attempt to reconcile Jewish thought and German philosophy, specifically regarding the Jewish nation and the Hegelian notion of national and absolute spirits—and the importance of a collective *Geist*. I address this in chapter 5; here, I focus on his use of reason.

In the first chapter of the *Guide*, Krochmal uses the language of pathology to argue that religion is prone to three interrelated psychological maladies: mystical enthusiasm, superstition, and excessive externalization of worship (ritualization). Mystical enthusiasm may trigger madness when it attempts ecstatic unification with God, and this, in turn, leads to antinomianism—a disregard for the commandments that held the community together. He adduces, as a prime example, the seventeenth-century case of the false messiah Sabbatai Zevi, who disrupted Jewish communities throughout eastern Europe and the Ottoman Empire, and whose use of the Zohar to promote his antinomian theology pushed the book further into disrepute. While Krochmal demands the firm rejection of mystical enthusiasm, he contends that mysticism itself needs to be reassessed; it cannot be completely detached from reason, the goal of which is to achieve greater abstraction. Mysticism creates a certain distance between man's mind and the sensual world, and this is how Krochmal's claim that mysticism "begins with reason" should be understood.

For Krochmal, then, if mysticism's tendency to succumb to a "feverish imagination" were reined in, Kabbalah could fulfill the role of a "science of faith" occupying a middle ground between pure sensuality and pure abstraction.[54] As *Religionsphilosophie*, it would thus be closer to the Hegelian concept of speculative Kabbalah (which seeks to explain the nature of God) and opposed to practical Kabbalah (arguably akin to magic).[55] Krochmal claims that Kabbalah is congruent with the philosophy of Maimonides—the religious rationalist par excellence[56]—making it possible to show that Judaism is rational and simultaneously indicate what is truly Jewish (*echt-jüdisch*) in it and what is not, while remaining within a German philosophical frame. In distinguishing between authentic and false Judaism, Krochmal was actually operating on a model established by the German rabbi Jacob Emden in 1780 in *Mitpachat Sefarim* (*The Shroud of the Books*), which distinguishes between earlier and later layers of Kabbalah, thereby allowing one to criticize some parts of it while accepting other parts, and which serves as a template for a criticism of Kabbalah that would not be its denunciation.[57]

ISAAC MIESES AND DAVID JOEL: INCORPORATING THE NONRATIONAL

Influenced by Krochmal's example, in 1863 Isaac Mieses undertook a similar comparison of Maimonides's teachings with mystical Jewish doctrines, insisting on the compatibility of the philosopher's thought with kabbalistic elements and thus downplaying Kabbalah's irrational nature.[58]

As Mieses's work attests, Krochmal's thinking gained currency in the second half of the nineteenth century, but several contemporaneous contributions by important figures, such as David Joel (1815–1882), marshaled similar arguments regarding the Jewish nature of Kabbalah.[59] After serving as a rabbi in the province of Posen in the kingdom of Prussia for twenty years, Joel joined the prestigious Breslau seminary in 1879, where he taught Talmudic literature until his death in 1882. His *Die Religionsphilosophie des Sohar* (*Religious Philosophy of the Zohar*, 1849) was a well-accepted defense of Kabbalah based on the premise that Kabbalah is not a heresy and that "the reconciliation of kabbalistic theories with truly-Jewish ideas" is possible, since "kabbalism and rabbinics [i.e., the literature from the Talmudic era] meet in most teachings."[60] More specifically, he saw no difference between medieval Jewish philosophy and Kabbalah, apart from Kabbalah's predilection for bold metaphors and symbolism. Joel acknowledged that Kabbalah, far from being heretical, called for reconciliation with rabbinical Judaism.

The *Wissenschaftler* mostly kept the conversation within the realm of their traditional apologetics, which were based on a certain primacy of rationalism, thought to be necessary to assess Kabbalah's worthiness. But works like those of Joel, Krochmal, or Mieses signal a transition into the incorporation of nonrational elements within their canon of Judaism—a canon reflecting more their own intellectual and historical perceptions of Judaism than the reality of Jewish practice, as Amos Funkenstein has pointed out.[61] What comes through, however, is the spectrum between the rational and the not-strictly rational, which is more complex than the outright irrational.[62] This should invite us to reconsider the enduring binary between the Enlightenment and the irrational or the occult.[63] Subsequent advocates of Kabbalah started defending it based on a worldview extending beyond reason—and where myths, symbolism, and typologies could help make sense of the mystical language. Indeed, the unconscious and its mystical refractions became a source for the defense of Judaism comparable to the notion of "ethical monotheism" for other Jewish thinkers at that time.

Myth, Symbolism, and Typologies: Expanding the Borders of the Wissenschaft des Judentums

Reassessing the treatment of Kabbalah by the WdJ illuminates the trajectory of the movement; in particular, it helps us fathom the expansion of the WdJ's topical borders and its new directions. These include the inclusion of the nonrational features of Judaism but also a reflection on myth that tacitly incorporated a Wissenschaft approach of philology and historicism, increasingly blending myth with a Schellingian worldview, and a more ahistorical one. The first publications of the generation immediately following the Wissenschaftler examined myth and the human efforts to represent the divine. What ensued was a new appreciation of Kabbalah as a manifestation of Jewish vitality, and—more universally—as insight into the human psyche and the quest for its religious core, in which the psyche mirrors itself.

PETER BEER: KABBALAH AS CONSTITUTIVE MYTH

One Jewish thinker in this period expressed an unapologetic and historical interest in Kabbalah in which the quest for origins resulted in a reflection on possible reforms of contemporary Judaism. This was the *maskil* Peter Beer (1758–1838) of Bohemia, a transitional figure between the Enlightenment and the *Wissenschaftler*.[64] Benefiting from Emperor Franz Joseph II's edict of tolerance (1782), he could attend the university in Vienna and became a teacher in modern Jewish schools as well as an active reformer of education and liturgy. Beer contributed to the journal *Sulamith*, the first German-language Jewish periodical, founded in 1806.[65] He published the two volumes of his *Geschichte, Lehren und Meinungen aller bestandenen und noch bestehenden religiösen Sekten der Juden und der Geheimlehre oder Cabbalah* (*History, Beliefs and Doctrines of All Once-Existing and Still Existing Religious Sects of the Jews and of Their Secret Teachings or Kabbalah*) in 1822 and 1823—just as Immanuel Wolf's programmatic essay was being read.[66]

Although his methods have drawn criticism, Beer's study has a pioneering quality: it traces Kabbalah to ancient times and denies it a purely Jewish character by emphasizing its non-Jewish elements.[67] For example, since he presents Kabbalah as Egyptian theology affixed on the holy scriptures, he contends that it could serve as a sort of map to return to an *Urreligion*, from which the sects that he describes had deviated as they went off in many different directions.[68] Rather than expressing anxiety about the non-Jewish nature of Kabbalah and blaming all sorts of perversions on these foreign accretions, Beer's narrative seeks to locate a religious core of humanity, the constitutive myth, and also the possibility of religious reform by revisiting an age of pure religion.

Though calling Hasidim "charlatans," in keeping with Joseph Perl's contemporaneous characterization and with the enlightened ideology of his time, in *History, Beliefs and Doctrines* Beer distinguishes them from earlier kabbalists, whom he abstains from depicting as manipulators and swindlers. He is also more lenient toward proponents of the Frankist sect and even gives an anthropological description of the movement and its families. Beer paints a psychological portrait of the kabbalists as insatiable seekers, but he also signals a judgment of possible hubris by comparing mystics to Icarus coming too close to the sun and a resulting downfall.[69] With his budding interest in the psychology of the mystic, whom he describes as "entangled in his own web," as well as in a core religion outside history that can be retrieved by peeling off its historical layers, Beer ushered in a new era in the study of Judaism. Indeed, the well-trodden path for explaining the ascent of Kabbalah, especially in the Middle Ages, had hitherto been to frame it as a response to either the dry rationalism of philosophy or Talmudic legalism at odds with metaphysical thought.

MEYER LANDAUER: KABBALAH AS INTERIORITY

The work of Meyer Landauer (1808–1841), already mentioned in chapter 2 for his proximity to Friedrich Schelling, broke new ground in Kabbalah scholarship. With Landauer, the premises of the philosophy of Schelling were turned into a scholarly endeavor mobilizing philology and symbolism alongside forays into comparative religion. His work was rightly hailed as the first scholarly survey of Jewish mysticism; its discoveries were based on his careful study of kabbalistic manuscripts.

After his untimely death, his notes and findings in the Munich library collection on medieval poetry and Kabbalah were published in 1845–46 by the Orientalist Julius Fürst (1805–1873) in the *Literaturblatt des Orients* (*Literary Journal of the Orient*), a periodical dedicated to study of the language, literature, and history of the Jews. It was the prime outlet for Kabbalah research during its decade of existence (1840–1851).[70]

Notable for its research breakthroughs, Landauer's work took shape at the intersection of existential and scholarly approaches.[71] In his first book,

Jehovah and Elohim, he accepts the rabbinical premise of a single-authored Pentateuch and examines the names of God as part of the theology of the Hebrew Bible, according to which Elohim and yhwh refer to different aspects of the divine. He also claims that the decision to name God Elohim and yhwh was incumbent on the redactor which emphasized his own role in interpreting the text and his choices when conveying the sacred text to the reader.[72]

By the time of his second book, *Essence and Form of the Pentateuch*, Landauer had evolved to the position that while there is no difference between yhwh and Elohim, this oneness can be separated into visible and hidden, subjective and objective. yhwh is the idea ("yhwh contains the first fundamental idea of the consciousness of God—the highest being as a living primary cause of the world") and Elohim its actualization.[73] Thus, the names of God do not simply denote different qualities of God, in the traditional rabbinical explanation, but also ways of experiencing the higher being.

Landauer's comparisons with Hinduism and his incorporation of manuscript studies into his scholarship were pioneering.[74] But his most important—and modern—contribution in *Essence and Form of the Pentateuch* might be his way of situating the redaction of the Pentateuch within broader cultural history and adducing kabbalistic hermeneutics to illuminate the creation of the cosmos, as captured and mirrored by Hebrew letters. As we have seen, the world is an expression of divine self-creation and the result of a contraction.

> The first action of the deity in creation, or in its emergence from itself, is represented in the Zohar either as a letter, a letter sign or as an act of copulation with the *Shechina* [literally, "dwelling" in Hebrew, a term used to describe the presence of God], and indeed using thoroughly sensual expressions—with Abulafia we have the solution to the puzzle. He compares the act of conception with the act of writing. What here is the erect member is the pen there, the seed flows here, the ink there. The ink comes onto a receptive matter, sticks, hardens—and the child of the spirit comes into the world.[75]

Without shying away from exposing the sexual content of the mystical tradition in a scholarly setting, Landauer emphasizes the nature of language as creation and procreation and consequently portrays interpretation as *imitatio dei*—a theological imperative and a process that could be experienced as a spiritual practice in which the psyche exhibits a contiguity with the divine. The sensuality of textual creation—and thus world creation—suggests an intimacy. This intimacy, or interiority, is what Kabbalah brings to Judaism, Landauer suggests, and this is why it is best suited for exploring the inner life of the mind.

ADOLPHE FRANCK: KABBALAH AS INNER LIFE

Though in a much more chaste way, at a scholarly distance and without using the language of the kabbalist, this inner sanctuary is also what Adolphe Franck meant when he described the place of Kabbalah in Judaism. Whereas Landauer pioneered manuscript studies, Franck is often credited with spreading knowledge of Kabbalah throughout Europe.[76] A scholar in his own right, Franck was an assimilated Jew and a prominent academic whose primary legacy in France was his *Dictionnaire des sciences philosophiques* (1875). His key contribution to Kabbalah scholarship is his study of Kabbalah from a philosophical perspective, but philological shortcomings—which led him to claim that the Zohar is indeed a work of the second century, when it actually is a medieval pseudoepigraphic text—weakened his work.[77]

Franck's desire to assert himself as both fully French and fully Jewish prompted him to seize every opportunity to describe Judaism as a pathway to universalism and to marshal Kabbalah as a bridge between Judaism and other philosophies. He specifically emphasized that Kabbalah's worldview deserved the consideration given to other major religious and intellectual systems. As he contended, "This transformation that we point out in the Kabbalah, this passing from symbol to ideas, is reproduced in all great philosophical and religious systems, and in all great conceptions of the human intellect."[78]

With unmistakable overtones of French revolutionary values, Franck anticipated the perception of Kabbalah as counterhistory—later posited by Gershom Scholem—as he highlighted the challenge kabbalists posed to various authorities. Kabbalah can thus appear "as a monument to the patient struggle of a people for intellectual freedom during a period of religious tyranny." But he also noted its influence, deeming it an "extremely important element in the history of human thought."[79] Franck thus rejected any notion that Kabbalah is an alien element in the religion: "We cannot possibly consider the Kabbalah as an isolated fact, as accidental in Judaism, on the contrary: it is its life and heart."[80]

This notion of Kabbalah as inner life is paramount, and it comes through in the review of Franck's work in translation by the lesser-known *Wissenschaftler* and activist Abraham Adler (1811–1856), who wrote, "Kabbalah is the truth in the form of pure inwardness." Adler flecks his review of Franck with both kabbalistic and Schellingian accents about Kabbalah originating in a darkness from which clarity emanates: "Her light finds its way in all directions, but she herself lives in the dark, denying access to the uninitiated."[81] Because reason comprehends neither itself nor the Absolute, it needs an oblique conduit, which Kabbalah provides.

Scholars such as Franck and Adolf Jellinek, Franck's German translator and a prominent scholar himself, unequivocally emphasized Kabbalah's importance in the spiritual development of humanity. So when Jellinek described Kabbalah as an element entirely alien to Judaism, he made sure to emphasize the difference between its importance in antiquity and its corruption in contemporary societies. Thus, he implicitly recognized the validity of Salomon Maimon's description of Kabbalah as a tradition whose keys had been lost.[82]

SALOMON MUNK: KABBALAH AS UNIFIER

A recurring motif among these thinkers is the Jewishness—either the alien nature or the purity—of Kabbalah or the lack thereof, which shows a degree of anxiety about borders and identity. The question of authenticity can be traced back to Jacob Emden's *The Shroud of the Books* (1780), mentioned earlier.

Like the unconscious, Kabbalah is a place where otherness may reside or creep in. Integrating Kabbalah into the canon meant expanding the boundaries of the traditional study of Judaism. This was the endeavor of Salomon Munk (1803–1867), who further contributed to the revived appreciation of Kabbalah by showing its unifying quality: its capacity to embrace and incorporate religious elements, myths, and doctrines of foreign origins and synthesize them in a form that accords with the tenets of Judaism.[83]

Born in Prussia, Munk trained in Berlin with Leopold Zunz and Abraham Geiger before resolving to abandon philosophy after attending Hegel's seminars. In reaction to the contempt in which he felt Hegel held Judaism and Islam, he set out to study Oriental philology with August Boeckh (1765–1867). Ineligible, as a Jew, for any academic position, he moved to

Paris, where he penned the first French translation of Maimonides's *Guide of the Perplexed*.[84] In his *Mélanges de philosophie juive et arabe* (*Essays on Jewish and Arab Philosophy*, 1857), Munk treats Kabbalah positively, depicting it as a bridge between East and West, a reflection of the Alexandrian Jewish milieu from which it emerged, a diasporic milieu that served as a barely disguised reflection of modern times. Such a milieu, he notes, showed Kabbalah to be an instance of Judaism's capacity for integrating elements of other cultures without losing its identity—a place of not-Other otherness.

ELYAKIM HAMILZAHGI: FROM THE SOUL OF JUDAISM TO THE HUMAN SOUL

We have seen that since Lazarus Bendavid, a psychology of Judaism had crept into the depiction of Kabbalah. This intimate—and therefore perpetually relevant—core of Judaism was essential to the work of Adolf Jellinek or David Joel, who interpreted this hidden meaning as the "inner kernel" or "metaphysical principle" of Judaism.[85] This view foreshadowed the task that Franck and then Scholem, the preeminent Kabbalah scholar of the twentieth century, would assign himself (as he described it to his publisher): unveiling "the inner life" of Judaism.[86] Whereas Kabbalah had been described as a fringe aspect of Judaism, the shared effort of these scholars was to return it to the center. Characterizing Kabbalah as the "inner life" of Judaism (or its heart) paved the way for an affinity with the inner life of the mind, which is the unconscious.

The movement, in this first generation, was beset by tensions, as we have seen. One of the most blatant sources of strain was that the very act of scrutinizing the contributions of the past could legitimize the present.[87] Subsequent proponents of a scholarly study of Kabbalah endeavored to solve this tension by reassessing the edifying value of kabbalistic hermeneutics, both past and present—with the inherent danger that their work would turn into affirmative apologetics at the expense of accuracy. This phenomenon of showcasing Kabbalah as an affirmation of Judaism, and the blurred borders between the critical study of Kabbalah and its apologetics, can be traced back to earlier periods, with instances found in the work of non-German scholars—which tends to decenter the standard narrative about the WdJ.[88]

Such was the enterprise of Elyakim Hamilzahgi (1780–1854), a Galician proponent of the Haskalah (Jewish Enlightenment) who sought to expand both the access to and the relevance of Kabbalah studies in order to deepen the meaning of Judaism and render it a source for a renewal of Jewish religious culture. In a sense, this endeavor resembles Peter Beer's earlier enterprise; he, too, was on the margins of the WdJ. Hamilzahgi had a distinct awareness of the margins and center, and of the power dynamics they implied. Indeed, he did not hesitate to call out the textual acumen of established scholars in his scathing *Sefer Rabiyah* (1837) (*The Book of Rabbi Eliakim ben Yehudah Hamilzahgi*, the title being the acronym of the author's name), in which he calls into question the German-centered focus of Jewish scholarship.[89] He preferred the perspective of eastern European research, which operated in a space free of the binaries created by the Berlin Haskalah—namely, the gap between halakha (Jewish law) and reason, which biased it against Kabbalah as a concept and rendered it blind to the difference between the true, original Kabbalah and its distortions.[90] An imperative task for scholars seeking to reinvigorate Judaism was thus to salvage the text, calling for a blend of erudition and militancy.[91]

This reappraisal of various forms of mysticism found its most explicit formulation in the previously mentioned essay by Samuel Abraham Hirsch, "Jewish Mystics: An Appreciation" (1907). Part of the reappraisal, he argues, consists of linking Kabbalah to psychology to see how both play their part "in the construction of that eternally inscrutable enigma which is called the human soul."[92] For all its inscrutability, the enigma was being increasingly scrutinized.

GEISTESWISSENSCHAFT: HERMENEUTICS AS AFFIRMATIVE APOLOGETICS?

The endeavor of shedding scholarly light on Kabbalah coincided with the emergence within both mainstream culture and academia of theories of the mind—and specifically the construction of the unconscious. The unconscious thus occupied a space comparable to Kabbalah's place in the Jewish tradition. A seemingly peripheral or liminal presence that is in fact central, it informs life in its entirety but may escape our perception unless given proper light or proper understanding. The concept proved instrumental in fostering new paradigms of universalism for Judaism and for religion in general in its struggles with secularism.

In 1869, Eduard von Hartmann, an interloper in philosophy, published his *Philosophy of the Unconscious*. The reception of the work, as I will show in the second part of the book, occurred largely outside academia, but the intellectual climate that he captured and promoted soon entered that world. The work of Wilhelm Dilthey (1833–1911) belongs to this ethos, in which a shadow had been cast on representations themselves in Michel Foucault's characterization of the unconscious, drawing attention to the previously unthought dynamics in the production of knowledge.[93] Dilthey worked under the assumption that the transparency of representation central to the classical period was gone. In the modern episteme, he believed, the relationship between signs and things is interrogated, every representation is the representation of a representation, humanity is simultaneously object and subject of its own knowledge. This prompted him to push against existing academic disciplines and open up the range of their investigations to the inner dimensions of experience.[94]

Dilthey's expansion of Georg Wilhelm Friedrich Hegel's *Wissenschaft vom Geiste* (*Science of the Spirit*) through his *Geisteswissenschaft*, in which the human sciences are grounded in and shaped by the moral sciences, certainly resonated with his readers in the WdJ.[95] As the holder of Hegel's chair at the University of Berlin, Dilthey proclaimed that the natural sciences' monopoly on the representation of the world is a contradiction in logic, since the impossibility of deriving mental or spiritual facts from those of the mechanical order of nature restricts the scope of human understanding to external matters and proves inadequate for grasping the inner experiences of hermeneutics. In a striking paradigm shift, because of a novel assessment of their scientific status, inner experiences (including mysticism) became a subject of research and a locus of cultural modernity at the end of the century.[96] Although Dilthey's work is often divided into two epochs—an earlier emphasis on psychology followed by a turn toward hermeneutics—psychology functions as hermeneutics and must be a "reflexive awareness." A new discipline emerged that sought to decipher mental images and representations as part of the exploration of humanity.[97] Dilthey's construction of the *Geisteswissenschaft* turned emotions and the unconscious into legitimate fields of study and anticipated later scholarly developments in that direction.[98]

Building on this edifice, Wilhelm Wundt's *Beiträge zur Theorie der Sinneswahrung* (*Contributions to the Theory of Sense Perception*, 1862) set up psychology as a discipline made up of three subfields. The first would be articulated along the principles of the *Naturwissenschaften*, based on experiments in empirical and inductive science for sensation, perception, and reaction stimuli observable in a laboratory. The second would be aligned with the *Geisteswissenschaften* (human or social sciences) and a description of mental processes such as customs, myths, or language, based on cultural productions and historical archives. This has often been termed the comparative-historical approach. The third division of psychology, *scientific metaphysics*, would seek to reconcile laboratory and scientific discoveries with key metaphysical tenets.[99]

This turn accompanied a new sense of purpose for Jewish universalism, predicated on the idea that Jewish thought was particularly adept at exploring the mind and the need to raise awareness of this ability. This approach aligned with Adolphe Franck's earlier connection between the human mind and kabbalistic musings: "a truly original system, and truly grand, which does not resemble any other systems, whether religious or philosophical, only in that it comes from the same source, in that it was called forth by the same causes, in that it responds to the same needs; in short, in that it rests upon the general laws of the human mind. These are the kabbalists."[100] The science of the mind vindicated philosophical approaches to Kabbalah and their intuitions.

When reflecting on the "threshold of modernity" in Jewish history, Amos Funkenstein has argued that this modernity implied a recognition of temporality in its constructs and self-understanding, which the WdJ promoted. Nonetheless, it had had little impact on Jewish communities and did not have a significant impact on the culture of its time or on culture writ large. Yet this new historical consciousness still highlighted its contribution to world culture as a sort of perennial contribution. And this, Funkenstein contends, resulted in a paradox by which "the Wissenschaft became as ahistorical as its predecessors."[101]

In another paradox, the construction of theories of the psyche and of the unconscious, aligned with mysticism, also nuances the notion of modernity: although seemingly resisting history, they enabled or demanded a *return* to history for the religiously minded. Indeed, the study of the unconscious, as part of the scientific advances of the time, appeared as a path of progressive revelation, mostly for those thinkers who sought to reconcile the Jewish tradition and a positivist, progress-oriented sensibility—since progress is a manifestation of the divine. Even absent a religious agenda, the concept of the unconscious illustrates a broader strategy for Jews of reappropriating scientific or philosophical concepts and of partaking in a broader conversation, thereby fulfilling the emancipatory agenda by which Jewish scholars hoped to prove the civic worth and universalism of their people.

This reappropriation might have already been timidly at play when it came to the Talmud. Indeed, Zunz acknowledges—in a footnote—that it was not his first choice to use the term *rabbinische* (rabbinical) in the title of his pamphlet *On Rabbinical Literature*. He would have preferred *neuhebräische* or *jüdische* (new Hebraic or Jewish).[102] But choosing *rabbinische* was important, because it was a matter of reclaiming it after it had been disparaged. This denigration can be chalked up to the long-lasting influence of the Christian Hebraist Johann Buxdorf's *Synagoga Judaica* (*The Jewish Synagogue*). In it, Buxdorf asserts that the true source of authority and practices in Judaism is the teachings not of Moses but of the rabbis. Following the Talmud, which, in his view, is filled with superstition and errors, could only lead Jews astray.[103] That gesture of rewriting a much-maligned history on Jewish terms was taken to the next level in the reappropriation of Kabbalah, increasingly placed at the forefront of the conversation in Europe because of its affinities with myth and with the making of the mind.

Reflecting on the emancipation era, scholars have turned to the concept of mimicry, as theorized by Homi Bhabha and his depiction of the relation of the colonized toward the colonizer, arguing that "Judaism as a religion is a modern invention, developed in mimicry of Christianity."[104] But was the recourse to a new scientific paradigm—specifically this unchartered territory in Jewish thought—a matter of mimicry? A key difference between the Jewish reappropriation of the unconscious and colonial mimicry, however, is that mimicry results in camouflage, which Bhabha describes as "a form of resemblance that differs/defends presence by displaying it in part, metonymically."[105] In contrast, the goal of proclaiming affinities between the concept of the unconscious formulated in the Jewish tradition and the main philosophers of the time, or of proclaiming these thinkers' indebtedness to Jewish thought, was not camouflage, which implies a dissimulation of one's features, but a proud manner of affirming Jewish worthiness. Those who believed that such a message was inaudible in Europe took it to the United States and grafted Kabbalah onto America, making it the new country's religious unconscious—the story to which I now turn.

* 4 *
Emerson's Oversoul, "American Religion," and Kabbalistic Motives

Ralph Waldo Emerson's "truest achievement," according to Harold Bloom, was to "invent the American religion."[1] Throughout his work, the poet, thinker, and founder of the transcendentalist movement of the mid-nineteenth century helped shape the American credo, most notably in his essay "Self-Reliance." Published in 1841, it serves as an injunction to assert one's individuality, famously proclaiming the need for everyone to look inward and to avoid conformity as well as false consistency. "A man should learn to detect and watch that gleam of light which flashes across his mind from within, more than the luster of the firmament of bards and sages," Emerson declares. "Yet he dismisses without notice his thought, because it is his. In every work of genius we recognize our own rejected thoughts: they come back to us with a certain alienated majesty."[2]

In this foundational text and in the process it describes—dismissing one's own thoughts—Bloom detects an instance of repression found in psychoanalytic theory and proceeds to connect Emerson to Sigmund Freud. Emerson, Bloom contends, anticipated and illustrated the Freudian notion of primary repression (*Verdrängung*), in which unwanted thoughts or feelings are pushed into the unconscious.[3] Emerson was indeed attuned to the notion of the unconscious—but to the Schellingian unconscious. And probing the writer's connection to pre-Freudian theories about it and their underpinnings in Jewish mysticism offers further insights into the intersection between the psyche and religious faith and its impact on the making of that American religion.[4] A churchless, literary-inflected faith, Emerson's American religion is actually a transposition of religious ideas into an American creed rather than their replacement.[5] And a key aspect consists of a knowledge of the self before the Creation, which was turned into a centeredness of the self.[6]

But in the religious tradition on which Emerson drew, this self is identified with the abyss and thus the unconscious: it is manifested in the freedom necessary to uncover the initial bond between the self and the abyss and to differentiate oneself from the abyss, thus turning one's relationship with the abyss into self-knowledge, followed by self-affirmation. And because everyone is linked to that protoself, best expressed in a language with kabbalistic overtones, the individual and the collective are connected.[7]

The first time Emerson mentioned the unconscious was in an earlier text with no clear connection to repression. In "The Philosophy of History," one of the lectures on human culture he gave in 1837–38 at the Masonic Temple in Boston, he assesses the "pleasure we derive from a description of some thought or passion" and claims that a large "portion of ourselves lies within the limits of the unconscious."[8] The text was never published in his essay collections, but parts of it were incorporated into "Self-Reliance."[9] Emerson's use of the very noun *the unconscious* signals the moment when the term gained currency in English.[10]

Through an examination of specific motifs in the Emersonian corpus, namely the abyss and what the essayist called the *oversoul*, I will argue that Kabbalah-inflected tropes, by way of German philosophy—in particular Friedrich von Schelling, whom Emerson read—infused Emerson's representations of the unconscious.[11] A chief reason for this is that Emerson did not interpret such tropes as an expression of mysticism, of which he was critical, but rather as a link between ontology and psychology as well as an articulation of the collective and the individual, based on and beyond reason. Such Kabbalah-inflected representations found their way into the Emersonian worldview, thus arguably defining the American religion.

Kabbalah left another mark by way of Schelling. Though he does not occupy a place of choice in the history of philosophy in America, he does so indirectly, in the religious thought or imagination mediated by Emerson.[12] But Schelling's influence was also channeled by a generation of rabbis born and educated in Germany, his former students, and his lecture auditors, whom we met in previous chapters. Some of them moved to the United States and translated Schellingian concepts into a worldview and theology of Judaism for the "land of the future" they were adjusting to.[13] In a transatlantic translation, Schellingianism, its kabbalistic atmosphere, and the notion of a collective unconscious found an afterlife in the spirituality of the American Jewish Reform movement.[14]

World Soul and Oversoul: Schelling, Emerson, and Early Mentions of the Unconscious in America

The influence of Kabbalah on the philosophical and religious thinking of nineteenth-century America did not escape the attention of Charles Sanders Peirce (1839–1914), the philosopher and logician often dubbed "the father of pragmatism." Pierce mockingly remarked, "I may mention, for the benefit of those who are curious in studying mental biographies, that I was born and reared in the neighborhood of Concord—I mean in Cambridge—at the time when Emerson, Hedge, and their friends were disseminating the ideas that they had caught from Schelling, and Schelling from Plotinus, from Boehm [sic], or from God knows what minds stricken with the monstrous mysticism of the East."[15]

The kabbalistic-inflected language of German philosophy infuses Emerson's writings about the psyche—and notably the term *abyss*, as it pertains to the soul and to the source of being. In the essay "Compensation," published as part of his *Essays: First Series* in 1841, Emerson calls the soul "the aboriginal abyss of real Being."[16] That same year, in *The Method of Nature*, he proffers, "The termination of the world in a man, appears to be the last victory of intelligence. The universal does not attract us until housed in an individual. Who heeds the vast abyss of possibility?"[17] Later, in 1850, the chapter of *Representative Men* dedicated to Plato holds that "the connection between our knowledge and the abyss of being is still real, and the explanation must be not less magnificent."[18] Emerson continued his investigation into the abyss well into his life. One of his journal entries in September 1866 mirrors the same concern: "There may be two or three or four steps, according to the genius of each, but for every seeing soul there are two absorbing facts, I and the abyss."[19] All these examples converge to show how Emerson appropriated the notion of a dynamic source of being that originates from a groundless ground called the abyss. In addition, they show how he embraced Schelling's reading of a process of self-creation that connects the divine and man, in a codependency alien to Jacob Boehme's thought.[20]

The proximity that Emerson perceived between the works of Schelling and Boehme is manifest in a journal entry in which he juxtaposes the two: "Unity, says [Boehmian] Schelling, is barren."[21] This identification of Schelling as Boehmian is owed to the sources used by Emerson, who until 1843 mostly read Schelling through secondary material that aligned him with Boehme.[22] In addition to the allusion to Schelling made by the

English poet, critic, and philosopher Samuel Taylor Coleridge (1772–1834) in *Biographia Literaria* (1817), other works influenced Emerson as well, such as Auguste Théodore Hilaire's *Histoire de la philosophie allemande* (*History of German Philosophy*, 1836) and Victor Cousin's *Introduction to the History of Modern Philosophy* (1832). I will return to Cousin later in the chapter.[23]

The Schellingian abyss (*Abgrund*) is not just a fiery pit into which one must gaze. It also provides a narrative of affirmation and negation (equated with restriction and expansion), duality and individuation, desire and differentiation, with which one must engage. An 1835 journal entry by Emerson attests to the importance of the creative nature of these oppositions: "The Germans believe in the necessary Trinity of God—the Infinite; the finite and the passage from Inf. into Fin; or, the Creation. It is documented in the art of thinking. Whilst we contemplate, we are infinite; the thought we express is partial and finite; the expression is the third part & is equivalent to the art of Creation. Unity, says [Boehmian] Schelling, is barren. Duality is necessary to the existence of this world."[24] This passage also illustrates the continuum from God to man's psyche, the dissociation principle necessary for the creation of both the universe and the mind, and the parallels between creation and human expression, which characterize Schelling's psychologizing of theology. Like Ludwig Feuerbach, who demonstrated the relevance of Boehme's intuitions regarding the human psyche, Emerson ascribed a psychologizing of theology to Schelling, which is probably why he described him as Boehmian.[25]

In 1844, the philosopher James Cabot gave Emerson his manuscript translation of Schelling's essay "Freedom," and Schelling's continued direct influence is documented in one of Emerson's journal entries from the following year: "Thus all philosophy begins from Nox & Chaos, the Ground or Abyss which Schelling so celebrates. And in every man we require a bit of night, of chaos, of *Abgrund*, as the spring of a watch turns best on a diamond."[26] This image of need, of a necessary night, is revealing, as is its igniting mechanism in the form of the spring of a watch. Chaos or the abyss thus functions as a possibility for, and repetition of, creation. Darkness and night stand for, and offer, a return to the sources of life and of light, supporting the notion of "abyss-radiance."[27]

In a later exchange with Cabot, however, Emerson sounds less favorably inclined toward the German philosopher: "Schelling continues to interest me, but I am so ill a reader of these subtle dialectics, that I let them lie a long while near me, as if in hope of an atmospheric influence when the Understanding refuses his task."²⁸ This sentence operates on two levels: it captures the influence of Schelling on Emerson—even though he ostensibly refuses it—but it also sheds light on Emerson's use of the concepts of understanding and reason. He did use the term *unconscious* (versus *consciousness*) on occasion, but he also resorted to *understanding* and *reason*, which Coleridge used in order to feature two key aspects of the psyche. In *Aids to Reflection*, Coleridge asserts that "reason indeed is far nearer to SENSE than to Understanding"—an intuition that is called revelation.²⁹ Coleridge's 1829 American edition, edited by the philosopher James Marsh, features a long and influential preliminary essay in which he elaborates on this proximity between understanding and reason and on the need to bring together philosophy and theology—ushering in the concept of what would be called transcendentalist philosophy.³⁰

Coleridge's reading contradicts the Kantian categories of *Verstand* (understanding) and *Vernunft* (reason). Indeed, it is Immanuel Kant who made these concepts central to his *Critique of Pure Reason*. In his construct, *Verstand*, "understanding," grasps the phenomena of the world—in other words, the experiences and things as they appear to an observer through their sense perceptions—while *Vernunft*, "reason," senses the noumenon—or *is* the noumenon, the thing-in-itself. However, since even *Vernunft* in Schelling cannot in fact apprehend the noumenon, this might be another instance of an uncited Schellingian influence and a strategic broadening of the role of reason that recombines it with the phenomenal world, a move that could align reason with God.

Emerson spells out his system in an 1834 letter to his brother Edward: "Reason is the highest faculty of the soul—what we mean often by the soul itself; it never *reasons*, never proves, it simply perceives; it is vision." To reason, he opposes understanding, which "toils all the time, compares, contrives, adds, argues."³¹ Emerson thus aligned the unconscious with reason and reason with God. His preoccupation with the topic shows in a journal entry that same year, where he describes "the passage from the Unconscious to the Conscious" as a movement "from maternal Reason to hard short-sighted Understanding; from Unity to disunion."³²

The unconscious remains far from any demonic irruption, even in the essay "The American Scholar," which describes the moment when the latent content of the unconscious becomes conscious as a sudden event.³³ If we return to Emerson's letter to Cabot, it might be that the unconscious is the "atmospheric influence" that he calls on when understanding is insufficient, leading him to a place where the divine resides. This question of the residence of the divine in humanity and/or in the world is also at the heart of Emerson's concept of the *oversoul* and the injunction to look inward as part of finding the divine: "We should distinguish the announcements of the soul, its manifestations of its own nature, by the term Revelation. These are always attended by the emotion of the sublime. For this communication is an influx of the Divine mind into our mind."[34] Religious revelation is thus not just an emotion but a moment of individualization—which would vindicate Harold Bloom's definition of the American religion: by experiencing the all-encompassing nature of the divine, one needs to actualize it in oneself, in an instance of self-assertion. The "oversoul" is both a collective soul and the container of every soul—a place from where individual souls emerge.

The Oversoul

Because it resists a robust conceptual nature or doctrine, the very notion of "oversoul" has at times been deemed not significant enough to illuminate Emerson's work and theology.[35] Its main definition appears in the following passage of his 1841 essay "The Over-Soul":

> The Supreme Critic on the errors of the past and the present, and the only prophet of that which must be, is that great nature in which we rest, as the earth lies in the soft arms of the atmosphere; that Unity, that Over-soul, within which every man's particular being is contained and made one with all other; that common heart, of which all sincere conversation is the worship, to which all right action is submission; that overpowering reality which confutes our tricks and talents, and constrains every one to pass for what he is, and to speak from his character, and not from his tongue, and which evermore tends to pass into our thought and hand, and become wisdom, and virtue, and power, and beauty. We live in succession, in division, in parts, in particles. Meantime within man is the soul of the whole; the wise silence; the universal beauty, to which every part and particle is equally related; the eternal ONE.[36]

The oversoul seems to represent a "monistic unity of creation" detached from any specific denomination.[37] This prompts Emerson to coin, as Robert Detweiler puts it, an "imaginative name that combines two aspects of the divine nature usually thought as mutually exclusive"—namely, immanence and transcendence resolved in unity.[38] Indeed, the term *oversoul* is used alongside locutions ("common heart," "overpowering reality," and the "eternal ONE") whose aggregation conveys the struggle to describe the experience of transcendence. In the context of antebellum American Christianity, however, Emerson's use of the oversoul and his many other mentions of the soul—as an entity that both encompasses and describes all the faculties of a subject, energy as well as character—are part of his efforts to de-Christianize its meaning.[39]

To be sure, the oversoul, as the "eternal ONE," with *one* all in uppercase, manifests Emerson's indebtedness to Neoplatonism. He had turned to Neoplatonism as an alternative to the conservative Christianity of his youth and had drawn on it to buttress the anti-ecclesiastical sentiment that had inspired him, and which he most famously expressed in his Harvard Divinity Address.[40] Additionally, the author of the quotation used by Emerson as an epigraph of "The Over-Soul" is none other than Henry More (1614–1687), the philosopher of the Cambridge Platonist school.[41] Placing the oversoul under his auspices signals the influence of perennial philosophy, Neoplatonism, and Christian Kabbalah, as well as a refusal of Cartesian dualism, which is constitutive of the Cambridge school.[42]

In order to grasp the significance of the oversoul as inner experience that leads to understanding the unity of all things and beings, it is useful to compare it to a seemingly cognate locution, the "world soul." This concept is found in many transcendentalist writings, helping anchor the central tenet of the movement—the likeness of God in every aspect of creation.[43]

World soul appears in Emerson's work in the title of an 1846 poem as well as in his famous ode to Mount Monadnoc, in which he pictures the mountain as yearning to disclose its mysteries to men and in which the soul is anthropomorphized.[44] In Neoplatonism, the world soul is the lower stage of the ideal world: it is distributed among individual souls, currently inhabiting this lower, seemingly disjointed world, and it must ascend to the ideal world and its oneness. But *world soul* in these instances points to more of an external, scattered reality, whereas the oversoul describes the unity realized, the locus of articulation of the individual and the collective.

Another possible source for this elusive oversoul is the Vedic tradition: Emerson's journals provide evidence that he read the Vedas, beginning in 1832. It is through the writings of the French philosopher Victor Cousin that Emerson was introduced to both the Vedic corpus and the work of Schelling.[45] For one of his contemporaries, however, there was no doubt that the term *oversoul* came not from the Vedas but from the eighth chapter of the Bhagavad Gita, verses 3 and 4.[46] This, however, might be an instance of an "atmospheric" influence, since Emerson did not read the Bhagavad Gita until 1845 in the Charles Wilkins translation, four years after the publication of the essay "The Over-Soul."[47] The passage quoted (but not cited) by Cousin, which stirred Emerson's curiosity, does not deal at all with the question of the oversoul but rather with one of the book's main characters, Arjuna, and his anxiety in battle (in chapters 1 and 2), violence on the battlefield, and the elusive nature of life.

Undoubtedly, Emerson's oversoul bears a resemblance to Brahman, the supreme god, which he describes in his 1856 poem "Brahma."[48] Both represent the divine not as personhood but as an entity transcending matter, thus constituting a realm in which duality does not exist: "shadow and sunlight are the same . . . I am the doubter and the doubt."[49] For all his fascination with Eastern literature, however, Emerson later grew defiant of any understanding of a religious worldview that would advocate a passive submission to fate, something that, in an Orientalist gesture, he associated with Oriental mysticism.[50] It is indeed through the self and through the action of seeing the world that the access to and experience of wholeness can take place and have a personal and collective impact on one's environment, as he argues in "Self-Reliance."

Emerson's oversoul is thus at the junction of multiple traditions and is also informed by a different *world soul*, one that had traversed philosophy since Plato's *Timaeus*, with its account of the formation of the world from earth, air, fire, and water. A tradition of Aristotelian physics identified as the "world-soul" the separate intellect found in the cosmos's outermost region.[51]

Accepted by the Cambridge deists Ralph Cudworth and Henry More, on the condition that it not form an alternative deity, the notion of a world soul was rejected by Gottfried Wilhelm Leibniz, who faulted it for the confusion between physics and metaphysics it could likely bring. It reappeared forcefully in German Romanticism and idealism, specifically in Schelling's *Anima Mundi*—"world soul."[52] A topic on which he had written an essay as a student in 1794, he expanded on it in this 1797 work. In it, he reflects on the interconnectedness of natural teleologies and on "the idea of an organizing principle" that turned "the world into a system." "Perhaps the ancients wished to intimate this with the world-soul," he speculates.[53] Schelling described the Absolute as will and as the impulse toward self-manifestation, and he turned the world soul into a locus of origins, bringing not only the I and the collective together but also the cosmic and the material.[54] This process was enshrouded in "ether," which was meant literally as a metaphysical substance that was created by a contraction (which we have previously encountered as *tsimtsum*).

From Emerson's references to ether in other texts, it is difficult to tease out whether these are more metaphorical than scientific and metaphysical.[55] In any case, with all the porosity between the literal and the figurative in Emerson's writings, ether is invoked a few times and furthers his connection with a Schellingian *anima mundi* when he connects the substance to the intellect: "We figure to ourselves Intellect as an ethereal sea, which ebbs and flows, which surges and washes hither and thither, carrying its whole virtue into every creek and inlet which it bathes."[56] Another reference occurs in his essay "History," where Emerson's mention of ether signals wholeness as an erasure of perceived reality: "Time dissipates to shiny ether the solid angularity of facts."[57] The transformation of facts into ether parallels the move from understanding to reason, of the individual to the impersonal yet dynamic, through a timeless intellect.

Based on this perception of the oversoul as an impersonal, universal intellect and a psychic system reflected in every individual, the oversoul has been associated with the Jungian collective unconscious, as a possible articulation of the collective and the individual, within a pre-Christianized or de-Christianized soul. In an Emersonian way, it is the duty and calling of human beings to become aware of it and to understand the unity of all things and psyches. The Emersonian oversoul may thus constitute a transition to a nonreligious worldview that still bears the mark of its religious origins, therefore foreshadowing a Jungian approach.[58]

From Ontology to Psychology

In his use of the ideas of abyss and oversoul, Emerson traced and signaled a passage between ontology and psychology that operates in a manner paralleling Cousin's eclecticism, defined as the application of psychology to philosophical systems, with a methodological priority given to psychology before establishing any ontology.[59] A popularizer of German idealism, Cousin (1792–1867) had an outsize impact in the 1830s and was one of the most widely read philosophers of his time; he was a public intellectual and statesman as well. Although his star soon faded, he was at the time applauded for refuting Lockeanism and the metaphysical anxieties produced by British empiricism.[60] Although long held to be a second-rate philosopher, Cousin's legacy has been reconsidered. Since eclecticism morphed into spiritualism, whose main figures like Félix Ravaisson (1813–1900) and Jules Lachelier (1832–1918) were mentors to Henri Bergson, he is also now credited with having paved the way for the alternative understanding of consciousness that Bergson developed.[61]

Like most of his contemporaries, Emerson was an avid reader of Cousin's *Introduction to the History of Modern Philosophy*, and despite subsequently speaking of this work with contempt, he was at one point immersed in Cousin's eclecticism.[62] Cousin held that our prereflective reason—our "spontaneous and instinctive thought"—already contains *everything*: "It gives us ourselves, the world, and God."[63] For him, the psyche is an organ through which one grasps the transcendent. Such a philosophy of the mind opens up a passage from psychology to ontology, while Emerson's reading of Schelling goes back the other way—from ontology to psychology through the study of the soul and the abyss. It is in this dynamic that prereflective reason—in other words, the unconscious—is best understood.

Indeed, in the absence in Schelling's work of any direct application of the unconscious on individual psyches, Emerson saw the German philosopher as paving the way to psychology. In a letter to John Heath, an American student who attended Schelling's lectures in Berlin in 1842, he wrote that "to hear Schelling might well tempt the firmest rooted philosopher away from his home and I confess to more curiosity in respect of Schelling's opinions than to those of any living psychologist."[64] This statement shows that the interpretation Emerson offers of the Schellingian *Naturphilosophie* is a reading in a nonphilosophical key—or rather, as a preclinical understanding of the science of the mind.

Emerson's diagnosis of a collective psyche identifies the characteristic of modernity as a splintered conscience. Variations on the sentence "We live in succession, in division, in parts, in particles" can be found throughout his work, especially in "The Transcendentalist," a lecture given in January 1842 at the Masonic Lodge in Boston.[65]

Foreshadowing Carl Gustav Jung, Emerson uses an archetype or collective image for diagnosing the ills of his times. In "The American Scholar," he resorts to the old Gnostic image of the *anthropos*, the primordial man (also understood as an allegory of humanity).

> There is One Man—present to all particular men only partially, or through one faculty ... [but] you must take the whole society to find the whole man.... Unfortunately, this original unit, this fountain of power, has been distributed to multitudes, has been so minutely subdivided and peddled out that it is spilled into drops and cannot be gathered. The state of society is that in which the members have suffered amputation from the trunk and strut about like walking monsters—a good finger, a neck, a stomach, an elbow, but never a man.[66]

The challenge that confronts the individual in modernity, Emerson is saying, is to find an organic whole, to recreate the articulation of humanity and the cosmos found in the anthropos, and indeed to connect the individual to the whole.

The use of a Gnostic image supports Bloom's claim that the American religion contains elements of Gnosticism, especially with regard to the presence of a divine spark trapped in every body, making salvation the liberation of that spark..[67] Yet, against Bloom's aforementioned diagnostic of a Freudian repression in Emerson, the pathologies that we see lurking in Emerson are the result not of repression but of negative dissociation, which is also found in Schelling and Jung as well as in a French lineage in the works of Pierre Janet, Henri Bergson, and Gilles Deleuze.[68]

God's self-restriction, described in Jacob Boehme's or Friedrich von Schelling's work and derived from the kabbalistic concept of *tsimtsum*, can be read as an instance of dissociation from oneself in order to make space for that which is not the self, for otherness—and, in the case of the divine, for creation. The previous self is not repressed but latent and hidden, just as the retracted divine is still present yet concealed. In that configuration, pathologies emerge when the subject cannot create a "personal synthesis" of the manifest and hidden selves, and a cure involves the reappropriation of these multiple aspects of the selves in order to recreate a sense of wholeness and of a conscious, multifaceted, yet stable self. This is what Emerson applauded in his 1837 lecture, "Philosophy of History": "Whoever separates for us a truth from our unconscious reason, and makes it an object of consciousness, draws that is to say a fact out of our lives and makes it an opinion, must of course to us be a great man. We hail with gladness this new acquisition of ourselves."[69]

As confident as Emerson appears in this claim, a tension might come to the fore if we juxtapose this assertion to the 1834 journal entry in which he describes the passage from the unconscious to consciousness as a passage "from careless receiving to cunning providing; from beauty to use; from omnivorous curiosity to anxious stewardship; from maternal Reason to hard short-sighted Understanding; from faith to doubt; from Unity to disunion."[70] In fact, the acquisition of one's self thus means that a deconstruction of the original unity needs to happen to identify the multiple strata of the self (instead of the delusional, "foolish consistency") and consciously articulate them, thus asserting one's individuality.

Does such a credo of self-contradiction explain the paradox by which Emerson almost shuns mysticism despite the abundant references to mystical-inflected themes? In "The Poet," composed between 1841 and 1843, the writer cautions against mysticism's edifying qualities: "Mysticism consists in the mistake of an accidental and individual symbol for a universal one. The morning-redness happens to be the favorite meteor to the eyes of Jacob Behmen [sic],[71] and comes to stand to him for truth and faith; and, he believes, should stand for the same realities to every reader."[72]

In this construct, the mystic's individual relation to God threatens the singularity and individuality of the expression of the divine in others, which is precisely what had driven Emerson away from organized religion. In spite of the emotional aspect of Boehme's mysticism and the challenge he mounted against an institutionalized Christianity, Emerson still lumped the thinker with the scientist and mystic Emanuel Swedenborg (1688–1772) and criticized them, and mystics in general, for falling prey to the same mistakes as religions, in delineating specific means of communication (ritual or verbal) with the divine and claiming that they are the prime way to embrace God. "All religious error," he wrote, "consisted in making the symbol too stark and solid, and, at last, nothing but an excess of the organ of language."[73] The outcome is a reification of both the object and the vehicle of worship.

Opposed to the Boehmian goal of recovering the stillness preceding creation, Schelling's and Emerson's philosophies of the mind are centered on the process of becoming: "The philosophy we want," Emerson wrote, "is one of fluxions & mobility; not a house, but a ship in these billows we inhabit."[74] Consonant with the notion of flux, which he made his philosophical cornerstone, are the kabbalistic tropes of divine emanations and their unceasing movement, the passage of the One into the multiple. These can be interpreted as the progressive revelation of the divine to mankind and of the psyche to the self. And this interpretation of the soul and the self, as the One into the multiple and of the multiple that invites individuation—which Emerson amplified in his work—certainly shaped the American religious perspective.

This also explains why Jungian (or analytic) psychology, with its emphasis on the articulation of, and harmony between, the collective unconscious and the self through individuation, long enjoyed greater popularity in the United States than in Europe.[75] Essential in that pursuit is the merging of one's consciousness with the collective unconscious by integrating symbols and archetypes whereby the self can be seen as a refraction of the divine in one's soul. Jung's work, heavily influenced by Schelling, as we will see in chapters 7 and 8, resonated with common themes and images introduced and magnified by Emerson. Jung's perspective was indeed, as Philip Rieff calls it, a "new message of salvation," a positive one in tune with the American creed of redemption and self-reinvention.[76]

If Emerson created "the American religion," as Harold Bloom argued, he did so by adopting kabbalistic motives (more specifically of Christian Kabbalah, introduced by way of Boehme and Schelling), manifested in the abyss and the oversoul. Because the origin is inscrutable, the Emersonian unconscious is future oriented and creates the endless possibility of self-reliance, of turning the dark side of the psyche into a self-affirming, positive one, grounded in religion and modeled for a secular world.[77] If Emerson did create the American religion, then Kabbalah is now part of its multifaceted nature, and of its unconscious.

Expanding the Boundaries of Reason: The Symbolism of Judaism and Its Universal Significance in the Eyes of the Reform Movement

Schelling may not occupy a choice place in the history of philosophy in the United States, and yet his influence was subterranean, as we have seen, and it also reverberated in the religious makeup of the country. Coleridge's confession about the philosopher in his 1817 *Biographia Literaria* ("In Schelling I first found a genial coincidence with much that I had toiled out for myself, and a powerful assistance in what I had yet to do"[78]) was able to capture the mindset of a few German-born rabbis who shaped the American Reform movement.[79] At some point, the main proponents of the Reform movement who emigrated from Germany had been influenced by the ideas of Schelling; the convergence of views is noteworthy. Chief among them, David Einhorn—encountered in chapter 2—moved to the United States in 1855 and was appointed rabbi to Har Sinai in Baltimore, founded a decade earlier as one of the first Reform congregations in the country.

Einhorn lacked the charismatic presence of his opponent Isaac Wise (1819–1900), whom he derided in his correspondence as "this Jewish Pope." Wise was more conciliatory with Orthodoxy, and Einhorn opposed his acceptance of the Talmud.[80] Moreover, Einhorn's reluctance to accept English as a vernacular for his sermons disconnected him from his contemporaries. The impact of his work is undeniable, however, and his legacy was further channeled by his two sons-in-law, Emil Hirsch (1851–1923) and Kauffman Kohler (1843–1926), both prominent figures of the Reform movement in the late nineteenth and early twentieth centuries.

Viewed as a radical, Einhorn indeed declared himself one. He wrote *Ner Tamid (Eternal Light)*, a book of popular theology subtitled *The Teachings of Judaism for School and Home*. He also edited the journal *Sinai*, for which he was the main contributor, and he wrote assiduously for the *Jewish Times* newspaper based in New York. Forced to flee Baltimore when a mob destroyed his printing presses as punishment for his abolitionist sermons, he went on to lead congregations in Philadelphia and New York.[81]

Shortly after his arrival in the United States, in 1858 Einhorn authored the Reform prayer book *Olat Tamid (The Continual Burnt Offering)*. First translated into English in 1872 and then in 1896 by Emil Hirsch, the book constituted the foundation for the *Union Prayer Book*, which the Reform movement in the United States would use until the 1970s.

The Continual Burnt Offering should be put in dialogue with Einhorn's *The Principle of Mosaism*, published in 1854 right before he left Europe. In it, he lays out his views on and for Judaism.[82] It should also be considered in view of his *Eternal Light*, with which he aimed to shape a popular theology. The main pillars of that work are a primordial revelation for all human beings and the importance of understanding symbolism in religion, from which will emerge a universal truth and spirit—all of which echo Schelling's teachings.

Einhorn adopted the notion of a prebiblical, primordial monotheism as the common possession of all humans. He held that the true essence of Judaism is its universal nature, which predates and exceeds its specific historical incarnation in a creed.

Judaism in its essence is older than the Israelites; as pure humanity, as the emanation of the inborn divine spirit, it is as old as the human race. The origin and development of the human spirit are also its own origin and its own development. It is rooted in Adam and culminates in a messianically perfected humanity. It was not a religion, but a religious people, that was newly created at Sinai, a priestly people called upon, first of all, to impress the ancient divine teaching more deeply upon itself and to bring it to universal dominion.[83]

This human spirit is contained in the figure of the "first Adam" found in biblical and rabbinical sources, such as Psalms 139:16 and Genesis Rabbah 8:1 (the latter probably written between 500 BCE and 300 BCE). These are frequently invoked to demonstrate the universalism of Judaism.

Invoking Adam as a universal ancestor is significant on multiple levels. It was a way to fend off racism when it took the shape of pre-Adamism, the notion of multiple human beings accounting for multiple races that populated the earth before Adam, before and around Einhorn's time.[84] Moreover, it constituted a rejection of the Christian doctrine of the Fall, because Adam represents human self-perfection in a construct where the Fall is not central. Emil Hirsch describes his father-in-law's philosophy.

> Einhorn ... was under the spell of Schelling's idealism. With his master, he believed in the original perfection of man, in primitive revelation. . . . With Schelling, Einhorn posits one principle applicable both for nature and self: for both of them, the real and the ideal are identical in their ultimate essence. This note of Schelling's system is clearly audible in Einhorn's anthropology. The account of man's creation as given in Genesis is a confirmation of this identical essence actualized in the personality of man. "Child of two worlds" is he, as Einhorn loves to put it. His freedom is the function of reason, and sin is not inherent in the body because it is "Unnatur"—against nature.[85]

This identity of nature and self conveys an identity between the divine and the self, which takes place within the soul. It rules out a fallen nature, thereby establishing the ethical nature of the self.

One of the key truths of Einhorn's *Principle of Mosaism* is the existence of a soul. All human beings possess a *nefesh* (the Hebrew term for an animal life force that he translates into German as *Seele*) as well as a spirit that is an emanation of God's absolute spirit captured by man. The *nefesh* is where free will—and the ethical in general—resides. This is the *ruah Elohim*, the channel for communication with God, which Einhorn translates as *Geist*. This dual soul instantiates the condensation or centralization principle, which implies a mutual and necessary relationship between the real and the ideal. Human reason is the encounter between these two life forces, the divinely emanated spirit (*Geist/ruah*) and the animal spirit (*Seele/nefesh*). It is a synthesis whose realm is and should be ever expanding. The truths of revelation, Einhorn preached, ought to be embraced first—sometimes in a mystical, ecstatic state. They will then lead to a reason-based acceptance. His acceptance of mysticism and his reliance on the medieval philosopher and kabbalist Nahmanides (1194–1270), particularly his *Commentary on Genesis*, for his interpretation of the *nefesh* as the locus of the divinely emanated knowledge demonstrates that Kabbalah was for him an acceptable aspect of tradition and one that did not shy away from reason as he saw it.[86] Revelation, for Einhorn, was a preamble to, not an antithesis of, reason.

In that construct, symbolism has a distinct role to play—it is what needs to be interpreted, a place for reason to unveil itself. Einhorn's focus on symbolism distinguished him from the other Reform rabbis. This comes to the fore in his prayer book *The Continual Burnt Offering* (1858). While he had advocated expurgating references to Jerusalem from the Reform liturgy since his days in Germany, his book does make reference to the Temple liturgy—namely, its sacrifices.[87] The *olah* is a burnt offering on the altar at the Temple (two male lambs, morning and night) mandated by Numbers 28:6: "A continual *olat tamid*, offered at Mount Sinai as a pleasing aroma, a sacrifice of fire to the Lord." It is thus a daily transposition of the meaning of past rituals. Using the Schellingian distinction of Form and Being, Einhorn shows how rituals (forms) are symbols for religious ideas (essence); this is the essence he tries to recapture and impart onto the community. To drive his point home, and despite his call to abolish all prayers mentioning the Jewish state and the theological centrality of the Temple, he sees value in invoking the trauma of the Temple's destruction. But instead of expressing a lamentation, he presents this historical event as an opportunity to expand the central ideas of Judaism beyond the spatial and historical confines of the Temple: "The sanctuary itself, Your immortal testimony [*Zeugnis*], remains intact, and only came forth ringing and gleaming brightly from the bitter, sorrowful conflagration, liberated from the city's walls, which had become a prison for it, and its glory obstructed to the view of millions of alien people [*Wesen*] who were created in Your image who wish to become Your people through Your Priests."[88]

For Einhorn, the memory of the suffering of the exiles was to lead not to a nostalgia or a dream of restoration but to an opportunity to reconsider Israel's mission to the world. While stripping the meaning of the word *Zeugnis* (testimony, historically linked to the notion of martyrdom) of its uniquely Christian overtones, Einhorn redefined the mission of Judaism as one of liberation and turned the catastrophe into an opportunity, the lament into a celebration.[89] By recasting rites as symbols, he also deflected the traditional Christian accusation of Jewish literalness. His son-in-law Hirsch goes on to explain this stance.

> In his "Prinzipien des Mosaismus," he shows that rabbinical misconstruction of the intent of the sacrificial ordinances approaches very closely the assumptions of Paulinianism. Sacrificial, or any other, ceremonies are meant to be helps and appeals for man. They symbolize the identity of the ideal and the real, inasmuch as through their sign-language they convey the call to man or to Israel, in whom the human must come to propaedeutic power for the guidance of others, to be mindful to strive for "holiness," i.e., that state of thought, feeling and willing, in which, indeed, the identity of the natural and the reasonable, flowers forth in signal beauty and strength.[90]

This convergence of the ideal and the real captures the moment of revelation. The condensation or centralization process, already described in chapter 2, conjures up *tsimtsum* but can also take on the kabbalistic meaning of a coincidence of opposites. According to Einhorn, the "principle of centralization brings together various phenomena without encroaching upon any particular one."[91] It implies proximity, codependency, and mutual relations, along with antinomies that find their resolution in the dissolution of their apparent contradictory relationships. It is also a political principle: "The soul of Mosaism is the centralisation of various existences without capricious infringement upon individual existence."[92]

Unlike Moses Mendelssohn, who rejected ceremonial laws as part of a national past of Judaism that he considered defunct, Einhorn professes that some ceremonial laws, properly explicated once the form unveils the essence, provide insights into the deeper truths shared by Judaism and beyond it. Judaism offers humanity the capacity of making obscure forms emerge into consciousness. It provides both the receptacle of the divinely emanated spirit and its decipherment.

From there, Einhorn derives his injunction to distinguish between form and truth. The greater the distinction between the "form" and "essence" of the teachings of Israel, the greater the development of the human consciousness. The rabbi often expressed similar anxiety when confronting a reification of the realm of the symbolic. Unlike Emerson, who ascribed "all religious error" to it, Einhorn does not blame such misguided tendencies on mysticism. On the contrary, he uses the metaphor of shattering the vessels—the *shevirat ha kelelim* of Lurianic Kabbalah—in order to describe Judaism's mission: the creative destruction of the "old, narrow and bulky vessels, so that their contents may be poured into larger and less opaque ones."[93] Einhorn, clearly resorting to a kabbalistic imagery of refoundation, also relied on Kabbalah's notion of the reparation and progressive revelation necessary to make a universal spirit emerge—one that was always present, beneath the realm of consciousness. Such for him was the true, unconscious bond of humanity needing to be revealed.

The penetration of symbolism and the early introduction of kabbalistic-inflected tropes into American philosophy and prayer books may explain the future appeal of a mainstream Kabbalah. The broad acceptance of the mystical tradition has been promoted by the Kabbalah Centre, which paints it as part of a universal wisdom, akin to New Age spirituality, with no prerequisite knowledge of Judaism.[94] In addition, Kabbalah has been used as a tool of outreach by the Orthodox movement, whose stated purpose is to deliver its teachings in an Emersonian style, thus coming full circle.[95]

In this circulation of ideas between Europe and the United States, the broadening of reason, of its meaning and of its realm, converged in the transcendentalist movement and more precisely in its understanding of revelation.[96] According to this belief, traditional paradigms are destabilized, and the unconscious is described not as the opposite of reason (itself the "infinite in faculty," as authoritatively defined by Immanuel Kant, which can also be understood as the "faculty of the Infinite"[97]) but as an instance beyond reason, in an erasure of opposites and a culmination of mystically-inflected references that place humanity and its psyche at Kabbalah's elusive center. In accompanying the emergence of Kabbalah as a mainstream philosophical reference and a discipline, the unconscious had turned from a philosophical concept into a psychological one—and it was now going to become increasingly political.

PART II

The Mind as Battleground

The Collective Psyche in Jewish Thought
and the Many Claims to the Unconscious

In his late writings, the twentieth-century Russian philosopher and literary critic Mikhail Bakhtin (1895–1975) briefly mentions the role of ethnopsychology in shaping the notion of collective unconscious.[1] Aside from this brief fragment, however, that connection has gone mostly unnoticed. The second part of this book focuses on this question and on the broader question of the politicization of the unconscious—the collective unconscious in particular.

I begin this exploration by examining the work, reception, and legacy of the two Jewish architects of the field of ethnopsychology (in German, *Völkerpsychologie*, also rendered as "the psychology of peoples" or "the science of national character"). Moritz Lazarus and Heymann Steinthal coined the term and attempted to establish the field. Understanding the impetus for their work helps us capture a moment when psychology was envisioned as a vehicle for ethics and signaled a short-lived hope for a liberal project in Germany: both men focused on the psyche as a human bond in order to counter the notions of national spirit and race that were increasingly being used as tools to exclude Jews from the nation. Their noble failure nevertheless solidified the notion of a collective dimension of the unconscious, which took a more explicit, albeit different, place in the work of Eduard von Hartmann.

Lazarus and Steinthal's work conveyed a sense of urgency in finding new grounds on which to proclaim the existence of a *Gesamtgeist*, a collective spirit—in the service of a universalism rooted in science. Judaism would have a role to play in this project, and it could address alienation both as a symptom of modernity and as the resurgence of the perennial accusations leveled at Jews.

The notion of a *Volksgeist*, the spirit of a people or a national spirit or mentality, gained prominence in German thought over the course of the nineteenth century and became instrumental in fostering a type of nationalism derived from an ethnic, Romantic, and quasi-mystical essence, in contrast to the French universalism brought about by the Revolution.[2] Yet at the same time, a handful of Jewish thinkers—such as Nachman Krochmal (see chapter 3) and later the aforementioned Moritz Lazarus and Heymann Steinthal—mobilized the very concept of *Volksgeist* in implicit counternarratives. In doing so, Krochmal sought to show Judaism's kinship with an absolute spirit, not just a national one. And through the field of *Völkerpsychologie*, Lazarus and Steinthal promoted the ideal of a common humanity: every nation had a legitimate role to play in fostering a collective spirit that would not involve ethnic superiority. Their work partook in a distinct psychologization and politicization of the *Geist*. In their version, it is a spirit specifically devoid of its nationalist exclusivism.[3]

From there, a universal psychology of culture could emerge across peoples, based on conscious or unconscious behaviors and creations. Lazarus elaborated a key aspect of the *Geist*: the process of condensation (*Verdichtung*). Condensation accounted for the modalities by which collective representations manifest themselves in groups. This notion in the work of Lazarus has not received the attention it deserves, both on its own terms and as part of a possible archaeology of a future epoch-making concept. Indeed, the concept is almost universally attributed to Sigmund Freud, who would go on to use it in *The Interpretation of Dreams* (as both *Verdichtung*, condensation, and *Verschiebung*, displacement) to describe the working of the individual's mind in dreams.[4] But Lazarus employs it to ponder a collective phenomenon.

Because of *Völkerpsychologie*'s methodological shortcomings, and despite some of Lazarus and Steinthal's scholarly contributions that would later influence anthropology and sociology, the field that they sought to create was unable to counteract the appropriation of the concept of *Geist* by ethnocentric and racist (*völkisch*) worldviews and rhetoric.[5] The psyche came to be instrumentalized and increasingly associated with ethnic traits: race-based psychologies became a tool against Jews, used to brand them as unassimilable. This was one of the arguments of the infamous *Antisemitismusstreit* (anti-Semitism controversy) of the late 1870s, when a high-profile academic, Heinrich von Treitschke, penned an article in which he called Jews "our greatest misfortune" and rallied scholars and public intellectuals behind him.[6]

While Lazarus and Moritz redirected their energies into writings on Jewish ethics (which were in fact apologetics—insofar as they sought to offer an intellectual defense of the values of Judaism), Eduard von Hartmann's immensely popular *Philosophy of the Unconscious* offered a narrative that espoused or repurposed many of the themes of *Völkerpsychologie*. Hartmann acknowledged the influence of Lazarus and Moritz, but he imbued this book with a mysticism absent from their writings. My argument here is that despite many differences, Hartmann's exploration of the psyche was a continuation of the work of Lazarus and Steinthal, and it enabled Jewish thinkers to avail themselves of the Hartmannian concepts they recognized as familiar.

One of the scholars' tactics was to read texts from the biblical, rabbinical, or kabbalistic tradition in light of these new conceptions of the unconscious and to claim that these texts had foreshadowed them. This process sometimes amounted to what I call a *retrospective* unconscious: when the concept of the unconscious is identified in hindsight and in unexpected places. Such a retrospective move helped solidify the concept of progressive revelation (in the work of Elia Benamozegh and Adolphe Franck), and for some advocates of Hasidism, it was instrumental in dismissing the charges of obscurantism leveled at the sect. By applying Hartmann's philosophical system to Hasidic theology, they claimed that it would vindicate both the thinker's worldview and the sect's core religious tenets. In addition, it would usher in a new discourse on Hasidism that would reevaluate its sociological, philosophical, and theological contributions to counter charges that it was insular and progress-adverse. From the standpoint of the unconscious, Hartmann, I contend, expressed concerns into which a young generation of Jewish thinkers such as Martin Buber and Ernst Bloch could insert their own political and religious ones: the meaning of a collective spirit for humanity; the role Judaism played in it; and the way the unconscious could challenge a narrative of reason as the sole means of uniting humankind while also opening up new ways to reconnect with their own tradition.

* 5 *
Jewish Spirit, National Spirit, and Absolute Spirit

Building Blocks of the Collective Unconscious and the Defense of Judaism

The incipient notion of a collective spirit of humanity—from which the concept of a shared unconscious emerged—appeared in the work of a handful of thinkers, including Giovanni Battista Vico (1668–1744), Johann Gottfried von Herder (1744–1803), and Georg Wilhelm Friedrich Hegel (1770–1831). These are the philosophers that the Jewish authors I examine in this chapter primarily drew on. Absent in their work, in contrast, are the French philosophers Montesquieu (1689–1755) and Voltaire (1694–1778), who also dealt with the formation of human societies in *The Spirit of the Laws* (1751) and *An Essay on Universal History, the Manners, and Spirit of Nations* (1756), respectively. These omissions not only signal differing sensibilities (especially given the French philosophers' hostile stance on religion); they might also have been a strategic move. The ambition of these Jewish writers was to display their loyalty to German identity and to foster a novel universalism that would not be indebted to French philosophy. By ushering in a new understanding of "Spirit," by which they meant the mind, they also sought to cast a new light on Judaism, which could be articulated through the themes of canonical authors.

Vico's Poetic Universals

In his *Scienza nuova* (*New Science*, 1725), Vico sought to establish a "social science" for modern times and took the "common nature of peoples" as its starting point. At the core of every people's identity is its relationship with language and myth, a *lingua mentale commune* (mental common language) reflecting the *universale fantastico* (poetic or imaginative universal). These can be defined as figments of a universal imagination: they are mental images formed in response to specific sensory stimuli; they constitute the structure of the world experienced by human beings as they create patterns of cognition. Vico took them to have an ontological meaning, arguing that "uniform ideas originating among entire peoples unknown to each other must have a common ground of truth."[1]

Vico's philosophy of history is equally important. His construct of history appears as a cyclical one of eternal laws, which are instantiated by the specific destinies and actions of nations.[2] The pattern of rise, decadence, and dissolution applies across nations, except for the Jewish people, whose very survival is evidence that they are not subject to the laws of history.[3] In Vico's natural succession of cycles, guided by Providence, there is no dialectical path toward progress, and this construct explains his reception as a Counter-Enlightenment figure.[4] Instead, history is an organic process in which the representation systems of the various peoples do not disappear with them: they survive extinction by being carried forward by other peoples.

These stages of evolution in the life of nations also display certain characteristics that Vico calls divine, heroic, and human, each linked to distinct modes of expression: metaphor, metonymy, and irony, respectively. Language is thus a function and a mirror of history. Equally pivotal in his laws of cultural history are the social origins and functions of myths as variations on the imaginative universals in fostering a collective identity based on social consensus.[5] Vico postulated that an empirical basis for metaphysics can be derived from historical and social circumstances that themselves manifested or took the shape of myths, customs, and language.

As subsequent thinkers duly noted, the importance of language and of these universals in Vico's thought constituted a significant basis for any exploration of the unconscious from a Freudian or Jungian perspective.[6] The philosopher and political theorist Isaiah Berlin and the Jungian analyst James Hillman (1926–2011) have remarked on Vico's groundbreaking ideas and their kinship with what Jung would call "archetypes," as they personify myths and take metaphors as "mini-myths."[7] While Hillman's analysis is rather cursory, Berlin's appreciation is justifiably more cautious, noting that Vico's writing is by no means systematic. Indeed, Berlin wonders whether his concepts can map onto subsequent psychological constructs in a rigorous manner: "When Vico speaks of 'our human mind,' 'our understanding,' 'a certain human mind of nations,' 'our human thought,' 'our spirit' and so on, do such phrases refer to what is common to all individual minds, or to some 'collective' mind, like Jung's collective unconscious, but with pantheistic implications? Or is the use of the term *nostro* merely metaphorical or distributive?"[8]

Even in the absence of an exact conceptual equivalence, these generalities constitute the subtext of how the collective workings of individual minds were understood as the other new science—psychology—was evolving into its twentieth-century form. Vico's insights into language-as-psychology have also been perceived as intuitions that would find their full expression as the unconscious. Such is Lionel Trilling's conclusion in a brief assessment within a more wide-ranging analysis of Freud's impact on literature: "In the eighteenth century Vico spoke of the metaphorical, imagistic language of the early stages of culture; it was left to Freud to discover how, in a scientific age, we still feel and think in figurative formations, and to create, what psychoanalysis is, a science of tropes, of metaphor and its variants, synecdoche and metonymy."[9] Yet this judgment once again reflects the long-prevailing invisibility of the pre-Freudian moment. The prefiguration of a recognizably modern psychology had emerged decades earlier, and a handful of scholars set out to explore the psychological meaning and significance of the collective tropes, as laid out by Vico.

The first German translation of Vico's *New Science* appeared in 1822.[10] In his 1837 introduction to Hegel's *Philosophy of History*, Eduard Gans credits Vico, alongside Friedrich Schlegel and Herder, with founding the philosophy of history and establishing its laws.[11] This edition is the one that likely introduced the Jewish philosopher Nachman Krochmal to Vico's work. I will demonstrate how it prompted Krochmal to elaborate on Vico's understanding of the significance of the Jewish and absolute spirit later in the chapter, after I probe the concomitant influence of Herder and Hegel. Herder, born in 1744, the year of Vico's death, had taken his thinking in another direction, suggesting that a shared humanity could derive from collective representations.

Herder and the Spirit of Humanity

Johann Gottfried von Herder was a towering figure of Sturm und Drang, the late eighteenth-century literary movement that exalted feeling and nature.[12] He is often characterized as the founding father of historicism and cultural nationalism. Heralded as a hero by multiple thinkers and irreconcilable schools of thought, his legacy was reclaimed by zealots of German blood and soil ideology as well as impassioned advocates of the improvement of mankind.

Herder based his concept of a *Geist des Volkes* primarily on the ideas of *Gefühl* (feeling) and national character organically conveyed by language and history rather than imposed by centralized institutions or revolutions.[13] *Geist* denotes an eternal spirit channeled in the *Volk*, the national unit that is a building block of humanity as a whole: it is the combination of distinct national spirits that shapes the plurality of mankind. Like Vico, Herder contended that the singularity of a people is best expressed through language, especially poetry.[14]

Herder expounded his views on humanity in his *Ideen zur Philosophie der Geschichte der Menschheit* (*Reflections on the Philosophy of the History of Mankind*, 1784–91), whose first three parts preceded the French Revolution, and in *Briefe zu Beförderung der Humanität* (*Letters for the Advancement of Humanity*), twenty-four letters written in 1792.[15] The two different terms used in the titles of these works—mankind (*Menschheit*) and humanity (*Humanität*)—are respectively descriptive and programmatic. *Menschheit* encompasses actual peoples of the past, present, or future.[16] *Humanität* portrays a lofty ideal, a potential force: "the abstracted concept from all exemplars of human nature in both hemispheres."[17] This abstraction does not equate to an erasure of differences: indeed, it is Herder's insistence on preserving differences that explains the appropriation of his thought by racialist ideologies in which ethnic and racial differences were reinterpreted into hierarchies.[18] His understanding of the "prototype of humanity [as lying] not in a single nation of a single region of the earth [but as] the abstracted concept from all exemplars of human nature in both hemispheres" is not unitary.[19] Herder's pluralism maintains that the real unity of mankind will arise from the self-realization of each distinct people.

Herder unquestionably operated within a Western-centric historicism and did consider certain nations more advanced, but he refused to either essentialize them or derive hierarchy and chauvinism from such difference. He harshly criticized claims to universality made on behalf of certain nations, because these could lead to an oppression of different cultures by dominant powers. Nor did he equate nation and state or see the perfect state as the end goal of history. In his view, doing away with the state would be the ideal manifestation of the spirit. To that end, he found the Jewish example noteworthy: it represents a formation in which the law does not need a state if it captures the ethics and spirit of the people, as he argued in *The Spirit of Hebrew Poetry* in 1782–83. Herder's positive perspective on Jewish culture was purposefully misread—and tainted—by Houston Chamberlain (1855–1927) in order to advance a stridently *völkisch* agenda in his best-selling *Grundlagen des neunzehnten Jahrhunderts* (*The Foundations of the Nineteenth Century*, 1899).

Herder's establishment of the contributing role of the discrete spirit of each people in the making of humanity, and manifesting its essence, which would be neither unitary nor derived from French philosophy, constituted a building block for psychology-based universalism. It inspired Moritz Lazarus and Heymann Steinthal's use of the concept of *Geist*, in its plurality, as a pathway to civic inclusion.

Hegel's Geist and Jewish Alienation

Jacques Derrida has argued for the importance of Georg Wilhelm Friedrich Hegel in Freudian psychology, but Hegel's impact on the pre-Freudian moment is equally significant, especially with regard to the *Geist*.[20] The multiplicity of cultures can be misleading in Hegel's philosophical system: what the plurality of humanity reveals is an underlying unity, manifested in his pivotal concept of *Geist*.[21] He contended that any given perception by individuals depends on a *Geist* that precedes them and will survive after them. The *Geist*, often mistaken for a metaphysical entity, should be understood as mind, Spirit, or self-consciousness—but situated in history.[22] With his articulation of unity and plurality, the individual and the collective, Hegel sought to break from the individualistic and ahistorical philosophical tradition of the West, which he subjected to severe criticism in the introduction to his 1807 *Phenomenology of Spirit*.[23]

Phenomenology charts the modalities of the *Geist*'s self-manifestation. The *Geist* necessitates the presence of an entity distinct from itself in order to actualize itself, which introduces otherness. It is also rational, but its rationality can be temporarily obscured by external phenomena and by human behavior: it will eventually be uncovered at the end of the actualization process.

The Hegelian *Geist* has multiple aspects: it can be subjective (which corresponds to the realm of psychology), objective (manifested in institutions), and absolute, which is the moment when the subject/object dichotomy is annulled and when the world and the consciousness of the world are reconciled. With the absolute *Geist*, humanity shows consciousness of itself and its destiny. Additionally, the *Geist* in its collective instantiations is divided along other lines: *Volksgeist* (the Spirit of a given people) and

Weltgeist (world Spirit). A nation can only attain its metaphysical principle once it is imbued with the absolute Spirit.

When a *Volksgeist* exhausts itself, it is sublated (*aufgehoben*).[24] But its contribution is absorbed into the *Weltgeist* and endures even after its disappearance: "The further existence of the national spirit [*Volksgeist*] is interrupted (inasmuch as it has exhausted itself and worked itself out to its conclusion), in order that world history and the world spirit [*Weltgeist*], may continue their course."[25] Specific national spirits are transient, whereas the absolute Spirit is eternal and reveals itself in all the spirits of every people over time. At this point, as his first biographer, Karl Rosenkranz, famously stated, the continuing existence of the Jews becomes a "dark riddle"[26] for Hegel: they are an exception to the rule of a *Volksgeist*'s limited life span and should have already disappeared, especially since Christianity claimed to have superseded Judaism and absorbed its message.[27]

Hegel's view of Judaism shifted over time: the philosopher's early writings envisioned it in a historicizing manner as the expression of a nation's soul or Spirit, one whose people, he claimed, displayed an "existence with no self-consciousness."[28] In 1795, he published *The Positivity of the Christian Religion*, in which he criticizes the authoritarianism into which the Christianity of his time had descended, which he blames partly on the religion's Jewish element.[29] In *The Spirit of Christianity and Its Fate* (1798–99), Hegel attacks the abstraction of Kantian universal law and seeks to define Christianity as a bond of love. This book contains his harshest critique of Judaism and explores a key theme of his philosophy: alienation. Based on his reading of Genesis, Hegel contends that the exclusive connection between Abraham and his God precludes any other relation than with a God who is fundamentally Other. He also asserts that the Jewish God, in his unknowability and in his demands, removes his followers from their environment (just as Abraham left Chaldea) and inscribes alienation (*Entfremdung*) at the core of Judaism. Abraham "became a stranger on earth, a stranger to the soil and to men alike."[30] Hegel even compares Judaism's relation to this world to the way Macbeth "stepped out of nature itself."[31] He likewise blamed Western negativity on Judaism, which he regarded as fostering rupture and discontinuity with an organic life.

Despite his modest knowledge of Judaism, Hegel did reference Maimonides in his analysis of the sublime. He characterized it not as an instance of a positive sublime—in the form of pantheism, traditionally much prized in German thought—but as a negative sublime, which highlights the unbridgeable difference between man and God.[32]

The hostile apprehension of Judaism was mitigated in Hegel's later writings, especially when he shifted from a historical and psychological approach to a concept-based one in the wake of *The Phenomenology of Spirit*. In this text, he classifies various religions, from Greek antiquity to Christianity, in relation to the absolute Spirit, to self-consciousness and manifestation, but chose to ignore Judaism altogether.

In *Philosophy of History* (1837), the posthumous publication of public lectures he had given between 1822 and 1830, Hegel contends that any religion possesses truth, even in an erroneous form, and that Jews do have a "world historical importance" because of their "unhappy consciousness."[33] This last concept, first used in *The Phenomenology of Spirit* in 1807, here indicates a split between the finite and the infinite that the Jews experience and that leaves them standing at the gate of salvation, alienated from this world and longing for a sublime and inaccessible kingdom of God.[34] Portraying such yearning for God demonstrates that Judaism goes beyond a slavish observance of statutory laws. This portrayal reversed the position Hegel had taken in *The Spirit of Christianity and Its Fate* and represented a break from the Kantian dismissal of Judaism as faith rather than religion. Despite its limitations, Judaism for Hegel in these lectures does exhibit a measure of subjectivity and interiority.

Hegel's more favorable reassessment comes about in his *Lectures on the Philosophy of Religion* (1827), in which he discusses the question of "determinate religion."[35] The object of religion, he argues, like the object of philosophy, is eternal truth. These two approaches, however, use different tools: whereas religion is based on representations (*Vorstellung*), philosophy uses concepts (*Begriffe*). Both approaches play an essential part, as a vehicle for manifesting the Spirit as well as by constituting an Other through which the Spirit can dialectically reveal itself over time. In order to do so, however, religion must externalize itself, and one of the modalities of this externalization is incarnation. This process explains the importance of Christianity, and the centrality for Hegel of Jesus made flesh.

Philosophers of the eighteenth and early nineteenth centuries thus depicted Judaism as a religion of alienation, no longer in terms of a theological agenda but now as a philosophical construct. Because the concept of alienation came to loom large in the nineteenth century, I argue that a generation of Jewish thinkers aimed to remedy this accusation as well as to refute the broader idea of a disharmony between Judaism and the world—and even affirm its belonging in the world. They proposed a Jewish-inflected philosophy of religion and created a counternarrative that turned the dominant discourse of alienation on its head. Nachman Krochmal was one of those thinkers.

Krochmal: Reconciliation or Alienation

The stated purpose of Nachman Krochmal's posthumously published *Guide for the Perplexed of Our Time* (1851) was to update Maimonides's *Guide of the Perplexed*, which addressed the quandaries of the man of faith in the twelfth century. The ambition of Krochmal's work was thus modeled after Maimonides's imperative to "give indications to a religious man for whom the validity of our Law has become established in his soul and has become actual in his belief," yet "the human intellect having drawn him on"—being versed in the sciences and philosophy—"he must have felt distressed by the externals of the Law."[36]

The underlying assumption here is that observance as external normativity will necessarily be shattered by the intellect and thus foster anguish and detachment—an incapacity to articulate the finite and the infinite, which is a modality of the estrangement that Hegel had described. Indeed, seven hundred years after Maimonides, the religious and societal confusion described by Krochmal resembled what the philosophers of his time, Hegel chief among them, depicted as alienation. Krochmal died before the publication of Ludwig Feuerbach's *Essence of Christianity* (1841) and Karl Marx's response in his *Theses on Feuerbach* (1845), both of which elaborated the concept further.[37] But in his defense of Judaism against an argument about alienation that was part of the ethos, Krochmal paved the way for a generation of Jewish thinkers who read the canon against the grain, in an effort to dispel any notion of Jewish alienation and of a universal Spirit to which Jews would have no access.

Since Leopold Zunz first mentioned Hegel's influence on Krochmal in his obituary of the latter in 1845, much has been written about the imprint of Hegelianism on the *Guide for the Perplexed of Our Time*—even if it only mentions Hegel once and other references are oblique.[38] The notions of a universal and particular Spirit certainly conjure up a Hegelian universe of references, especially in the book's sixth chapter. Consider the following passage: "And at this point he [the reflective person] will understand

JEWISH SPIRIT, NATIONAL SPIRIT, AND ABSOLUTE SPIRIT   117

that intellection is the perfection of inner speech, that is, spirit becoming known to itself, just as the symbols in their totality are the perfection of outward speech, that is, [one spirit] becoming known to another spirit."[39] Here, Krochmal details what would be the typical workings of the Hegelian Spirit with the development of self-consciousness in time. However, his objective was not to claim a specific tradition but to synthesize multiple authors into a pragmatic work that could constitute an apology for the wisdom of Torah-derived knowledge and a reconciliation between multiple planes of knowledge and of existence, to which, in his view, Judaism offered the best approach.[40]

The architecture of Krochmal's *Guide* intertwines culture and metaphysics and posits Judaism as the synthesis between eternity and temporality. Chapters 1 through 7 are devoted to the philosophy of religion and of history, chapters 8 through 11 survey the history of the Jewish people, and chapters 12 through 15 provide an overview of Jewish literature. The two concluding chapters, left unfinished by Krochmal's untimely death, sketch out his philosophical system. The placement of chapter 6, on the Spirit, is revealing: the Spirit borders history (and the retelling of history by the *Guide*), and it also shapes it. It is on the margins, and yet it is a driving force.

In this section, Krochmal says that the *ruḥani ha-muḥlat*, absolute Spirit, is reality itself. Using Hegelian categories, he claims that this absolute Spirit has to do with the question of representations, more precisely with the initial moment of representations or thoughts (*tziyyurei teḥilat ha-maḥshavah*). Krochmal's notion of "ideas of incipient thought" is key to what defines a Torah-based knowledge of reality: a specific approach to the world and the psyche. It also foreshadows future reflections on the concept of *kadmut ha sekhel*, "the beginning of the intellect," found in Hasidic texts, which were later interpreted as a variation or prefiguration of the unconscious, as the next chapters discuss. Knowledge gained from the Torah is not based on intellectual, conceptual categories or philosophical concepts—*maḥshevot ha-sekhel*, or *Begriffe*, in the German terms Krochmal uses.[41] It is a representation that can then call for its own philosophical analysis.

In the seventh chapter, as he ponders the significance of the *ruah ha umma*, the spirit of the people, which explains the eternity of that people while contrasting it with the extinction of others, Krochmal reframes the Hegelian *Geist*.[42] The Jewish people constitute an exception to the law of the

Volksgeist in that they should have disappeared when Christianity claimed to have superseded and absorbed the message of Judaism. Yet they never exhausted themselves. The only possible reason, Krochmal advances, is that the *Volksgeist* of the Jews is the *Geist* itself. History is thus evidence of the specific bond between the Jews and the absolute Spirit and of their distinct capacity to suspend the rules of history. To demonstrate his proposition, however, Krochmal had to return to history. The construction of his argument can thus appear contradictory, since his metaphysical principles seem at odds with his immanent cultural-historical analyses. Yet, as Amos Funkenstein shows, this is precisely the contribution of the Haskalah (Jewish Enlightenment) and its thinkers: "the introduction of the historical, evolutionary dimension which these [medieval and Neoplatonic] older insights lacked."[43] And while Funkenstein is certainly right, history is not enough. Krochmal interweaves theology and culture, just as Giovanni Battista Vico had done.[44] Though it is likely impossible to conclusively determine whether Krochmal actually read the Italian philosopher, the resemblances are striking, and his categories do echo Vicoean universals.

> From what we have explained, the wise person will understand that these metaphorical usages are not just matters of pure convention fixed by those who invented or enlarged the language, but are grounded in the intellect and the nature of the spiritual, which is all encompassing, and immediately when it reveals itself and develops its signs, these signs encompass [the levels of] sense, intellect, and Reason. Therefore, we see that almost the exact same metaphors are found in different languages.[45]

Properly understood, metaphors dissolve the dichotomy between the intellect and the spiritual: they are just metaphysics waiting to be culturally interpreted. Krochmal envisioned the notion of Spirit as a mitigation of the supposed alienation plaguing the Jews—of being torn between intellect and sentiment, group and individual. Krochmal's *Geist* is a totality, a connective force.[46] The manifestation and progress of the Spirit can only take place within and among a collective social formation on which individuals can then draw to establish a sense of unity and of continuum between them and the group, the finite and the infinite, which should remedy any possible alienation. A variation of this interconnection, expressed in a decidedly more psychological idiom, would undergird Lazarus and Steinthal's *Völkerpsychologie*, to which I will now turn.

✳ 6 ✳
Völkerpsychologie
A Psychology of Culture against a Race-Based Spirit

Völkerpsychologie is a psychology of social life, but at the same time a theory of sociocultural evolution drawing on linguistics, law, literature, religion, myth, and customs ushered in by Moritz Lazarus (1824–1903) and Heymann Steinthal (1823–1899). Lazarus first developed his notion of Völkerpsychologie in a semischolarly journal.[1] Later, however, he did acknowledge his indebtedness to Giovanni Battista Vico and especially his "universals," which Lazarus called the "generalities of spiritual life" in his best-selling monograph, *Das Leben der Seele* (*The Life of the Soul*, 1855–57).[2]

Lazarus and Steinthal also expanded on the work of Johann Gottfried von Herder—along with the philosopher Johann Friedrich Herbart and the historian and philologist Wilhelm von Humboldt—in an effort to reclaim German philosophy while reinscribing the Jewish tradition in a psychological key. This construct aimed to showcase a universal Spirit in which the Jewish spirit played an integral part. Such was their ambition.

The lives and works of Lazarus and Steinthal were so intertwined on multiple levels that most of the scholarship barely differentiates between them.[3] The two young men, who hailed from traditional Jewish families, met in the class of the linguist Karl Heyse (1797–1855) at Friedrich Wilhelm University in Berlin. They became friends, and even relatives after Steinthal's marriage to one of Lazarus's sisters.[4] Steinthal was more scholarly minded and had greater language skills, while Lazarus was a popular lecturer. But it is as the founders of *Völkerpsychologie* that their names, and sometimes their reception, are inseparably linked. The term *Völkerpsychologie* itself was coined by Lazarus in an 1851 article.[5] Nine years later, the two of them founded and edited the *Zeitschrift für Völkerpsychologie und Sprachwissenschaft* (*Journal of Ethnopsychology and Linguistics*), whose twenty issues appeared between 1860 and 1890. From the first issue, they sought to define the contours of a field.⁶ Their respective approaches and their work for the journal showed how the diversity of nations or peoples contributed to the "development of the human Spirit," in David Einhorn's words; constituted a foray into collective psychology; and expanded the notion of shared consciousness that transformed into the idea of the collective unconscious.

From Psychology to Ethics
MORITZ LAZARUS: CULTURE AS MULTIPLICITY

Moritz Lazarus was the son of a learned merchant who had been the student of the prominent Talmudic scholar Akiva Eger (1761–1837). He grew up in the province of Posen in East Prussia, which had recently been annexed to the kingdom of Prussia and would be ceded back to Poland after the First World War.⁷ The region's social environment brought together Jews, Polish Catholics, and German Protestants. Such ethnic, religious, and linguistic diversity made an impression on him and seeded, he believed, the "personal beginnings of his *Völkerpsychologie*."⁸ Lazarus studied law and philosophy in Berlin—and, like Steinthal, counted the historian Leopold von Ranke as well as the philologist August Boeckh among his teachers.⁹ Since in German lands Jews were barred from academic positions, he pursued a career as an independent lecturer and scholar, quickly gaining recognition.¹⁰ His popular three-volume monograph, *The Life of the Soul*, landed him an offer of a teaching position at the University of Bern, where he stayed until 1866. This position was followed by one at the Royal Military Academy in Berlin between 1868 and 1872 and an honorary chair at the University of Berlin in 1873, though Lazarus never became full professor. Despite the popularity of his books and his renown, his multiple unsuccessful attempts to secure academic positions illustrate the fate of Jews as outsiders in academia and the ambivalences of civil society in general, which percolated into his work.¹¹

Lazarus's first pamphlet, published in 1850, was titled *Die sittliche Berechtigung Preussens in Deutschland* (*The Moral Authority of Prussia in Germany*). In it, he defends the superiority of Prussia in a future German state.¹² He subsequently abandoned this chauvinistic approach, as demonstrated in the aforementioned *Life of the Soul*, in which he takes a philosophical and psychological approach to both individuals and the notion of a collective Spirit, while making no mention of ethnicity. "The real culture lies in multiplicity," he now claims.¹³

Yet in German politics and culture from the mid-nineteenth century onward, the question of the formation of communities and the possibility of maintaining differences within these communities became increasingly contentious and racialized.[14] The turns and new tone of Lazarus's work in the later part of his life certainly illustrate a more combative stance. His 1879 lecture at the Hochschule für die Wissenschaft des Judentums (Higher Institute for Jewish Studies) was "What Does National Mean?"[15] In it, Lazarus responds to the Lutheran theologian and court chaplain Alfred Stoecker (1835–1909) and to his recent inflammatory speech, "Our Demands on Modern Jewry," in Berlin.[16] Stoecker's diatribe was directed against social democracy and was brimming with anti-Semitic tropes, accusing Jews of disloyalty and being agents of regime change. In striking an emotional note in his response, Lazarus also rebukes earlier attacks on Jews made by Heinrich von Treitschke in his 1879 article "The Jews Are Our Misfortune."

Lazarus took a stand against a growing anti-Semitic climate in the culture at large: "This blood-and-race theory is in its entirety a product of a general coarsely sensualist-materialist worldview."[17] He thus turned long-standing tropes associated with Judaism on their head and highlighted the fixation of anti-Semites on blood and on the so-called carnal nature of Jews. His accusing non-Jews of materialism and quoting Martin Luther's very rare favorable appreciations of Jews (in his 1523 essay, "That Jesus Christ Was Born a Jew") against a Lutheran theologian made for a powerful counterpunch that turned traditional anti-Jewish tropes against anti-Semites.[18] Initially directed to a Jewish audience and meant to reinforce their sense of belonging, Lazarus's address was later published for the broader public. Fueled by a sense of urgency, he hoped to make his message accessible to all.

In "Was heisst national?" ("What Does National Mean?"), Lazarus argues that nations spring from their members' collective desire to be part of a community of shared destiny.[19] The French philosopher, historian, and religious scholar Ernest Renan's famous 1882 Sorbonne conference of nearly the same title ("What Is a Nation?")—which has become a cornerstone of the French understanding of the nation as resting on a common will and as an ever-renegotiated construct, rather than based on immutable characteristics such as language or race—is indebted to Lazarus. Without attribution, Renan borrowed key elements of *Völkerpsychologie* for his speech. Although it might have been inspired by a German Jewish thinker, Renan's "What Is a Nation?" has been taken as the antithesis of German worldviews that were grounded in a mythical essence and distinctiveness.[20] This opposition has come to represent the two nations' irreconcilable perspectives, explaining their enmity and wars. Lazarus's talk and pamphlet have a poignant tone to them—and evince a growing feeling of powerlessness.

It was in that climate, where political and racial, science-based anti-Semitism was gaining ground, that the term *Antisemitismus* itself was coined by the journalist Wilhelm Marr in 1880 in order to replace *Judenhass* (hatred of Jews) with a more scientific-sounding word.[21] Given the rising marginalization of his views and ideals, Lazarus increasingly started to speak from a Jewish perspective. This stance comes through in his 1887 collection of speeches and lectures, *Treu und Frei (Faithful and Free)*.[22]

The emphasis on ethics shifted from a more historical perspective in *Über den Ursprung der Sitten (On the Origins of Morals)*, published in 1860 and 1867, to the ahistorical *Die Ethik des Judentums (The Ethics of Judaism)*, in which Lazarus claims that Judaism embodies universal, timeless values.[23] The book was hailed as an instant classic in Jewish circles and was translated into many languages, including English in 1900 by Henrietta Szold, a well-known thinker and future prominent figure of American Zionism. But Gershom Scholem dismissed Lazarus's ethics as the compromise of a liberal theology that ignored the social reality, the ethos and mentality of the Germany of his time, "in the service of an abstraction" and of lofty, universalistic ethics.[24] This argument is a variation of Scholem's broader critique of his coreligionists for fostering the myth of a German-Jewish dialogue and of a symbiosis that never was.[25] While Lazarus's work prompted criticism from one of his students, the philosopher Hermann Cohen, Cohen's subsequent fight against anti-Semitism was predicated on the affinity between the German and the Jewish spirits, so it was still imbued with his teacher's worldview.[26]

In addition to his scholarly work, Moritz Lazarus held positions within the Jewish community as president of the Jewish synods in Augsburg and Leipzig in 1869 and 1871 and president of the Higher Institute for Jewish Studies founded by Abraham Geiger, where many luminaries of German Judaism taught. Their students included future towering figures such as Abraham Heschel, Emil Fackenheim, and Leo Baeck. Lazarus's posthumous book *Die Erneuerung des Judentums (The Renewal of Judaism,* 1909) tackled the challenges faced by the Judaism of his time.[27] And it was now from the sources of Judaism itself that he sought to establish the moral pillars of a more inclusive society: promoting a discourse of psychology-based universalism had failed to deliver the moral message Lazarus believed in.

HEYMANN STEINTHAL: THE DIGNITY OF DIVERSITY

Heymann Steinthal took a similar path. Toward the end of his life, he wrote disillusioned lines in his *Allgemeine Ethik* (*General Ethics*), prefaced with an address to his friend Lazarus about the climate of the times: "The pillars of their *Weltanschauung*, whose strength we never tested, or not in a long time and never feared that we should ever test it, are decayed and worm-eaten." Moral values seemed to have retreated: "The most beautiful stars of moral culture seem to fade away in the heavens above our fatherland.'"[28] From there follows a call for a new ethics, which was the impetus for the book. His initial ambitions, however, were to mesh morality and science: the ethical aspect of folk psychology was not self-contained and was taken for granted—grounded in German thought, applicable across nations, and doing justice to Judaism.

Born in 1823 into a lower-middle-class and learned family, Steinthal studied philology and philosophy at Friedrich Wilhelm University in Berlin, where he completed his doctoral thesis on Humboldt and Hegel while learning multiple languages.[29] He then became a *Privatdozent* and, between 1852 and 1856, resided in Paris after receiving the prestigious Prix Volney, the highest award granted in France for a work in the field of philology.[30] He used the prize to improve his Mandarin and further reflect on linguistics, as he had started doing in his book *Der Ursprung der Sprache im Zusammenhange mit den letzten Fragen alles Wissens* (*The Origin of Language with Regard to the Ultimate Questions of All Knowledge*, 1851).[31] His prolific contributions always brought together the science of language and of the mind, as did *Grammatik, Logik, Psychologie: Ihre Prinzipien und ihre Verhältnis zu Einander* (*Grammar, Logic, Psychology: Their Principle and Relation to One Another*, 1855), as well as the programmatic *Philology, History and Psychology in Their Mutual Relations* (1864), *Overview of the Sciences of Language: Introduction to the Psychology and the Science of Language* (1871), and *Outline of Linguistics* (1881).[32]

In 1862, Steinthal became a professor of the comparative science of language, but he did not climb the traditional echelons and his career remained mostly on the margins of academia.[33] From 1872 onward, he also lectured on the philosophy of religion at the College of Jewish Studies in

Berlin and collected his various contributions in *Über Juden und Judentum* (*On Jews and Judaism*), in which he defines himself as a "philosopher, free thinker and pious Jew."[34] He took a more textual approach in *Zu Bibel und Religionsphilosophie* (*On the Bible and Philosophy of Religion*, 1890).[35]

A disciple of Wilhelm von Humboldt, whose *Works on the Science of Language* he edited and published in 1884, Steinthal shared his belief that language represents the data of experience—which he pitted against an abstract Hegelian system of philosophy.[36] He also shared Humboldt's belief in the dignity of the diversity of languages.[37] Language, both men held, is a product of the common spirit of a people and denotes its capacity for creating a worldview that Steinthal ascribed to a degree of self-confidence.[38] His trust in the power of such a worldview, however, seemed fragile: "This book is dedicated to the living and future members of the Humboldtian faith in the ideal of Humanity," he wrote in his introduction to Humboldt's collected works, while hoping that their number would expand in time.[39]

Both Lazarus and Steinthal were thus firmly grounded in a German Jewish identity and became increasingly eager to show that this identity was not based on particularism. From its very inception, their *Journal of Ethnopsychology and Linguistics* made it clear that the concept of *Volk* could not and should not be based on ethnicity. The psychology of the people was but a step toward universal psychology. The scope of *Völkerpsychologie* was thus twofold: finding not only the laws governing the specific history of peoples but also the overarching essence and theories, or patterns of cultural evolution. And although an absolute Spirit was regarded as the "essence of all inner and higher activity," it could not be imbued with a metaphysical principle—a fine line that didn't make it immune to contradictions.[40] Continuing to draw on the work of Giovanni Vico, Johann von Herder, and Georg Hegel, especially with the notion of absolute Spirit, the new field was also at the intersection of the psychology of Johann Friedrich Herbart and the linguistics of Wilhelm von Humboldt.

WILHELM VON HUMBOLDT: BETWEEN A "MENTAL WHOLE" AND INDIVIDUATION

Steinthal's appreciation of Humboldt fluctuated over time, but he certainly was among the most prominent proponents of his theories. For Humboldt, language was not a representation but the "formative organ of thought" (*das bildende Organ des Gedankens*).[41] Steinthal elaborated on this idea as early as 1851 in *The Origin of Language*.⁴² That book offers a psychological philology based on the Humboldtian notion of language as *energeia*. Energeia is an Aristotelian category; connected to the active intellect, it is what actualizes potential qualities. Language is thus an actualization, an activity of production (*Erzeugung*): the psyche is the internal process by which a people creates itself through its language activity.⁴³

Humboldt should be credited, Steinthal claimed, with moving the understanding of language from a quest for origins with potential racist implications to an emphasis on its continually self-creating and self-created activity.⁴⁴ He was thus more interested in a synchronic—rather than diachronic—study of language.

This understanding of language as activity is where the Humboldtian distinction between *Weltansicht* and *Weltanschauung* becomes operative. The latter literally means a worldview that unifies experiences and feelings; it has a retrospective, explicative quality to which we will return in chapter 7.⁴⁵ A *Weltansicht*, on the other hand, shapes our perception of the world and language: it is not a reflection but a "vehicle" to use to "drive through the diversity of the whole world."⁴⁶

That diversity is best understood as the articulation between the individual and a collective whole and as a process of individuation. The individual psyche is part of a mental whole, and each specific mental structure of speakers depends on the organization of their language. The articulation between language structure and national Spirit is key in Humboldt's writings: "Man is by birth a member of a *Volk*, and is thus determined in his mental development in manifold ways. The individual cannot be completely comprehended without regard to the mental whole [*die geistige Gesamtheit*] in which it has been created and in which it lives."⁴⁷

One of the manifold ways to gain this comprehension is language: Humboldt provides the link between linguistic relativism and psychology because of the instability of representations, which are anchored in language. Since this faculty is so formative, Humboldt refutes the divide between the sciences ("natural history") and the human sciences (or "history of mankind"), thereby vindicating Steinthal's ambition to make his Völkerpsychologie a multidisciplinary approach. However, Steinthal increasingly perceived a dualism in Humboldt's thinking—a chasm between speculative and empirical knowledge that he ascribed to the legacy of medieval thought.⁴⁸ In his article "Zur Religionsphilosophie" ("On the Philosophy of Religion," 1877),[49] Steinthal also laments what he regarded as Humboldt's tendency to hypostatize concepts instead of examining them in their specific dynamics and in relation with one another, which he thought was more central in the field of psychology, and which was why he grew particularly attracted to Herbart.

Breaking into Consciousness: The Role of Herbart in Völkerpsychologie

Johann Friedrich Herbart (1776–1841) inspired the work of both Lazarus and Steinthal, as amply demonstrated in their journal.[50] Upon taking over Immanuel Kant's chair at Königsberg, he rejected parts of his predecessor's system, notably the concept of innate ideas. He also rejected the notion that the mind could be composed of multiple, independent faculties best suited for specific subjects and that it could be trained accordingly. Herbart's theory of knowledge is based on experience and on "facts of consciousness."[51] Psychology—which he saw as the mechanics of the mind—must be empirical, although not based on experiment, as he held in his treatise *Psychologie als Wissenschaft* (*Psychology as Science*, 1824).[52]

Herbart's concept of "the real" was informed by the Newtonian physics of inner and outer pressure and of infinitesimal calculus—the mathematics he used were meant to exhibit "the universal laws of psychological phenomena" and were thus rather speculative.[53] At the same time, he did not shy away from using the word *soul* to describe the entirety of the workings of the mind. He held the soul to be made up of entities comparable to Leibnizian monads (from the Greek, meaning "unity"— that which has no part and is therefore indivisible), the basic substances making up the universe. Because these entities are likely to violently collide with others given the narrowness of the mind (which shows his indebtedness to John Locke), they must strive for their own self-preservation (*Selbsterhaltung*) and can do so through *Vorstellungen*— mental representations.[54]

It is through these representations, which have a specific and measurable duration and intensity, that a soul can be timeless and preserve itself. Herbart claimed that mental life results from the collision of the representations inside a psyche and that the structure of human experience and the development of the psyche are based on such dynamic states.

The mind, an "apperceptive mass," is an agglomerate of representations fighting one another—these are forces capable of coalescing in order to break through the threshold of consciousness. Or they can impede one another, thus constituting "inhibiting sums" (*Hemmungsume*). When they do leave consciousness, that inhibition recedes. The mind also includes areas of sensations that disappear, while their former presence leaves a trace. Herbart postulated that blockages are ubiquitous—the terms *repression, suppression,* and *inhibition* populate his work, and their activity could be measured algebraically. *Apperception* is another aspect of the working of the mind: building on Gottfried Wilhelm Leibniz, it is the capacity for old experiences to inform new ones. Successful learning is thus achieved when preexisting knowledge can be accessed and built on—hence his legacy in modern pedagogy.

Lazarus and Steinthal's principal criticism of Herbart's psychology was his limited focus on the psyche as the realm of the conscious. It is indeed precisely the thesis of the "narrowness of consciousness" that makes it essential to analyze what is behind and beyond it in the unconscious. Lazarus thus takes Herbart to task: "The exclusion of the unconscious from the subtle psychological process constitutes the greatest flaw in Herbart's basic view."[55]

In fact, for Lazarus and Steinthal, it is only by bringing together language and psychology that one can make sense of the conscious and the unconscious. This is what Steinthal expresses in his programmatic *Einleitung in die Psychologie und Sprachwissenschaft* (*Introduction to Psychology and the Science of Language*, 1881): "The philologist understands the speaker and poet better than he understands himself and better than his contemporaries understood him, for he brings clearly into consciousness what was actually, but only unconsciously, present in the other."[56] Humboldt and Herbart must thus be read in conjunction; philology was understood as the proper hermeneutics for psychology. Language is, once again, the royal road to the mind.

Herbart died in 1841, and despite the criticism regarding his speculative models, his presence loomed large in psychology throughout the century and in the making of social psychology.[57] With his theory of representations as dynamic, associative forces, he paved the way for the work of Moritz Lazarus and Heymann Steinthal and especially for Lazarus's concept of condensation.

The Concept of Condensation: Collective Inscriptions of the Unconscious

The paternity of the term *Verdichtung* (thickening, compression, or condensation) has been almost universally attributed to Sigmund Freud, but its genealogies have been mostly ignored.[58] It is thus worth attending to the ways the concept in the work of Lazarus conveys an exploration of collective psychology and the unconscious workings of communities across time.

According to the dictionary of the Brothers Grimm, the occurrence of the term *Verdichtung* can be traced to the philosopher and poet Jean Paul, who used it in conjunction with the notion of incarnation (*verkörpert*) to describe the qualities and the persona of a prince, and thus to convey sovereignty.[59] The condensation of virtue and wisdom and their incarnation were meant for the edification of the people.[60] In later works, not mentioned in the Grimm dictionary, Jean Paul invokes the artistic vision sustaining this process: "The ethereal world of the poet must first condense itself [*sich verdichten*] in order to become the cloudy world of the dream."[61] Indeed, *Verdichtung* is built on the word *Dichtung* (poetry), whose root, *dicht*, expresses a phenomenon of condensation. This is precisely what is at work in poetic expression.[62] Condensation here is an aspect of the world-making task of the poet—and of the world-deciphering of the observer.[63]

The term also appeared in cosmology, notably in the works of Alexander von Humboldt (the brother of Wilhelm, the natural scientist and polymath) as well as in Friedrich Albert Lange's influential *History of Materialism*, published in 1865, which deals with the origins of the celestial bodies. As discussed in the first part of this book, the notion of divine compression that led to the creation of the universe is the kabbalistic concept of *tsimtsum*, and *tsimtsum* is sometimes translated as "Verdichtung."[64] Lazarus was certainly the first to employ *Verdichtung* in the psychological realm as a hermeneutical tool fundamental to *Völkerpsychologie*, with its emphasis on language and dynamic forces.

Let us return to Lionel Trilling's claim that Vico prefigured Freud (see chapter 5): "It was left to Freud to discover how, in a scientific age, we still feel and think in figurative formations, and to create, what psychoanalysis is, a science of tropes, of metaphor and its variants, synecdoche and metonymy."[65] This is incorrect: before psychoanalysis became associated with these literary figures of speech, Lazarus's *Verdichtung* systematically captured the poetic workings of both language and the mind into which Jean Paul had offered a glimpse, showing the intimate link between condensation and poetry.[66]

Lazarus sought to uncover what had become condensed over time and across nations: the poetic universals. As he makes it clear in 1855 in his programmatic statement in *The Life of the Soul*, "I directly express the spirit of continuity and the continuity of spirit [*der Geist der Continuität und die Continuität des Geistes*]," and he asserts that Vico was "one of the earliest people to have penetratingly grasped the generalities of spiritual life [*die geistige Lebensbewegung der Gesammtheiten*]."[67] He thus linked poetry and psychology.

> Poetry [*Verdichtung*], although it is a psychological process, can nonetheless be more or less perfect in both a logical and a psychological respect. Discussing this will be one of the most interesting and pedagogically important tasks for advancing psychology.[68]

Lazarus often belabored this concept of *Verdichtung*, which he clearly linked to the unconscious.

> Consciousness . . . in what it performs, however much its psychological quality may be different from that of the unconscious, is nevertheless not isolated; it is in cooperation and resonance that it carries out its own activity. Or, if, in order to accord with the truth, we call Spirit [*Geist*] the active subject, we must say that its conscious activity is always accompanied, fulfilled, and supplemented by unconscious activity. The Spirit thus also overcomes the narrowness of consciousness. This happens in many ways, and we will concern ourselves only with a few, to the extent that they impact knowledge of the processes. The narrowness of consciousness comes first in the condensation [*Verdichtung*] of thinking.[69]

Lazarus drew a causal link between the inadequacy of the mental space postulated by Herbart and the condensation process, which is how the psyche adjusts to these limitations. For Herbart, unless the condensation has reached a critical level, its contents remain unconscious, and he failed to attend to the unconscious mass. For Lazarus, however, the process is more capacious, with a dynamic and ongoing connection between the conscious and the unconscious. Compression denotes the relationships of ideas in the unconscious state, which Lazarus made central to the collective Spirit that manifests in various forms of culture.[70]

In the Spirit of nations, compressed contents—the result of *Verdichtung*—constitute an expansive category that includes the representations of thoughts or concepts, unconsciousness, language, and material objects.[71] *Verdichtung* occurs "when concepts and series of concepts, which have been discovered in earlier times by the most talented individuals and could only be grasped and understood by few, become slowly appropriated by whole classes of peoples and ultimately by the entirety of the people."[72] This is akin to a process of progressive revelation, with top-down social overtones: condensation happens first among the elite/the initiates and then is disseminated across nations and across social classes within nations. This process means greater access to what had originally been the privilege of the few. Equally noteworthy for the time is that Lazarus needed to specify the true universalism of the concept, since its access is not delimited by gender: "In all human conceptions . . . the process of condensation and fluency is carried out for the whole sexes as well as for each individual through language."[73]

Two aspects are worth noting: the notions of free circulation and of time are key to that condensation. First, the free circulation belongs to an economy of the mind that Lazarus deploys in his book *Über die Ideen in der Geschichte* (*On Ideas in History*, 1865), in which the vocabulary of economic exchange applied to the psyche reflects his time. He also lays out the substitution process that creates "an economy of the spiritual force without which man would be always stuck at the lowest level of a life that is but a representation."[74] Energy and economy are thus closely linked, and the Herbartian categories of forces detailed earlier, whose collisions make them prevail or recede, play themselves out here: the forces and frictions of the psyche are transposed on a social level.

Second, the process leading to condensation consists of a stratification through time: the mental labor of prior generations is condensed (*verdichtet*) in what may become preconceived ideas; because these concepts or sentences have become shallow, or lost their initial meaning, they impede any deep engagement with them by the new generation, since these individuals cannot fathom their true significance—and this can lead to a lack of intergenerational understanding and thus social cohesion. Clichés or slogans are one such example. Even if Lazarus warned against the potential dangers of such compressed ideas, these compressions are indispensable so that each generation does not have to start conceptualizing the world anew. They are a form of inherited cognition, which Lazarus illustrates by marshaling examples of what the words *state* or *Bible* immediately elicit in anyone's mind: "You have a condensation of multiple kinds of knowledge, feelings and judgments in mind when you think of the 'Bible.'"[75]

Using later categories sheds further light on Lazarus's construct. The structure of language is organized around the two poles of metaphor and metonymy. This psychopathological framework, introduced by Roman Jakobson (1896–1982), was transposed by Jacques Lacan, who juxtaposed the metaphor/metonymy binary to the one established by Freud as the basic functions of the unconscious: repression/displacement.[76] Thus, metaphor functions to suppress, and metonymy functions to coalesce: there is a combinatory process at work in condensations such as metonymy, which invites a plurality of meanings along with the interpretative work needed to tease them out.

Condensation is "saturated by the whole content," but precisely because it is symbolic and metonymic, it is "a mere indication of the manifold content that comes into play for the creation of the present thought."[77] It leads to a clustering of mental phenomena, and it has been equated with memory groups. Indeed, one of the lectures at the Third International Congress of Psychology of 1896 held in Munich addressed the formations of such systems, and the conversations signal Lazarus's weight in the scholarship of the time.[78] A more significant paper was "Der Begriff des Unbewussten in der Psychologie" ("Concept of the Unconscious in Psychology") by Theodor Lipps, Freud's main acknowledged influence.[79] The conference proceedings sum up the highly praised paper as follows: "The condensed ideas are also called masses of ideas for, the forces that in the act of apperceiving awaken and guide the masses of ideas are the secret powers of the emotional soul; to understand them means to recognize the deepest motives and causes of apperception."[80]

Condensation is descriptive—it is an aggregation, but absent a proper disentanglement or interpretation of its layers, it can become symptomatic. It needs apperception to be properly channeled into the psyche. As we have seen in its Herbartian valence, apperception is defined as the mind's consciousness of its own perceptions and an awareness of the workings of the past: it is from the reflective or attentive apprehension of one's inner states—possibly a condensed one—that judgment is formed. But when the *Verdichtung* has become too thick, the individual loses access to the essence of the concept or phenomena and no appropriation can happen, leading to a process akin to alienation, which Steinthal identified as one of the perils of his time.[81]

For all its nebulous contours, the term *Verdichtung* is noteworthy. Coupled with *Verschiebung* (displacement), the very word *Verdichtung* has become a cornerstone of Freudian psychology.[82] It is one of the main processes of the dreamwork (*Traumdeutung*), as elaborated in chapters 6 and 7 of Freud's *The Interpretation of Dreams*.[83] As Jean Laplanche and Jean-Bertrand Pontalis have noted, for Freud, condensation is mostly defensive: it is a "consequence of the censorship and . . . a means of avoiding it," which is very different from Moritz Lazarus's understanding of it.[84]

Freud's archaeology of the concept does not acknowledge Lazarus, and Lazarus's collective focus is certainly different from Freud's. Mourning the death of his father, Freud was not present at the 1896 Congress of Psychology. Nonetheless, Lazarus's public stature and the attention his work drew make it unlikely that he could have ignored his contribution and the possible symptoms that emerge from an absent or improper interpretation of aggregated ideas.

Additionally, in Lazarus's work Verdichtung is combined with *Representätion* or *Vertretung*—meaning the act of representation, of substitution.[85] Unlike condensation, representation "appears to be thoroughly devoid of the actual content"[86]—it is an empty shell that future content will occupy and fill in what is latent; it is a place of futurity. *Vertretung* appears less often than *Verdichtung*—only three times in *The Life of the Soul*—and seems to be less of a theoretical interest for Lazarus. However, it is worth mentioning this correlation with Verdichtung as well as the possible echoes in the Freudian concept of *Vertretung* (used interchangeably with *Representänz*), which acts as delegation: "an act of delegation," or Lacan's "*tenant lieu*," or placeholder.[87] Whereas representations are a future-oriented projection, condensation is an after-the-fact phenomenon.[88]

The Lazarusian unconscious as a place of layers and memory elicits comparisons with the structure of the unconscious described by Henri Bergson (1859–1941).[89] It is a repository of the past, mostly static, whose impact on everyday life is virtual. Gilles Deleuze noticed this in his attempt to rekindle interest in a Bergsonian unconscious and offer alternatives to the hegemonic Freudian theory of the unconscious.[90] Bergson's unconscious becomes actual only when the past becomes so sedimented that it cannot be accessed anymore and hampers a person's psyche.[91] In addition, this construct is assessed from a collective vantage point, which would not be Freud's focus until later in his life, notably in *Totem and Taboo* in 1913 and the post–First World War corpus, *Civilization and Its Discontents* (1930) and *Moses and Monotheism* (1939).

During the 1896 Congress of Psychology, the writer and journalist Georg Hirth gave a paper dealing with the associations of perceptions that remain below the threshold of consciousness, while being actively in conflict with each other. These *Merksysteme*, as he called them, could take possession of an individual without his being aware of it. According to the minutes, "In the discussion following the conference, the Rector Ufer commented that the *Merksysteme* were Herbart's *Vorstellungsmassen*, and [Johannes] Trüper said that they were identical to Lazarus's condensations, but Hirth took them in another direction."[92] That same year, Hirth founded the magazine *Jugend* (*Youth*), which was dedicated to art nouveau in all its dissonances (hence the term *Jugendstil* used to describe the art movement known as the Vienna Secession). This paper and moment in time thus signal a new direction: when the Berlin conceptions of the unconscious migrated to Vienna, psychology became a testament to a fractured self and to the inevitability of discordance rather than the harmony that Lazarus and Steinthal pursued.[93]

This difference between the personal and the collective unconscious might well also be the difference between the Viennese and the German Jewish approaches to the unconscious. Deciphering the psychological process of condensation enables one to decipher the "objective Spirit" (*objektiver Geist*), which comes from Hegelian philosophy and theorizes the collective nature of cultural life in the broader sense—illuminating the psychological underpinnings of the laws governing collective behavior.[94]

Simmel and the Reinterpretation of Condensation in Sociology

Many concepts of *Völkerpsychologie* reappeared in sociology, especially in the work of Georg Simmel, a student of Lazarus. One was the objective Spirit as law of the social order as well as of the interaction between individual and community (*Wechselwirkung*) and condensation.[95] This is a key aspect of Simmel's *Philosophy of Money*. Published in 1900, the same year as *The Interpretation of Dreams*, it examines money as the hidden underlying structure of life: "This extension of the power of money ... is manifested here as the condensation of the purely formal cultural energy that can be applied to any content in order to strengthen it and to bring about its increasingly purer representation."[96]

Simmel mobilizes the language of energy and representation, as well as the mention of condensation, to describe one of the most significant layers of symbolic culture along with the power structure that he details: "Objective culture is the historical presentation or more or less perfect *condensation of an objectively valid truth which is reproduced by our cognition* ... the objectification of the mind in words and works, organizations and traditions is the basis for this distinction by which man takes possession of his world, or even of any world at all."[97]

Simmel does not use the Hegelian term *objective Spirit* to describe the laws governing observable phenomena. Instead, he introduces the concept of *objective culture*, which implicitly stems from the former: objective culture reflects the collective values of societal production, such as art, economy, and religion. These collective representations may end up existing objectively and separately from the culture and groups that created them; but in order to exist as subjective representations, they must be actualized by the subject. "For even where the mind is tied to matter, as in tools, works of art and books," Simmel explains, "it is never identical with that part of them that is perceptible to our senses. The mind lives in them in a hardly definable potential form which the individual consciousness is able to actualize."[98] In his writings, an excessive production of cultural and social goods inevitably leads to estrangement, since no actualization can happen—the condensation, which initially created the shared references and experience for a collective existence, becomes impossible to unravel.[99]

In a remarkable bridge between symbolic projections, the concept also appears in the article "A Contribution to the Sociology of Religion" (1908), in which he claims that "social relations condense or refine themselves into a system of religious ideas or add new elements to existing ideas."[100] He returns to this notion in order to claim that the idea of God is actually the reflection of previous layers of dependence. The deification of ancestors is thus an "expression of the individual's dependence on the previous life of the group" and "the condensation and the transformation of those relations."[101]

It thus behooves philosophy or psychology to take on the task of analyzing and unpacking the condensed layers of representations, which, if left unexamined, may render an individual powerless—lost in his condition of alienated subject. Simmel's attention to excessive condensation draws on Lazarus and Steinthal's concepts but calls for even greater caution toward the products of society as well as a skeptical approach toward the achievements of modern society. In their simultaneously historical and forward-looking approach, Lazarus and Steinthal relied on the tools of *Völkerpsychologie* to neutralize the alienating effects of modernity with a confidence that seemed to elude the generation that had come of age with the fin de siècle ethos. Simmel's stance rejected the materialism of his time and linked economic objectification and cultural objectification, which he came to describe in his essay "On the Concept and Tragedy of Culture" (1911).[102]

The necessity and peril of condensation in creating a shared universe of references for humankind also subsequently appeared in Ernst Cassirer's *An Essay on Man: An Introduction to the Philosophy of Human Culture*, but in a more optimistic key.[103] Cassirer defines humanity as working toward a common purpose and showcasing a universal character "in which [cultures] all agree and harmonize."[104] It is thus incumbent on philosophy to be even more proactive toward this purpose and harness all forms of cultural production, including religion. "Philosophy cannot, on the other hand, stop here," Cassirer declares. "It must seek to achieve an even greater condensation and centralization. In the boundless multiplicity and variety of mythical images, of religious dogmas, of linguistic forms, of works of art, philosophic thought reveals the unity of a general function by which all these creations are held together."[105]

The centrality of the condensation of representations as an operative concept signals an intersection between *Völkerpsychologie* and the philosophy of culture, of which Cassirer might be one of the last representatives.[106] Whereas the philosophy of culture expresses the possibility of human agency by finding unity, *Völkerpsychologie* aims to unpack these condensed representations and shed light on the process that led to their condensation—a process in which specific individuals had no part, but that needs to be disentangled in order to transcend possible forms of alienation.

These characteristics, which run through *Völkerpsychologie* and later conceptions of the psychology of culture, are also apparent in Carl Gustav Jung's distinction between the individual and the collective unconscious: "While the personal unconscious is made up essentially of contents which have at one time been conscious, but which have disappeared from consciousness through having been forgotten or repressed, the contents of the collective unconscious have never been in consciousness, and therefore have never been individually acquired but owe their existence exclusively to heredity."[107]

The philosophical system of Moritz Lazarus and Eduard von Hartmann—with their construct of inherited forms of cognition and an external "objective Spirit" that can cripple individuals or societies when they are unaware of them or cannot access them—does indeed offer a glimpse into what Jung would model as the collective unconscious. They thus vindicate Mikhail Bakhtin's observation on the lineage of the idea of a collective unconscious and psychology of culture, or ethnopsychology, which he clearly traced back to Lazarus and Steinthal: "It was retained in the unconscious (if only the collective unconscious) and was fixed in the memories of languages, genres, and rituals; from here it penetrates into the speech and dreams (related, consciously recalled) of people (who have a particular psychic constitution and are in a particular state)."[108]

These collective representations would also subsequently be elaborated as cultural anthropology and psychology.[109] Probing a collective conscious, or unconscious representations of communities based on *Gemeinschaft* (i.e., on kinship and personal ties), also meant interrogating the possibility and modalities of coexistence—a coexistence soon imperiled by anti-Semitic and racist forces.

Rejecting Race: Völkerpsychologie, *Anthropology, and the Politics of German Academia in the Nineteenth Century*

Not only did Freud never directly acknowledge Lazarus in his writings, but *Völkerpsychologie* soon turned into, as Woodruff Smith puts it, "a case study of a deserted science."[110] Indeed, Lazarus and Steinthal seem to have fallen into relative oblivion. The lack of methodological and topical clarity of the science they strove to create and its hesitations between historicism and natural science, between national specificities and general laws presiding over humanity, help explain why the legacy of *Völkerpsychologie* was so limited. But other choices are what primarily account for this noble failure. Although they marshaled the resources of other disciplines, Lazarus and Steinthal resisted associations with other scholarly endeavors, such as anthropology, because in German academia racist worldviews increasingly permeated them. The science of the mind still appeared relatively untouched, but that field never recognized *Völkerpsychologie* as a legitimate endeavor.[111] The brief rise and fall of *Völkerpsychologie* closely followed the crisis of the humanities and the shattering of Jewish hopes in German liberalism.

One of the ambitions of *Völkerpsychologie* was to promote a psychological philology: a psychology that invokes language, in all its various layers, in order to paint a robust picture of the mind, its development, and its activity.[112] As such, psychology is at "the border of history and philology."[113] In its emphasis on language, this endeavor closely resembled what August Boeckh, Lazarus's teacher, detailed as his goal for philology in general: "Erkenntnis des Erkannten"—that is, "the acknowledgment of what is produced by the human mind, which is the known."[114] In its exploration of the productions of the mind, philology is an activity in which "one gives the highest consideration to universality."[115] It operates at a double level: it is a window onto the individual and the collective psyche—which Friedrich Nietzsche would pursue—and it also paves the way for a philosophy of culture.[116] Both Steinthal and Boeckh highlighted the process of the creation of meaning—what would be known in the twentieth century as philosophical hermeneutics and would be famously deployed in Hans-Georg Gadamer's *Truth and Method* in 1960: a debt acknowledged by the German philosopher, who credited those who influenced him, including Steinthal and Boeckh.[117]

The approach to philology developed by *Völkerpsychologie* carried a political weight: it went against a certain "linguistic turn" in the nineteenth century that was integral to the German nationalist project. For that undertaking, nationhood came to be defined as the expression of an ethnic and linguistic community, in which the emergence of the mother tongue came to be scrutinized and almost sacralized.[118] But in the case of Lazarus and Steinthal, acknowledging sedimented layers of knowledge is ideologically different from exploring the origins of language. As we saw in the first chapter of this book, the inscrutability of the unconscious discourages an origin narrative. So, too, does philology in their approach, as it highlights the plurality of genealogies rather than the univocity of an elusive objectivity. The philological work prescribed by Leopold Zunz in the agenda of the *Wissenschaft des Judentums* had already pointed toward an expansive understanding of philology. In his programmatic pamphlet *On Rabbinical Literature* (1818), he characterizes the new "science" as a retrospective inventory of the riches of Jewish history.[119] But the subsequent efforts of Lazarus and Steinthal were even more pointedly geared toward encompassing a broader community, beyond religious fault lines.

The philological part of *Völkerpsychologie*, however, also lent itself to perilous reinterpretations at a time when nationalist and racist appropriations of philology were gaining further traction and getting enmeshed with psychology.[120] For most of the nineteenth century, philology was connected to the "spirit of modernity," as Ernest Renan proclaims in his book *The Future of Science* (1890), but modernity took different turns.[121] Houston Chamberlain, the infamous theoretician of *völkisch* worldviews and author of the best-selling *Foundations of the Nineteenth Century*, claims in that book that it had been the "century of philology," one that promoted his racist agenda.[122]

Lazarus and Steinthal's conceptualization of humanity, which they proclaimed in the first issue of their journal, implied diversity, though *Völkerpsychologie* mostly dealt with Western nations and inscribed itself in the legacy of an ethnocentric type of humanism. Belief in progress did come with a hierarchy between primitive and developed peoples, albeit without an essentialization of differences.[123] In a context of increased focus on biology and race, especially within the Berlin school of anthropology, Lazarus and Steinthal's voices became increasingly dissonant.[124] In their view, the school's outright dismissal of the notion of *Geist* reeked of materialism.

Their rejection of the double lens of race and materialism, through which a significant part of anthropological research was being conducted, explains why Lazarus and Steinthal did not envision anthropology as a possible cognate discipline and left their own discipline with no academic affiliation. They nevertheless had an indirect impact on the field, through two of its towering figures in Germany and in the United States. One of the future fathers of German anthropology, Adolf Bastian (1826–1905), attended Lazarus's lectures. From the 1860s onward, he extensively cited Lazarus's work while refining his own theories, notably those regarding "the psychic unity of mankind," for which he came to be known.[125] This notion is based on his notion of "elementary ideas" (*Elementargedanken*)—which in turned influenced Carl Gustav Jung's and Joseph Campbell's comparative mythology.[126] Bastian's emphasis on this, and on how the elementary ideas can and must be extracted from past representations, relied more on a sense of method than Lazarus and Steinthal did. Their ultimate inability to carve out a scholarly field arguably led to their relative obscurity despite their legacy, which was carried forward by their students and disciples.[127] This lineage can be found in the work of Franz Boas (1858–1942), who introduced cultural anthropology to the United States and whose anti-racism is certainly indebted to Lazarus and Steinthal's earlier ethnouniversalism. A student of Bastian, he credited "folk psychology" and specifically the work of Steinthal with the linguistic framework that he judged essential to the field of anthropology.[128]

Lazarus and Steinthal's commitment to universalism was aptly captured by their former student and disciple Hermann Cohen, who despite his critique came to understand both the foundations and the ambiguities of the non-racial universalism that the two sought to promote.[129] "The concept of this national Spirit [*Volksgeist*] is not based on a racial unit, but, objectively, on the uniformity of this religious literature," he wrote in his magnum opus, *Die Religion der Vernunft aus den Quellen des Judentums* (*Religion of Reason: Out of the Sources of Judaism*, 1919).[130] The project was doomed, however, by its very tenets and by the fragility of any appropriation mechanism. Indeed, the appropriation of the *Geist*, a key aspect of the philosophical and cultural discourse of its time, and pivotal for *Völkerpsychologie*, highlights the limitations of such strategic fluidity.[131] The term *Geist*, in its *Absolute Geist* or *national Geist* variants, was used to promote and safeguard the process of Jewish integration into German society by showing the specificity and universalism of the Jewish *Geist*. But it was also employed by anti-Semites to emphasize the irreducible difference and unassimilable character of Jewish people. *Völkerpsychologie*'s failed efforts thus demonstrate that any particularistic universalism is an especially fragile construct.

Though the *völkisch* critique of the promotion of universalism was expected, the attacks also came from Jews themselves. In a book entitled *Der Sinn der Geschichte* (*The Meaning of History*), the influential Zionist thinker Max Nordau (1849–1923) argues that while Lazarus and Steinthal "believed they had founded a science," Völkerpsychologie is in fact no different from the psychology of the masses popularized by Gustave Le Bon's *The Crowd: A Study of the Popular Mind* (1895).[132] Nordau also criticizes them for downplaying the importance of the individual and, more important, for ignoring "race" as a factor with which to characterize nations.[133] The increasing use of the concept of race—and the misunderstanding around Lazarus and Steinthal's project—permeated discussions within mainstream Judaism as well. The entry on Steinthal in the 1906 *Jewish Encyclopedia* wrongly defines the *Zeitung für Völkerpsychologie* as the outlet where "the new science of racial psychology" was established.[134]

The influence of *völkisch* ideas on a younger generation was also a marker of a generational divide. Whereas Lazarus rejected it, it fueled Martin Buber's initial return to Judaism, as we will see in chapter 8.[135] Along the same lines, turning ethnopsychology into an arguably ethnocentric agenda or using the ambiguities of particularistic universalism became paramount for a key figure of the Religious Zionist movement, Rav Zvi Yehuda Kook (1891–1982), who praised *Völkerpsychologie* as a source for Jewish difference.[136]

On the other hand, some followers of Moritz Lazarus and Heymann Steinthal adopted stances that did align more closely with their teachers. The core tenets of *Völkerpsychologie* were adopted by the Chicago school of sociology in order to refute the findings of Cesare Lombroso (1835–1909), the founder of anthropological criminology, whose theoretical underpinnings were based on race.[137] The legacy of Lazarus and Steinthal's Völkerpsychologie and its uses by or against nascent theories of race is thus complex.

The "Abstraction" of a Collective Psyche?

Regardless of the question of race, many scholars at the turn of the century denied the new field any value and even refused to consider *Völkerpsychologie* an autonomous discipline. The question and relevance of a collective psyche also loomed large in its dismissal as an irrelevant field, especially considering the mere feasibility of any study of a collective psyche. The linguist Hermann Paul (1846–1921) argued that it was an epiphenomenon of the philosophy of history and would soon be reabsorbed by it, since real philosophy could only be at the individual, not the group, level. In addition, he dismissed "the hypostatization of a series of abstractions."[138]

Another critique was offered by the German philosopher Wilhelm Dilthey, who held the chair of philosophy at the University of Berlin from 1882 to 1911; his influence on Gadamer and twentieth-century hermeneutics cannot be overstated.[139] Dilthey introduced the distinction by which psychology should be considered Geisteswissenschaft rather than as *Naturwissenschaft*.[140] He famously distinguished between nature and soul: "We explain [*erklären*] nature [but] we understand [*verstehen*] the life of the soul."[141] This distinction led to distinct forms of hermeneutics: on the one hand, nature is defined by objective causal necessity and scientific laws; on the other, the *Geisteswissenschaften* are based on inner experience, an empirical character, and an inner, quasi-intimate comprehension (*Verständnis*). From this, he concluded that psychology, as *Geisteswissenschaft*, stands closer to philosophy and poetry than it does to experimental science. Dilthey's *Geisteswissenschaften* acknowledge the dynamics of collective forces but do not essentialize them and articulate them in relation to the individual.[142] *Völkerpsychologie*'s concept of a collective soul is "no more usable in history than is the concept of life-force in physiology."[143]

Wilhelm Wundt (1832–1920) is widely recognized as the father of experimental psychology, having set up his first laboratory at Oxford in 1879.

He is now sometimes mistakenly identified as the founder of folk psychology as well.[144] Wundt did acknowledge the work of Lazarus and Steinthal and their role in paving the way for the exploration of "universal mental creations,"[145] but he failed to properly credit them with their innovation. Unlike them, he regarded the field as a work in progress and a tool rather than an end in itself.[146]

> All those developments that emerge from mental life in community constitute problems for an autonomous psychological investigation, for which one will properly retain the name *Völkerpsychologie*. . . . *Völkerpsychologie* is, in its turn, a part of general psychology, and its results frequently provide valuable explanations for individual psychology, too. For language, myth, and custom, as products of the collective Spirit, offer together material from which inferences about the mental life of individuals can be drawn. . . . Thus, just as individual psychology serves, on the one hand, to elucidate problems of *Völkerpsychologie*, so the facts of the latter become an extremely valuable objective material for explaining the phenomena of individual consciousness.[147]

Despite his reservations, Wundt preferred the term *Völkerpsychologie* over *social psychology* or *sociology* in order to indicate greater breadth of vision.[148] He argued that those disciplines were too focused on contemporary society, lacked psychological insight, and ignored the developmental, historical character of civilization.

The Interplay between Psychology and Ethics

Another facet of the discipline, as Lazarus and Steinthal hoped to promote it, was its porosity with ethics.[149] The presence of ethics was in fact at the core of their interest in psychology: they presented both as closely related, even necessary and complementary objects of study. Wundt acknowledges this proximity in his *Ethik* (*Ethics*), which also explores this interconnection of mind and ethics. He uses an architectural metaphor to describe the introductory quality of folk psychology: "I regarded *Völkerpsychologie* as the vestibule of ethics which, among other tasks, has to deal with the history of traditions and of moral representations from a psychological point of view."[150]

That work was even more pressing for Lazarus and Steinthal: as politics became radicalized over the course of the 1880s and 1890s, *Völkerpsychologie* gave way to straightforward ethics.[151] "The topic of the psychology of morals has been truly life changing in various epochs and different nations," Lazarus wrote in *The Life of the Soul*. "The task of ethics is to reveal the eternal, unchanging ideals of morality unconcerned with all aberrations in life."[152] But he did anchor his ethics in his time: just as his *Völkerpsychologie* was not just historical but also forward-looking, so did his endeavor possess a hybrid nature.

This explains Simmel's regret that *Völkerpsychologie* was not descriptive enough.[153] The difference in his and Lazarus's analysis of the figure of "the stranger" is a case in point. The imperative of caring for the stranger, a cornerstone of both ethics and self-representation in Judaism, appears in Lazarus's *Ethics of Judaism*: this, he argues, should lead contemporary societies to welcome the stranger (and thus the Jews) in their midst and lead Jews to seek assimilation. "We Jews immigrated as strangers; but did we come in order to remain strangers?" he asks in his "What Does National Mean?"[154] This exhortation foreshadows Simmel's eight-page essay, "The Stranger," in which he famously describes the stranger as the one who stays but who will be viewed with distrust (as opposed to the wanderer, who will continue his journey).[155] By reflecting on the meaning and symbolism of strangeness and otherness, both men explore the social and psychological mechanisms of alienation.

Moritz Lazarus and Heymann Steinthal are noteworthy because they did provide the building blocks of the unconscious, as Mikhail Bakhtin observed—but also because they articulated the unconscious in an ethical manner. Such a continuity between disciplines was highlighted somewhat differently in the characterization of the emergence of the human sciences from the moral sciences—but here, the movement goes further: it comes from the moral sciences and returns to them.[156]

Völkerpsychologie's methodological shortcomings and lack of an academic or institutional home account for its disappearance. Yet some of its intuitions also explain how its legacy morphed into key tenets of sociology, in the writings of Georg Simmel, and anthropology, in the work of Adolf Bastian and Franz Boas; all three established the importance of their linguistic framework and the linguistic turn in the humanities.[157]

It also paved the way for the concept of a collective unconscious, as well as for the Freudian concept of condensation. Quite poetically, *Völkerpsychologie* is now part of the sedimentary layers that Lazarus and Steinthal described as the process of the emergence of ideas, specifically the idea of the unconscious. It bespeaks a turn to universalism—from a Jewish perspective—that insisted on the ethical aspect of the collective psychology but also reinforced the forces it sought to combat.

Although Lazarus and Steinthal both criticized other projects that were too metaphysical in essence, the same type of argument was leveled at them. The influential writer Fritz Mauthner (1849–1923), for instance, whose theories of language reverberated in Ludwig Wittgenstein's work, critiqued *Völkerpsychologie* for being a belief system designed to hide its true purpose: the quest for a secular modernity claiming to reject its religious roots but secretly eager to retain them.[158] Ironically, the reservations toward this endeavor were the same as the suspicions that the notion of the unconscious elicited. And, as we will now see, Eduard von Hartmann's philosophy of the unconscious would only radicalize these positions.

* 7 *

The Unconscious as Mystique?
Hartmann's *Philosophy of the Unconscious* and Its Jewish Critics

The concept of the unconscious offered an intellectual justification and framework to those eager to prove the compatibility of Judaism with philosophy in general and with current debates in particular, and the driving force behind these conversations was unquestionably Eduard von Hartmann's *Philosophy of the Unconscious*.

The Jewish thinkers that availed themselves of the concept of the unconscious examined in this chapter were interested in a modality of accommodation that can be understood as monism. Monism is the affirmation of a unifying principle in this world against the fracturing individualism of modernity. It is indeed "a symptomatic expression of a century that was marked by a secularism but that was not yet secular," as Todd Weir has put it. The pre-Freudian unconscious, in its attempts at wholeness, exemplifies such an expression.[1] Other thinkers, who were closer to Orthodox Judaism, as we will see in the next chapter, sought to validate their faith by retrospectively detecting scientific elements in their tradition—and they specifically reinscribed the Hartmanian unconscious in the Talmudic or Hasidic tradition.[2] Both modalities underscore Hartmann's impact on Jewish thought and self-definition.

The publication of Hartmann's *Philosophy of the Unconscious* in 1869—and the unity of mankind that it championed—could have fostered a dialogue, or at least elicited a certain affinity, with Moritz Lazarus and Heymann Steinthal's *Völkerpsychologie* and its universalism. But this was hardly the case.

In an 1882 letter to his favorite student, Steinthal excoriated *Philosophy of the Unconscious* as "rubbish," using the derogatory word *drekke*, which, interestingly, exists in both Yiddish and German.[3] With this scathing assessment of the best-selling book, he joined the camp of Hartmann's detractors. The positivist scientist and philosopher Eugen Dühring (1833–1921) also had some choice words for Hartmann's pessimism and mysticism, ranging from "phony mystic" (*Schwindelmystik*) to "higher nonsense" (*höherer Blödsinn*) and "metaphysical humbug" (*metaphysischer Humbug*).[4]

The weighty tome rapidly drew sarcasm from Friedrich Nietzsche as well. In his essay "Vom Nutzen und Nachteil der Historie für das Leben" ("On the Use and Abuse of History for Life") (1874), the philosopher calls Hartmann an "amalgamist" and his work a "philosophically roguish prank."[5] In his unpublished writings, Nietzsche derides the enterprise further: "In the entire world, one does not speak about the unconscious since, according to its essence, it is unknown; only in Berlin does one speak of and know something about it, and explain to us what actually sets it apart."[6] Yet the unconscious was already on its way to becoming part of a continentwide conversation, and not only in Berlin.[7] For all his mockery, Nietzsche did read Hartmann's work and acknowledge its significance.[8] The philosopher even addressed him in a way that might indicate veiled admiration: "Rogue of all rogues, you give voice to the longings of contemporary mankind."[9] Indeed, Hartmann captured his time, and Nietzsche realized as much when he said that the unconscious "was in the air."[10]

Toward the Centrality of the Unconscious: From Carus to Hartmann

Yet the unconscious had been in the air for a few decades. In *The Archetypes and the Collective Unconscious* (1959), Carl Jung specifies the concept's genealogy: "Although various philosophers, among them Leibniz, Kant, and Schelling, had already pointed very clearly to the problem of the dark side of the psyche, it was a physician who felt impelled, from his scientific and medical experience, to point to the unconscious as the essential basis of the psyche. This was C. G. Carus, the precedent that Eduard von Hartmann followed."[11]

Carl Gustav Carus (1789–1869) was a polymath, a friend of Johann Wolfgang von Goethe's, and a student of the painter Caspar David Friedrich. He was also a philosopher, physician, and physiologist. And, as Jung noted, he was one of the key thinkers of the unconscious in the nineteenth century. His book *Entwicklungsgeschichte der Seele* (*Psyche*, 1846) was the first to assert the hidden centrality of the notion of the unconscious, declaring in its opening sentence, "The key to understanding the conscious life of the soul lies in the realm of the unconscious."[12] Although he never gained the audience that Hartmann and Jung would later reach, he was an inspiration for both men. Carus represents the acme of Romantic psychology, or perhaps the "testamentary executor of romantic philosophy," as one of his most perspicacious exponents, the literary critic Albert Béguin, argued. Indeed, he used all the tropes of Romanticism without resorting to the "banal esotericism" of its conservative form, which ignores the possibility of progress and is based on the pure exaltation of the individual.[13] For Carus, consciousness derives from the unconscious, which is a part of an organic whole as well as a symbol and expression of nature.[14] He also established bold links between natural and mental phenomena, such as dreams: personal identity cannot be separated from a cosmic whole. Life in all its forms obeys a principle that he called the Idea—and the Idea acts in the realm of the unconscious.

With his idiosyncratic blend of biology, philosophy, and the arts, Carus's analysis paints a multifaceted unconscious. He divides it into the absolute unconscious (which is inaccessible to the human spirit and constitutes the texture of the universe), the partial absolute unconscious (which is unindividuated), and the relative unconscious (which becomes conscious momentarily but recedes back into unconsciousness). It is this latter part of our mental life that we can get a glimpse of in somnambulistic states or in sleep. The relative unconscious shapes and creates the organs of life: it is organic, whereas the absolute unconscious is metaphysical.[15]

Carus also argued that the study of the unconscious can help predict human behavior, because the unconscious has its own laws: it is relentless and likely to manifest itself as instincts. It behooves science to shed light on the unconscious, in order to escape its rule and thereby elude necessity—to decipher it in a way that would prove liberating: properly analyzed, knowledge of the unconscious could lead to freedom. Carus does not ascribe any superiority to the unconscious, even if it is conducive to the inspiration traditionally hailed as genius by the Romantics. Rather, he calls for keeping both forces in balance and understanding that the unconscious affects reality because it influences our perceptions.

Though Hartmann offered only tepid praise for Carus, he certainly drew on his predecessor and used one of his remarks—"The key to insight into the nature of conscious psychic life lies in the region of the unconscious"—as the epigraph of the second part of his book.[16] He also conceived of the unconscious as having a comparable tripartite structure—the absolute unconscious, the physiological unconscious (from which the evolution of mankind derives), and the relative unconscious—and, just like Carus, his work brims with references from a wide range of fields.

Carus is mostly absent from the writings of Jewish philosophers and thinkers, whereas Hartmann occupies a significant place, just as he did in public life and conversations mostly across Europe and, to a lesser extent, even in the United States. The gap between the two men and how each was received—one quietly exerting his influence on a select group of thinkers that included Fyodor Dostoevsky, the other a literary sensation—captures the difference in the scope and ambition of their work as well as a changed zeitgeist.[17] In *Psyche*, Carus sought to theorize the process of the unconscious, whereas Hartmann was out to establish a worldview. Hartmann's vision was aligned with a pessimism about the state of religion and culture that had first been expressed by Arthur Schopenhauer (1788–1860). It also exhibited a specific brand of metaphysical pessimism, grounded in a distinct appreciation of mysticism that a handful of Jewish thinkers would reappropriate and challenge.

The World according to Hartmann: The Unconscious as Worldview

The son of an army officer, Eduard von Hartmann (1842–1906) briefly followed in the footsteps of his father but left the military after an injury and dedicated himself to his philosophical work. He was twenty-seven years of age in 1869 when he published *Philosophy of the Unconscious*. The book brought him instant fame.[18]

Hartmann's contradictory views reveal a complex figure. Politically conservative and a vocal admirer of the German Empire, he was nevertheless liberal on religious issues. He believed in the need to separate church and state, and he favored Jewish emancipation (and the emancipation of religious minorities in general). However, his book *Judaism in the Present and Future* (1885) shows how, like many such advocates of his time, his otherwise liberal stance remained grounded in anti-Jewish prejudices. In his view, anti-Semitism must be fought merely because it impedes Jewish assimilation. But his motivations for such an assimilation had the same impetus: deploying clichés about race, power, and sexuality and describing Jews as a "parasitical breed" (*Schmarotzerbrut*), he deemed assimilation necessary only because it would eventually lead to the disappearance of Jews as a people.[19] One may thus wonder how Jewish thinkers ignored that aspect of Hartmann's thought, but such a stance was quite prevalent in philosophy in general at the time. The same question stands for Jewish followers of Immanuel Kant, Georg Hegel, or Friedrich Nietzsche who chose to co-opt these thinkers' broader philosophical proposition and inscribe their own stance into it.

To Hartmann, the unconscious is more than a psychological construct: it is a thought experiment and a worldview, as conveyed by the subtitle of his book (absent from most translations): *Versuch einer Weltanschauung (Attempt at a Worldview)*. The term *Weltanschauung* reveals a fundamental aspect of his intellectual system: it is an aspect of monism, the view that the universe can be explained by a single and irreducible principle intrinsic to it, the unity and identity of all individual or distinct existences in one substance.[20] Hartmann's use of *Weltanschauung* might explain Sigmund Freud's later objection to the term: "I must confess that I am not at all partial to the fabrication of *Weltanschauungen*. Such activities may be left to philosophers."[21]

Rejecting both theism and atheistic materialism, Hartmann envisioned this philosophy as the underpinning of a new and urgent religious construct. Notably, it is the first instance of an approach he would go on to characterize as "spiritual monism," a unifying mechanism, which he professes in his book *Die Selbstzersetzung des Christenthums* (*The Self-Destruction of Christianity*, 1874).[22] The term *monism* describes the unity of reason and revelation, which he divides into two different orientations: "spiritual monists" and "material monists," for those who located the unifying substance either in the mind (or soul) or in the body (matter).[23] He continued his analysis of this need for monism as a replacement for religion in *Das religiöse Bewusstsein der Menschheit im Stufengang seiner Entwickelung* (*The Religious Consciousness of Mankind in the Stages of Its Development*) seven years later.[24] None of these subsequent books brought him the same fame as *Philosophy of the Unconscious*, which launched his career as a public intellectual.

The use of the term *monism* and the philosophy it undergirded became increasingly popular in the second part of the nineteenth century, driven by the work of Ernst Haeckel (1834–1919), who presented it as the proper concept needed to comprehend modernity and who, in his *Generelle Morphologie der Organismen* (*General Morphology of Organisms*, 1866), postulated "the unity of nature and the unity of science."[25] His manifesto, *The Riddle of the Universe*, came out in 1899, thirty years after *Philosophy of the Unconscious*. It contains echoes of Hartmann's text, and it was equally a best seller. Over the course of Haeckel's lifetime, monism developed political, religious, and societal connotations.[26] He spoke of a "monistic religion," or at least offered a credo that aimed to provide a new vision of the world. And indeed, a short-lived association of monists was briefly set up as a political organization. With its all-encompassing philosophy, monism went on to form the bedrock and operating principle of twentieth-century totalitarianisms.[27]

The unconscious as a monistic principle encompassing the relationship between the individual and the universal is the central idea of Hartmann's *Philosophy of the Unconscious*: the All-One Unconscious is the internal essence of life itself, the unconscious as a unity principle in which traditional oppositions do not apply. Hartmann claims that binaries like "Thought and Thing... Spirit and Nature, Ideal and Real, Subjective and Objective" do not apply, and that "Spirit and Nature are no longer different."[28] In the book's translation, the term *the Unconscious* was capitalized, further emphasizing the specificity of the unconscious as an essence.[29]

Concerned about the future of religion, which he ties to the future of civilization more broadly, Hartmann regards monism as a regenerative force. "The tendency to the monistic purifying of Christianity has always emerged in greater strength and has been ever gaining in influence over discerning minds," he asserts. He also identifies monistic impulses across faiths and claims that only oppressive religious institutions resist it. With little modesty, he professes that the "involuntary tendency of great minds toward Monism cannot be denied."[30]

His genealogy of monism is religious and philosophical as well as overreaching: he traces it to Kant's concept of the thing-in-itself (*Ding an sich*) and thus to the philosopher's distinction between a phenomenon, an observable fact or event, and what exists independently of any observation, as theorized in Kant's *Prolegomena to Any Future Metaphysics*.[31] Hartmann claims that because he was "timid in his inferences," Kant only unknowingly promoted the monism that Schopenhauer would be the one to fully express, albeit in a pessimistic version.[32]

The Unconscious and the Allure of Pessimism

In his response to the "pessimism controversy" sparked by his own work in the 1870s, Hartmann defends and recapitulates his vision in *Zur*

Geschichte und Begründung des Pessimismus (*On the History and Justification of Pessimism*, 1880), which demonstrates Schopenhauer's enduring influence.[33] In his prolific writings, he continued exploring the intersections of philosophy, psychology, and religion, expounding on the crisis of the latter. But he also fought against accusations that the pessimism pivotal in his work was immoral because it implied a worldview in which the will might assume different forms in the phenomenal world but nonetheless left no room for individuality and plurality. He rejected the notion that his concept of the unconscious came down to such a blind force, and he faulted Schopenhauer for that misconception. Conversely, Hartmann offered repeated and multifaceted defenses of his "optimistic pessimism," of which an important aspect was that this shared unconscious, as he understood it, had allowed for, and explained, connections between individuals who expressed it in a variety of philosophies or religions throughout history.[34]

For all Hartmann's critique of Schopenhauer, his *Philosophy of the Unconscious* must be read in light of Schopenhauer's *The World as Will and Representation*. First published in 1819, it was initially met with indifference. It was not until the 1850s that Schopenhauer's work gained attention. The German novelist Thomas Mann (1875–1955) described the experience of encountering the book as "drinking that metaphysical magic potion," and it had that effect on many readers.[35] Schopenhauer's late-found fame may have stemmed from the fact that his philosophy was suited to the post-1848 mood and the pessimism resulting from the failed 1848 revolutions, as the psychologist Paul Janet later contended.[36]

According to Schopenhauer, the real has two aspects: will and representation, which correspond respectively to the Kantian categories of the thing-in-itself and the phenomenon. The will refers to the blind, unconscious, dynamic forces presiding over the universe and humankind alike. These forces push for self-conservation and, as a result, fuel a sexual drive that is an affirmation of life. The will, however, is impersonal and lacks a conscience: in the Schopenhauerian system, irrationalism prevails, thus producing the worst of all possible worlds, which should lead to nonexistence as a preferred choice.[37] The only truth is the inevitability of future destruction.

Hartmann's *Philosophy of the Unconscious* fluctuates between somber Schopenhauerian diagnosis and more optimistic passages affirming the ethical value of mysticism as an aspect of, or channel to, the unconscious.

The book is divided into three parts: a metaphysical teleology of nature, an interpretation of the unity of the alogical Will and the logical Idea, and a system of world history. It has been rightly described, in many respects, as a "Schellingian synthesis of Schopenhauer with Hegel."[38] Indeed, instead of *opposing* will and representation, as Schopenhauer did, Hartmann strives to *reconcile* them, arguing that they are mere attributes of a single substance, the All-One. Their very substance is "this One Absolute Subject," which he characterizes as the unconscious, and from which will and representation emanate. Envisioning a highly intelligent universe akin to the Hegelian Idea, Hartmann carries out the reconciliation with Schopenhauer by adducing Schelling's late positive philosophy and his *Philosophy of Mythology*. But it behooved him to bring this principle to the world's consciousness, and thus, Hartmann wrote, "it may be said . . . that the theme of the present book is mainly the elevation of Hegel's unconscious Philosophy of the Unconscious into a conscious one."[39]

Hartmann's ambition was to make the unconscious emerge and be part of consciousness. But since, in his view, the unconscious cannot be measured empirically, it must be observed in all its forms. He thus marshals evidence from a variety of disciplines, as Carus had done before him, in order to capture the unconscious at work in its cultural, social, and natural manifestations. Concurrently, assessing these manifestations requires a move from *Selbstgefühl* (sentiment of the self) to *Selbstbewusstsein* (consciousness of the self), modeled after the Hegelian imperative of the self-consciousness of the *Geist* because the collective *Geist* is refracted in the individual one. This is where individuation needs to occur—a process that would be at the core of Jung's collective unconscious.[40] If one substitutes the *Geist* for a Spirit inhabiting nature—possibly a divine Spirit, or nature itself—the unconscious amounts to no more than sheer modern-day pantheism, cast as a new philosophy or even theology. The accusation of veiled deism or pantheism is one of the criticisms leveled at Hartmann's philosophical system, as we will see later in the chapter, with Adolphe Franck.

The Jewish Reception of Hartmann's Unconscious in Germany

Hartmann recognized the convergences or similarities between monism and pantheism, but regardless of the denominations, he insists on the merits of his system. Since every being is part of only one self, he argues, each individual is distinct but linked to everyone else and in the *Gesamtgeist*, the collective Spirit. *Philosophy of the Unconscious* is thus the "reconciliation of monism and pluralistic individualism."[41] Hartmann claims to be in agreement with Gottfried Wilhelm Leibniz's theory of monads—the basic entities making up the substance of the universe. According to Hartmann, Leibniz "declares unconscious ideas to be the bond 'which unites every being with the rest of the universe,' and explains by their means the pre-established harmony of the monads, in that every monad as microcosm unconsciously represents the macrocosm and its position therein."[42] This unity exists, Hartmann acknowledges, but it can only be viable if grounded in metaphysics. And this is a point of fundamental divergence between Hartmann and the philosophy of Moritz Lazarus and Heymann Steinthal. Let us return to *Völkerpsychologie*. What can we learn by comparing that account of the psyche with Hartmann's? Do their distinct psychological assumptions explain the gap between them? How does Lazarus and Steinthal's work differ from Hartmann's?

For Lazarus and Steinthal, a difference of degree exists between consciousness and the unconscious. They understand the unconscious in Leibniz's terms, as "petites perceptions," whereby the unconscious consists of perceptions below the threshold of consciousness. In Hartmann's view, in contrast, there is a difference of nature between consciousness and the unconscious, a fundamental discontinuity that inscribes him in the idealist tradition. In the introduction to *Philosophy of the Unconscious*, which serves as a survey of previous thinking about the concept, he negates any continuity between consciousness and the unconscious. After praising Leibniz for affirming the existence of thoughts that escape our consciousness and for his theory of monads as foregrounding the harmony of the universe, Hartmann criticizes the "weak side" of his theory, specifically the concept of *petites perceptions*, and claims that Leibniz "destroyed with one hand what he seemed to have built with the other—the true notion of the Unconscious as a province opposed to Consciousness, and its significance for feeling and action."[43]

Ernst Bloch, an avid reader of Hartmann, sums up this major difference in the 1918 version of *Geist der Utopie* (*The Spirit of Utopia*), in a passage removed from later editions: "What separates [Hartmann] from Husserl, but also from Kant and Hegel, is first his refusal to eavesdrop [*belauschen*] directly with the consciousness itself on the preconscious emergence of the conscious content."[44] With his reference to the founder of phenomenology, Edmund Husserl (1859–1938), Bloch stresses that Hartmann is interested not in the phenomenology of the unconscious but in how the noumenon, the thing-in-itself, can be felt in this world. Hartmann highlights the paradox by which the infinitesimal nature of these "petites perceptions" cannot be reconciled with the results they effect in human behavior: "For if, as Leibniz himself maintains, natural disposition, instinct, the passions—in short, the mightiest influences in human life—take their rise in the sphere of the Unconscious, how are they to be shaped by ideas which are withdrawn from consciousness simply on account of their weakness? Would not the more *powerful* conscious ideas prevail at the decisive moment?"[45]

Bloch's questioning highlights what led to Hartmann's metaphysical monism as well as how his interpretation and description of the nature of the *Geist* separate him from Lazarus and Steinthal, though they inspired him. In Hartmann's view, *Völkerpsychologie* can only be legitimate if it were based on the assumption that the *Gesamtgeist* is a "secret, unconscious connection between individuals."[46] While Hartmann's use of *gesamt* closely follows Steinthal's, he imbues his *Geist* with spiritual—if not esoteric—overtones thoroughly absent from the work of his predecessors.

The chapter in *Philosophy of the Unconscious* titled "The Unconscious in the Emergence of Language" showcases this chasm. Here, Hartmann acknowledges Steinthal's insights in calling language the "product of unconscious mental activity" in order to promptly reject them: "H. Steinthal, in his celebrated book, *The Origin of Language,* concludes his excellent objective criticism of his predecessors with the following formulation of the problem: 'Language is not innate in man, not revealed by God—man has produced it; but not the mere organic nature of man, but his *mind*: and finally, *not* the thinking *conscious* mind. What mind then in humanity, i.e., what form of action of the human mind has produced language?'"[47] Hartmann then offers his own response: "What other answer is conceivable to this than that of the *unconscious* spiritual activity?"[48] Yet for Lazarus and Steinthal, Geist was precisely neither spiritual nor metaphysical.

This is the reason why Lazarus, too, dismissed Hartmann's work: while Lazarus critiqued Johann Friedrich Herbart for his scarce attention to the unconscious, "the greatest flaw in Herbart's basic view," he commended him for not making it "as it was later with Hartmann, a metaphysical but merely a psychological category."[49] *Völkerpsychologie* posits *Volksgeist* as a fact, a reality documented in each language, "a veritable monad in the Spirit of the people." It manifests a subjective "interconnectedness," but according to Lazarus and Steinthal, this subjectivity is not metaphysical, much less mystical.[50]

Even in his treatment of ethics, Lazarus's antipathy toward any form of mysticism led him to distance himself from one of the classical texts of Jewish ethics, Ḥovot Ha-levavot (*The Duties of the Heart*) by the eleventh-century philosopher Bahya ibn Paquda. Lazarus claimed that the author's engagement with ethics was limited, favoring a retreat into mystical musings.[51] Ironically, the reproach of mysticism was nevertheless leveled at Lazarus and Steinthal by those contemporaries who emphasized the very racial theories that the pair sought to combat, such as the Zionist Max Nordau, who rejected the abstraction of a collective organism as a "mystical delusion" (*mystische Verirrung*).[52] A similar criticism was voiced by the erstwhile influential Sorbonne professor Théodule Ribot (1836–1916), a key exponent of German philosophy and psychology, who described Lazarus and Steinthal's style as "a tad mystical."[53] He faulted the lack of experimentation in their methods (unlike in British psychologists'), which in fact revealed the deep moralistic and metaphysical underpinnings of Völkerpsychologie.[54]

Finally, Hartmann's methodology also set him apart from Lazarus and Steinthal. They used a deductive method, in which details test an existing theory, whereas Hartmann made an inductive method a cornerstone of his writing, as affirmed on the title page of *Philosophy of the Unconscious*: "speculative results according to an inductive-natural scientific method." Induction, in which generalizations are made from specific observations, fits Hartmann's monism, since any phenomenon is but a manifestation of the general Spirit.

In his attempt to ground that old metaphysics on a new method, he advocates a metaphysical realism in which "the radical difference between spirit and material [is] abolished ... and not by killing the spirit, but by vivifying the matter."[55] It is at these types of junctures that Hartmann conjures up the role of mysticism in history.

> Mysticism has also performed priceless civilising services for the human race. Without the mysticism of Neo-Pythagoreanism, the Johannean Christianity would never have arisen; without the mysticism of the Middle Ages, the spirit of Christianity would have been submerged in Catholic idolatry and scholastic formalism; without the mysticism of the persecuted heretical communities from the beginning of the eleventh-century, which, in spite of all suppressions, ever sprang up again with renewed energy under another name, the blessings of the Reformation would never have dispelled the darker shades of the Middle Age [sic] and opened the portals of the new era. [...]

> As for the human race as a whole, so also for the individual. So long as it keeps free from sickly and rank outgrowths, mysticism is of inestimable worth.[56]

Despite seemingly promoting a collective unconscious, the elevation of the material and the universal mysticism he extols were aimed at a specific nation. These are two of the tensions that riddle his work and run across many constructs of the universalism of Jewish mysticism that turn into ethnocentrism (found, for instance, in the theology of Rav Kook and of Habad Hasidism).[57] Indeed, the unconscious was seen as a remedy against French thought in general, since Hartmann accused French militant rationalism of having devolved into materialism. More generally, in *Philosophy of the Unconscious* he calls for a reassessment of "rational intelligence" (*vernünftige Intelligenz*) as a characteristic of the unconscious and of mysticism's approach to grappling with it: "Without mysticism in the mind of the German people, and among the heroes of modern German poetry and philosophy, we should have been so completely inundated by the shallow drifting sand of the French materialism in the last century, that we might not have got our heads free again for who knows how long."[58] The unconscious had become political, and even a tool for nationalists.

An Unpatriotic Unconscious? Franco-Judaism and the Rejection of Hartmann's Pessimism

Eduard von Hartmann's impact made the unconscious part of the public conversation in the late nineteenth century. But the term and the concept also raised such suspicions of covert metaphysics that it led one of the pioneers of scientific psychology, Pierre Janet (1859–1947), to claim that he had coined the word *subconscious* in 1889 in an effort to differentiate his science-based concept from a Hartmann-inflected characterization.[59]

In his introduction to and early survey of the reception of Hartmann's work, his French translator highlighted the lingering presence of a theistic form of religion, more specifically Christian theism, which regarded Hartmann's mysticism as a justification of its own.[60] But the stakes were even higher in academic circles and among French Jews eager to emphasize their assimilation. Of particular interest for probing the reception of Hartmann's work is the review written by the first prominent Jewish academic, Adolphe Franck.[61] As we saw in chapter 3, Franck set out to highlight the philosophical, universal aspect of Kabbalah in *The Kabbalah: The Religious Philosophy of the Hebrews*. One would thus have expected him to welcome Hartmann's embrace of mysticism as philosophy, but he did not view *Philosophy of the Unconscious* favorably.

Franck's critique contains two elements. First, Hartmann's philosophical system is merely a form of pantheism under the guise of this novel category of monism. Second, the new deity it created is potentially a mechanistic, oppressive one—one that suppresses autonomous consciousness and freedom, leading to a pessimism at odds with the French-Jewish ideals Franck fiercely championed.[62]

In the same review, Franck asserts that Hartmann's unconscious, the "One-All" (Un-Tout), has the attributes of a divine absolute: "The unconscious possesses the clairvoyance that theologians call omniscience, absolute wisdom."[63] But though he praises Hartmann's intellectual agility, Franck questions his very motivations, denouncing them as serving "an odious and thoroughly repulsive cause."[64]

The cause repulsing Franck is Hartmann's unconscious being less metaphysical than mechanical, as he explains in a letter to the famous esoteric author Papus (1865–1916). In this short text, the professor professes his "tenderness" toward esotericism as an acceptable method of knowledge that enables emotional, human participation, whereas Hartmann's system, among others, precludes this. "If God does not penetrate inside us, if He is not the secret engine of our thoughts and actions, He is not what the Bible so accurately calls the living God," Franck declares. "He amounts to an algebraic or logic formula comparable to Spencer's Unknowable, Hartmann's Unconscious, or even the Premises of pure reason invented by Kant."[65] In Franck's opinion, Hartmann's dry principle of the unconscious, and the theology that can be derived from it, is almost akin to Gnosticism. The result is a demiurge—a God who has stopped caring for his creation, thus resembling the Gnostic gods that attracted increasing interest in the first half of the twentieth century.[66]

Franck claims that Hartmann's strand of mysticism actually distorts it by trying to make it pass as the unconscious, but "it does not prove, it cannot prove that mysticism is one of the forms, one of the manifestations of the Unconscious."[67] Indeed, he still considers Hartmann's unconscious to be little more than blind will and thus comparable to the philosophical pessimism of Arthur Schopenhauer and his followers, positing the inner nature of the world as an aimless and blind driving force that merely wants. Mystics, on the other hand, see will and intelligence as a dual force that leaves human beings the consciousness of their actions and is at the core of the divine, albeit in a form inferior to love.

A related aspect of Franck's criticism points to the accidental and subordinate nature of individual consciousness in Hartmann's philosophical system. This, in turn, implies that any individuality will eventually be subsumed by the collective principle. Hartmann wrote, "If one imagined the union of the brains of two men possible by a bridge as capable of conduction as is that between the two hemispheres of the same brain, a mutual and indivisible consciousness, including the thoughts of both brains, would immediately embrace the hitherto separate consciousness of both persons; each would no longer be able to distinguish his own thoughts from those of the other."[68]

What is at stake is the very question of individuality and, further, of freedom. The unconscious articulates the relationship between freedom and necessity, but it is a faulty one—and, for Adolphe Franck, Hartmann's unconscious is a case of misunderstood ontology. If human freedom is predicated on the consciousness of justice and injustice, then the unconscious eradicates the possibility of freedom and thus makes a mockery of the arc of human history.[69]

What Franck regarded as a strand of pessimism would be fought by the prominent French liberal intellectuals of the late nineteenth century, who were often steeped in positivism and invested in the values of the fledgling republic.[70] French Jewish intellectuals who saw themselves as products of a symbiosis known as Franco-Judaism belonged to this generation and embraced its credo.[71] At the very same time, conservatives and nationalists turned to Germany as a foil for the French secular and individual-based political and social model.[72]

The embrace of the concept of the unconscious became a marker of a generational divide as much as a national one. The older generation of Lazarus and Franck, along with the advocates of the *Wissenschaft des Judentums* or of its French version, the *Science du Judaïsme*, was still committed to the centrality of rationality and ethics in describing and understanding societal constructs, aimed at a symbiosis between Judaism and the host nation.[73] Increasingly, the invocation of the unconscious became an instrument of cultural criticism. If reason was the linchpin and jewel of the Enlightenment and of the French Revolution by extension, and if the unconscious destabilized it, the unconscious could be made into a political or ideological statement against the Enlightenment.[74] Beyond representing a new aesthetic (found in the poetry of the symbolist Jules Laforgue (1860–1887), for instance, and his "Propitiatory Complaint to the Unconscious" of 1894), making reference to the unconscious suggested an alternative worldview.[75] The collective principle of the Hartmannian unconscious was anchored in a specific soil (the French *terroir*) and an ethnic identity, which should subsume the will of the individual. Maurice Barrès (1862–1923), one of the most strident French nationalists and anti-Semites of his time, specifically invokes the unconscious in *Le jardin de Bérénice* (*Berenice's Garden*) of 1891 as an emanation of the people from which the narrator will find his soul.[76] But this could not be further from the idea of the unconscious as a collective principle representing humanity as a whole, as Jewish writers would come to defend.

The unconscious was thus both a battleground and a Rorschach test. The positions taken in relation to the unconscious, defined on Hartmann's terms, reveal the worldviews of those who engage with it. The notion thus differs from the odyssey of the individual psyche that the Freudian unconscious would soon set in motion, but it bespeaks, or betrays, collective self-understanding and self-representations.

For all his criticism, Franck acknowledged that Hartmann's was a more nuanced pessimism than Schopenhauer's and one that sought to offer fresh perspectives and solutions not only to the spiritual crisis but to the social ills of his time.[77] He noticed, though, that Hartmann seemingly contradicted himself in calling for increased social participation—a conscious, collective decision that would result in social organizations meant to lift the yoke of capitalism.[78] But in marshaling socialist ideas borrowed from Pierre-Joseph Proudhon (1809–1865) or Charles Fourier (1772–1837) and presenting them in a rather cursory manner, Hartmann was suggesting that the newfound consciousness could indeed propel political and social progress. However, such a proposition ran against his pivotal predicate, that the unconscious is an all-encompassing force. The possibility of progress either implies temporary suspension of the unconscious or—in order to remain consistent with the notion that the unconscious is the secret principle of the world—it postulates an illusory consciousness that is in fact manipulated by the unconscious, thus precluding human agency.

Franck voices a vision of Judaism revolving around its contribution to philosophy, reading it and religion in general as ethics and an invitation to civic participation in a modern society frequently at odds with Hartmann's worldview and philosophy of religion. But another generation would articulate that force of the unconscious as a godless god and make it a placeholder for modernity.

Between Marxism and Messianism: Bloch's New Reading of the Unconscious

The disdain for Eduard von Hartmann and his mystical bric-a-brac is also the reflection of a generation that held the notion of rationality to be central to its belief system and to the promise of a symbiosis between Jews and their environment. Another generation, however, proved more receptive to a worldview objecting to rationalism as a value. This resistance resulted not from a conservative interpretation of the Jewish tradition, which had little purchase for rationalism, but rather from the fact that the assumption of rationality as a social good and shared purpose had to be challenged. In a striking paradigm shift, mysticism and its disruptive power became a locus of cultural and political modernity at the turn of the twentieth century.

The turn to Kabbalah as the proper hermeneutics for capturing the new zeitgeist has often been credited to Gershom Scholem, as he himself famously declares in his aforementioned 1937 letter to his publisher.[79] His motivation for studying these obscure sources, which ran afoul of the petty respectability of the *Wissenschaft des Judentums*, was to break new ground. And indeed, the language he uses reveals triumphing over the abyss. As he explains, "To be sure the key to the understanding of these things seems to have been lost. . . . And perhaps it was not so much the key that was missing but courage: the courage to venture out into an abyss, which one day could end up in ourselves, courage also to penetrate through the symbolic plane and through the wall of history."[80] The language here, whereby the external abyss is threatening and may become a devouring, internal one, has clear Schellingian overtones while charting a distinct Scholemian path.

Scholem's claim is only partly accurate. Other thinkers, around that time and even before him, were also redirecting their gaze toward a nontraditional narrative of Judaism. But the question of their initial exposure to kabbalistic sources has often been neglected. How, then, did a new generation of thinkers—most of whom, like Scholem, Ernst Bloch, or Martin Buber, were assimilated and detached from the sources of Jewish mysticism, as they readily admitted—find its way back to Kabbalah?[81]

Their return is almost always taken for granted, raising the question of the missing piece that would explain this shift.[82]

Among this generation, Ernst Bloch (1885–1977) acknowledged the influence of Hartmann on multiple occasions.[83] It is with him that the young man corresponded in his late teens before returning to the Jewish texts themselves. He also had exchanges with Theodor Lipps, Wilhelm Wundt, Wilhelm Windelband, and Ernst Mach—all of whom were either influential philosophers or the key figures of psychology before Freud.[84] The presence of such figures among Bloch's intellectual references—and the absence of Freud—shows that it took time for Freud's influence to extend beyond his psychoanalytical circles and become an unmatched reference.

From his youthful essay "On Force and Its Essence" to his last work, *Experimentum mundi*, in 1975, Bloch directly claimed Eduard von Hartmann's influence.[85] Arguably, this was more evident in his early work—the 1918 version of *The Spirit of Utopia*, in which he devotes a chapter to Hartmann and Friedrich Nietzsche that was left out of later editions, as well as *Spuren* (*Traces*), written between 1910 and 1929. In *Traces*, a series of literary and philosophical fragments, he revisits the intellectual awakening of his childhood and youth. The part entitled "Geist, der sich erst bildet" ("Spirit Still Taking Shape"), and specifically "Der Lebensgott" ("The God of Life"), brim with the Romantic tropes of nature as an all-consuming force and are inflected with the presence of the unconscious.

> What one called God was nothing but the infinite sum of matter, energy, and (unconscious) reason; all consciousness is mere combustion, like lights in the night, behind which the dark dynamo stood. Indeed, consciousness itself seemed dearly purchased; on one's youthful bosom, or rather deep within it, one could feel a peculiar weight, the slight but persistent weight of life, speaking figuratively, yet not only figuratively.... For it was physically quite exactly focused and palpable; this slight pain, so it seemed—was the seat of consciousness, or the source. It also heals, but likewise outwardly, in outward unconsciousness, above all in natural beauty, especially inorganic beauty, in the beauty of rivers, mountains, and cliffs.[86]

The isomorphism between man and nature that Bloch evokes here belongs to the repertoire of a German mystique popularized by the *völkisch* movement.[87] This also attracted Bloch as a solution to alienation.[88] Further, it evokes Jacob Boehme, and with its motifs of combustion links this incandescent landscape back to psychology—recall that Ludwig Feuerbach had identified Boehme as a protopsychologist.[89] The link between German mysticism and psychology was consolidated in Hartmann—and Bloch would only deepen that link, attaching a more consciously Jewish mysticism later on.

The title of the piece quoted above, "Spirit Still Taking Shape," indicates this continual emanation process informing the utopian psychology that Bloch sought to create in his early writings: an ontology of the "not there yet."[90] Such a construct of the liminal is designed to avoid the alienation stemming from the fetishization of cultural objects or forms, which could even be seen as a corrective for Marxism, inflected with the messianism that came to define Bloch's thought—as well as Walter Benjamin's. And the hyphenating nature of a Jewish reinterpretation of German idealist philosophy, according to Jürgen Habermas, should not be ignored. Habermas was adamant about the subterranean presence of Jewish contributions to German thought and its need to be known. In his view, Bloch created "an amazing reconciliation of traditions that, especially in Germany, seem to have been separated along religious lines. The Jewish sensibility in Marxism brings to life certain perspectives that once were the province of cabbala and mysticism; likewise, it unearths the Pythagoreic and Hermetic traditions that often were cut off and rarely were refined to the level of official philosophy."[91] This mediation may come across as an instance of the misleading "symbiosis" maligned by Scholem. Or, in a more positive light, it could be read as an "alliage": the elective affinities when two elements, as Michael Löwy puts it, "are looking for one another, are attracted and seize each other . . . and then resurge from this intimate union into a regenerated, new and unexpected form."[92]

The alliance of Jewish messianism and the worldview of the unconscious, both as a godless god and as a blind, inflexible realm, was also a catalyst for other German Jewish activists and philosophers, notably Gustav Landauer (1870–1919), the theoretician of anarchism and leading figure of the socialist movement and the short-lived Bavarian Social Republic in the wake of First World War, to whom I will only briefly turn. Mysticism informed his activism, and the liberation from the unconscious, viewed as a yoke that had oppressed prior generations, is a road map to his trajectory. In his *Skepsis und Mystik* (*Skepticism and Mysticism*), published in 1903, Landauer ponders the role of an unconscious that weighed down human activity. Anarchism must bring humanity into the realm of self-determination and remove it from the "unconscious necessity," thus enabling "conscious, voluntary, purposeful smaller or larger communities" to take over, in a break from the past. "The previous history of the human race is composed of innumerable instances of unconscious, dull, blind development," he insists.[93]

Against the blind violence of anarchism that he came to condemn at the turn of the twentieth century, Landauer favored a mystical renewal based on ancient communitarian traditions that remain inscribed in a collective memory or in a collective unconscious. As Franck had observed, Hartmann contradicted the pessimism he championed by proposing that mysticism is a framework that enables active participation and by connecting the community to this unifying principle, rather than foreclosing all possibility of coexistence in a society atomized under the weight and the domination of a principle that annihilates freedom and could resemble a Gnostic God.

Against the daemonic principle, called the unconscious—which would devolve into a destruction of human consciousness and agency, and the eradication of the legacy of the Enlightenment—Bloch opposed a principle of hope. This is why he spoke of the "rationalism of the irrational" to describe his philosophy. It acknowledges a realm beyond reason that would not devolve into the irrational, which is somewhat reminiscent of Hartmann's reassessment of this binary.[94] Bloch's principle of hope would consider the granularity of human experience; a cold, mechanical rationalism would only amount to the mirror image of a mechanical unconscious lamented by Franck. Reclaiming the unconscious was an opportunity to promote a new understanding of Jewish humanism in modernity.

Although a number of Jewish thinkers nonetheless rejected it for its monism which bore a clear resemblance to pantheism, Moritz Lazarus, Heymann Steinthal, Adolphe Franck, and Ernst Bloch represent a specific Jewish engagement with Hartmann's unconscious that provides the triumph of a metaphysical entity over the individualism believed to be consuming modernity.

8

The "Retrospective Unconscious"

Reading the Jewish Tradition as Psychology

Having detected the concept of the unconscious in the scriptures or in texts from the Jewish tradition, or having claimed that Judaism had been able to anticipate modern scientific discoveries, a generation of Jewish thinkers was projecting a later concept onto tropes or attitudes that did not clearly express it yet—or that at best had foreshadowed it.

In its Hartmannian key, the unconscious became a source of affirmative apologetics and reappropriation. Using a now-widespread term, thinkers like Elia Benamozegh in Italy, Israel Salanter in the Russian Empire, Ahron Marcus in Germany, and others established the precedence of Jewish thought for understanding the concept—in what appeared to be a retroactive imputation. Regardless of its epistemological accuracy, the term *unconscious* was used to further reject alienation. Martin Buber's I-Thou concept went on to become the culmination of a Jewish ethical humanism in which the unconscious plays an important role both as an identification with philosophy and as an identification with Jewish (and kabbalistic) sources.

For all their differences, all these thinkers reappropriated the unconscious in a Jewish register through Eduard von Hartmann's work, which enabled them to read texts from the Jewish tradition in light of these new conceptions of the unconscious and to claim that the tradition had foreshadowed them. The mechanism that I describe as the "retrospective unconscious" is this distinct effort a generation of thinkers made to showcase the prescience of Judaism regarding the concept of the unconscious as a strategy for affirmative apologetics.[1] The unconscious was thus turned into a marker of the insights of the Jewish tradition into the workings of the mind, thereby indicating that it is a participant in the cultural conversation, in a culture that it has actually subterraneously shaped and that it behooved Jewish thinkers to unveil.

These thinkers had a double focal point. They sought not only to shape the perception of Judaism for a non-Jewish audience but also to reevaluate the theology of Hasidism for Jews and to rehabilitate its image. They professed that the sect, described as insular and progress-averse by advocates of Jewish emancipation, had in fact been able go beyond the binaries of reason and the irrational, thus transcending the binaries of modernity. This *retrospective* unconscious bolstered the idea that Jewish insights into psychology demonstrate the validity, plurality, and universality of Jewish thought.

The retrospective unconscious is very much in opposition to what the philosopher and psychologist William James (1842–1910) described as "medical materialism" in his time, whereby religious, particularly spiritual, experiences were considered to be a mere reflection of pathologies.[2] What I propose is the opposite: a case in which spiritual notions shed light on, and foreshadowed, scientific or therapeutic concepts. This phenomenon also differs from what Gershom Scholem called "historical psychology," in which, he argued, the historian can detect how "the metaphysical and psychological elements are closely intertwined; or, to be exact, they are one."[3] It is worth noting that this kind of endeavor follows in the footsteps of Friedrich Schelling: like them, he sometimes called it "historiosophy."[4] Such a cross-pollination is aligned with Scholem's stated self-assessment in his diary, written at age seventeen: "All my knowledge only reproduces my metaphysical existence. I am, as it were, a metaphysical psychologist."[5] The proclamation of his youth arguably captured his intellectual project. Indeed, he endeavored to show how Jews resorted to metaphysics to exert an analytical grip on, or even reify, the course of history from which they had been excluded after the expulsion from Spain. Another case in point is his biography of Sabbatai Zevi, the seventeenth-century false messiah from the Ottoman Empire whose erratic acts, which Scholem diagnosed as maniacal, came to stand for religious transgression and antinomianism writ large, capturing a collective psyche and a particular moment in Jewish history. With what I call the retrospective unconscious, the gaze of these various thinkers was not historical. It was an affirmation of the present, in the present—a case of affirmative apologetics. Indeed, they aimed to intervene in the culture through a concept that was part of a nascent epistemological discourse, the unconscious, and to which their tradition could legitimately lay claim, and reclaim as its own.

Deciphering the Unconscious as Progressive Revelation and Cohesion

Among the advocates of the value of Judaism for addressing the social, political, and religious tensions of modernity, the Italian rabbi Elia Benamozegh (1823–1900) availed himself of the scientific discoveries of his day to demonstrate their accordance with his faith.

A prolific writer, Benamozegh is best known for his *Jewish and Christian Ethics* and his magnum opus, *Israel and Humanity*, published posthumously in 1914, in which he sought to chart a new path toward religious coexistence. The notion of a collective psyche or collective unconscious plays a significant role in that construct. Benamozegh had a keen interest in psychology in general, and in the new theories of the unconscious and Hartmann in particular. He saw them as an entry point into the study of the psyche as well as a locus of the revelation of God himself in and as the human mind—and a defense of Kabbalah.[6]

Benamozegh was no late arrival in his efforts to draw on theories of the unconscious, which he regarded as a "confused perception of the wider field of shared consciousness."[7] As early as 1877, he closed his 250-page *Dogmatic and Apologetic Theology* with a credo, affirming, "I believe that man is not aware of his whole self, which is much more than he knows he is, and thus I believe that the philosophy of the unconscious which gets so much publicity, not only with Hartmann but before, has much truth in it."[8] A few lines later, he claims, "I believe that consciousnesses create a hierarchy among themselves, and at the top is God, the consciousness of consciousness."[9] The very date of 1877 shows that he had availed himself of the work of Hartmann remarkably quickly—1877 is the year the French translation of *Philosophy of the Unconscious* came out, predated by a few excerpts and journal articles beginning in 1874. His interest grew rapidly and never abated. Indeed, twenty years later, in one of his last works published, Benamozegh wrote,

> I have long been at work on perfecting my theory of concentric consciousnesses that culminate in God, the consciousness of consciousnesses as the first protological principle of the universe, in the place of intelligence, will, etc. . . . Now that the Unconscious is playing an increasingly important role, we may allow that it is the sense or the awareness of the greater field of shared consciousness; it has at least been proved that we do not have total consciousness of ourselves and that our consciousness has no insurmountable boundaries.[10]

In both passages, Benamozegh reworks a classic notion, found in Aristotle and Maimonides, that God is the active intellect and as such can be said to be the intellect of intellects; Benamozegh simply replaces *intellect* with *consciousness*.[11]

In addition, in using the phrase "first protological principle," Benamozegh employs the terminology of the prominent Italian theologian and philosopher Vincenzo Gioberti's posthumous *Della protologia*, published in 1857. In it, Gioberti contends that the real significance of revelation is not to repair human sin but to bring the natural and the supernatural closer together, as they had been artificially and wrongly separated by the church.[12] Like Gioberti, Benamozegh wove together the Enlightenment understanding of progress—which he collapsed with human perfectibility, as defined by Condorcet—and his own religious beliefs, as expressed in his statement "Everybody realizes how this capacity of God for disclosure is the origin of human perfectibility—of progress."[13] The boundaries between the micro- and macrocosm, science and religion, and between human beings were thus abolished. In *The Future of Science*, Ernest Renan, whom Benamozegh read assiduously, argues that this deeper consciousness is part of future science, but also that it is incumbent on the future religion of humanity to "constitute a greater consciousness, or, as it used to be expressed, 'the greater glory of God.'"[14]

For Benamozegh, the social and theological agendas converge and can be translated into the unconscious, as long as it behooves religion to unpack its meaning. But he also contends that "this rapprochement between the social and the physical world, and the laws, revolutions, forms, creations, and procedures of each, was attempted even before Mr. Hartmann. To sum them all up, it suffices to quote Quinet and his book on Creation."[15] Hartmann seems here little more than a token of intellectual legitimacy; Benamozegh brushes him aside in favor of a reference to Edgar Quinet's *Création*, published in 1870—a year after Hartmann's study was first published in German. Quinet (1803–1875) was a historian, philosopher, politician, and key figure of French liberalism. In this book, he offers an instance of popular science that seeks to close the gap between science and spirituality, but also between the ideal and the real, in a way that Hartmann does not attempt.[16]

This explains the Italian rabbi's affinity for Quinet: Benamozegh used the unconscious as a jumping-off point for the rapprochement of the microcosm and the macrocosm—and more important for the ideal and the real, which for him is the true ambition of Judaism.[17] Through the concept of the unconscious, he sought to capture the collective expressions of metaphysical aspirations, distilled in kabbalistic language and hermeneutics.[18] His goal was to demonstrate how their implementations should foster religious coexistence or social justice and thus lead to using mystical concepts in the political arena to address the fractures of modernity.[19]

Ignoring the underlying pessimism decried by Heymann Steinthal, Moritz Lazarus, and Adolphe Franck, Benamozegh zeroes in on the significance of the unconscious as a shared feature of humankind. He challenges his readers, "When [Hartmann] tells us that the 'Unconscious is the common subject that feels both [pleasure and suffering] since it is at the bottom of all individual consciousnesses,' shouldn't we listen to the Bible or the Rabbis when they tell us about the joy or the pain that God derives from our actions?"[20] For Benamozegh, scientific inquiry can only affirm the validity of previous knowledge already contained in Kabbalah. Expanding knowledge of the psyche should thus depend on increasing knowledge of the Torah, in a dynamic that captures the asymptotic nature of the human mind toward the divine—continually approaching it but never meeting it at any finite distance.

By adopting the main theses of *Philosophy of the Unconscious* and highlighting the as-yet-untapped resources of Judaism, Benamozegh also sought to show that the Jewish tradition, as the real origin of modern humanism, had established its spiritual and intellectual worth through its compatibility—and even harmony—with modern science. He noted its particular compatibility with the nascent discipline of psychology: the unparalleled understanding of the psyche it provided was ample evidence of that.

Starting in the mid-nineteenth century, advocates of Jewish mysticism, broadly defined, availed themselves of the new but ubiquitous notion of the unconscious in order to establish Kabbalah as a form of hermeneutics and proclaim it both a reflection of the human psyche and a tool for its future exploration. The idea of the unconscious thus offered a key for reconciling science and religion, religion and modernity. Such is the claim Franck makes in *The Kabbalah: The Religious Philosophy of the Hebrews* when he describes Kabbalah as operating in accordance with psychological principles: "A truly original system, and truly grand, which does not resemble any other systems, whether religious or philosophical, only in that it comes from the same source, in that it was called forth by the same causes, in that it responds to the same needs; in short, in that it rests upon the general laws of the human mind. These are the kabbalists."[21]

This claim announced a new understanding of the Jewish universalism that is key to Benamozegh's worldview and that would go on to define Levinasian ethics: the more original and particular a system, the more universal it can be. The respected philosopher and psychologist Jean-Philibert Damiron (1794–1862), whom Benamozegh quoted liberally, believed that to ground moral sciences anew, one cannot do without psychology—and if psychology had its roots in the Jewish tradition, then that was a scientific demonstration of the value of Judaism.[22]

Additionally, certain notions were fruitfully used as adjoining concepts between theology and the science of the mind. Such is the case with the process of "afterwardness," of *Nachträglichkeit*, found in Schelling, which corresponds to the notion of progressive revelation, as seen in chapter 2. It is the theological concept that best captures the notion of progress and of scientific developments.[23] If God's blueprint for the world is progressively unveiled by the human psyche, which seeks to perfect itself (following the precept of the imitation of God, who is the supreme intellect), the advance of scientific knowledge of the mind and of the unconscious will follow from this self-perfection. Beyond being evidence of progressive revelation, a more precise understanding of the workings of the psyche also offers the possibility of a greater understanding of the soul, and thus of the revelation of God *in* the mind.

The unconscious, as perceived in the Jewish reception of Friedrich Schelling and Eduard von Hartmann, resists a narrow localization. It highlights the possibility of a continuity between the I and the world—and thus of an updated holism—through a more precise knowledge of the self. The concept was mobilized in the opposition between holism and atomism in the philosophy of science, dating back to Aristotle's teleology, in which each organ has its own purpose. The new iteration of this debate in the modern era was vitalism. Indeed, the unconscious was taken up as a form of vitalism, the eighteenth-century principle according to which living organisms cannot be reduced to chemical or physical factors but possess a distinct vital principle.[24]

Vitalism had been disputed by Immanuel Kant, who saw evidence of the limits of human cognition in the belief that certain phenomena and biological functions are driven by a telos. In this controversy, phrenology was a case in point. Developed by the physiologist Franz Josef Gall (1758–1828), who first discovered that gray matter is associated with active tissues (neural components) and white matter with conducting tissues, phrenology proposed a physiological theory of the brain, ascribing specific functions to specific locations. Gall understood psychic development to be a consequence of the development of the organs, thus applying natural categories to the notion of Spirit. But unlike other physiologists, such as Frédéric Cuvier, Gall resisted localizing the soul. His hesitancy stemmed from the importance he ascribed to the concept of Spirit, which was a testament to Johann Gottfried von Herder's influence on him.[25]

This new holism was also a defense against atomism, which was increasingly being taken as a broader metaphor for a disjointed society and for modernity. Atomism was one of the causes of the alienation described by Ludwig Feuerbach and for which Jews stood accused. Consequently, Jewish thinkers were led to defend themselves by mobilizing their own tradition to show that it could create the bonds lacking in society: if the unconscious was evidence of holism, they must find evidence of that concept in the Jewish tradition.

These forays into the discovery of the unconscious are a marker of societal and religious progress, according to the advocates of a Jewish reclamation of the unconscious. Whereas Schelling's interest in the dark side of the psyche has been ascribed to a conservative turn and his interactions with Franz Xaver von Baader, the exploration of the unconscious by theorists of Judaism subsequently came to be construed or heralded as a promise of its universalism and of its role in fostering a new understanding of ethics.[26]

The Edifying Unconscious: Channeling the "Dark Forces" of the Psyche in the Jewish Ethics Movement

Beyond intellectual circles, two popular forces in nineteenth-century Judaism, the Musar and the early Hasidic movements, availed themselves of what they called the "dark forces" of the psyche, believing in their potential for teaching and edification. The approaches these movements took to the unconscious reveal their theological and ideological fault lines. I will first focus on the Musar, or Jewish Ethics movement, which never had the appeal of a mass movement and whose influence on Jewish communities and thought was much more limited than that of Hasidism.[27]

The term *musar* has two connotations. It is at once a genre of spiritual guidance, ethical teachings, and treatises elicited from the Bible (Prov. 1:2—"to know wisdom and instruction [*musar*]") and also an ethical and educational movement that originated in Lithuanian Orthodoxy.[28] The Musar movement focused on Torah study, deeming the Talmud insufficient for creating a deep emotional attachment to Judaism, and it sought to strengthen Jewish values, which its proponents considered to have been imperiled by the Haskalah (the Jewish Enlightenment). While the movement shared with Hasidism an emphasis on emotions and a critique of Talmudic studies, the two strands were at odds. This complex opposition cannot be attributed to a wholesale rejection of Kabbalah by the Musar movement, since this would disregard how indebted the ethical (*musar*) tradition—on which parts of the Musar relied—was to Kabbalah.[29] Nevertheless, scholars widely accept that the founder of the movement, Rabbi Israel Salanter (1809–1883), was indeed estranged from kabbalistic materials.[30] With some nuances, this would also broadly describe the movement's first generation.[31] Indeed, Salanter was less invested in a metaphysical reading of his sources than in psychology and ethics.[32]

The rabbi's early writings, composed when he lived in Lithuania, are more homiletic in nature and show little non-Jewish influence, but the prose of his years in Germany—where he took refuge after opposing the Russian imperial regime—manifests a concern for greater clarity in his writing and exhibits a degree of porosity with his new environment.[33] Although he did not cite his sources, his German texts, particularly the later ones, are permeated by philosophical concerns. In his mention of the problem of "obscure forces," he uses a terminology absent from his previous writings but found in the works on the unconscious penned by Christian Wolff and Immanuel Kant—possibly the "researchers of the powers of the soul of man" he invokes in his study.[34]

But instead of validating his claim by clamorously adducing sources outside the realm of Judaism, Salanter followed the lead of Mendel Lefin (1749–1826). A figure of the Jewish Enlightenment in Galicia, Lefin appropriated the concepts of the eighteenth-century philosophy of the mind, which he termed *ḥokhmat ha-neshamot* (the science of souls).[35] He created a de facto bridge between secular knowledge and religious thought. For instance, in an effort to win support from more traditional communities, Lefin underscored a continuity between the medieval tradition of Jewish rationalism and ethics.[36] This method undergirds his treatise entitled *Sefer Ḥeshbon ha-Nefesh* (*Book of Moral Accounting*), published in 1808.[37]

Salanter explicitly used the method, adopting Lefin's comparison of character training with animal training in the ethics journal *Tevunah*, and using the word *taming* to denote the power exerted by the will on humans' "evil nature."[38]

The possibility of a transformation of human nature is pivotal in Israel Salanter's thought. Such change is individual and has a degree of solemnity. Though ultimately informed by the awe of the divine (*yirat Elohim*), its path is anthropological, not metaphysical or cosmological, and the concept of awe is actually closer to the definition of elementary morality than an imperative based on the presence of the divine.[39] Indeed, Salanter's critique of Hasidism excoriated the movement's emphasis on the *tsadikkim* (the righteous) as *axis mundi* (center of the world).[40] He also targeted its reliance on mediators between the average man (*beinoni*) and the divine—because this arguably enabled human beings to divest themselves of their ethical responsibility and could be self-aggrandizing.[41] Instead of trusting the *tsadikkim* with the task of showing the average man how to achieve greater moral rectitude, Salanter suggested that it is the responsibility of the individual to observe and discipline the mind in a methodical, quasi-scientific fashion.

As for evil tendencies within individuals, Salanter imputed these not to the realm of the Kabbalah's *siṭra aḥra* (the demonic other side) but to the *yeṣer ha-ra* (usually rendered as "evil inclination").[42] He placed the responsibility for these tendencies squarely within the individual's mind and milieu, and with this responsibility comes the possibility of improvement.

In *Tevunah*, printed in the second half of 1861, Salanter's *derushim* (expositions) depict mental interiority as a "muddy well ... hidden in its latency, ready to gush forth its waters under the impact of a great cause ... that from out of their hiding places the waters reveal themselves, spread out, and destroy."[43] If Torah is often read as living water, the imagery is here turned on its head—with the image of soiled and destructive waters. Later, Carl Gustav Jung unequivocally associated this trope with the unconscious: water is not a "figure of speech, but a living symbol of the dark psyche" and "the commonest symbol for the unconscious."[44] The prevailing vision is rather pessimistic: these dark and clear forces are more powerful than men, at least initially.

Salanter fleshes out these forces in *Eṣ Pri* (*Fruit Tree*), a three-part pamphlet addressing man, theodicy, and education. In the first part, on man, he aligns the concept of dark and clear forces with the categories of inner and outer forces: "The psychologists [*ḥoqrei nefesh ha-adam*] have found that 'two types of forces reside in the soul of man: outer and inner forces.' The outer forces [*ḥiṣoni*] are also called evident [*barur*]. The other type [*penimi*] are obscure [*keheh*] (*ganz dunkel*)."[45]

It is both a moral and a religious imperative for an individual to retrieve clarity, to make these dark forces become evident. The findings of the "researchers of the powers of the soul," whom Salanter never identifies, are no different from the task the observant individual should set out to do, since they consist in an illumination of what had been previously left in the darkness of the soul or the psyche, thus creating a continuity between science and religion.

A more intriguing passage in this pamphlet is Salanter's treatment of the biblical episode of the binding of Isaac (in Hebrew, *aqedat Yiṣhaq* or simply *Aqedah*). The rabbi used the exegetical tradition that portrays Abraham weeping as he lifts his knife to sacrifice his son; drawing on that example, Salanter claims that such tears betrayed the "dark" or "obscure forces" that the patriarch was able to overcome. His views on the biblical episode differ from the prevailing interpretation in the first generation of Hasidim.[46] In that interpretation, Abraham seems alienated from his emotions. Yet in both cases, obscure mental states function as the expression of a connection with the divine, though of a different nature.

In the course of writing his pamphlet, Salanter examined the *Yalkut Shimoni*, a thirteenth-century haggadic compilation of older sources.[47] This text describes Abraham's body as being covered with tears while binding Isaac and sees him as acting "with his whole heart," since he seems resolved to perform the sacrifice.[48] But, Salanter asks, "how can these accounts be in contradiction with each other—how, after he bound Isaac with all his heart, can tears pour from his eyes?" The inner forces, in Salanter's view, are represented by Abraham's tears. Next, he underscores such coexistence of conflicting forces within a human being.

> Seen in the light of what we have earlier explained... they can both be true, for when the *Yalqut Shimoni* says "he bound [him] with all his heart," this means with the outer forces, which were at their highest level in Abraham and in fact were accessed to overcome the inner forces, while the tears were falling from the inner forces, whose action is the most potent of all human characteristics. From this, we see clearly that even with Abraham

our father, who is greater than us in faith and righteousness, and despite this, the inner forces exerted such a strength on him that it caused tears to fall even though he fully carried out his deed and did it with all his heart.[49]

Positing the heart as the vessel of outer forces seems counterintuitive, and yet the heart does not in fact systematically convey a purely emotional (and thus an inner or subjective) disposition. It is seen in Maimonides—and expanded on in early systems of religious-based psychology—as the seat of wisdom, of knowledge of the divine, and of conscience.[50] In that construct, the heart can thus be linked to external forces; it functions as the place where the consciousness of transcendence occurs. So in Salanter's reading of the midrash, the dark forces are revealed by tears and reined in by the heart in an opportunity to face one's dark forces and to test and establish one's faith—which leads to self-improvement. Faith, as a modality of self-improvement, is thus a form of habituation—the internalization of outer forces, norms, or practices.[51]

Salanter's analysis of an episode that ultimately negates the role of inner (or obscure) forces constructs a figure of Abraham as one who prevails over instincts that most human beings are unable to control: it behooves the man of faith to become aware of these instincts.[52] In Salanter's construct, liminal states of consciousness signal the moment when man is likely to fall prey to these obscure forces, whereas religious fervor acts as an intensifier of consciousness, heightening the awareness of the dark forces present within the soul in order to conquer them. This intensification is part of the cure that Salanter offers, as *hitpa'alut*—an intensification of the power of religious emotions in order to get rid of the other forces.[53] The detour into the inner forces only happens in order to reconnect with the outer forces, which determine ethical conduct and should be a lesson. Salanter continues: "And he placed him on the altar. Abraham's eyes gazed on Isaac and Isaac's eyes gazed at the heavens. Tears welled up and fell from Abraham's eyes until the pool of tears was as high as he was tall."[54]

This description of Abraham's distress and solitude (he cannot make eye contact with his son) also points to a new emphasis on the individual and on existential angst—a paradigm shift for a religion whose tradition is centered on community. And this turn toward the individual corresponds to a new focus on self-improvement.[55] It is not, however, an exploration of inwardness for its own sake, or in a Romantic fashion: Salanter's heart and the "outer forces" it describes are closer to the concept of a hylic intellect. The hylic intellect is a traditional concept present in medieval

Jewish philosophy, notably in the writings of Maimonides. It refers to an agent that actualizes knowledge in human beings or functions as a form of intellectual consciousness of the transcendent.[56] In addition, the exploration of the unconscious can be seen as a possibility of ethics through a test of these outer forces but also as a relation to the Other. All this explains Salanter's effacement of Satan and the angels, and of any cosmic presence that can be found in the passage of the *Yalkut Shimoni* he discussed but that he chose to ignore, and his insistence on Abraham's relationship and dialogue with Isaac, notably absent from the text itself. Here, faith is a triangulation—it is an articulation of the relationship between the self, brought to heightened consciousness; the Other, which makes this consciousness emerge; and the divine, which created that test.[57]

The manifestation of the unconscious through this motif of tears instantiates the discontinuity between inner mental states and outer behavior.[58] Yet these conflicts and discontinuities are eventually acknowledged and overcome; the way the dark psyche is reined in is displayed as a measure of faith and of self-improvement, where both are intertwined and serve the Musar's ideology.

Mapping the term *unconscious* on the Musar's "obscure forces" mostly occurred in the 1970s with the scholarship of Hillel Goldberg.[59] Other thinkers also sought to demonstrate that the Musar movement (which had lost countless members in the Holocaust) could rival Hasidism's psychological accuracy. This revival within Orthodoxy was signaled by the publication of Goldberg's *The Fire Within* on the popular ArtScroll imprint. It is a defense of the Musar for the times, tacitly proposing it as an alternative to Hasidism.[60] But ironically, this emphasis on Salanter's psychological insights along with the prefigurations of the unconscious in his writings, a case of the retrospective unconscious, bears a clear resemblance to prior reappraisals of the Hasidic movement, which had come be associated with self-knowledge and even the increasingly popular self-help genre.[61]

Hasidism and Its Discontents

In *Major Trends in Jewish Mysticism*, Gershom Scholem famously characterizes Hasidism as "mystical psychology."[62] He lauds the acuity of its insights.

> The distinctive feature of the new school is to be found in the fact that the secrets of the divine realm are presented in the guise of mystical psychology.... With every one of the endless stages of the theosophical world

corresponding to a given state of the soul—actual or potential, but at any rate capable of being felt and perceived—kabbalism becomes an instrument of psychological analysis and self-knowledge, an instrument the precision of which is not infrequently rather astounding.[63]

In the wake of Scholem, other scholars have likewise focused on the sharpness of Hasidism's psychology.[64] Yet, before him, the movement had already received a reappraisal along the same lines, recognizing the value of the insights it offered on an enigma seemingly on the verge of being solved: the unconscious.

The hypothesis, then—based on the psychological intuitions of the Maggid of Mezeritch, and of a nascent theory of the unconscious— was that Hasidism can be envisioned not just as a religious force but as a powerful philosophy and psychology beyond its religious confines. Arguably, it represents yet another instantiation of the magnitude of the mystical Jewish current that swept eastern Europe from the eighteenth century onward.

Hasidic affirmative apologetics were developed in the late nineteenth century by Ahron Marcus in *Hartmann's Inductive Philosophie im Chassidismus* (*Hartmann's Inductive Philosophy of Hasidism*, 1889) and *Der Chassidismus* (*Hasidism*, 1901). Marcus (1843–1916) was a key figure in the attempt to articulate a new Jewish identity politics based on Hasidic Orthodoxy and later on Zionism in the early stage of the movement.[65] Born in Hamburg, he was a student of Isaac Bernays, the rabbi we met in chapter 2 who left no writings but whose students described and perpetuated his Judaism, which was imbued with Schellingian and kabbalistic references. Widely considered an *illuy*, a prodigy, Marcus grew frustrated with the German Jewish ethos and went to study with Hasidic masters in Poland, joining the court of Radomsk, one of the great Hasidic dynasties. He became a figure of the Zionist movement while supporting Hasidic Orthodoxy and is mostly remembered for his book *Hasidism*. Published under the pseudonym Verus, it exerted an influence on Franz Rosenzweig.[66]

But the book that interests us here is Marcus's *Hartmann's Inductive Philosophy of Hasidism*, a monograph that both piqued Scholem's interest and drew his scorn. In it, Marcus explicitly avails himself of Eduard von Hartmann's inductive method and demonstrates its prevalence in Hasidism. As a preamble, he discusses the concept of the unconscious as developed by

Hartmann and then sets out to prove that it had been discovered earlier by Talmud scholars.[67]

> My efforts are geared toward showing that in the whole Hartmann system, which is considered to be a model of the most modern science, there is no reasonable proposition, which means that there is nothing in the rabbinical science that cannot be found and whose origin—before it collapsed in confusion and degeneration—could not be located in that science. As a trial case, we begin with the theory of evolution, the foundation of the modern *Weltanschauung*.[68]

Aligning inductive reasoning with the rabbinical tradition was consonant with contemporaneous religious studies.[69] Marcus's mention of collapse and degeneration comes across as a preemptive defense along Salomon Maimon's line of argument, that Kabbalah had devolved into obscurantism, while proclaiming the value of the thought mechanism itself, thus catering to multiple audiences while mounting an Orthodox apology for Jewish thought. But he expanded his argument to mysticism, in an affinity first discussed by Sergei Bulgakov (1871–1944), widely regarded as the greatest Orthodox theologian of the twentieth century. Bulgakov's *Unfading Light*, published just before the Russian Revolution of 1917, offers a combination of Orthodox theology and sophiology (the theological and philosophical conceptions pertaining to the wisdom of God) as well as of Friedrich Schelling's later philosophy.[70]

Marcus's book was also aligned with his era's taste for scientific popularization: amateur scientists and popular enthusiasm for science had supplanted earlier rarefied discussions in maskilic circles.[71] This appetite swept across both the non-Jewish and the Jewish world and was taken up by the prolific Hayyim Selig Slonimski (1810–1904), who saw it as a religious duty to decipher and proclaim God's greatness.[72] He, too, ventured into psychology as he tried to scientifically prove the immortality of the soul.[73]

Resorting to one of the main strategies of modern Jewish apologetics, Marcus next argues in *Hartmann's Inductive Philosophy of Hasidism* that Jewish thought anticipated major scientific discoveries, but what in fact was at stake was kabbalistic hermeneutics: "We assert the laws of mystical conceptions, which, according to Hartmann, shape the sources of philosophical systems and more generally of genius, and this is how Newton captured it in the exact sciences (see also Leibniz's infinitesimal theory) and came to use these theories of evolution and movement in the anthropological realm."[74] The mention of Gottfried Wilhelm Leibniz and his infinitesimal theory describes the idea of *petites perceptions* beneath the threshold of consciousness—and thus, as we have seen, the first exploration of the unconscious.

Marcus placed the study of the mind within both anthropology and nature. He also alluded to mesmerism in another instance and to the "validity of 'animal magnetism,'" which is "a scientific problem in nature."[75] The scientific theory of the German physician Anton Mesmer (1734–1815), which relied on fluids as a purported cure for both mental and physical illnesses, is often perceived as an instance of obscurantism, but it was initially consonant with other scientific theories of fluids in nature and their impact on human bodies and minds, as shown in Wilhelm von Humboldt's musings on the magnetic force of the moon or Luigi Galvani's animal electricity.[76] Marcus's own reflection on the substance of ether in Kabbalah, as a medium that in the wave theory of light permeates all space and impacts the world and humanity, is no different.[77]

Beyond its purely therapeutic aspect, mesmerism had two main political and cultural implications.[78] First, it signaled disdain for institutions and medicine, which led to its surveillance by the Old Regime in France as it announced the egalitarianism of the French Revolution.[79] Second, after the Revolution, the esoteric nature of the practice came to the fore: its stance against the narrative of the triumph of reason that had nevertheless led to the murderous excesses of the Terror signaled the end of the Enlightenment and the turn to Romanticism.[80] The visionary mesmerism of the early nineteenth century became increasingly mired in occultism and symbolism.[81] This new turn effaced the memory of a time when mesmerism had the aura of a scientifically sound discipline. Also known as animal magnetism, it was a pathway into the secrets of nature, and it led to the demonstrated presence of God, pictured as a triangle with the word *Dieu* (God) at the top and *la matière* (matter) and *le mouvement* (motion) along the sides. "Animal magnetism, in M. Mesmer's hands, seems to be nothing other than Nature herself," wrote Mesmer's apologist, the physician Charles Deslon.[82]

Mesmerism appeared to be an illustration of metaphysical assumptions: at the heart of science and religion but also of religion and philosophy lies the question of the soul. Thus, it should not come as a surprise that Marcus used mesmerism mostly in order to assert that the existence of a soul can be scientifically established—a question shared not just by religious apologists like him but also by philosophers such as Georg Wilhelm Friedrich Hegel, who used it in order to emphasize the world's underlying spiritual unity: "In experience too the phenomena of *animal magnetism* in particular have given, in recent times, a visible confirmation of the *substantial unity* of the soul, and of the power of its ideality. Before these phenomena, the rigid distinctions of the intellect are thrown into disarray; and the necessity of a speculative examination for the dissolution of the contradictions is displayed more directly."[83]

In a different key, Arthur Schopenhauer devoted a whole chapter of *On Will in Nature* (1836) to animal magnetism, which he called "practical metaphysics." He saw it as a "corroboration" (*Bestätigung*) likely to reveal the "will" at the source of the world—the basis for what Hartmann would later call the unconscious.[84]

The religious overtones of these theories of animal magnetism resonated across faiths and philosophical traditions. While the interest in magnetism was not specific to Judaism, the politics of mesmerism accorded with those of Hasidism in its opposition to traditional authorities (replacing rabbis with *tsadikkim*) and in light of the connection between Hasidism and healing practices—especially those attributed to the founder of Hasidism, Rabbi Israel ben Eliezer (1698–1760), known as the Baal Shem Tov (the Master of the Good Name).[85] Mentions of mesmerism in relation to Orthodox rabbinical figures also suggest a greater degree of porosity between the Orthodox Jewish communities and secular culture than routinely assumed. Each of these cultures made its own attempts to deal with the individual's spiritual or psychological unrest of the era.

Mesmer's technique of quieting the mind (also known as magnetism) actually relies on the natural order and shows the continuity between the two realms, the psyche and nature, in a quest for harmony that could extend to the realm of politics. Ahron Marcus's invocation of Kabbalah likewise highlights the necessity of harmony: "The primeval concept of man comes from the world of harmony of the mineral, vegetal, and animal realms, as it is said in the *Idra*: 'Without the principle of man there is no harmony. This manifests itself in the differences, by which man distinguishes himself from other creatures, on which he exerts his dominion.'"[86]

The reference to the *Idra* is noteworthy, since it references the *Idra Rabba* (*The Great Assembly*), a part of the Zohar describing the meetings of the sages and their discussion of the most secret teachings of Kabbalah, the face of God. The *Idra* includes bold anthropomorphic representations as well as a dive into the layers of divine consciousness.[87] Its mystical premise is that God is a force that continually fills the world with divine energy. This part of the Zohar gave modern scholars an opening to see parallels between divine energy and contemporary discoveries about the physics of fluids. More generally, it underscored the harmony between the world, man, and God, all defined in terms of the fluids sent or received. This could only lead Marcus to assert, "Just as Hartmann characterizes the religious element of modern philosophy . . . it is not out of question that, in its newest direction—psycho-magnetism—the current research in the natural sciences will lead to places that Jewish cosmology had long identified as such."[88] Thus, he pronounced the psyche both philosophical and cosmological.

Another limit that Marcus explored between the natural world and the mind was somnambulism. Nineteenth-century scientists were obsessed with a condition that they hoped could produce insights into the transcendental subject—that part of the human mind that controls the body while it sleepwalks, the liminal state in which, in Hartmann's philosophical system, the unconscious is an undifferentiated absolute.[89] Attempts to read occultism in light of psychology by the now-forgotten German occultist and philosopher Carl du Prel (1839–1899) profoundly influenced many thinkers and writers, including Marcus and an admiring Sigmund Freud.[90] Du Prel wrote approvingly of Hartmann and claimed that somnambulism proves that "that of which our personal Ego is unconscious is not *in itself* unconscious; and further, that between our personal selves and the Universal Substance, there must be interposed a transcendental subject, a knowing and willing being. Thus, man's individuality extends beyond his passing phenomenal form, and life on earth is but one of the forms of existence possible to his true self."[91]

According to du Prel, the subject is by nature double: it is a transcendental subject that lives in two worlds—the world of experience and of nature and the world of dreams and the mind—through which it can gain access to the thing-in-itself, the noumenon, as defined by Kant. Du Prel thereby reconciled Kantianism and mysticism: "If, even in our highest ecstasies, consciousness does not exhaust our whole being, but rather leaves behind an immeasurable foundation of the Unconscious, which can create new fissures, then certainly man appears as a being of groundless depth [*von abgründiger Tiefe*], reaching with his individual roots into the metaphysical region. . . . Man [is] a double being, with one foot on the earth, the other in the realm of spirits."⁹² In his depiction of the duality and insatiability of the human experience, of its cleavages, he also inserted the groundless nature of man (close to the abyss), which conjures up an inversed kabbalistic tree that has its branches in earth and its roots in the sky.

Paramount for Marcus is being able to establish the identity between the self and nature by recognizing and embracing this dynamic within the Jewish tradition. In reconciling the science of the mind and of nature, as well as religion and philosophy, he even called the traditional rabbinical stances *Identitätsphilosophie*, a nod to the fundamental identity of Spirit and nature in Friedrich Schelling's metaphysical theory of absolute identity: in his endeavor to create a *Naturphilosophie* from 1797 onward, Schelling sought to illuminate in new ways the identity between thinking processes and the workings of nature. In his words, "Nature is to be invisible mind, mind invisible nature," which conveys the necessity of this absolute identity.⁹³ Marcus, in his apology for Kabbalah and Judaism, affirmed the same, while proclaiming the centrality of both evolution and revelation.

Gershom Scholem, who read Marcus early in his formative years and cited him twice in diary entries in 1916, later criticized him as a disguised defender of Orthodoxy.⁹⁴ He nonetheless recognized a "seed of truth and something worth exploring" in the similarities that Marcus had sensed between the unconscious and the Hasidic concept of *kadmut ha sekhel*—the beginning of awareness—in the work of a Hasidic master, the Maggid of Mezeritch (1704–1772), a disciple of the Baal Shem Tov (Besht).⁹⁵

The topography of the mind found among the first generations of Hasidic thinkers, notably the Maggid of Mezeritch, is a theosophic locus, especially in the studies of the Hasidic masters' sayings, notably the collections *Liqqutei Amarim* (*Collection of Statements*) and *Or ha-Emet* (*The Light of Truth*).⁹⁶ These have invited comparisons with the unconscious, but it is in fact in the heart that the unconscious resides, and it is the heart's connection to the divine that matters: "The force of intelligence has its seat in the heart, corresponding to the saying 'the heart is intelligent,' for it receives [its content or influence] from the uppermost level, [i.e.] the beginning of consciousness [*me-qadimat ha-sekhel*]."⁹⁷ The heart is thus the residence of that which is before or beyond comprehension. The "beginning of consciousness" can be rendered as "supraconsciousness" or "metaconsciousness" as well as "the unconscious." In any case, the shared essence of the intellect is a precondition: "preexistence of the intellect [*qadmut ha-sekhel*] in order to think."⁹⁸

In 1944, in discussing the key term *qadmut ha-sekhel* as preexistence of the intellect, preconscious, or unconscious, Scholem refuted the claim that the Maggid had actually discovered the concept by arguing that the resemblances were fleeting and that the concept had fallen into oblivion after him.[99] Despite his more cautious assessment of the putative discovery and his reservations about Marcus's agenda, however, Scholem did acknowledge an entity similar to the unconscious in the work of the Maggid of Mezeritch.[100] In this construct, the human mind is mapped onto the emanation system of the divine; is organized as the sefirotic tree, the diagram that represents this circulation of potencies; and is invested with mystical and cosmological valence. "Without any cessation, it is constantly giving [vitality] to what is below it and receiving influx from that which is above it, like the blink of an eye, instantaneously," the Maggid explains. "This cannot be grasped. For example, the letters of thought [i.e., the Sefirah of *Binah*] flow without interruption from *qadmut ha-sekhel*, meaning *Ḥokhmah*."[101] In the kabbalistic tree, *Keter* (the crown, the realm of the divine) is linked to *Ḥokhmah* (wisdom), which connects to *Binah* (understanding). Hence the Maggid claims, "Understanding is in the heart, because it receives it [this understanding] from higher levels through the unconscious" [*mi-qadmut ha-sekhel*: literally, from the beginning or depths of consciousness]."[102] The unconscious is thus a point of contact with the primordial intellect, which can be accessed through meditation and the will of the soul—that is, through greater inwardness, where the divine reveals itself. The unconscious, as a vessel for divine emanations, is thus a dynamic process.

Additionally, the heart and the unconscious are an instance of the isomorphism between the human and the divine realms, and part of the kabbalistic tradition.[103] The unconscious is a point of passage between these realms. Such a reading and the multiple passages in the teachings of the Maggid collected in *Or ha-Emet* echo Rivka Schatz-Uffenheimer's assessment: "It is astounding to what extent the boundaries between the discussion of Divine thought on the transcendent plane and the psychological discussion are blurred."[104] In this construct, divine emanations reflect the self-unfolding, self-revealing God, and the unconscious is a place where one can cleave to the divine through the nullification of speech and thought that takes place in states of meditation, for which outer forces seem irrelevant.[105]

Yet Scholem resisted Marcus's views and dismissed the similarities that Marcus had sensed between the unconscious and the Hasidic concept of *kadmut ha sekhel*—the beginning of awareness—as far-fetched. Another point of overinterpretation, in Scholem's mind, is Marcus's reading of *Or ha-Hayim* (*Light of the Life*), the biblical commentary by the eighteenth-century Moroccan-born rabbi, talmudist, and kabbalist Haim ibn Attar (1696–1743). Ibn Attar is the rare Sephardi author who was widely read and revered in the Hasidic world and whose commentaries exerted a significant influence in the circles of the Maggid.[106] Marcus also read the importance of the soul into texts whose usual interpretations seemed to have little purchase for it, notably in his interpretation of the Creation story and of Genesis 2:2.

> God created the soul [*nefesh*] of the world on the Sabbath day. This is the deeper meaning of the verse: "And on the seventh day He rested [*shavat*] and infused [*va-yinafash*]." From this the Sages taught that the additional soul mourns when the Sabbath departs [*b. Beitza* 16a] but theirs is only a homiletical interpretation ... the plain-sense of the verse is that ... "and infused" refers to "God's vital effluence pouring into all created beings" since before Shabbat everything lacked a soul.[107]

Va-yinafash here is not a reflexive moment following the completion of a task.[108] Nor does it show God desisting from formative work or taking a refreshing pause. Marcus's construct is closer to the commentary of Samson Raphael Hirsch (who was, like him, a student of Isaac Bernays), according to whom God's *vayinafash* means that he withdraws into his own essence. Thus, since all human beings possess a *nefesh* (the Hebrew term for an animal life force that he translates as *Seele*, soul), *vayinafash* means to withdraw into one's own soul.[109]

In his depiction of the unconscious, Marcus quotes the following passage as evidence of a prefiguration of the unconscious:

> What all these modern philosophers obscurely guessed and the new researchers have found, was what the ... *Or Hahayim* of Rabbi Chaim ben Atar 1696–1743 had said. ... I will tell whoever contemplates *the interiority of the intelligence* [*Begriffsbildung*] of the intelligible that the intelligence of the intellect instructs intelligences, and by comprehending through his intelligence, he will understand that the intelligible is unintelligible.[110] And when he will understand through the awakening of oneself and not oneself, he will understand that this intelligible is understandable only through the intelligible unintelligible toward the

intellect. *Thus, through the unity of his intelligence, teach the secret of the very depths of the soul to the intelligent.*[111]

The stylistic prowess here, which borrows from the philosophy of the intellect (*sekhel*) and adds the dizzying alliterations, which Marcus calls *Wortspiele* (plays on words), captures the mystical experience, that liminal state of the unconscious. This comes after ibn Attar's musings on the death of the righteous (*parasha Aharei mot*), which he assesses in terms of incommunicability but also effacement or nullification.

> The nature of this [experience] cannot be grasped. It lies beyond intellectual comprehension and cannot be expressed in words either spoken or written. It cannot even be imagined. In order understand it even to some small degree, one must remove the Evil Inclination that is holding one back. [Growing spiritual awareness] will allow one to see the signs of the accursed Inclination, and one can then nullify it and prevent it from getting in one's way ... as this ability increases within one, one's soul will despise one's flesh and will depart back to the house of its Father.[112]

Scholem dryly questions the logic of such a deduction from the *parasha* (the Torah portion) on the death of the righteous and disputes the conclusions drawn from the reading of ibn Attar. But Marcus reframes the same questions differently in his 1905 monograph, *Barsilai*, with the arresting subtitle *Sprache als Schrift der Psyche* (*Language as the Writing of the Psyche*). Marcus uses the same quote from the Maggid, but this time he argues that Wilhelm Wundt's *Contributions to the Theory of Sense Perception* (1862) comes to the same conclusion.[113] He quotes from Wundt and responds.

> "The first act of becoming conscious, which still falls into unconscious life, is already a final process, so that with it the law of logical development is also demonstrated for unconscious life (?).[114] It has been shown that there is not just a conscious, but also an unconscious thinking,["][115] although it translates into the conscious life, the psychic processes of perception take the form of the conclusion. Therefore the unconscious logical processes carry themselves out with so much certainty and steadiness. Our soul is so happily laid out that it prepares the most important foundations of knowledge for us, while we have no idea of this work. This unconscious soul stands there like a strange creature, which creates for us in order to throw the ripe fruit into our lap.[116]

This depiction of the unconscious, in which human agency is overpowered by an unidentified creature, undoubtedly carries echoes of the demonic that fascinated Scholem and drew him to the study of Kabbalah. However, he did not venture in this direction here. His reluctance to use psychoanalytical categories might be explained by his distaste for the "amateurish character of psychological research into the History of Religion, especially of both the Freudian and the Jungian branch... caused by the lack of philological basis for their contentions" that he witnessed and lamented.[117]

Subsequent scholarship, especially that of the Jungian psychoanalyst Siegmund Hurwitz (1904–1994) in "Psychological Aspects in Early Hasidic Literature," would follow Ahron Marcus's lead in this, but also take issue with his characterization of the legacy of the Maggid. Trained by Carl Jung, Hurwitz was a member of the psychoanalytic school of Zürich. He brought together Jungian analysis and Hasidism and wrote a few monographs on the intersection between Jewish lore or mysticism and analytical psychology.[118] Like Scholem, Hurwitz downplayed the parallel between the concept of *qadmut ha-sekhel* and the unconscious, arguing that no other student had pursued—at least fully—that aspect of the Maggid's thought, so Marcus probably had been exaggerating it.[119] The fact that it had no real enduring quality in Hasidic literature could be disproved, however, by the example of one early disciple of the Maggid, Rabbi Baruch of Kosov. In *Yesod Ha-Emunah* (*The Foundation of Wisdom*), Baruch identifies the *sefira hokhmah* with human wisdom—one of the ten sefirot of the human soul that possesses its own sefirot—as reflections of the divine, making these sefirot both apart from and a part of the cosmic ones. But he turns this into an expression of the hylic intellect—that is to say, he reduces it to the concept of potential intellect, thereby reintroducing Maimonides's categories and dispensing with the innovations of the Maggid.[120] Whether the specific identification between qadmut ha-sekhel with the unconscious is inflated, the interest in the workings of the mind remained present in the work of the Maggid's son, Avraham ha Malakh, who expands on the dialogue between Kabbalah and the mind in his commentary on the Torah, *Hesed le-Avraham*. According to both men, the Godhead is the source of thought, a hidden life within the life of man; but there is no real continuation of the concept of qadmut ha-sekhel, which Marcus had interpreted as the unconscious.[121]

The apology for Hasidism as a foreshadowing of the discovery of the unconscious aimed to dismiss the accusations of obscurantism leveled at it by the *maskilim* (proponents of the Jewish Enlightenment) and the

Wissenschaft des Judentums. Scholarly demonstrations of its intuitive grasp of a complex concept showed the necessity for a greater understanding of Hasidism and the acknowledgment that its system of thought and representation called for engagement with it rather than condemnation. Notably, Marcus neglected to address an important aspect of the Maggid's thought, which could be understood as an irruption of the unconscious, along with the work suggested by the Maggid to restrict the possible impact of this on devotional life. The practices that he instituted and that acknowledge the inner workings of the human mind are called *ha'ala'at mahshavot zarot*—the raising of strange thoughts. They became a focus of early Hasidic thinking.

These uninvited thoughts, including libidinal ones, likely to perturb prayers, must be raised up to the Creator: even lust can—and ought to—be understood and restored to the love of God.[122] The Maggid did not downplay the disruptive nature of these thoughts, and he went so far as to compare them to transgressing shabbat. Yet, given the accusations of lewdness traditionally leveled at Hasidim, it might be the case that Marcus abstained from such mentions—even if they belong to a theological construct that exposes a symptom in order to cure it—because they might have lent themselves to highlighting the antinomian character of Hasidism. His mention of eroticism pertains to the "labyrinth of errors and the erotic abyss," which he attributes to Gnosticism.[123] This prudish rejection of eroticism also indicates how the Jewish pre-Freudian conception of the unconscious as presented by Marcus and a new generation, including thinkers such as the lesser-known Samuel Alexandrov and the towering Martin Buber, was turned into an exercise aimed at establishing the respectability of the Jewish sect and of Judaism more broadly.[124]

Though treading a fine apologetic line, Marcus's thinking illustrates a new ethos that affirmed the primacy of Judaism as foreshadowing scientific discoveries. It is a corroboration, an inversion of epistemological legitimacy by which the authoritative sources—of philosophy or psychology—are said to derive from Jewish sources.

In light of the discredit Hasidism suffered among the educated public, the impetus for drawing these corroborations grew even greater for proponents of a more nuanced approach to its practices and beliefs. Another figure to weigh in was the rabbi, mystic, and philosopher Samuel Alexandrov (1865–1941), who was eager to foster a cultural and spiritual renewal of Judaism that would bolster religious practice by demonstrating its relevance.¹²⁵ Like many of the figures in this study, Alexandrov defied categories, chief among them the divide between the secular and the religious: he sought to expand the boundaries of Judaism and advocated for a dialogue between Judaism and neighboring cultures, including Christianity, while claiming its universal mission.¹²⁶ He was trained at the prestigious Volozhin Yeshiva in the Russian Empire (now Belarus) but was also self-taught in European philosophy. Though he never became a pulpit rabbi, he was a sought-after Torah teacher who sustained himself mostly thanks to support from his wife's family and, beginning in his forties, by working as a bank clerk. Beyond his circle of students, Alexandrov conveyed his views as a literary critic after becoming a contributor in the 1890s to the prestigious *Hamagid*, the first weekly Hebrew-language newspaper (it had been founded in Lyck, East Prussia, two decades earlier and by the 1890s had become a daily), which circulated across the Jewish world. One of his most prominent interlocutors was Rav Kook, who would go on to become the first rabbi of Mandatory Palestine and an advocate of a complex Jewish universalism.

Baruch Spinoza, Friedrich Schelling (whom Alexandrov dubbed "the father of modern philosophy"), and Nachman Krochmal ranked among Alexandrov's main philosophical influences, in addition to his contemporary, the Orthodox theologian and polemicist Vladimir Solovyov (1853–1900). Solovyov was a staunch defender of Jews in an increasingly anti-Semitic Russia. He formulated a syncretic religious philosophy called sophiology (bringing together Hellenistic philosophy, Kabbalah, and Christian Gnosticism) and emphasized the concept of *sobornost* (organicity or the spontaneous integration of disparate elements).¹²⁷ Solovyov thus articulated a spiritual monism that resonated with Alexandrov's worldview and the intimate connection he saw between philosophy and religion.

In *Mikhtevei Meḥqar u- Viqqoret* (*Letters on Research and Criticism*), Alexandrov draws on Fabius Mieses's analysis of the proximity between Habad and Schelling (discussed in chapter 2), claiming that Schelling's source was the "Habad masters and the kabbalists, and even if we presume that the source for the foundations of the wisdom of the Kabbalah is in the words of the ancient Gnostics, nevertheless it appears that *these images circulate in the human species without dependence on place and time*."¹²⁸ Alexandrov thus shows his cognizance of the scholarship that conflated Kabbalah and Gnosticism but deflects the criticism out of hand while professing that Habad Hasidism was the source of modern philosophy.¹²⁹ In doing so, he gestures toward Giovanni Battista Vico's poetic universals and archetypes, untethered to temporality and geography, or rather returning to a primordial characteristic of humanity, an atemporal, intuitive self-knowledge that was only diminished in history. The rest of the text explains as follows:

> No wonder that the foundations of the scholars of the new philosophy, which originated in the ancient human mind, are found even in the words of the *Tannaim*. Of course, in and of itself, not all wisdoms and not all imaginations are equal, because such things were not said only about investigations that are beyond nature or the wisdom of the soul whose foundations depend on man's self-understanding—indeed, from the day man began to shake off his slumber, he began to know himself. . . . In the same way that the ancient man, born of nature, could have pitted himself against the self-knowledge of the present man, I will say that that man, in his innocence, was able to know himself more than the present man, who has already distanced himself a bit from his innocence and soul.[130]

In other instances, Alexandrov specifically calls Kabbalah a primitive and intuitive knowledge.[131] Such a reading ushered in the notion of Hasidism as a form of intuition, or unmediated insights into the human psyche—the metaphysics of intuition soon to be taken up by Henri Bergson, whom Alexandrov also cited. These intellectual exchanges also help us reassess the boundaries between Hasidic theology and the wider world.

Alexandrov's monism, combined with dialectics inspired by Krochmal, enabled him to make sense of the early years of the Soviet Union by establishing a dialectical affinity between Judaism and Marxist materialism, even claiming that Marxism, as a form of monism, would lead to a welcome rupture with Christian dualism, shape minds, and pave the way for a world in which unnecessary binaries would be abolished.[132] In spite of the regime's persecutions, he maintained a steady correspondence with fellow rabbis.[133] In his construct, modern philosophy and politics were not in opposition to Judaism but offered a means of strengthening it by emphasizing the quality of its intuitions and its relevance. Alexandrov was murdered by the Nazis when they invaded his town of Bobruisk, Belarus, in 1941.

Although Gershom Scholem ignored or dismissed his predecessors, this new approach to Hasidism as a source of insights into philosophy or psychology is reflected in the words of his *Major Trends in Jewish Mysticism* (quoted in the preceding section) regarding the precision of this "mystical psychology."[134] Indeed, Hasidism neutralizes the messianic element by turning its emphasis on the collective back onto the individual. Herein lies the paradox: by focusing on the individual, the depoliticization of mysticism as a collective phenomenon lends itself to being political. If theosophy was now understood to mirror the individual and not the community, this theological shift nevertheless emerged from a mass movement. Depending on the observer, the relationship between the individual and the collective could be hailed as a reconciliation or as a contradiction.

Ahron Marcus strove to show that Hasidism has an intuitive grasp on philosophical and moral concepts and thus refashioned the perception of the sect. Soon it was popularized by Martin Buber, who praised both its mythical and its ethical aspects. This in turn ushered in the emphasis on psychological insights in Hasidic literature. These tendencies were radicalized by Buber, with whom Scholem shared his view of Hasidism as cultural criticism but from whom he diverged on its essence. Scholem accused Buber of eschewing historical accuracy in favor of strategically mythical misreadings. This Buberian psycho-mythical approach was amplified by the analyst and scholar Erich Neumann, informed by Jungian therapy, constituting an ironic turn in light of Buber's disagreement with Jung's representations of the self.

Buber, Jung, and the Twentieth-Century Abyss

Martin Buber's groundbreaking and influential book *Ich und Du* (*I and Thou*, 1923), introducing his I-Thou philosophy, makes relationality central in the human as well as the divine experience of the world. These experiences are predicated on the possibility of a dialogue with the non-I, the existence of which he first deciphered in the relationship between the human and the abyss, an ultimate Thou present in Hasidic literature.

In 1904, Buber (1878–1965) completed his dissertation on the principle of individuation in the works of Nicholas of Cusa and Jacob Boehme. Under the auspices of his advisor Wilhelm Dilthey, he examined how these "two founders of the more recent metaphysical individualism" could illuminate modern conceptions of personality.[135] Buber also looked to Ralph Waldo Emerson for ways of anchoring the individuation process within a communal framework.[136] That same year, he wrote that he had "begun collecting material for a book on the Jewish soul which shall provide a survey of the Jewish folk psyche [*Volkspsyche*]."[137] As a student of Georg Simmel, Buber must have been familiar with the writings of Moritz Lazarus and Heymann Steinthal.[138] Their dual endeavor of documenting a *Volksgeist* and establishing Jewish ethics resonates in his coinage of the notion of *interhuman* (*das Zwischenmenschliche*). The term *interhuman* conveys the ontological nature of sociology as it derives from *Völkerpsychologie*—it is based on communities, *Gemeinschaft*, not simply exchange-based individual relations.[139] The advent of a new community, based on dialogue, could happen through the novel understanding of mysticism he was able to propose by reading Boehme and the Baal Shem Tov together.[140]

Two years after completing his doctorate Buber published *Die Geschichten des Rabbi Nachman* (*Tales of Rabbi Nachman*, 1906). He prefaced the book with two short essays: a biography of Rabbi Nachman, the founder of the Hasidic dynasty of Braslov (now in Ukraine), and an introduction to Jewish mysticism.[141] In 1908, he published *Die Legende des Baal-Schem* (*The Legends of the Baal-Shem*), in which the motif of the abyss figures prominently. It's especially important in "Die Offenbarung" ("The Revelation"), an essay about Israel ben Eliezer's revealed path as both a *baal shem* ("master of the name," a healer whose cures are based on the secret knowledge of the ineffable names of God) and a *tsadik*, centralizing the link between mysticism and the mind in his theology.[142] This piece captures the convergence of the Hasidic tradition, of which Buber would become an exponent and popularizer, and the German mystic and idealist philosophy whose Jewish contribution the prior generation had started retrieving. The following passage from "The Revelation" illustrates the nature of the abyss as a broader metaphor for how the workings of the mind of the rabbi are connected to the universe:

> While the rabbi spoke thus to himself, he shut his eyes for happiness. But when he opened them, the first thing that he saw was the sinking downward of an enormous veil. Then the world lay before him like an abyss. Out of the abyss emerged the solar disk in silent torment. In agonized birth pangs the earth brought forth trees and plants without number, and many animals ran and flew in senseless motion. Each creature suffered because it must do what it did, could not get free, and gasped in its pain. All things were enveloped by the abyss, and yet the whole abyss was between each thing and the other. None could cross over to the other, indeed none could see the other, for the abyss was between them.[143]

With one exception, the German term Buber chooses to render as "the abyss" across these collections of stories is not *Ungrund* but the more turbulent *Abgrund*, which conjures up pain and pangs in Boehme but also corresponds to the mystical concept of *ayin*, the state of nonbeing.[144] The divine self-alienation is transposed into an existential vision of human alienation, in which people are separated from one another, from nature, and from the divine—but this is a divide that can be bridged. If the Nietzschean tone and influence on Buber and his generation have been copiously and correctly noted, the articulation and echoes of Boehmian thought—its kabbalistic sources and Schellingian echoes—are paramount.[145] As we have seen in the writings of Schelling and Boehme, despite or because of this turmoil that precedes creation, God (the infinite) experiences the need and desire for the finite—this world. In addition, the abyss is not just between man and God but within and between men themselves. Human relations and the human psyche both suffer a similar disconnection from the primordial unity and need to find a way back to it.

In Buber, the abyss is mythologized and psychologized—and applied to the times and to Judaism—in the most straightforward way. In *Vom Geist des Judentums* (*Of the Spirit of Judaism*, 1916), Buber returned to the motif of the abyss (*Abgrund*) a few times, writing, "No man knows the abyss of inner dualism so well as the Jew, but neither does anyone know so well the miracle of unification, which cannot be accepted on faith but must be experienced."[146] He thus turns against modern alienation—and against the perception of Judaism as an alienating force. In fact, he goes on to show that the return to Judaism should be done by "everyone, alone and from his own depth," and they "must strive for divine freedom and unconditionality."[147]

Buber makes the abyss—the depth—into an existential experience of dissociation from which individuation can happen, based on the recognition of the need for the Other: the construct is comparable to the protocreation at work in the kabbalistic and Schellingian contraction. Since the abyss is the place of the infinite calling for the finite, it leads to the "the myth of I and You, of the caller and the called, the finite which enters into the infinite and the infinite which has need of the finite."[148]

The role and presence of the Thou imply a dialogue and a prominent role given to language: "The word is an abyss through which the speaker strides," remarks the Baal Shem Tov.[149] He thereby emphasizes the creative process of this abyss, in which the not-being is brimming with pain but also pregnant with possibility and filled by the locutors who contain the infinity of the divine within them. From this place of protoconsciousness emerges a philosophy of language and of creation as a manifestation of otherness within oneself. And if the abyss is in fact the unconscious, the motif of the abyss reveals the ethical aspect of the unconscious as a place of and for the Other within oneself. Although the abyss thus seems to represent a peril, it is in fact an opportunity in which the I demands a not-I and is expanded by it. The abyss, and thus the unconscious, establishes the necessity of I and Thou, central to Buber's philosophy of dialogue.

This use of the phrase "I and Thou" can be traced back to the eighteenth-century philosopher Friedrich Heinrich Jacobi, who criticized Immanuel Kant for replacing the self with an abstract, illusory I and professed that the recognition between two individuals, the I needing a Thou, can only happen through the presence of a transcendental God.[150] It was as an advocate of conservative values that Jacobi established this articulation in order to express a stable relationship between the individual and their environment. The I-Thou of Buber is of a different nature, part of his design for a new community: a *Gemeinschaft* that is in itself the "revolution" he called for, a place where society and mysticism meet.[151]

The imperative necessity of an awareness of the Other provided grounds for Buber to criticize Jung, who in his assessment reduced God to an aspect of the self: if God is understood to be a projection of the self, Buber held, then the divine is reduced to an abstract concept—rather than a lived presence—in the service of self-knowledge. Jung, he wrote, "proclaims the new religion, the only one which can still be true, the religion of pure psychic immanence."[152] Although this controversy extended well into the 1950s, the seeds of the disagreement were planted in the earlier writings of both authors and color their understanding of the unconscious as articulation or reflection of the religious in the psyche.

Because Jung viewed religious symbols as a collective human expression of a religious content that occurs empirically in the individual psyche, Buber claimed that the Jungian construct subsumes not just God but the Other into the self, "as contents of the individual soul that shall, just as an individual soul, attain its perfection through individuation."[153] He thus argued that this instrumentalization of the Other returns it to an I-it relation, which is the opposite of the inner nature of religiosity based on I-Thou. To this, Jung retorted,

> Analysis of the unconscious has long since demonstrated the existence of these powers in the form of archetypical images, which, be it noted, *are not identical with the corresponding intellectual concepts*. One can, of course, believe that the concepts of the conscious mind are, through the inspiration

of the Holy Ghost, direct and correct representations of their metaphysical referent. But this conviction is possible only for one who already possesses the gift of faith. . . . I have merely expressed an opinion about something that can be experienced, that is, about one of the very palpable "powers of the unconscious." These powers are numinous "types"—unconscious contents, processes, and dynamisms—and such types are, if one may so express it, immanent-transcendent. Since my sole means of cognition is experience I may not overstep its boundaries, and cannot therefore pretend to myself that my description coincides with the portrait of a real metaphysical archangel. What I have described is a psychic factor only, but one which exerts a considerable influence on the conscious mind. Thanks to its autonomy, it forms the counterposition to the subjective ego because it is a piece of the *objective psyche*. It can therefore be designated as a "Thou."[154]

He thus framed the I-Thou dialogue as between the unconscious and the objective psyche.

Buber rejected this argument on a phenomenological basis, highlighting the divide between the man of faith and the philosopher.

Neither psychology nor any other science is competent to investigate the truth of the belief in God. It is the right of their representatives to keep aloof; it is not, within their disciplines, their right to make judgments about the belief in God as about something which they know. The psychological doctrine which deals with mysteries without knowing the attitude of faith towards mystery is the modern manifestation of Gnosis. Gnosis is not to be understood as only a historical category, but as a universal one.[155]

By shifting the definition of Gnosis to identify it as a concept rather than a fact, Buber also subtly accused Jung of a double Gnosticism—an ignorance of the true meaning of the existential notion of faith in addition to the assumption of an absence of God.

Certain strands of mysticism, Buber asserted, could be plagued with solipsism. But rather than read Hasidism as a solipsistic soliloquy, which would create the false dialogue for which he faulted Jung, the sect's teachings must be marshaled and read anew as an invitation to dialogue—insofar as it recognizes the Other, which the unconscious came to represent.[156] Buber needed the Boehmian-Schellingian triangulation to give Jewish mysticism its mythopoetic dimension—even at the expense of the absolutizing lamented by Gershom Scholem.[157]

Toward the end of his life, Buber also expressed misgivings about what he called

> the psychologizing of God and the psychic effusiveness of the egotist who has cut himself off from the totality of the actual world[.] I find [these] noteworthy only as spectacles, as a dance on a tightrope between two cliffs. . . . To make the human element absolute means to tear it out of life's totality, out of reality; and if I have at any time contributed to this "absolutizing"—so far as I know, unintentionally—I now feel duty-bound to point out all the more emphatically the dimensions of reality.[158]

Martin Buber's remorse—stemming from the theologization of psychology in order to create an absolute self and distance it from the concreteness of human experience—seemed to have found an echo and a resolution in the work of Erich Neumann (1905–1960). A Berlin-born psychoanalyst who immigrated to Palestine in 1934 after training with Jung, Neumann sought to reconcile Buber's and Jung's thinking in the second volume of his *Roots of Jewish Consciousness*, dedicated to Hasidism.[159] His books *The Great Mother* and *Depth Psychology and the New Ethics* are central texts in the corpus of the Jungian school. They focus on the question of ethics, which was not a central concern of Carl Jung himself, but which Neumann tried to establish as a mainstay of Jungian-based psychology—the recognition of individuation as part of a larger, collective self. With the limitations that came from relying mainly on Buber's translations and his writings on Hasidism, Neumann asserted that Hasidism can be a means to achieve both psychological and spiritual wholeness—a wholeness which—in Neumann's work, unlike that of Scholem and Buber—meant that the scope and significance of its symbolism expanded to the feminine.

Despite this positive view, in the final chapter of *The Roots of Jewish Consciousness*, "Hasidism and the Birth of the Modern Jew," Neumann offers a harsh critique: "Hasidism was also ruined because its self-awareness was not radical enough, and it knew too little about the real message that it brought."[160] The sentence is striking—it reeks of Orientalism or of the *Wissenschaft des Judentums*. While acknowledging Hasidism's contribution, it still contains language about Hasidism exhibiting a lack of understanding of its own merits and insights, and its need for an exponent capable of translating the message for both the Hasidic community and the wider world. Neumann also laments a broader phenomenon of amnesia that would negatively impact the world. If Hasidism, or Judaism in its entirety, ceased to remember its own tradition, he maintains, "the memory loss extends to the entire layer of the collective unconscious."[161] Here a tension is palpable: if the memory loss affects the unconscious, it follows that the collective unconscious is made up of the sum total of conscious traditions, which does not accord with the Jungian unconscious—it more closely resembles Lazarus and Steinthal's condensation process.[162] But Neumann's anxiety about the disappearance of a whole world probably accounts for the lack of rigor in the categories he used.

The text was not published. Its completion in 1945 coincided with the discovery of the magnitude of the Holocaust and questioned the very possibility of the reflection on evil—especially evil folded into goodness—as part of Hasidic theology. In the wake of the First World War, Sigmund Freud's *Civilization and Its Discontents* centered the death drive in a way that resonated with the world's trauma. The death drive of the clinical, Freudian unconscious was characterized by what Jacques Lacan called its "impediment, failure, split."[163] This construct seemed more apt to capture reality than the pre-Freudian, philosophical, myth-based, metaphysical, and somehow positivist unconscious, with its progressive revelation and divinely inspired human progress. In Jewish thought, strategies for assimilation in the interwar period had already taken on a more disruptive, messianic turn. The abyss, then, was the abyss of Gnosticism—of a God that had estranged himself and veiled his face. After the Second World War, the contraction of God, the *tsimtsum*, would become, in Buber's expression, the eclipse of God—a metaphor not for creation but for destruction, of which our collective unconscious would have to bear the traces.

Coda

In nineteenth-century Jewish thought, the unconscious served to unveil Judaism's subterranean presence within systems of thought that did not acknowledge its significance. It also served to validate Judaism's insights—especially those of Kabbalah—into the human psyche. Studying it presents an invitation to ponder the many, and often hidden, cross-pollinations between Kabbalah and our systems of representation, such as language or myth, about which the unconscious has become a discourse. Just as the unconscious became a legitimate object of knowledge and of conversation over the course of the long nineteenth century, so did Kabbalah. This was a turning point for Jewish philosophy, which could now rely on kabbalistic tropes and reclaim them. It was also a turning point for Orthodox circles, where psychology as a validation of Jewish insights continues to play itself out in the works of the influential Shimon Gershon Rosenberg (1948–2006), known in Israel as Rav Shagar, who turned to Jacques Lacan and postmodern theory as a validation of the tenets of his faith, especially with regard to Lacan's theory of the Real as a locus of the coincidence of opposites—thus revisiting the kabbalistic concept and positing the unknown that exists at the limit of our symbolic universe and the constant tension with it.[1]

This book has explored the modalities and rationales for claiming a Jewish imprint on the discourse of the unconscious, including metaphysical overtones and their overcoming, in the era before Sigmund Freud became, in the words of W. H. Auden, "no more a person now but a whole climate of opinion."[2] Freud's unconscious undoubtedly signaled a new turn. Instead of the Schellingian unconscious modeled after the *tsimtsum* and thus an initial retraction, Freud's unconscious was one of repression.[3]

In many ways, however, the Freudian, Viennese, individual unconscious, where traces of mysticism have been ostensibly effaced, supplanted a German, collective unconscious born out of kabbalistic tropes made visible by a generation eager to reclaim this tradition. The continuity between these two constructs is beyond the scope of this study.[4] One may wonder, however, if the pre-Freudian Jewish unconscious could be an instance of the "paleonomy" described by Jacques Derrida, in which "strategic necessity . . . requires the occasional maintenance of an old name in order to launch a new concept"—especially in light of Freud's skepticism about the prior emphasis on philosophy and mysticism.[5] Yet what links the two can be elicited from the words of Marcel Proust (1871–1922) for an interview given in 1913 before the release of *Swann's Way*, the first volume of *In Search of Lost Time*, in which the novelist called his work "an attempt at a series of 'Novels on the Unconscious.'" He added, "In every epoch, literature has tried to attach itself—after the fact, naturally—to the reigning philosophy."[6]

In many instances, as we have seen, this was also the case for the proponents of Jewish thought, who attached it to the philosophical unconscious. I have called this the retrospective unconscious as a way to describe affirmative apologetics for Judaism, especially Hasidism. What this tendency also signaled is that the therapeutic or metaphysical search for time and wholeness through literature and memory was mirrored in the search for wholeness in religion. And it indicated that the unconscious had become its locus: that search for wholeness engages the enigma of the Other and the self—and seeks to alleviate the feeling of alienation, acutely felt by Jewish thinkers both in their individuality and as part of a community on the margins.

The relationship of Jewish thought to the pre-Freudian unconscious can be seen as a case study of a minority group mobilizing a new scientific paradigm in order to modify both its perception and self-perception, and advance its participation in the polity; such an instrumentalization of the unconscious happened, as we have seen, in the second half of the nineteenth century.[7] The increasing transposition of the psyche into politics and activism also can be surmised in the use of the term *double consciousness* by W. E. B. Du Bois. From the 1820s and until the late 1870s, *double consciousness* meant double personality; the concept appeared in Ralph Waldo Emerson's *The Transcendentalist* (1842), where he wrote about the split between our reflective self, in the realm of ideas, and our active self, in the here and now: "The worst feature of this double consciousness is that the two lives, of the understanding and of the soul, which we lead, really show very little relation to each other."[8] In his memoir, *Dusk of Dawn*, Du Bois acknowledges,

> The meaning and implications of the new psychology had begun slowly to penetrate my thought. My own study of psychology under William James had pre-dated the Freudian era, but it had prepared me for it. I now began to realize that in the fight against race prejudice, we were not facing simply the rational, conscious determination of white folk to oppress us; we were facing age-long complexes sunk now largely to unconscious habit and irrational urge, which demanded on our part not only the patience to wait, but the power to entrench ourselves for a long siege against the strongholds of color caste.[9]

Striving to make the majority group aware of the subsurface influences shaping its representations results in fracturing its dominant narratives, and the unconscious thus played an ideological and a political role. But the recognition of similar processes, specifically of a double consciousness for racially oppressed minority groups beyond Judaism, went mostly ignored by the generation of Jews at the beginning of the twentieth century, even those who professed the need for cultural pluralism in the United States.[10] The exploration of other models of self-assertion and affirmative apologetics deserves further scrutiny. Indeed, the pre-Freudian unconscious seemed better suited to an exploration of otherness, as it tried to articulate a place of not-I in the I, whereas in Freudian theory, this unconscious seemed to make little space for models of otherness, of the feminine or the non-Western.[11] This a key aspect of the critique of Freudian theory, and this is also why the other unconscious and the theories of the unconscious before Freud are worth revisiting.[12]

The uses of pre-Freudian stances on the unconscious by Jewish thinkers undoubtedly raise a question familiar to modern Jewish thought: how to proclaim the particularism and universalism of the unconscious at the same time. They also raise further questions—while offering opportunities—about the mere possibility of going beyond traditional models of belonging and of creating other bonds through the promotion of a universal unconscious. There are questions, too, about the exportation of psychology, and of its role in emancipation narratives and strategies that rely on the affirmation of particularism, which could extend beyond the Jewish instance, as shown in the work of W. E. B. Du Bois.

It is thus worth revisiting the legacy of these nineteenth-century Jewish thinkers who understood the potential of the concept of the unconscious as they reached toward emancipation by highlighting the notion's textual and cultural beginnings in their own tradition. Trying to return the unconscious, a rhizomic concept, to its roots might have been an impossible task, but their gesture and their quest for emancipation bespoke the urgency of finding a place to exist, even on the edge of the abyss.

Acknowledgments

This project began as a talk I gave while a postgraduate fellow at the Katz Center of the University of Pennsylvania. I am grateful to its director, Steve Weitzman, and to all the fellows from the *Wissenschaft des Judentums* year for helping me lay the groundwork for the book.

My colleagues at Columbia's Department of Religion and at the Institute for Israel and Jewish Studies have been an invaluable source of support throughout the writing of the manuscript, a process that overlapped with my path to tenure. I also had the good fortune of becoming acquainted with the faculty at the University of Michigan's Frankel Center; I deeply appreciate the illuminating insights they shared on my work as well as their kindness.

Sections of several chapters were published earlier; each of these has been substantially revised for inclusion here. Part of chapter 3 appeared in "From *Wissenschaft des Judentums* to *Geisteswissenschaft*: Early Kabbalah Scholarship and the Construction of the Unconscious," *Journal of Religion* 99, no. 3 (2019): 288–311. Some of chapter 4 is included in "The Abyss, the Oversoul, and the Kabbalistic Overtones in Emerson's Work: Tracing the Pre-Freudian Unconscious in America," in *Kabbalah in America: Ancient Lore in the New World*, ed. Brian Ogren, Studies in Jewish History and Culture, 64 (Leiden: Brill, 2020), 51–71. A section of chapter 8 was featured in "Abraham Unbound: The Prefiguration of the Unconscious in the First Generation of the Musar and Hasidic Movements," in "Mysticism, Pietism, Morality," ed. Patrick Koch, special issue, *European Journal of Jewish Studies* 14, no. 2 (2020): 334–54.

I am thankful to Dov Weiss for encouraging me to submit the article to *JOR*, as well as to Brian Ogren for convening the "Kabbalah in America" conference at Rice University and for his meticulous editing of the resulting volume. I also appreciate the helpful comments provided by the other conference participants. My thanks as well to Patrick Koch, who invited me to be a contributor to the special issue of the *EJJS*.

Once again, this book owes an immense debt of gratitude to Paul Sager, who reined in some of the manuscript's most egregious instances of free association and whose edits are unfailingly sharp and thoughtful.

I am profoundly grateful to Kyle Wagner of the University of Chicago Press for believing in this project from the outset and for his vision for the book. I'd like to thank my team at the press for so diligently shepherding it to publication: Kristin Rawlings and Nathan Petrie, along with Stephen Twilley, who oversaw the copyediting, and Sandra Hazel, whose edits were insightful. The anonymous reviewers of the manuscript provided thought-provoking feedback.

As always, I have been privileged to be able to count on the generous support of Elliot Wolfson. Elli Stern and Shaul Magid have likewise been formidable supporters through the years, and my conversations with Chloe Aridjis, Devorah Baum, Nathaniel Berman, Pierre-Emmanuel Dauzat, Yoni Garb, Sam Glauber-Zimra, Moshe Halbertal, Ruth Kara-Kaniel Ivanov, George Yaakov Kohler, Hartley Lachter, Ariel Mayse, Elly Moseson, George Prochnik, Ruby Namdar, Katalina Rac, Tom Reiss, Zalman Rothschild, Simon Schama, and Tsachi Slater have enriched both my thinking and my writing.

"When you gaze long into the abyss, the abyss gazes back at you." So observed Nietzsche in *Beyond Good and Evil*. This book is for my loved ones and for those who gaze into the abyss.

Notes

Unless otherwise noted, all translations are mine.

Introduction

1. Freud, *The Interpretation of Dreams*, 4:54.
2. The eighteenth-century Scottish philosopher Henry Home (1696–1782) coined the English adjective *unconscious* in the phrase "being quite unconscious of the impression." Home, *Essays on the Principles of Morality*, 210. In 1776, Ernst Platner coined the German noun *Unbewusstsein*, spelled at the time as *Unbewusstseyn* (unconsciousness), in *Philosophische Aphorismen*, § 141, p. 86. But this was hardly seen as a paradigm shift, as Lancelot Whyte observes in *The Unconscious before Freud*. The theoretical framework of the concept itself can be traced back to Gottfried Wilhelm Leibniz's "petites perceptions." See Leibniz, *New Essays on Human Understanding*, 54. For the prehistory of the concept before Schelling, see chapter 1.
3. Beyond the autobiographical elements, studies that have been devoted to Freud's Judaism include Grollman, *Judaism in Sigmund Freud's World*; Bakan, *Sigmund Freud and the Jewish Mystical Tradition*; Klein, *The Jewish Origins of the Psychoanalytic Movement*. In a more recent article, Gilad Sharvit tried to foreground the Oedipus complex in Jewish mysticism, the motives of which Freud would have been made aware by way of Schelling. See Sharvit, "Luria, Schelling, and Freud."
4. Jonathan Garb's *Yearnings of the Soul* is a compelling analysis of the metamorphoses of the concept of the soul in the development of psychology, but it has a broader focus and does not precisely center on the pre-Freudian unconscious. In contrast, my project aims at a granular survey of the cultural, intellectual, and political landscape in which the dialogue between the Jewish and the non-Jewish world preceding the psychoanalytic paradigm took place.
5. I adopt here the historians' term *long nineteenth century*, which stretches the century to the end of the First World War. This is not because of the dual revolution (industrial and political) described by Eric Hobsbawm, but because Freud's theories did not resonate beyond certain circles—even in Jewish thought—until after the war. See Blackbourn, *The Long Nineteenth Century*; Hobsbawm, *The Age of Revolution*.

6. Whyte, *The Unconscious before Freud*; Ellenberger, *The Discovery of the Unconscious*; Henry, *Généalogies de la psychanalyse*; Hemecker, *Vor Freud*; Gödde, *Traditionslinien des Unbewussten*; Mills, ed., *Rereading Freud*; Völmicke, *Das Unbewusste im Deutschen Idealismus*; Nicholls and Liebscher, eds., *Thinking the Unconscious*. See also, for a focus on Schelling, Arens, *Structures of Knowing*; McGrath, *The Dark Ground of Spirit*; Ffytche, *The Foundations of the Unconscious*; Fenichel, *Schelling, Freud, and the Philosophical Foundations of Psychoanalysis*.
7. Kolakowski, *La philosophie positiviste*; Steinmetz, *The Politics of Method in Human Sciences*.
8. On the concept of progressive revelation, which emerged in the nineteenth century in order to reconcile science and faith, see Solomon, *Torah from Heaven*, 212–14. See also the work of Elia Benamozegh, specifically his *Teologia dogmatica e apologetica*, 271.
9. Fechner, *Elemente der Psychophysik*, 2:438.
10. Janet, *Principes de métaphysique et de psychologie*.
11. "The theory of dreams has remained what is most characteristic and peculiar about the young science, something to which there is no counterpart in the rest of our knowledge, a stretch of new country, which has been reclaimed from popular beliefs and mysticism." Freud, *New Introductory Lectures* (1933), 22:6. Despite claiming the mantle of science, Freud nevertheless chose to use *Seele* (soul) rather than *Geist* (spirit, mind) in order to describe what is routinely translated as "the mind," because *Geist* conveyed too clearly a notion of consciousness. Bruno Bettelheim notes this choice in *Freud and Man's Soul*, 77.
12. Lipps, *Grundtatsachen des Seelenlebens*. An influence on Freud, Theodor Lipps remains known for being a popularizer of the notion of empathy, *Einfühlung*.
13. "The concept of the unconscious in psychology . . . is neither hypothetical, nor mystical, it is the expression of established facts. I can add that it includes in itself the renunciation of metaphysical suppositions in psychology, and consequently the adherence to the psychological point of view of observation and the humble recognition that one cannot know everything." Lipps, "Der Begriff des Unbewussten," 12.
14. Jonte-Pace and Parson, *Religion and Psychology*; Parson, *The Enigma of the Oceanic Feeling*.
15. Histories of the reception of the idea of the unconscious (and other psychological concepts) by other religious communities have been written for a later period—the Freudian moment. See, for instance, Desmazières, *Comment les Catholiques ont reçu la psychanalyse*; Tyler, *The Pursuit of the Soul*; El Shakry, *The Arabic Freud*.
16. Thirty years earlier, the lesser-known philosopher Albert Lewkowitz did offer an overview of the cross-pollination between Judaism and the spiritual currents of the nineteenth century. A rabbi and philosopher, Lewkowitz (1883–1954) taught at the Breslau seminary until its closure in 1938 and was invested in the academic study of Judaism. Coming on the heels of two volumes on the Renaissance and the Enlightenment, his overview of the interrelations between German philosophy and Jewish thought came out in 1935, a time when the symbiosis between Jewish and German cultures was all but disrupted. Salo Baron, the towering figure of modern Jewish history who was adverse to a "lachrymose" narrative of the Jews' interaction with their environment, praised the thick volume as

"pioneering," calling it, despite some shortcomings, a "much-needed reinterpretation of the position of the Jew in the world." Baron, "Review of *Das Judentum*," 83. In his book, Lewkowitz proclaims that "like the philosophy of the Greeks, that of the nineteenth century is the self-knowledge of man," but only devotes a scant portion of the text to the impact of the later, mystical Schelling on Jewish thought. Consequently, he does not envision the Schellingian unconscious in his study. Lewkowitz, *Das Judentum*, vii. In his otherwise favorable 1936 review of the book, the Russian-born, German-trained French philosopher Jacob Gordin (1896–1947) laments the paucity of his analysis. The unfortunate result, in his view, was to obscure a whole range of figures (such as Landauer or Hirsch, featured in the present study) who focused more specifically on Kabbalah. Gordin, "La pensée juive." Nevertheless, Lewkowitz depicts the currents of nineteenth-century thought as a rich tapestry woven from both Jewish and non-Jewish threads. See Lewkowitz, *Das Judentum*, esp. 27 and 410–11.

17. Habermas, *Philosophical-Political Profiles*, 21.
18. On categories of self-assertion, see Blumenberg, *The Legitimacy of the Modern Age*, 47; Mendes-Flohr, *Divided Passions*, 77–132. See also Hecht, "Self-Assertion in the Public Sphere"; Boulouque, *Another Modernity*, chap. 15.
19. Ricœur, *Freud and Philosophy*, 4.
20. Bloom, *Kabbalah and Criticism*, 22. Regarding interpreting the unconscious in a "Jewish key," see the related notion of a "Jewish twist" in Schwarzschild, "An Agenda for Jewish Philosophy."
21. Ricœur, *Hermeneutics and the Human Sciences*, 185.
22. Rosenzweig, *Gesammelte Schriften*, vol. 1, *Briefe sund Tagebücher*, citing entry of April 3, 1922, in vol. 2 (1918–29), 770. The concept of dissimilation has been applied to German Jewish literature, where, as Jonathan Skolnik has explained, it has been perceived as an integral accompaniment to assimilation in writing "Jewish history into German history and into new notions of universal history historical fiction, surveying expressions of literary dissimilation." Skolnik, *Jewish Pasts, German Fictions*, 67.
23. Rose, *Jewish Philosophical Politics in Germany*, 18; Heschel, *Abraham Geiger*; Hess, *Germans, Jews, and the Claims of Modernity*.
24. Rose, *Jewish Philosophical Politics in Germany*, 18.
25. Asad, *Formations of the Secular*, 26ff; the narrowing between the self and the world is what Charles C. Taylor calls the "buffered" self in modernity, in *Sources of the Self*. On the question of myth as discourse, see Lincoln, *Theorizing Myth*. I concur with Jason Josephson-Storm that the line between myth and metaphor is thin and that the work of Hans Blumenberg illuminates the discursive function of the two. See Blumenberg, *Paradigms for a Metaphorology*; Josephson-Storm, *The Myth of Disenchantment*, 31–32.
26. *The Oxford Dictionary of Jewish Religion* defines the purpose of apologetics as "a reaction against criticism, whether from hostile objective sources or from self-questioning." Berlin and Grossman, eds., *The Oxford Dictionary of Jewish Religion*, 60. Adele Berlin and Maxine Grossman find its origin in second-century-BCE Alexandria, a diasporic environment where Jews were compelled to explain themselves. Given the impact of the diasporic condition, it has been argued that Jewish thought is apologetic in essence. Jacob Gordin has further suggested that post-emancipation, the greater interaction with a non-Jewish

environment favored a return of the apology as a genre. However, because it is combined with the growing self-assertion of modernity, it seems warranted to coin the expression "*affirmative* apologetics." See Gordin, "La pensée juive," 74–75.

27. The embrace or rejection of reason based on the unconscious was an ideological marker for right-wing thinkers, as I explain in chapter 7 (see the section "An Unpatriotic Unconscious?").
28. This claim has been increasingly challenged, and rightly so. See, for instance, Josephson-Storm, *The Myth of Disenchantment*.
29. Biale, "Gershom Scholem and Anarchism." See also chapter 3 of this book.
30. On these transformations, see Garb, *A History of Kabbalah*; Weinstein, *Kabbalah and Jewish Modernity*; Huss, Pasi, and von Stuckrad, eds., *Kabbalah and Modernity*.
31. Bloom, *Kabbalah and Criticism*, 42.
32. Weiss, "*Tsimtsum* between the Bible and Philosophy."
33. Levinas, *Difficult Freedom*, especially "Separation and Absoluteness," 102–4. As Daniel Weiss notes, Emmanuel Levinas does not invoke Kabbalah here (he had a complex relationship with it) but situates the discussion of separation alongside Plotinus and Neoplatonism. The Schellingian tradition, based on *tsimtsum*, achieves the same result. Wolfson, "Secrecy, Modesty, and the Feminine."
34. Levinas, *Totality and Infinity*, 103.
35. Krell, *The Tragic Absolute*.
36. Lacan, *Le moi dans la théorie freudienne*; Lacan, *Le séminaire*, 5:18; Gorog, "L'identité est 'de l'autre.'"
37. Lacan, *Le séminaire*, 11:35.
38. Bell, *The German Tradition of Psychology*, 2. Scholars of the ancient world have reflected on the epistemological caution needed when applying psychoanalytical concepts to their subject while still claiming the importance of those concepts for textual hermeneutics.
39. Freud, "On Psychotherapy," 7:265.
40. 1952 interview with Carl Gustav Jung in Jung, *C. G. Jung Speaking*, 208.
41. Such is also Jonathan Garb's proposition regarding Kabbalah studies and psychoanalysis: "The way forward is to release our dependence on psychoanalysis, and instead bring to the forefront the indigenous psychological theories developed in the kabbalistic world that shared the modern period with psychology." Garb, *Yearnings of the Soul*, 11–12.
42. The underlying concept of the "retrospective unconscious" differs from Richard Rorty's "rational reconstructions," in which, despite their correct insights, ideas need to be restated so that they accord with current conceptions. Rorty, "The Historiography of Philosophy."
43. Bergson, *Essais et conférences*, 95–96. On the two types of unconscious, see Sitbon-Peillon, "Bergson et l'inconscient."
44. This is demonstrated by the writings of Alexander Kristianpoller (1884–1942) in his compendium on dreams and their Talmudic interpretation, finished in 1915 and published in Vienna in 1923 in the *Monumenta talmudica*, a learned and ecumenical journal. Published in German in Vienna, the study shows the importance of dreams in the Jewish tradition and not simply in the Greco-Roman world, with writers such as Artemidorus, but it makes no mention of Freud's

The Interpretation of Dreams. See the first (and only) translation (into French): Kristianpoller, *Les rêves et leur interprétation dans le Talmud.* See also Wolfson, *A Dream Interpreted within a Dream.*

45. On the reception of Freud, see Burnham, ed., *After Freud Left;* Heinze, *Jews and the American Soul;* Hale, *The Rise and Crisis of Psychoanalysis.* For the Jewish reception specifically, see Meyer, *Response to Modernity,* 314–17.
46. Joshua Liebman subsequently described his engagement with psychoanalysis in his best-selling book *Peace of Mind,* published in the immediate aftermath of the Second World War. Liebman, *Peace of Mind.* See also Heinze, "*Peace of Mind* (1946)." See as well the part entitled "Rabbi Liebman and the Psychic Pain of the World War II Generation," in Heinze, *Jews and the American Soul,* 195–239; also see Herzog, *Cold War Freud.*
47. Gay, *Freud for Historians,* esp. 144–80. See also Freud, *A Life for Our Times;* Merleau-Ponty, *La structure du comportement;* Nicolas and Fedi, *Un débat autour de l'inconscient,* 48–53.
48. The philosophical concept of the rhizome (and of its opposite, arborescence) was first formulated by Gilles Deleuze and Félix Guattari in 1980 as a way to describe the principles of connection and heterogeneity at work in their new model of culture. See Deleuze and Guattari, *A Thousand Plateaus.*
49. On this "reoccupation of positions," to borrow from Hans Blumenberg, see his *The Legitimacy of the Modern Age,* 47–51.

Introduction to Part I

1. Schelling, *The Ages of the World (1811),* 83.
2. Schelling, 122.
3. Schiller, *Das verschleierte Bild zu Sais;* Hadot, *The Veil of Isis.* See also Gombrich, "The Symbol of the Veil."
4. Ffytche, *The Foundation of the Unconscious,* 141; Feuerbach, *Thoughts on Death and Immortality.*
5. Schelling, *The Ages of the World (1811),* 141; Baczko, *Utopian Lights.*
6. Hadot, *The Veil of Isis,* 51.
7. Schelling, *Historical-Critical Introduction;* Beach, *The Potencies of God(s).* See also Dupré, "The Role of Mythology"; Marquet, "Schelling."
8. Schelling, *The Ages of the World (1811),* 83.
9. Schelling, *Die Weltalter,* 8:200. See also Schelling, *The Ages of the World (1811),* 41, which translates *mit-wissenschaft* as "participatory knowledge."
10. Dupré, *Religion and the Rise of Modern Culture;* Dupré, "The Role of Mythology."
11. Nassar, *The Romantic Absolute,* esp. 185–86; Krell, *The Tragic Absolute.*
12. Mine, *Ungrund und Mitwissenschaft.*
13. Schelling, *The Schelling Reader,* 386. See Schelling, "Philosophy of Revelation," 256.
14. Schelling, *The Ages of the World: (Fragment),* 4; Mine, *Ungrund und Mitwissenschaft.*
15. Schelling's lectures from 1821 to 1830 on mythology gesture toward myths as protorevelation: his 1841–42 lectures on the *Philosophy of Revelation* finally embraced the question of revelation itself and the liberation of human consciousness from myths in order to embrace the Absolute. See Dews, *Schelling's Late Philosophy.*

Chapter One

1. Feuerbach, *Geschichte der neueren Philosophie*, 3:177.
2. Gödde, *Traditionslinien des Unbewussten*, 27.
3. Leibniz, *New Essays on Human Understanding*, 54. See also Leibniz, *Principes de la philosophie ou Monadologie* (1714), para. 14; Coudert, *Leibniz and Kabbalah*. Another idea of Locke's that Leibniz refuted was his theory of tabula rasa, in which the human mind is a blank slate at birth.
4. Locke, *An Essay concerning Human Understanding*, 113.
5. Leibniz, *New Essays on Human Understanding*, 57.
6. "Each soul knows the infinite, knows everything, but confusedly. Just as when I am walking along the shore of the sea and hear the great noise it makes, though I hear the separate sounds of each wave of which the total sound is made up, I do not discriminate them one from another; so our confused perceptions are the result of the impressions which the whole universe makes on us." Leibniz, *Principles of Nature and Grace*, 211.
7. Leibniz, 208.
8. Leibniz, *New Essays on Human Understanding*, 173.
9. Richards, "Christian Wolff's Prolegomena"; Wolff, *Psycholologia Empirica*; Blackwell, "Christian Wolff's Doctrine of the Soul."
10. Kant, *Theoretical Philosophy*, 203–6; Leland, "Unconscious Representations in Kant's Early Writings."
11. Kant, *Anthropology from a Pragmatic Point of View*, 24.
12. Kant, 24–26.
13. Foucault, *Introduction à l'anthropologie de Kant*.
14. On Herder's reading of Spinoza, see Hampton, *Romanticism and the Re-Invention of Modern Religion*, 89–107; Lord, "Herder and Spinozistic Naturalism." On Goethe's understanding of Spinoza, see Lange, "Goethe and Spinoza."
15. Klages, *Goethe als Seelenforscher*.
16. Johann Wolfgang von Goethe, conversation with his literary assistant, Riemer, in 1805, quoted in Nicholls, "The Scientific Unconscious," 108. For Goethe, the unconscious is what enables artistic production and thus closely relates to his conception of the "daemonic"—a refuge and source of inspiration. The image of plunging into the unconscious, where our roots lie, is also noteworthy—it connotes a tree, likely to be an inverted tree, which is found in many mystical traditions, including the Bhagavad Gita and the Kabbalah—with which Goethe was familiar. Romanticism emphasizes the layers beneath or preceding consciousness—the artist, divinely inspired, has special access to it or can tap into it. On the geological aspect, see Groves, *The Geological Unconscious*.
17. Goethe, *Conversations with Eckermann*, 358, entry for Tuesday, March 8, 1831. In addition, the 1807–8 sonnet "Mächtiges Überraschen" [Mighty Surprise] provides an initial insight into the idea of the *daemonic*. Goethe explores this in his collection of autobiographical essays, *Dichtung und Wahrheit* [*Poetry and Truth*], written between 1811 and 1833. See Goethe, *The Autobiography*, 157–59. The more personal example of the daemonic is arguably the 1823 "Elegy from Marienbad," in which he defines the word. See Nicholls, "The Philosophical Concept of the Daemonic." On the broader question of the unconscious in that period, see Bishop, "The Unconscious," 39; Nicholls, "The Scientific

Unconscious," esp. 104–5; Naumann, *Philosophie und Poetik des Symbols*; Holub, "From the Pedestal to the Couch"; and Peters, "Goethe und Freud."

18. Schelling, *The Ages of the World: (Fragment)*, 4.
19. Steigerwald, "Rethinking Organic Vitality in Germany"; D'Anna et al., eds., *Morfologie del rapporto parti-tutto*; Thumiger, introduction to Thumiger, ed., *Holism in Ancient Medicine*. This holism is not to be confused with the sociological homonym, which distinguishes it from individualism. See Gellner, "Holism versus Individualism."
20. Georg Lukács laments the "disparagement of understanding and reason, an uncritical glorification of intuition, an aristocratic epistemology, the rejection of socio-historical progress, the creating of myths and so on," which "are motives we can find in virtually any irrationalism." In his view, after Hegel, modern thought had become sharply divided into the opposing tendencies of Marxist dialectics and of bourgeois "irrationalism." Lukács, *The Destruction of Reason*, 10. See also Lukács, "Schellings Irrationalismus"; Snedeker, "The Politics of Epistemology."
21. Freud mentions Schelling in the first chapter of *The Interpretation of Dreams*, marking him as a precursor (but only for his *Naturphilosophie*). He does not venture to accuse Schelling of irrationalism. "We may leave on one side pietistic and mystical writers—who, indeed, are perfectly justified in remaining in occupation of what is left of the once wide domain of the supernatural so long as that field is not conquered with scientific explanation. But apart from them, one comes across clear-headed men, without any extravagant ideas, who seek to support their religious faith in the existence and activity of superhuman spiritual forces precisely by the inexplicable nature of the phenomena of dreaming. The high esteem in which dream-life is held by some schools of philosophy (by the followers of Schelling for instance), is clearly an echo of the divine nature of dreams which was undisputed in antiquity. Nor are discussions of the premonitory character of dreams and their power to foretell the future at an end. For attempts at giving a psychological explanation have been inadequate to cover the material collected, however decidedly the sympathies of a scientific cast of mind may incline against accepting such beliefs." Freud, *The Interpretation of Dreams*, 39.
22. Boehme, *Forty Questions of the Soul* (1620), III 11/1 1.5, as cited in Mills, *The Unconscious Abyss*, 24n16. The book is also known under the title *Forty Questions regarding the Nature of the Soul*.
23. The decision was made by the editor Werdenhagen, who was responsible for its Latin translation. Eckmeyer, "Johann Angelius Werdenhagen."
24. Hessayon and Apetrei, eds., *An Introduction to Jacob Boehme*.
25. On Hegel's views of Boehme, see Magee, "Hegel's Reception of Jacob Boehme"; Muratori, *The First German Philosopher*; Magee, *Hegel and the Hermetic Tradition*, 229; Schmidt-Biggemann, "Jakob Böhme und die Kabbala," 2:157–81. On Schelling's and Feuerbach's views of Boehme, see Mayer, *Jena Romanticism*; Vieillard-Baron, "Schelling et Jacob Böhme"; Weeks, *Boehme*.
26. Boehme, *"Aurora,"* 681.
27. The term *grunt* (the old spelling of *Grund*) indeed appears about 140 times in his work. See McGinn, *The Harvest of Mysticism in Medieval Germany*; McGinn, "Lost in the Abyss"; Dobie, "Meister Eckhart's 'Ontological Philosophy of Religion.'"

28. Eckhart, *Meister Eckharts Predigten*, 1:90. On the reciprocity between the soul and the ground, see Berggren, "Anmerkungen zu Einem Eckhartstudium," as well as Kern, *Der Gang der Vernunft bei Meister Eckhart*. On the continuity and differences between Eckhart and Boehme, see Pektas, *Mystique et philosophie*.
29. Tauler, *Die Predigten Taulers*, 174.
30. This is why the twentieth-century French philosopher Alexandre Koyré, whose work reintroduced Boehme in France and introduced him to Jacques Lacan, preferred the term *absolute*, and even *indeterminate absolute*, to *abyss*. Koyré, *La philosophie de Jacob Boehme*. It has been suggested that the famous mirror stage in the psychological development of a child was inspired by that bohemian dissociation: a bifurcation followed by an identification with one's self, through a vision of oneself as a non-Other Other. Dufour, *Lacan et le miroir sophianique de Boehme*; Roudinesco, "The Mirror Stage." A further instance of the influence of Boehme on Lacan during these years is found in the poem "Hiatus Irrationalis," which conjures Boehme's theories of signatures, in which the signature supersedes the sign in the production of knowledge. This foreshadows Lacan's theory of the Real, which posits the inability of the signifier in language to relate to the signified, hence the centrality of the symbolism of representations in the process of unveiling the meaning of the Real, whereby something is always missed. See Tardits, "La mélancolie du hiatus."
31. Boehme, *"Aurora,"* 58.
32. Gnosticism is a diverse set of theological and philosophical beliefs, systems, and movements that coalesced and gained prominence in the first century CE. On the presence of Gnosticism in Boehme's writings, see O'Regan, *Gnostic Apocalypse*.
33. Pektas, *Mystique et philosophie*.
34. Koyré, *La philosophie de Jacob Boehme*, 280.
35. Böhme, *"The Forty Questions of the Soul" and "The Clavis"*, 23.
36. Boehme, *Von der Menschwerdung Jesu Christi* [The human genesis of Christ], pt. 4, pp. 120–21; translation from Boehme, *"Aurora,"* 58. *Magia* is a primordial will and its hidden workings, a chain of causality inaccessible to the five senses. It is also the knowledge of these hidden workings. On *magia* in Boehme's writings, see Andrew Weeks's introduction in Boehme, *"Aurora,"* 57–58.
37. It has also been compared to the nothingness of Zen Buddhism. See Paslick, "From Nothingness to Nothingness."
38. This was noted as early as 1885 by Hans Martensen, *Jacob Boehme*. According to Andrew Weeks, Boehme was taught Kabbalah in Prague by the Maharal, the towering figure of early modern Kabbalah (Weeks, *Boehme*, 27). I concur with Elliot Wolfson's objection to this hypothesis, however attractive it may be. Despite his universalist proclivities, the Maharal was unwilling to share kabbalistic knowledge with non-Jews. See Wolfson, *Heidegger and Kabbalah*, 25n95.
39. Boehme, *"De Electione Gratiae" and "Quaestiones Theosophicae"*, cited in Wolfson, "The Holy Cabala of Changes"; Necker, "'Out of Himself.'"
40. Boehme, *The Key*, 17, cited in Wolfson, "The Holy Cabala of Changes," 23.
41. Scholem, *Major Trends in Jewish Mysticism*, 232–33.
42. Meroz, "Faithful Transmission versus Innovation."
43. Christoph Schulte traces the arborescence of the concept in his book *Zimzum*.

44. In *Heidegger and Kabbalah*, Elliot Wolfson probes the Lurianic references while pondering the implications of Boehme's and Schelling's ideas in the work of Heidegger.
45. Magid, "Origin and Overcoming the Beginning."
46. Boehme, *Forty Questions of the Soul* (1992), 35-36.
47. Boehme, *Six Theosophic Points*, vii and 33.
48. Boehme, *The Way to Christ*, 209.
49. Koyré, *La philosophie de Jacob Boehme*, 314.
50. Boehme, *"Aurora,"* 58.
51. Boehme, *The Threefold Life of Man*, 14, cited in Wolfson, "The Holy Cabala of Changes," 41.
52. Ludwig Feuerbach devoted chapter 9 of *Essence of Christianity*, "Of the Mystery of Mysticism, or of Nature in God," to Jacob Boehme.
53. Feuerbach, *Geschichte der neueren Philosophie*, 3:177.
54. Maimon, *An Autobiography*, 94-95.
55. Schelling, *System of Transcendental Idealism* (1800), 331. On the question of the world soul in German idealism, see Bowman, "Nature, Freedom, History."
56. Schelling, *System of Transcendental Idealism* (1800), 600. Here, I have used the translation written by Andrew Bowie in Bowie, *Schelling and Modern European Philosophy*, 50.
57. Some prefer "that which is eternally unconscious." This translation, however, misses Schelling's contribution and the fact that he coined the noun, whereas the adjective already existed. Using *ewig* as an adverb ("eternally") instead of an adjective, however, is a more compelling proposition. See Brès, "Home, Carus, Hartmann," 229n5.
58. Schelling, *System of Transcendental Idealism* (1800), 209.
59. Brown, *The Later Philosophy of Schelling*; Wolfson, *Heidegger and Kabbalah*.
60. The text was based on drafts and on the notes taken at his public lectures in Berlin, which constituted an intellectual and social event that attracted the likes of Kierkegaard, Engels, and Bakunin. Schelling, *The Grounding of Positive Philosophy*.
61. Schelling, "Stuttgarter Privatvorlesungen," 7:429-30. For a translation of the Stuttgart Seminars, see Schelling, *Idealism and the Endgame of Theory*, 195-243.
62. Faivre, "La critique boehmienne de Franz von Baader."
63. Koslowski, ed., *Die Philosophie, Theologie und Gnosis Franz von Baaders*. Boehme had little purchase for Lammenais and Joseph de Maistre, and the audience in France was very limited. Louis Claude de Saint Martin, the so-called unknown philosopher, translated Boehme into French, and his own work, deeply influenced by the German mystic, never garnered a significant audience.
64. Jaspers, *Schelling*, 98. See also Fackenheim, "Schelling's Conception of Positive Philosophy."
65. Schelling, "Stuttgarter Privatvorlesungen," 7:432-33; Schulze, "Zum Verständnis der Stuttgarter Privatvorlesungen Schellings." See also Franks, "The Midrashic Background," 56.
66. Schelling, *The Ages of the World: (Fragment)*. For the 1813 intermediary text, see Žižek and Schelling, *The Abyss of Freedom/Ages of the World*. For the long, 1811 version, see Schelling, *The Ages of the World (1811)*.
67. Schelling, *The Ages of the World: (Fragment)*, 181.

68. Here I concur with Sean McGrath's analysis of the dissociation process and what he calls "speculative psychology." McGrath, *The Dark Ground of Spirit*. See also Snow, "The Role of the Unconscious"; Buchheim and Hermanni, *Alle Persönlichkeit ruht auf einem dunkeln Grunde*.
69. Rosenzweig, "'Urzelle' to the *Star of Redemption*," 56–57. Original German phrase in brackets added here. See Bielik-Robson, "'The Story Continues . . .'"; Bielik-Robson, "God of Luria"; Bielik-Robson, *Jewish Cryptotheologies of Late Modernity*; Horwitz, "From Hegelianism to a Revolutionary Understanding."
70. Hart, *God Being Nothing*.
71. Schelling, "Philosophischen Untersuchungen," 7:407–8.
72. Žižek and Schelling, *The Abyss of Freedom/Ages of the World*, 114.
73. Wolfson, *Language, Eros, Being*, 392–93n2; Wolfson, *Heidegger and Kabbalah*, 18–19n40; Franks, "Mythology, Essence, and Form"; Franks, "From World-Soul to Universal Organism"; Franks, "Inner Anti-Semitism or Kabbalistic Legacy?"; Franks, "Rabbinic Idealism and Kabbalistic Realism"; Franks, "'Nothing Comes from Nothing.'"
74. Schelling, *Über die Gottheiten von Samothrake*. This pamphlet was based on a paper he had read at a public meeting of the Bavarian Academy of Science on October 12, 1815. See also Franks, "The Midrashic Background," 55 (note that Franks incorrectly cites vol. 7 of *Friedrich Wilhelm Joseph von Schellings Sämmtliche Werke*; the correct volume number is 8).
75. The Zohar, a foundational text of Jewish mysticism, is a commentary on both the Pentateuch and a pseudepigraph written in thirteenth-century Castile by Moses de Leon. It is attributed to Rabbi Shimon bar Yochai (also known by the acronym Rashbi), a sage of the Talmud who lived in the second century.
76. Kunitz, *Sefer Ben Yohai*. Often exclusively held to be a defense of the alleged authorship of the Zohar by Shimon bar Yochai against the case for a medieval authorship, the erudite yet quite controversial work is an inventory of all mentions of bar Yochai in the Talmud. On Kunitz, see Fahn, *Pirke Haskalah*, 2:70–99; Chajes, "Romanticising Rashbi."
77. Coudert, "Henry More"; Di Biase, "Henry More's Panentheism."
78. Schelling, *Historical-Critical Introduction*, lecture 9, 144–45.

Chapter Two

1. Cahnman, "Schelling and the New Thinking of Judaism."
2. Franks, "Mythology, Essence, and Form."
3. Gershom Scholem saw him as the last author to have penned a Kabbalah-inflected commentary, *Tore Zahav*. Scholem, "Zur Literatur der letzten Kabbalisten"; Bach, "Bernays und Schelling."
4. Herder, *The Spirit of Hebrew Poetry*. See also Stolzenberg, "What Was Oriental Studies in Early Modern Europe?," 365.
5. Based on these inconsistencies, Rivka Horwitz argues that a Christian scholar, H. A. Kalb, authored the work, and that Bernays assisted him or coauthored it. See Horwitz, "On Kabbala and Myth," esp. 139–56. Hans Bach and Isaac Heinemann argue that Bernays was the author or at least coauthor. See Bach, "Der

Bibel'sche Orient und sein Verfasser"; Heinemann, "The Relationship between Samson Raphael Hirsch and His Teacher Isaac Bernays."
6. Horwitz, "On Kabbala and Myth," 157.
7. *Der Bibel'sche Orient*, 18–19 (translation Horwitz).
8. *Der Bibel'sche Orient*, 19 (translation Horwitz).
9. Leiman, "Rabbinic Openness to General Culture," 166–76. Bollack, "Un homme d'un autre monde," 196. See also J. J. Schacter, ed., *Judaism's Encounter with Other Cultures: Rejection or Integration?* (Northvale, NJ: Maggid, 1997), 1–56.
10. Graetz, *History of the Jews*, 5:574; Duckesz, "Zur Biographie des Chacham Isaak Bernays," 298.
11. Kohler, "Biographical Essay," 407.
12. Sigmund Freud, letter, July 23, 1882, quoted in Bollack, *Jacob Bernays*, 15; Toury, "German Jewry in Mid-nineteenth Century."
13. Asked for his opinions about Jewish emancipation, Schelling encouraged the king to pursue this agenda and to create a consistory with Christian and Jewish faculty, for which he thought Löwengard well suited. "Without the political changes that have occurred, he might have been able to find a position in Prussia that would have been in line with his capability; I will hope that he has preserved himself mentally under the pressure of the miserable conditions in which he has had to make a living." Cahnman, "Schelling and the New Thinking of Judaism," 25. See also Cahnman, "Friedrich Wilhelm Schelling über die Judenemanzipation."
14. Löwengard, *Beiträge zur Kritik der Reformbestrebungen*.
15. Löwengard, *Auch einige Worte über das neue Gebetbuch*.
16. Löwengard, *Jehova, nicht Moloch*; Gotzmann, "Reconsidering Judaism as a Religion," 362.
17. Bauer, *Die Judenfrage*.
18. Löwengard, *Jehova, nicht Moloch*.
19. Löwengard, *Beiträge zur Kritik der Reformbestrebungen in der Synagogue*, 7.
20. Roth, *On the End of the World*.
21. Löwengard, *Jehova, nicht Moloch*, as translated in Cahnman, *German Jewry*, 226.
22. Landauer, *Jehova und Elohim*; Landauer, *Wesen und Form des Pentateuchs*.
23. Geiger, review of M. H. Landauer, *Jehova und Elohim*, 405.
24. Landauer, *Wesen und Form des Pentateuchs*, ix.
25. Landauer, 47ff. and 59ff.
26. On the motif of a "world soul" in the Jewish esoteric tradition, see Brown, "Glimmers of the World Soul."
27. Samuel Hirsch was a scholar and the author of a Hebrew grammar as well as studies on Francis Bacon.
28. Hirsch, "Jewish Mystics," 51.
29. Hirsch, 59.
30. Wiese, "Samuel Holdheim's 'Most Powerful Comrade in Conviction'"; Kohler, ed., *David Einhorn: Memorial Volume*; Cohen, "David Einhorn."
31. Kohler, "Biographical Essay," 407.
32. Görres, *Mythengeschichte der asiatischen Welt*; Görres, *Die christliche Mystik*.
33. Wagner, *Mein Leben*, 315; Jung, *Memories, Dreams, Reflections*, 99.

34. Creuzer, *Symbolik und Mythologie der alten Völker*. See also Feldman and Richardson, *The Rise of Modern Mythology*, 387–96; Szymkowiak, "La symbolique de Friedrich Creuzer." The idea that the Greek tradition overlapped with Judaism had been floated by Johann Gottfried von Herder without the critical apparatus used by Friedrich Creuzer.
35. Creuzer, *Symbolik und Mythologie der alten Völker*, 1:xv.
36. Schelling, *The Schelling Reader*, 386. See Schelling, "Philosophy of Revelation," 256.
37. Creuzer, *Symbolik und Mythologie der alten Völker*, 1:435. See also Greenberg, "Religionswissenschaft and Early Reform Jewish Thought," 126.
38. Einhorn, *Das Prinzip des Mosaismus*, 178–79. For an earlier Christian reading of the symbolism of Mosaism, see Bähr, *Symbolik des Mosaischen Cultus*.
39. Einhorn, *Das Prinzip des Mosaismus*, 13. This theme would reappear in the work of Elia Benamozegh and Franz Rosenzweig, who use the image of Judaism as the sun, with other religions as the sun's rays.
40. Molitor, *Philosophie der Geschichte*, 1:83–85; Koch, *Franz Joseph Molitor*; Mertens, "'The True Words of the Mystic'"; Mertens, "'This Still Remarkable Book'"; Greenberg, "Religionswissenschaft and Early Reform Jewish Thought," 126.
41. Schulte, "'Die Buchstaben haben . . .'"; Mertens, "'The True Words of the Mystic.'"
42. Scholem, *Walter Benjamin*, 53, as translated in Mertens, "'This Still Remarkable Book,'" 167.
43. Schubert, *Die Geschichte der Seele*, 5–6.
44. Roelcke, "Jewish Mysticism in Romantic Medicine?"
45. Noyes, "The Voice of History." Freud references Gotthilf Heinrich von Schubert in *The Antithetical Meaning of Primal Words*; Jung, *Collected Works*, 4:841.
46. The Emden-Eibeschütz controversy erupted in 1751 when the rabbinical scholar Jacob Emden accused Hamburg's chief rabbi, Jonathan Eibeschütz, of Sabbateanism, based on some amulets he possessed. The suspicions tore the community apart. See Emden, *Megilat Sefer*.
47. On Isaac Mieses, see Glasenapp and Horch, *Ghettoliteratur*, 372–76.
48. The comparison of Friedrich Wilhelm von Schelling and Habad can also be found in Mieses, *Geschichte der neuern Philosophie*, 155–56.
49. Mieses, *Korot ha-Philosophia ha-Hadashah*, 155–56n, as translated in Franks, "Mythology, Essence, and Form," 81. An earlier version, published in the Warsaw newspaper *Hatsefira*, June 18, 1878, is more specific and reads: "how this concept of [the *Sprung*] in its nature, origins, and implications coincides with the words of Schelling and his students."
50. Reconstructionism holds that Judaism is a religious civilization whose religious elements are in fact human. Peoplehood must be a central element in it, and Kabbalah plays the role of holding its people together. See Stern, "Pragmatic Kabbalah."
51. Joseph Judah Löb Sossnitz, cited in Stern, *Jewish Materialism*, 100.
52. Schelling, *Philosophy and Religion*, 26. I have adopted Elliot Wolfson's changes to the translation in "Tsimtsum, Lichtung, and the Leap," 148.
53. On the "leap" in Hasidism in light of Schelling, see Wolfson, "Achronic Time."
54. Lacan, *Écrits*. See, in particular, the chapters "Au-delà du principe de réalité" and "Réponse au commentaire de Jean Hyppolite."

55. Dov Ber Schneersohn, *Torat Hayyim*, Bereshit, 153c, as quoted in Wolfson, "Achronic Time," 49–50.
56. Gershom Scholem wrote the following about the "leap" or, in this translation, the "jump": "Every 'jump' opens a new sphere, defined by certain formal, *not* material, characteristics. Within this sphere the mind may freely associate. The 'jumping' unites, therefore, elements of free and guided association and is said to assure quite extraordinary results as far as the 'widening of consciousness' of the initiate is concerned. The 'jumping' brings to light hidden processes of the mind." Scholem, *Major Trends in Jewish Mysticism*, 135–36. Abraham Abulafia's techniques of free association have been compared to the psychoanalytic process. See Kagan, "God and the Psychiatrist in Psychotherapy"; Szafran, "Aspects socio-culturels judaïques de la pensée de Freud," 50.
57. Sossnitz, *Aken Yesh Adonai*; Büchner, *Kraft und Stoff*. See Stern, *Jewish Materialism*, 88–112.
58. Stern, *Jewish Materialism*, 99–100. A significant part of the work of Emil du Bois-Reymond (1818–1896) concerned the electricity in living beings—what was then the field of electrophysiology, which foreshadowed neuroscience. The first proponent of Darwinism in Germany, and an enemy of the monist Ernst Haeckel, he was mostly known as a public figure as well as for lectures that combined literature, philosophy, and science. See Finkelstein, *Emil du Bois-Reymond*.
59. It was Søren Kierkegaard, attending Schelling's conferences, who took notes on the concept of afterwardness. See Hühn, *Kierkegaard und der deutsche Idealismus*; Norman and Welchman, eds., *The New Schelling*, 101–2.
60. Robinson, "Kabbala and Science in *Sefer ha-Berit*."
61. On the history of *Sefer ha-Brit*, see Ruderman, *A Best-Selling Hebrew Book*.
62. Jankélévitch, *L'odyssée de la conscience*, 311.
63. Scholem, *On Jews and Judaism in Crisis*, 283. On the nuances of the notion of void, see Podmore, "'Abyss Calls unto Abyss'"; Franks, "The Midrashic Background," 39–60.
64. Franks, "The Midrashic Background," 41.
65. Idel, "Major Currents in Italian Kabbalah"; Idel, "Italy in Safed, Safed in Italy"; Idel, "Conceptualizations of *Tzimtzum*."
66. Vital, *"The Tree of Life,"* as quoted in Bielik-Robson, "Introduction: An Unhistorical History of *Tsimtsum*," 12; Franks, "The Midrashic Background," 41–42.
67. Scholem, *Major Trends in Jewish Mysticism*, 260–61.
68. Ronit Meroz has nuanced this claim, arguing that another Lurianic school in Safed was more philosophically minded. Meroz, "The School of Sarug" [in Hebrew].
69. Dweck, *The Scandal of Kabbalah*.
70. The term *panentheism* has long been thought to have been coined by the theologian Karl Friedrich Krause (1781–1832) in his *Vorlesungen über das System der Philosophie*. Because of the reconciliation he proposed, Krause attracted many followers across Europe, including the "Krausistas" in Spain. However, it first appeared in Schelling's *Philosophical Investigations*. See Clayton, "Panentheisms East and West"; Göcke, *The Panentheism of Karl Christian Friedrich Krause*.
71. Scholem, *Major Trends in Jewish Mysticism*, 257.

72. Also translated as "bemusement"; see Wolfson, *Heidegger and Kabbalah*, 100–102.
73. The divine emanations or powers called *sefirot*, through which God the Creator was said to become manifest, are organized in the form of a tree and have various attributes—in this instance, *din* (judgment) is paralleled with *hesed* (compassion).
74. Franks, "The Midrashic Background," 56.
75. See Gregory and Kosman, "Ḥesed."
76. See Schmidt-Biggemann, *Geschichte der christlichen Kabbala*, 3:76–85, 3:127–30, and 3:132–34.
77. The textual basis for this interpretation is found in the book of Isaiah: "For the sake of my name I will postpone my wrath and my glory I will hold in for you so that I will not destroy you" (48:9). Wolfson, *Alef, Mem, Tau*, 132–33.
78. Marcionism, a Christian Gnostic sect of the third century CE, accepts part of the Gospels but refuses the corporeality of Jesus and the God of the Hebrew Bible. See O'Regan, *Gnostic Return in Modernity*. Marcion was an early interest for Schelling; the young philosopher dedicated one of his theses to the Gnostic figure during his studies in Tübingen in the early 1790s. On the significance of Marcion in perceptions of Judaism in the nineteenth century, see Kinzig, *Harnack, Marcion und das Judentum*. On this subject in the early twentieth century, see Lazier, *God Interrupted*, 28–33.
79. Baur, *Die christliche Gnosis*, 544–740. See Drecoll, "Ferdinand Christian Baur's View"; Brenner, "Gnosis and History."
80. Deleuze, *Logic of Sense*, 106–7; originally Deleuze, *Logique du sens*, 130.
81. Franks, "Inner Anti-Semitism or Kabbalistic Legacy?"; Mack, *German Idealism and the Jew*, 120 and 132.
82. Zohar 1.15. On the analysis of the reversal, see Berman, *Divine and Demonic*, 251.
83. Nathan of Gaza, *Derush ha Taninim*, 19.
84. Zohar 2.34a–35b; Nathan of Gaza, *Derush ha Taninim*. See Berman, *Divine and Demonic*, 250–70.
85. Talmud, tractate *Sukkot*, 49a, 53a: "the drainpipes that are concealed within the altar . . . are like the links of a chain [ḥala'im]"; "they are hollow [meḥolalin] and descend to the depths."
86. The *'even shetiyah* is mentioned in Zohar 3.61. See Koltun-Fromm, "Imagining the Temple in Rabbinic Stone." The location of the Holy of Holies is according to the midrash in *Midrash Tanhuma*, 10.
87. Nathan of Gaza, *Derush ha Taninim*, 19. *Borer* is the verbal form of a concept that generally conveys clarification in Lurianic Kabbalah, and *berur* (clarification, the singular of *berurin*) is almost always connected to the abyss in the *Treatise on the Dragons* with such expressions as *berur ha-tehiru, ha-tehom* (clarification of the abyss).
88. Nathan of Gaza, 18.
89. See Scholem's "Redemption through Sin" (1937).
90. Nathan of Gaza, *Sefer Haberiya*, fols. 82a–b.
91. Wolfson, *Heidegger and Kabbalah*, 240.
92. Derrida, *Dissemination*, 344.
93. Magid, "Origin and Overcoming the Beginning."

94. I am purposely excluding Emmanuel Levinas here, given his lack of mystical proclivities, but remnants of kabbalistic teachings can be found in his philosophy. See Levinas, "The Trace of the Other."
95. See Tillich, *Mysticism and Guilt-Consciousness*. See also Elliot Wolfson's critique of Tillich in Wolfson, *Venturing Beyond*.
96. Scholem, *Major Trends in Jewish Mysticism*, 262. What the *tsimtsum* signals is, in Wolfson's words, the "otherness of the not-other" (*Heidegger and Kabbalah*, 197), which perfectly drives home the process.
97. Wolfson, *Heidegger and Kabbalah*, 197. Wolfson's reflection on otherness in Jewish thought is most specifically addressed in chapters 1 and 2 of his *Venturing Beyond*.
98. Schelling, *The Ages of the World: (Fragment)*, 6; Schelling, *Die Weltalter*, 8:211–12.
99. Idel, "Italy in Safed, Safed in Italy," 255–56. See also Bielik-Robson and Weiss, *Tsimtsum and Modernity*, vii–ix.
100. Lazier, *God Interrupted*, 28–29.
101. On the *sitra aḥra* in the medieval period, see Haskell, *Mystical Resistance*, chap. 2. This ascription persists to this day—see the treatment of otherness in Carlo Ginzburg or religious Zionism. See Ginzburg, "Selfhood as otherness."
102. Žižek and Schelling, *The Abyss of Freedom/Ages of the World*.
103. Lacan, *Le séminaire*, 11:34. See also Campos Moura, "Notes on an Ontology in Lacan."
104. On "Je est un autre" (I is another) and the decentered subject, see Lacan, *Le séminaire*, 2:60. See also Green, *Narcissisme de vie, narcissisme de mort*, 20, in which he explicitly used Jacques Lacan's phrase about desire without citing the source.
105. Schelling, *The Ages of the World: (Fragment)*, 91.
106. Schelling, *Philosophical Investigations*, 47. I have modified this translation. The original reads: "Die Angst des Lebens selbst treibt den Menschen aus dem Centrum, in das er erschaffen worden." Schelling, "Philosophischen Untersuchungen," 381.
107. See Johnston, "Ghosts of Substance Past."
108. Ricœur, *Hermeneutics and the Human Sciences*, 185.
109. Prickett, *Origins of Narrative*.

Chapter Three

1. Scholem, *On the Possibility of Jewish Mysticism*, 4–5. For the German original, see Scholem, *Briefe I*, 471–72.
2. Schulte, "Die Wissenschaft des Judentums."
3. Wolf, "On the Concept of a Science of Judaism."
4. In fact, the quote appeared in an obituary for Moritz Steinschneider in the Zionist newspaper *Der Israelit* (Mainz, Germany). It came from the pen of his student, the Orientalist Gotthold Weil (1882–1960), future director of the National Library at the Hebrew University. Weil was a Zionist who, like Gershom Scholem, had a vested interest in claiming that the WdJ's approach had left Judaism moribund. See Myers, *Re-inventing the Jewish Past*.

5. "A Jewry which, in Steinschneider's words, regarded it as its chief task to make a decent exit from the world." Scholem, *Major Trends in Jewish Mysticism*, 2; see also Scholem, *The Messianic Idea in Judaism*, 307.
6. Hirsch, "Wie gewinnen wir das Leben für unsere Wissenschaft?"
7. Idel, *Kabbalah*, 10; Fenton, "Qabbalah and Academia"; Hanegraaff, *Esotericism and the Academy*; Myers, "Philosophy and Kabbalah."
8. Huss, "Admiration and Disgust" [in Hebrew].
9. Meir, "The Origins of Hevrat Mekize Nirdamim"; Meir, "Haskalah and Esotericism"; Meir, "Haskalah and Esotericism in Galicia" [in Hebrew].
10. George Kohler's monograph, the first overview of Kabbalah research by Wissenschaftler between 1820 and 1880, further weakens the widely accepted Scholemian narrative and paints a more complex picture of the WdJ. Kohler, *Kabbalah Research*.
11. As Kohler notes, reason was not an ultimate value in and of itself. This very fact elucidates the Wissenschaft's criticism of Maimonides, which faulted the dryness of his argumentation as being stifling for Judaism, thus explaining the allure of Kabbalah as a response.
12. The term used for the translation is often *science*, even though, as I mentioned earlier, *scholarship* is more accurate.
13. Zunz, *Etwas über die rabbinische Literatur*, 36; Glatzer, "The Beginnings of Modern Jewish Studies"; Livneh-Freudenthal, "Jewish Studies" [in Hebrew]. The historian Yosef Yerushalmi (1932–2008) described this kind of project as "the faith of the fallen Jews." Yerushalmi, *Zakhor*, 86. However, the scholarly endeavor was matched by a growing sense of nostalgia, as the new generation felt increasingly disconnected from the tradition as lived experience. See Bourel, "Nostalgie et 'Wissenschaft'"; Meyer, *The Origins of the Modern Jew*.
14. Jacobson, "The Future of the Kabbalah."
15. See Makkreel, *Dilthey*; Makkreel, "Wilhelm Dilthey and the Neo-Kantians" (1969).
16. Rose, *Jewish Philosophical Politics in Germany*, 44–89.
17. Ascher, *Die Germanomanie*, 45–70; Rose, *German Question/Jewish Question*, 135–70.
18. Born Loeb Baruch, Ludwig Börne changed his name when he converted to Lutheran Protestantism in 1818. His satires were suspended in 1821 and in 1830 he moved to Paris, where he could enjoy political freedom; it was there that he wrote his famous *Letters from Paris*. Regarded as a piercing analyst of his time, "The Art of Becoming an Original Writer" was one of Freud's favorite reads in his youth. He later credited it with inspiring the notion of *Einfall*, free association, in the psychoanalytic method. See letter 804, April 9, 1919, in Freud and Ferenczi, *The Correspondence*, 344; Freud, "A Note on the Prehistory of the Technique of Analysis." See also Jones, *The Life and Work of Sigmund Freud*, 1:246.
19. The Verein zur Verbesserung des Zustandes der Juden im deutschen Bundesstate (Society for the Improvement of the Conditions of Jews in the German Federal State) replaced a more scholarly Wissenschaftszirkel established by Jewish students at Berlin University in 1816. This group was renamed the Verein für Kultur und Wissenschaft der Juden (Society for the Culture and Science of Judaism) in 1822. See Schorsch, "Breakthrough into the Past"; Zwiep, "Scholarship of Literature and Life."

20. Wolf, "On the Concept of a Science of Judaism," 204. See also Meyer, *Ideas of Jewish History*, 154–55.
21. Wolf, "On the Concept of a Science of Judaism," 204.
22. The Essenes were an ascetic and mystic Jewish sect active in Palestine during the second Temple period, from the second century BCE until the second century CE. They lived in highly organized groups and held property in common. The Sadducees were a sect of the upper Judean society during the second Temple period and held prominent political, social, and religious positions, including the maintenance of the Temple.
23. In his book *Gershom Scholem: Kabbalah and Counter-history*, David Biale argues that Zunz shared the same views and that those two thinkers' agenda was directed against the rabbinical establishment of their time. Zunz's pamphlet *Etwas über die rabbinische Literatur* also signals an estrangement from mainstream rabbinical dogmas.
24. Breckman, "Eduard Gans and the Crisis of Hegelianism"; Wolfson, *Venturing Beyond*, 2; Wolfson, "Imagination and the Theolatrous Impulse."
25. See Katzoff, "Salomon Maimon's Critique."
26. Maimon, *An Autobiography*, 95 (emphasis in original). See also Melamed, "Salomon Maimon et l'échec de la philosophie juive moderne"; Melamed, "Salomon Maimon and the Rise of Spinozism."
27. Heinrich Graetz spells out the greatest risk in his exposition, especially in the case of the Zohar. He claims it to be possibly amoral: "The Zohar sowed the seeds of unclean desires . . . created a visionary world, in which the souls of those who zealously occupied themselves with it were lulled into half-sleep, and lost the faculty of distinguishing between right and wrong." Graetz, *History of the Jews*, 4:23. On the depiction of Hasidism by the Wissenschaftler, see Krone, *Wissenschaft in Öffentlichkeit*.
28. Perl, *Joseph Perl's "Revealer of Secrets."*
29. See Seidman, *Faithful Renderings*; Benes, *In Babel's Shadow*, 13.
30. Perl, *Joseph Perl's "Revealer of Secrets,"* 17.
31. Scholem, *Major Trends in Jewish Mysticism*, 327.
32. On the notion and its limits, see Benor, *Ethical Monotheism*.
33. The Frankist movement was an eighteenth-century heresy in eastern Europe and the Ottoman Empire that led to mass conversion to Christianity. It was led by the eighteenth-century religious leader and self-proclaimed messiah Jacob Frank (1726–1791). Frank claimed to be a reincarnation of Sabbatai Zevi, advocated purification through transgression, and eventually encouraged his followers to convert to Christianity.
34. See Schäfer, "'Adversus cabbalam.'" A more traditional critique of Kabbalah was found in Heinrich Graetz's *Geschichte der Juden* [*History of the Jews*], published between 1820 and 1829. Isaak Marcus Jost, one of the key historians in the WdJ, took a negative approach toward Kabbalah by repeating a widespread allegation that the Zohar was a forgery and dismissing the whole tradition as inauthentic.
35. Meyer, "Abraham Geiger's Historical Judaism."
36. Fichte, "A State within a State (1793)."
37. Dietrich and Lohmann, "'Daß die Kinder aller Confessionen"; Bourel, "Lazarus Bendavid."

38. Guttmann, "Lazarus Bendavid"; Bourel, "Eine Generation später"; Bourel, "A l'origine du kantisme juif."
39. On the journal, see Davies, "Karl Philipp Moritz's *Erfahrungseelenkunde.*"
40. Dohm, *Über die bürgerliche Verbesserung der Juden.* See also Bernardini and Lucci, *The Jews, Instructions for Use,* 89–138.
41. Bendavid, *Etwas zur Charackteristick der Juden.*
42. This does not mean that Nietzsche embraced the nascent antisemitic ideology of his time. On the complexity of his stance, see Holub, *Nietzsche's Jewish Problem.*
43. See Rose, "Lazarus Bendavid's and J. G. Fichte's Kantian Fantasies."
44. Hegel, *The Phenomenology of Spirit,* 453. See also Lauer, *A Reading of Hegel's "Phenomenology of Spirit,"* 79–81.
45. Hegel, *Wissenschaft der Logic,* 1:44, as quoted in Josephson, "Specters of Reason," 207.
46. The esoteric influences in the work of Georg Hegel have recently come under scrutiny. See Magee, *Hegel and the Hermetic Tradition.*
47. Copleston, "Hegel and the Rationalisation of Mysticism."
48. Bendavid, "Über den Glauben der Juden an einen künftigen Messias."
49. "Having embraced my topic in all its breadth, I let the hitherto little-known sentiment of the Kabbalists enter it." Lazarus Bendavid, letter to Baron Silvestre de Sacy, September 17, 1822, in Bourel, "Trois lettres inédites de Lazarus Bendavid," 133.
50. Said, *Orientalism,* 123–48.
51. "There is no longer any middle ground for them between superstition and religion." Bourel, "Trois lettres inédites de Lazarus Bendavid," 135.
52. Espagne, Lafi, and Rabault-Feuerhahn, eds., *Silvestre de Sacy.*
53. Krochmal, *Moreh Nevukhe ha-Zeman.* On Krochmal, see Harris, *Nachman Krochmal.* On Krochmal and the Young Hegelians, see Avineri, "The Fossil and Phoenix."
54. See Krochmal, *Moreh Nevukhe ha-Zeman.*
55. Biale, "The Kabbala in Nachman Krochmal's Philosophy of History"; Harris, *Nachman Krochmal*; Rawidowicz, "Nachman Krochmal als Historiker."
56. See Fackenheim, "Hirsch and Hegel."
57. On Jacob Emden's strategy, which he had previously applied to discredit Maimonides, see Funkenstein, *Perceptions of Jewish History,* 239.
58. Mieses, *Darstellung und kritische Beleuchtung,* 4, 18, 20, and 65. See Kohler, *Reading Maimonides' Philosophy,* 64.
59. Schweid, *A History of Modern Jewish Religious Philosophy,* 2:26–28.
60. Joel, *Die Religionsphilosophie des Sohar,* 140–41. On David Joel, see Kohler, *Reading Maimonides' Philosophy,* 83–93.
61. Funkenstein, *Perceptions of Jewish History,* 248.
62. On these categories, see Davidson, "Paradoxes of Irrationality."
63. See Kléber Monod, *Solomon's Secret Arts*; Benz, *The Mystical Sources.*
64. On Peter Beer, see Hecht, *Ein jüdischer Aukflärer in Böhmen*; Brenner, "Between Haskalah and Kabbalah," 389; Goetschel, "Peter Beers Blick auf die Kabbala."
65. The full title of the journal was *Sulamith, eine Zeitschrift zur Beförderung der Kultur und Humanitat unter der jüdischen Nation* [A periodical for the advancement of culture and humanity among the Jewish nation]. See Grossert, *"Sulamith."*

Sulamith had a modest readership, but it was mostly read by wealthy and influential members of the community, financiers, or court advisers.
66. Beer, *Geschichte, Lehren und Meinungen*.
67. Praised at the time of his death, Beer's reputation was tainted by the historians Isaak Marcus Jost, who dismissed him, and Heinrich Graetz, whose chief reproach was Beer's "special liking" of the Frankist heresy. In fact, it was Beer who ended up providing the best insights into the sect. More recently, Ismar Schorsch has characterized Beer as "an assembler of scattered and inaccessible sources for convenient perusal." But a reexamination of his work is in order: Michael Meyer correctly remarks that despite its flaws, *History, Beliefs and Doctrines* remains "the first comprehensive Jewish history of the modern religion written by a Jew." Schorsch, *From Text to Context*, 304; Meyer, "The Emergence of Modern Jewish Historiography," 165n13; Graetz, *Frank und die Frankisten*, 3.
68. Beer, *Geschichte, Lehren und Meinungen*, 1:14–18.
69. Beer, 2:v.
70. Fürst, "Vorläufiger Bericht," 324; Scholem, *Bibliographica Kabbalistica*, 91–92; Goodman-Thau, "Meyer Heinrich Hirsch Landauer: Bible Scholar"; Goodman-Thau, "Meyer Heinrich Hirsch Landauer—eine Brücke"; Kohler, *Kabbalah Research*, 60–78.
71. Meyer Landauer unearthed and shed light on the work of Abraham Abulafia, one of the most important medieval kabbalists, who was until then practically unknown. He was mistaken in identifying Abulafia as the author of the Zohar, but he correctly situated the book in the Middle Ages.
72. Landauer, *Jehova und Elohim*; Landauer, *Wesen und Form des Pentateuchs*.
73. Landauer, *Wesen und Form des Pentateuchs*, 107ff.
74. Landauer also brought together Hinduism and Judaism—a staple in German Romantics' interest in their Indo-European roots (later to be weaponized in Aryanism)—and proposed a symbolism of the three primary names of God (El Roi, Shaddai, and El Koneh), thereby connecting them to Brahma, Vishnu, and Shiva (the Creator, the Preserver, and the Destroyer) as paradigms, bringing mythology and psychology together.
75. Landauer, "Interim Report on My Study" (posthumous installments), *Literaturblatt des Orients*, no. 34 (August 20, 1845), 542–44.
76. Franck, *The Kabbalah*, 8; Rothschild and Grondeux, eds., *Adolphe Franck*.
77. Adolphe Franck became influential through his published writing, but he lent himself to criticism because of his lack of command of Aramaic. David Joel discussed Franck's thesis and rejected his historical dating. More important, he repudiated Franck's suggestion of a Persian, Gnostic, or Christian influence on Kabbalah. See Joel, *Die Religionsphilosophie des Sohar*. In 1852, Samuel David Luzzatto's rejection of the antiquity of the Zohar in his *Vikkuah al Hokhmat ha Kabbalah* [Disputation on the wisdom of Kabbalah] was based on its punctuation system. In fact, the bulk of scholarship aims to disprove the authorship. This goal is perfectly formulated by Ignaz Stern in "Versuch einer umständlichen Analyse des Sohar," 267: "'With the increase in the deleterious effects [of Kabbalah] on the religious life of Judaism, the opposition against the Zohar became more and more implacable.' For that reason, 'the Zohar is now forced to take refuge in disinterested, unbiased and objective Higher Criticism.'" As quoted in Kohler, "Judaism Buried or Revitalised?," 56. In spite of this exhortation,

for those who championed Franck, the significance of the Zohar—and its symbolism—was more important than its date of origin.
78. Franck, *The Kabbalah*, 93.
79. Franck, 62.
80. Franck, 164.
81. Adler, "Die Kabbala," 185; as quoted in Kohler, *Kabbalah Research*, 70. See Meyer, "Religious Reform and Political Revolution."
82. Atlas, "Solomon Maimon's Philosophical Exegesis."
83. On the contribution of Salomon Munk, see Graetz, *The Jews in Nineteenth-Century France*, 50, 57, and esp. 66–70, where he draws a parallel with Adolphe Franck and compares the ideological underpinnings of their scholarship. See also Fenton, "Salomon Munk."
84. Maimonide, *Le guide des égarés*, 1:7n1.
85. Joel, *Die Religionsphilosophie des Sohar*, viii.
86. Gershom Scholem's letter to his editor, Zalman Schocken, 1937, as quoted in Biale, *Gershom Scholem*, 32; see also note 1 in this reference.
87. Myers, "Philosophy and Kabbalah," 64–71.
88. Huss, *The Question about the Existence of Jewish Mysticism* [in Hebrew]. See also Huss, "The Theologies of Kabbalah Research."
89. The work was subtitled "Critiques concerning the book by the wise, knowledgeable, and famous Rabbi, our Rabbi and teacher Lipman [Leopold] Zunz from Berlin, and regarding the wise, sharp Rabbi, the famous critic, our Rabbi and teacher Solomon Judah Leib Hacohen Rapoport from Lvov." As translated in Meir, "Haskalah and Esotericism," 158.
90. Meir, "Haskalah, Kabbalah and Mesmerism."
91. Meir, "Haskalah and Esotericism."
92. Hirsch, "Jewish Mystics," 51.
93. Foucault, *The Order of Things*, 355.
94. On Wilhelm Dilthey, see Makkreel, "Wilhelm Dilthey and the Neo-Kantians" (2009); Dilthey, "Berlin Plan," "Althoff Letter," "Sociology," and "Presuppositions or Conditions of Consciousness or Scientific Knowledge," in Dilthey, *Selected Works*, vol. 1.
95. The term *Geisteswissenschaft* is often—erroneously—thought to have been introduced in the translation of John Stuart Mill's discussion of the logic of moral science, in chapter 6 of his *System of Logic* (1843). The human sciences/moral sciences dynamic is convincingly explored in Makkreel, "The Emergence of the Human Sciences." On Dilthey's influence on the WdJ, see Meyer, "Two Persistent Tensions," 83; Dowden and Werner, eds., *German Literature, Jewish Critics*, 41 and 98.
96. Weber, "Carl du Prel"; Sharp, "Rational Religion"; Monroe, "Evidence of Things Not Seen"; Owen, *The Place of Enchantment*.
97. Tanner, "Unfassbare Gefühle."
98. Johach, "Dilthey, Freud"; Wiese, *Wissenschaft des Judentums*.
99. Wundt, *Beiträge zur Theorie der Sinneswahrnehmung*. See also Freitas Araujo, *Wundt*.
100. Franck, *The Kabbalah*, 39.
101. Funkenstein, *Perceptions of Jewish History*, 255.
102. Zunz, *Etwas über die rabbinische Literatur*, 2n.

103. Buxdorf, *Synagoga Judaica*. On Buxdorf and the works of early Hebraists, see Zunz, *Zur Geschichte und Literatur*; Miletto, "Leopold Zunz and the Hebraists."
104. Bhabha, "Of Mimicry and Man"; Heschel, "Revolt of the Colonized," 62; Heschel, *Abraham Geiger*.
105. Bhabha, "Of Mimicry and Man," 131.

Chapter Four

1. Bloom, "Emerson: The American Religion," 33.
2. Emerson, "Self-Reliance," 249.
3. Bloom, "Introduction: The American Sublime," 6.
4. The impact of Kabbalah in colonial America has been probed by Brian Ogren in his compelling study of the Protestant uses of Jewish texts from the mid-1680s to the mid-1780s. He pored over the work of several Protestant thinkers: the theologian George Keith, who helped shape the Quaker movement; the Puritan minister Increase Mather and his son Cotton, Increase viewed as the father of Congregationalism; the convert Judah Monis, who taught at Harvard; and the president of Yale, Ezra Stiles. The phenomenon Ogren describes through these idiosyncratic figures might not have been widespread, as he himself concedes, but their thought, with their peculiar interpretations of Kabbalah, did have an impact. See Ogren, *Kabbalah and the Founding of America*. See also Ogren, *Kabbalah in America*. Other studies focus on the influence of the Hebrew Bible, but not of mystical texts, in the nascent republic; see Shalev, *American Zion*.
5. Bloom claims that "it cannot become the American religion until it first is canonized as American literature." Bloom, "Emerson," 97.
6. This is a pivotal argument advanced by M. H. Abrams and quoted in Bloom, 38. It holds that secular thinkers did not foster "the deletion and replacement of religious ideas but rather the assimilation and reinterpretation of religious ideas." It also maintains that the Romantic era had focused on the reformulation of the relation between subject and object, ego and non-ego, consciousness and nature. Although I won't analyze the Romantic tradition per se here, the same mechanisms are certainly at play in the work of Emerson. Abrams, *Natural Supernaturalism*, 13.
7. Bloom, *The American Religion*, 96.
8. Emerson, "The Philosophy of History," 2:56.
9. Richardson, *Emerson*, 257.
10. As attested in a review of Emerson's work by the philosopher Francis Bowen (1811–1880), who lamented the grafting of the word from German into English, which he judged ill suited for such concepts: "Among the innovations made by the writers of the Transcendental school, we may instance the formation of a large class of abstract nouns from adjectives—a peculiarity consonant with the genius of the German language, as it is foreign to the nature of our own. Thus we speak of the *Infinite*, the *Beautiful*, the *Unconscious*." Bowen, review of Emerson, as quoted in Steele, *Unfolding the Mind*, 2.
11. Wellek, "Emerson and German Philosophy"; Wolfson, "The Holy Cabala of Changes"; Greenham, "'Altars to the Beautiful Necessity.'"

12. As Joel Rasmussen has rightly noted, Schelling is mentioned only once in Kuklick, *A History of Philosophy in America*. Rasmussen, "Schelling and the New England Mind."
13. Meyer, "America." Eliyahu Stern has charted these interactions between eastern Europe and the United States in "Pragmatic Kabbalah."
14. Against the myth of American exceptionalism, Daniel T. Rodgers aptly captures this transatlantic circulation of progressive ideas from the 1870s to the mid-twentieth century in *Atlantic Crossings*. This notion of translation as metamorphosis is inspired by Mark Taylor's *Last Works*: "When modern European philosophy crossed the Atlantic, Hegelianism was translated into the Transcendentalism of Emerson and Thoreau, and Kierkegaardism became the dark Romanticism of Poe, Hawthorne, and Melville." Taylor, *Last Works*, 7. On these transfers, see Wellek, *Confrontations*.
15. Peirce, "The Law of Mind," 1:12–13. Despite this quip, the influence of Kabbalah on Peirce himself is unnegligible. See Franks, "Peirce's 'Schelling-Fashioned Idealism.'" On the affinity between Peirce and Kabbalah, see Wolfson, "Theosemiosis through a Peircean Lens."
16. Emerson, "Compensation," 299; Keating, "Renaming the Dark," 305. I disagree with Joanne Feit Diehl's reading of the abyss as a fiery pit, comparable to what is found in Emily Dickinson, in "Emerson, Dickinson, and the Abyss." A Romanticism of the abyss bearing a closer resemblance to Emerson's version appears in the work of the poet William Wordsworth, equally influenced by Schelling and an influence on Emerson: "There I beheld the emblem of a mind / That feeds upon infinity, that broods / Over the dark abyss, intent to hear / Its voices issuing forth to silent light / In one continuous stream; a mind sustained / By recognitions of transcendent power, / In sense conducting to ideal form, / In soul of more than mortal privilege. / One function, above all, of such a mind / Had Nature shadowed there, by putting forth, / 'Mid circumstances awful and sublime, / That mutual domination which she loves / To exert upon the face of outward things, / So moulded, joined, abstracted, so endowed / With interchangeable supremacy, / That men, least sensitive, see, hear, perceive, / And cannot choose but feel." Wordsworth, *The Prelude, or Growth of a Poet's Mind*, 356. See Hirsch, *Wordsworth and Schelling*; Moore, "Emerson on Wordsworth." On other representations of the abyss, see Madden, "Images of the Abyss."
17. Emerson, "The Method of Nature," 122.
18. Emerson, "Plato: New Readings," 658.
19. Emerson, *Journals*, 10:171.
20. Braham, "Emerson and Boehme," 31.
21. Emerson, *The Journals and Miscellaneous Notebooks*, 5:30.
22. René Wellek traces Emerson's first mention of Schelling to an 1831 journal entry titled "Some minds think about things; others think the things themselves," in which Emerson quotes Schelling approvingly. The source might have been the aphorisms of Augustus William and Julius Charles Hare's *Guesses at Truth*, published in 1827. The writings of Thomas De Quincey—and his fascination for Samuel Taylor Coleridge's unattributed quotes of Schelling—might have been another source. Wellek, *Confrontations*, 198.
23. For the allusion in *Biographia Literaria*, see Coleridge, *Biographia Literaria*, 92–93. The scathing comment reads: "The coincidence of Schelling's system

with certain general ideas of Behmen, he declared to have been *mere* coincidence." Indeed, Schelling barely cites Boehme, but the irony lies in the fact that Coleridge lifted entire passages from Schelling in his magnum opus. See also Vieillard-Baron, "Schelling et Jacob Böhme"; Penhoën, *Histoire de la philosophie allemande*. Hilaire, an *homme de lettres* and friend of the novelist Honoré de Balzac's, translated from the German and published articles, including reviews of Schelling's *Philosophy of Nature*, in the prestigious and influential *Revue des deux mondes*, based in Paris.

24. Emerson, *The Journals and Miscellaneous Notebooks*, 5:30.
25. In his *Geschichte der neueren Philosophie* [History of modern philosophy, 1833–37], Feuerbach thus wrote, "Jakob Böhme is the most profoundly unconscious and uneducated psychologist [Jakob Böhme ist der tiefste unbewußte und ungebildete Psycholog], the most instructive and also the most interesting proof that the mysteries of theology and metaphysics find their explanation in psychology, that metaphysics is nothing but 'esoteric psychology.'" Feuerbach, *Geschichte der neueren Philosophie*, 3:177.
26. Emerson, *The Journals and Miscellaneous Notebooks*, 9:101.
27. Bloom, *Essayists and Prophets*, 87.
28. Emerson, *The Letters*, 1:lviii.
29. Coleridge, *Aids to Reflection*, 451.This is part of what has been called the broadening of the scope of reason in New England, as found in the works of Coleridge and Marsh. Menand, *The Metaphysical Club*.
30. Marsh, "Preliminary Essay to Coleridge's *Aids to Reflection*," 105. Frederick Henry Hedge was the first to use the term (*transcendental philosophy*) in "Coleridge's Literary Character." In the *Metaphysical Club*, Louis Menand also claims that this is the introduction of Romanticism in America. Menand, *The Metaphysical Club*, 247–48.
31. Cabot, *A Memoir of Ralph Waldo Emerson*, 218.
32. Emerson, *The Journals and Miscellaneous Notebooks*, 4:348.
33. "Suddenly, without observation, the selfsame thing detaches its beautiful wings." Emerson, "The American Scholar," 61.
34. Emerson, "The Over-Soul," 392.
35. Detweiler, "The Overrated Oversoul."
36. Emerson, "The Over-Soul," 385–86.
37. Fromm, "Overcoming the Over-Soul," 78.
38. Detweiler, "The Overrated Oversoul," 67.
39. Bishop, *Emerson on the Soul*, 19–25.
40. Cameron, *Young Emerson's Transcendental Visions*, 578. Emerson delivered a scathing address to a group of Harvard students about to enter the ministry. Trueblood, "The Influence of Emerson's Divinity Address"; Letham, "Newborn Bards of the Holy Ghost."
41. Taken from More's *Psychozoia, or, The Life of Soul*, the quotation itself conveys a community of destiny, and a shared identity, between the divine and the Creation: "But souls that of his own good life partake, / He loves as his own self; dear as His eye / They are to Him: He'll never them forsake; / When they shall dye, then God Himself shall die; / They live, they live in blest Eternity." More, *A Platonick Song of the Soul*, 187. (The capitalization of the pronouns for God in this quotation is erratic but reproduced accurately here.)

42. Cassirer, *Platonic Renaissance in England*, esp. 98–110.
43. Walls, "The World Soul in American Transcendentalism."
44. The 1846 poem is Emerson, "The World Soul." The ode reads: "The World-soul knows his own affair, / Forelooking, when his hands prepare / For the next ages, men of mould, / Well embodied, well ensouled." Emerson, "Monadnoc," 51.
45. Cousin, *Introduction to the History of Modern Philosophy*, 71–73; Riepe, "Emerson and Indian Philosophy"; Versluis, *American Transcendentalism and Asian Religions*, 57, 103, and 208. On the influence of Charles Wilkins's translation, see Nakdami, *The Bhagavad Gita for the Modern Reader*; Christy, *The Orient in American Transcendentalism*.
46. Harris, "Emerson's Orientalism," 376. (First published in 1884.) "The mention of the Over-Soul, or Adhyatma, an expression which Emerson used as a title for one of the greatest of his essays. In the eighth chapter we read: 'The supreme universal spirit is the One simple and indivisible; and my own nature is called Adhyatma (*Adhi*, meaning above, superior to, or presiding over; and *atma*, the soul, not the soul that presides over all, but that which is above the soul itself).'" In the Charles Wilkins translation of the Bhagavad Gita, that would be *Adeeatma*, "the over-ruling spirit" (pp. 73 and 142).
47. As attested to by Emerson's letter to Elizabeth Hoar dated June 17, 1845, where he says that he has read an "extract from" the Gita, "which I have often admired but never before held the book into my hands." Emerson, *The Letters*, 3:289–90.
48. Christy, *The Orient in American Transcendentalism*, 73–112; Emerson, "Brahma."
49. Emerson, "Brahma."
50. Emerson, *The Journals and Miscellaneous Notebooks*, 9:313.
51. Mohr, "The World-Soul in the Platonic Cosmology." The world soul is the intersection of two cosmic circles representing sameness and difference (whose X shape went on to be interpreted by Justin and other Christian exegetes as Jesus)—and functioning as a regulating mechanism. See Latura, "Plato's Visible God."
52. Vassányi, *Anima Mundi*, 363–92; Franks, "From World-Soul to Universal Organism"; Zachhuber, "World Soul and Celestial Heat"; Zachhuber, "The World Soul in Early Christian Thought."
53. Schelling, "System des transcendentalen Idealismus."
54. Mayer, *Jena Romanticism*, 188–89.
55. Emerson is especially expressive about ether in an 1840 journal entry: "I dreamed that I floated at will in the great Ether, and I saw this world floating also not far off, but diminished to the size of an apple. Then the angel took it in his hand & brought it to me and said, 'This must thou eat.' And I ate the world." (*The Journals and Miscellaneous Notebooks*, 7:525). Another key passage is in *The Journals and Miscellaneous Notebooks*, 5:336, where the conflict between the world soul and the self is mediated by the ether. See Greenham, *Emerson's Transatlantic Romanticism*, 170–71. On the attraction of ether for other writers at the time, see Freeman, *Emily Dickinson and the Religious Imagination*, 84.
56. Emerson, "Natural History of Intellect," 12:15.
57. Emerson, "History," 240.
58. Cowley, "A Note on the Selections," xxxiv. See also Jung, "The Concept of Collective Unconscious," 43.
59. Cousin, *Fragments philosophiques*, 287–88.

60. Cousin, *Elements of Psychology*, 78.
61. Vieillard-Baron, *Le spiritualisme français*.
62. Emerson, *English Traits*, 24; Emerson, *The Journals and Miscellaneous Notebooks*, 5:455 and 458.
63. Cousin, *Introduction to the History of Modern Philosophy*, 168.
64. Ralph Waldo Emerson, letter dated August 4, 1842, in Emerson, *The Letters*, 3:76.
65. The quotation is from Emerson, "The Over-Soul," 386; for the lecture, see Emerson, "The Transcendentalist."
66. Emerson, "The American Scholar," 53–54.
67. Bloom, *The American Religion*, 4.
68. On negative dissociation in Schelling, see McGrath, "Schelling and the Unconscious"; McGrath, "Schelling and the History of the Dissociative Self"; McGrath, "The Psychology of Productive Dissociation"; Ellenberger, *The Discovery of the Unconscious*, 199–223. On negative dissociation in Jung, see Ffytche, *The Foundation of the Unconscious*; Bishop, "Jung's Red Book"; Noll, "Multiple Personality and the Complex Theory"; Ulanov, "Jung and Religion." On negative dissociation in Deleuze, see Kerslake, *Deleuze and the Unconscious*. On negative dissociation in Bergson, see Miller, "The Religious Implicates"; Sitbon-Peillon, "Bergson et l'inconscient"; Courcelles, "Bergson et les grandes traditions religieuses." On negative dissociation in Janet, see Hart and Horst, "The Dissociation Theory"; Campbell, *Psychoanalysis and the Time of Life*.
69. Emerson, "The Philosophy of History," 2:57.
70. Emerson, *The Journals and Miscellaneous Notebooks*, 4:348.
71. Emerson often spells *Boehme* "Behmen," as does Coleridge.
72. Emerson, "The Poet," 464.
73. Emerson, 464.
74. Emerson, *The Journals and Miscellaneous Notebooks*, 9:222–23.
75. Sherry, *The Jungian Strand*.
76. Rieff, *The Triumph of the Therapeutic*, 91.
77. Hence the striking Emersonian injunction in "Self-Reliance": "When we have new perception, we shall gladly disburden the memory of its hoarded treasures as old rubbish." Emerson, "Self-Reliance," 271.
78. Coleridge, *Biographia Literaria*, 92–93.
79. Samuel Adler and Samuel Hirsch, as well as the next generation of rabbis, among whom were Bernhard Felsenthal. Stolz, "Bernhard Felsenthal."
80. David Einhorn, letter to Bernhard Felsenthal, dated May 25, 1862, Felsenthal Papers, Center for Jewish History, New York City; quoted in Greenberg, "The Significance of America," 165.
81. See the sermons in Einhorn, *Ausgewählte Predigten und Reden*, in Kohler, ed., *David Einhorn: Memorial Volume*: "Ich bin ein Hebräer!," given in New York, 1879, pp. 85–92; "Der Sieg des Ideen der Unabhaengigkeitserklaerung Amerikas," given at Keneseth Israel in Philadelphia, July 4, 1861, pp. 95–104; "Die Krebschaden unseres Landes," given at Keneseth Israel in Philadelphia, 1863, pp. 114–20.
82. Einhorn, *Das Princip des Mosaismus*.
83. As quoted in Meyer, "America," 73. For a discussion of Einhorn's monotheism, see Meyer, *Response to Modernity*, 245–46.

84. Livingstone, *Adam's Ancestors*.
85. Hirsch, "David Einhorn," 472.
86. From Nahmanides's *Commentary on Genesis*: "The virtue or excellence of the soul [*ma'alat ha-nefesh*], its source and its mystery . . . it did not come from the physical elements or by mediation of the disembodied intelligences. Rather, it is the spirit of the Great Name, from his mouth, knowledge and understanding. For it is from the foundation of Understanding [*binah*], by way of Truth and Faith [*emet ve- 'emunah*]." As quoted in Novak, *The Theology of Nahmanides*, 25–30. This passage is replete with symbolism later taken up by kabbalists to chart the flow of the divine into the human soul. See also Wolfson, "By Way of Truth."
87. Einhorn famously opposed Zacharias Frankel on these two questions at the Rabbinical Conference in Frankfurt in 1845.
88. Einhorn, *Olat Tamid*, 396.
89. For a detailed analysis of Einhorn's interpretation of the Temple symbolism, see Cohen, "David Einhorn."
90. Hirsch, "David Einhorn," 472–73.
91. Einhorn, *Das Prinzip des Mosaïsmus*, 13–65, as quoted in Greenberg, "The Significance of America," 167. On the "law of centralization," see Einhorn, "Abschiedspredigt."
92. Einhorn, *Das Prinzip des Mosaïsmus*, 13–14, as quoted in Greenberg, "Mendelssohn in America," 286. See also Cohn, "David Einhorn"; Greenberg, "The Significance of America"; Greenberg, "Mendelssohn in America."
93. As quoted in Greenberg, "The Significance of America," 175.
94. Huss, "All You Need Is LAV."
95. Myers, "Kabbalah as a Tool of Orthodox Outreach."
96. See Taylor, *Last Works*, 7, 274, 276, 300, 303.
97. The phrase is from Shakespeare, *Hamlet*, act 2, scene 2, lines 323–24: "How noble in reason! How infinite in faculty!" On the use of the phrase "infinite in faculty" in Kantianism, see Moore, *Noble in Reason*, 78–79 and 193.

Introduction to Part II

1. See his notes from 1970 to 1971: "The attempt to understand the interaction with another's word by means of psychoanalysis and the 'collective unconscious.' What psychologists (mainly psychiatrists) disclose existed at one time; it was retained in the unconscious (if only the collective unconscious) and was fixed in the memories of languages, genres, and rituals; from here it penetrates into the speech and dreams (related, consciously recalled) of people (who have a particular psychic constitution and are in a particular state). The role of psychology and of the so-called psychology of culture." Bakhtin, *Speech Genres and Other Late Essays*, 144. What he called psychology of culture corresponds to ethnopsychology as it emerged—but the overlap was frequent. On the turn from the psychology of people to the science of culture, see Trautmann-Waller, *Aux origines d'une science allemande de la culture*; Kalmar, "The Völkerpsychologie of Lazarus and Steinthal." I return to this shift later in chapter 5.
2. Kohn, "The Eve of German Nationalism."

3. It was Heymann Steinthal's contention that John Stuart Mill's phrase "science of national character" was the most accurate English translation of *Völkerpsychologie*. The translation has been an object of controversy: "cultural psychology" and "ethnopsychology" are both closer but still open to various objections, according to Urs Fuhrer in his *Cultivating Minds*, 41. In the English translation of his *Ethics of Judaism*, Moritz Lazarus refers to himself as an "ethno-psychologist." Lazarus, *The Ethics of Judaism*, 1:x. The term *social psychology* aptly describes the enterprise, but it was not referenced until 1864, in the journal of the philosopher and politician Carlo Cattaneo (1801–1869). See Jahoda, *A History of Social Psychology*, 57.
4. Freud, *The Interpretation of Dreams*, chap. 4, "The Dream-Work," 295–511, esp. 295–326.
5. Students of Lazarus and Steinthal's include Franz Boas, who went on to define the field of anthropology in American academia, and the sociologist and theorist Georg Simmel. Adolf Bastian, arguably the father of German anthropology, audited Lazarus's lectures and acknowledged his influence on his work, as we will see over the course of chapter 6.
6. Treitschke, "Unsere Aussichten" [Our prospects], reprinted in Krieger, *Der Berliner Antisemitismusstreit*, 1:14.

Chapter Five

1. Vico, *New Science*, axiom 13, par. 144.
2. See Rotenstreich, "On Cyclical Patterns," 187.
3. In the words of Ernst Cassirer, Giovanni Battista Vico understood "the methodological uniqueness and distinctive value of historical knowledge." Cassirer, *The Logic of the Humanities*, 52.
4. On the relevance of the Counter-Enlightenment category, see Berlin, *Against the Current*; Sternhell, *The Anti-Enlightenment Tradition*.
5. Cassirer, *An Essay on Myth*; Maier, "Vico and Critical Theory."
6. Saint Girons, "Vico, Freud et Lacan."
7. Hillman, *Re-visioning Psychology*, 16, 156. See also Hillman, *Plotinus, Ficino and Vico*.
8. Berlin, *Three Critics of the Enlightenment*, 128. Isaiah Berlin's first essay on Vico and Herder came out in 1976.
9. Trilling, *The Liberal Imagination*, 51. See also Grassi, "Vico versus Freud."
10. Vico, *Grundzüge einer neuen Wissenschaft*.
11. Gans, "Vorwort zur ersten Ausgabe."
12. Johann von Herder's text on Shakespeare and his collection of folk songs, both published in 1773, ushered in a new Romantic sensibility toward literature as a break from Enlightenment ahistoricity and a new hermeneutical turn of self-understanding through historical situatedness. See Herder, *Shakespeare*. He was then rejected by the Romantic movement on accusations of pantheism after the publication of *God: Some Conversations*, in which he proposes that Spinozism be understood as a form of vitalism compatible with Christian faith and makes nature a central aspect of his thought. Baruch Spinoza's philosophical system and its dynamic relationship between substance and finite modes, as described

13. Herder, *Ideen zur Philosophie der Geschichte der Menschheit*; Barnard, *Herder on Nationality, Humanity, and History*. Herder wrote that "not revolutions, but evolutions are the course of nature by which she awakens slumbering powers, develops germs, makes premature age youthful, and often changes apparent death to new life." As quoted in Schmidt, "Cultural Nationalism in Herder," 409.

by Herder, became an inspiration for Friedrich von Schelling's *Naturphilosophie*, as we saw in the first chapter.

14. Fox, "J. G. Herder on Language"; Beiser, *Enlightenment, Revolution, and Romanticism*.
15. Herder, *Ideen zur Philosophie der Geschichte der Menschheit*, bk. 5, chap. 4; bk. 12, chap. 3; Herder, "Letters for the Advancement of Humanity."
16. Clark, *Herder*, 314; Adler, "Herder's Concept of *Humanität*."
17. Herder, "Letters for the Advancement of Humanity," 395.
18. Linker, "The Reluctant Pluralism of J. G. Herder."
19. Herder, "Letters for the Advancement of Humanity," 395.
20. Derrida, *Glas*. See also Gearhart, "The Remnants of Philosophy."
21. In keeping with the traditional translations, I will refer to it as *Spirit* when not using the German term.
22. Geuss, "Kultur, Bildung, Geist"; King, *The Structure of Social Theory*.
23. Magee, *The Hegel Dictionary*.
24. *Aufgehoben* is the past participle of the verb *aufheben*, from which derives the noun *Aufhebung* (sublation). On *Aufhebung*, see Derrida, "Qu'est-ce qu'une traduction 'relevante'?" In this work, Jacques Derrida introduces the concept of stricture and not abolishing or canceling, thus creating a rational self-consciousness that is also beyond reason, equating it with repression at the individual level.
25. Hegel, *Lectures on the Philosophy of World History*, 82.
26. Rosenkranz, *Georg Wilhelm Friedrich Hegels Leben*, 49. See also Yovel, *Dark Riddle*; Yovel, "Sublimity and Ressentiment."
27. Rotenstreich, "Hegel's Image of Judaism"; Hegel, *The Phenomenology of Mind*, 366–67; Fackenheim, *The Religious Dimension in Hegel's Thought*.
28. Hegel, *The Spirit of Christianity and Its Fate*, 69.
29. *Positivity* here refers to any external authority and is the opposite of *subjective*. See Hegel, *The Spirit of Christianity and Its Fate*, 67–181. On alienation in Hegel, see Ormiston, "'The Spirit of Christianity and Its Fate'"; Bloch, "'Entfremdung, Verfremdung'"; Bloch, "Symbole: Les Juifs."
30. Hegel, *The Spirit of Christianity and Its Fate*, 186. *Erdefremdheit*, which is negative in Hegel, would be construed by Franz Rosenzweig as a positive category, and this strangeness to the soil would be transformed into the "very condition for eternity." See Kochan, *The Jew and His History*, 107.
31. Hegel, *The Spirit of Christianity and Its Fate*, 205.
32. On G. W. F. Hegel's knowledge of Judaism, see Lissa, "Deux modèles philosophiques de l'antijudaïsme." On his treatment of the sublime, see Fischbach, "Transformations du concept d'aliénation."
33. On the consequences of Hegel's claims about any religion possessing truth, see Perkins, "Hegel and the Secularisation of Religion." For "world historical importance," see Hegel, *The Philosophy of History*, 7. For "unhappy consciousness," see Hegel, 197–201. For the 1830 second draft, in which he collapses Islam and

Judaism in their incapacity to separate the finite from the Absolute, see Hegel, *Lectures on the Philosophy of World History*, 105–6.
34. Hegel, *The Phenomenology of Spirit*, 126–31.
35. Hegel, *Lectures on the Philosophy of Religions*, 201–387.
36. Maimonides, *The Guide of the Perplexed*, 5–6. See also Amir, "The Perplexity of Our Time," 267.
37. Sayers, *Marx and Alienation*; Ollman, *Alienation*. For a discussion of various occurrences of alienation in the social sciences, see Geuss, *The Idea of a Critical Theory*.
38. Landau, *Nachman Krochmal*; Katsh, "Nachman Krochmal and the German Idealists."
39. I thank Lawrence Kaplan for sharing his in-progress translation of the *Guide for the Perplexed of Our Time*.
40. This is also the position taken by Jay Harris in *Nachman Krochmal*, 125.
41. Schweid, *A History of Jewish Thought* [in Hebrew], 196–98.
42. On Krochmal's thinking on the extinction of peoples, see Nussbaum, "Nachman Krochmal." On Hegel and Jewish nationalism more broadly, especially regarding Israel, see Avineri, "Hegel and the Emergence of Zionism," 12.
43. Funkenstein, *Perceptions of Jewish History*, 243–47.
44. Lawrence Kaplan aptly writes that "Krochmal translates speculative, theological language into the language of collective cultural awareness." Kaplan, "Yehezkel Kaufmann." 145.
45. Lawrence Kaplan, in-progress translation of *The Guide for the Perplexed of Our Time*.
46. Simon Rawidowicz calls it "unitary." See Rawidowicz, *Nachman Krochmals Werke*; Kochan, *The Jew and His History*, 69–87.

Chapter Six

1. Lazarus, "Über den Begriff." In that same issue, the all-but-forgotten historian Eduard Cauer in 1851 highlights the kinship between social sciences and psychology.
2. Shortly after the foundation of Völkerpsychologie, Italian thinkers, in a display of national pride, claimed a measure of Italian influence on the new field and established a direct link between the thought of Vico and the German Lazarus and Steinthal, to whom I will now turn. Carlo Cantoni (1840–1906) described it as "a science of the shared nature of the nations, a science of a certain general Spirit of humanity, a *Völkerpsychologie* (psychology of the people), as some Germans would say and for which they claim to be the first inventors, whereas the idea and the word were most clearly expressed in Vico, a century earlier." Cantoni, *G. B. Vico*, 120–21. For an introduction to Cantoni's thought, see Genna, *Carlo Cantoni*. See also, more generally, Trautmann-Waller, *Aux origines d'une science allemande de la culture*. The phrase "generalities of spiritual life" is from Lazarus, *Das Leben der Seele*, 1:401.
3. Bumann, *Die Sprachtheorie Heymann Steinthals*, 6. Both Lazarus and Steinthal, however, were deemed worthy of an entry in Sabato Morais's dictionary of the major figures of the nineteenth century, albeit a shallow one in the case of Lazarus, as if Morais were unable to assess his work and only enumerated his

writings. See Morais, *Eminent Israelites of the Nineteenth Century*: see "Lazarus," 192–95, "Steinthal," 233–335.

4. Lazarus, "Wie Steinthal und Lazarus Bruder wurden," 152.
5. Lazarus, "Über den Begriff."
6. Lazarus and Steinthal, "Einleitende Gedanken über Völkerpsychologie," in Steinthal, *Kleine sprachtheoretische Schriften*, 321.
7. On his childhood, see Lazarus, "Eine kleine Gemeinde/Elternhaus und Jugend."
8. Lazarus, *Treu und Frei*, 133 and 174.
9. Hackel and Seifert, *August Boeckh*, 20, 121–23, and 230; Bunzl, "*Völkerpsychologie* and German-Jewish Emancipation," 66; Lazarus, *Moritz Lazarus' Lebenserinnerungen*, 422, 434, and 489–90.
10. Achelis, *Moritz Lazarus*, 3–4.
11. Sieg, "Der Preis des Bildungsstrebens," 74; Rahden, "Jews and the Ambivalences of Civil Society"; Rahden, "Germans of the Jewish Stamm."
12. Lazarus, *Die sittliche Berechtigung Preussens*, 58.
13. Lazarus, *Treu und Frei*. See Beiser, *The Berlin Antisemitism Controversy*, 123.
14. On the religious legitimation of race-based anti-Semitism, see Anidjar, *Semites*, esp. 30–33. On the racialization of Jews, see Nahme, "Ghosted," 205–10.
15. Originally published as Lazarus, *Was heißt national?*
16. Stoecker, "Our Demands on Modern Jewry"; Green, "Adolf Stoecker"; Hartston, *Sensationalizing the Jewish Question*.
17. Lazarus, "What Does National Mean?," 330.
18. Lazarus, 330. Moritz Lazarus recognizes the violence of Martin Luther's anti-Jewish writings in a footnote where he chalks it up to the pastor's illusions. The Luther essay he quotes from, "That Jesus Christ Was Born a Jew," emphasizes lineages but is also regarded as theological instruction toward Jews, albeit a friendly one: "We may think highly of ourselves, but we are still heathens, while the Jews are of the lineage of Christ; we are in-laws and strangers; they are kin, nephews and brothers of our Lord. If it were proper to boast of flesh and blood, the Jews belong more to Christ than we; the Jews are blood-relations of our Lord" (see Luther, *Dr. Martin Luther's Sämmtliche Werke*, 29:47).
19. Emphasizing the subjective quality and essence of nationalism, "What Does National Mean?" is in many ways similar to Benedict Anderson's concept of "imagined communities," though Anderson does not reference it. Anderson, *Imagined Communities*. On the paradigm proposed by Lazarus and the possibility of multiculturalism, see Hacohen, *Jacob and Esau*, 284–85 and 393–94.
20. As expressed by Fichte, for instance. See Kohn, "The Paradox of Fichte's Nationalism," 336–38.
21. The term *anti-Semitism* appears in 1880 in the pamphlet *Der Weg zum Siege des Germanenthums über das Judenthum* (*The Path to the Victory of Germanism over Judaism*), in which the polemicist Wilhelm Marr (1819–1904) claims that the irreducible difference between Jews and Germans would not be solved by assimilation and that Jews, as agents of liberalism, would be the end of Germany. Marr, whose political views were aligned with the Left but who became an inspiration for the conservative parties, offered to send Jews to Palestine.
22. Lazarus, *Treu und Frei*.

23. Lazarus, *Über den Ursprung der Sitten*; Lazarus, *Die Ethik des Judentums*; Ben-Pazi, "Moritz Lazarus and the Ethics of Judaism"; Koch, "'Universalist Particularism.'" See also Gordin, "Moritz Lazarus."
24. Scholem, "Zur Neuauflage," 229.
25. Scholem, "Wider den Mythos" ["Against the Myth"] and "Noch einmal" ["Once More"].
26. Myers, *Resisting History*, 46–53.
27. Lazarus, *Die Erneuerung des Judentums*; Scholem, "Juden und Deutsche."
28. Both quotations are from Steinthal, *Allgemeine Ethik*, v–vi.
29. Wiedebach and Winkelmann, eds., *Chajim H. Steinthal*.
30. A *Privatdozent* was an unsalaried faculty lecturer, affiliated with the university but paid by students directly.
31. Steinthal, *Der Ursprung der Sprache*.
32. Steinthal, *Grammatik, Logik, Psychologie*.
33. Pénisson, "Heymann Steinthal." See also Pénisson, "Steinthal."
34. Steinthal, *Über Juden und Judentum*, viii.
35. Steinthal, *Zu Bibel und Religionsphilosophie*.
36. Steinthal, *Die Sprachphilosophischen Werke Wilhelm's von Humboldt*.
37. Steinthal, *Abriss der Sprachwissenschaft*, 29.
38. Steinthal, 386.
39. Steinthal, *Die Sprachphilosophischen Werke Wilhelm's von Humboldt*, 3.
40. Lazarus and Steinthal, "Einleitende Gedanken über Völkerpsychologie," 305; Eckardt, ed., *Völkerpsychologie*; Köhnke, "Einleitung."
41. Humboldt, *Gesammelte Schriften*, 6:152.
42. Steinthal, *Der Ursprung der Sprache*.
43. Steinthal, 5 and 39. See Trautmann-Waller, *Aux origines d'une science allemande de la culture*, 58.
44. Olender, *The Languages of Paradise*; Steinthal, *Der Ursprung der Sprache*.
45. See Naugle, *Worldview*.
46. Humboldt, *Briefe an Friedrich August Wolf*, 250. See also Humboldt, *On Language*.
47. Steinthal, *Grammatik, Logik, und Psychologie*, 388; translation in Klautke, "*Völkerpsychologie* in Nineteenth-Century Germany," 245.
48. On the three stages of Steinthal's reading of Humboldt, see Krauss and Massimilla, "La lettura steinthaliana"; Steinthal, *Philologie, Geschichte und Psychologie*, 2.
49. Steinthal, "Zur Religionsphilosophie." On this divide and the accusation of mysticism, see Benes, *In Babel's Shadow*, 252–54; Bumann, *Die Sprachtheorie Heymann Steinthals*, 18.
50. Lazarus, *Ideale Fragen in Reden und Vorträgen*, 1–13; Steinthal, *Allgemeine Ethik*, 75 and 141. The founder of French psychology, Théodule Ribot, categorized them as part of the Johann Herbart school in his overview of contemporary German psychology, and he called them the true founders of "ethnic psychology." Ribot, *La psychologie allemande contemporaine*, 49–50.
51. Hoeschen and Schneider, "Herbartianismus im 19. Jahrhundert."
52. Herbart, *Psychologie als Wissenschaft*.
53. Herbart, 139 and 140.

54. On the narrowness of the mind, see Locke, *An Essay concerning Human Understanding*, pt. 1, chap. 6, para. 9.
55. Lazarus, *Das Leben der Seele*, 2:80.
56. Steinthal, *Die Arten und Formen der Interpretation*, 535–36.
57. Jahoda, *A History of Social Psychology*, 47–70 and 121–37.
58. The history of the concept by Alberto Meschiari is mostly descriptive. Meschiari, "Per una storia del concetto di 'condensazione.'" For an examination of the process of condensation in Lazarus, see Graevenitz, "'Verdichtung.'"
59. The Brothers Jacob (1785–1863) and Wilhelm (1786–1849) Grimm were among the founders of comparative folklore and historical linguistics. They edited the *Deutsches Wörterbuch*, a thirty-two-volume dictionary, from 1838 until their respective deaths. The project was abandoned and then finally completed in 1961. To this day, the *DWB* is the most comprehensive dictionary of the German language; it reflects the Grimms' intellectual and scholarly pursuits.
60. "How virtue and wisdom are embodied in a teacher of virtue and wisdom before the young man, how the divine becomes a personal god for him: so the fatherland or the idea that it inspires in his princes is condensed and embodied in front of the people." Jean Paul, *Dämmerungschmetterlinge oder Sphinxe* [Dusk butterfly or sphinx], 160.
61. Jean Paul, *Choix de rêves*, 45. On the relationship between the condensation of the dream and psychoanalysis, see Kahn, "Car à présent tout est processus."
62. Kluge, *Etymological Dictionary of the German Language*, s.v. *dicht*; Ripalda, "Philosophie als Dichtung und Verdichtung."
63. Freud acknowledges his youthful readings of Jean-Paul Richter in "A Note on the Prehistory of the Technique of Analysis," 18:265.
64. See Kilcher, *Die "Kabbala denudata."*
65. Trilling, *The Liberal Imagination*, 51.
66. Leary, *Metaphors in the History of Psychology*.
67. Lazarus, *Das Leben der Seele*, 1:402. Here, Lazarus refers to Vico's claim that the burial rituals of the corpses are a cornerstone in the structure of human culture. See also Lazarus, "Verdichtung des Denkens." See Pinchard, "Diis Manibus, ou Vico chez les morts."
68. Lazarus, *Das Leben der Seele*, 2:231.
69. Lazarus, 1:229.
70. Steinthal, "Assimilation und Attraction, psychologisch beleuchtet," 110.
71. Lazarus, "Verdichtung des Denkens," 57–58; Graevenitz, "'Verdichtung.'"
72. Lazarus, "Verdichtung des Denkens," 57.
73. Lazarus, *Das Leben der Seele*, 2:214.
74. Lazarus, *Über die Ideen in der Geschichte*, 75. Hoeschen, "Die 'Zirkulation der Ideen,'" 207. The ideas of Lazarus and Steinthal became important in Russian and later Soviet culture, and this economy of circulation might be one of the reasons. See Brandist, "The Rise of Soviet Sociolinguistics."
75. Lazarus, *Das Leben der Seele*, 2:235.
76. Jakobson, *Studies on Child Language and Aphasia*, 49–74.
77. Lazarus, *Das Leben der Seele*, 2:245.
78. Hirth, "Thesen zu einer Lehre von den 'Merksystemen,'" 473.
79. Lipps, "Der Begriff des Unbewussten in der Psychologie."
80. As quoted by Hans Ellenberger in *The Discovery of the Unconscious*, 774.

81. Steinthal, *Philologie, Geschichte und Psychologie*, 70 and 149.
82. *Verdichtung* is sometimes used by Freud as synonym for "Kompression." See Freud, "On Dreams" (1901).
83. Laplanche and Pontalis, *The Language of Psychoanalysis*, 82–83. Condensation also appears in Freud's *The Psychopathology of Everyday Life* (1901) and *Jokes and Their Relation to the Unconscious* (1905).
84. Laplanche and Pontalis, *The Language of Psychoanalysis*, 82–83.
85. "In the everyday train of thought in life and knowledge, condensation and representation tend not only to stand alongside, but also for one another; but a somewhat closer observation would recognize the different character of both." Lazarus, *Das Leben der Seele*, 2:246.
86. Lazarus, 2:246.
87. Laplanche and Pontalis, *The Language of Psychoanalysis*; Kahn, "Car à présent tout est processus"; Lacan, *Le séminaire*, 11:59.
88. A sentence in the third edition of Freud's 1917 *Lectures* reads: "Nicht nur, dass der Sinn der Symptome regelmässig unbewusst ist; es besteht auch ein Verhältnis von Vertretung zwischen dieser Unbewusstheit und der Existenzmöglichkeit der Symptome." Freud, *Vorlesungen zur Einführung in die Psychoanalyse*, 316. This has been translated as "Not only is the sense of the symptoms regularly unconscious, but there is an inseparable relation between this fact of the symptoms being unconscious and the possibility of their existing." Freud, *Introductory Lectures on Psycho-Analysis*, 16:279. The crucial implication of that sentence and, for that matter, of psychoanalytic theory as a whole, is the emerging theory of complementarity. See Devereux, "Freud, Discoverer of the Principle of Complementarity."
89. Bergson, *Matière et mémoire*; Sitbon-Peillon, "Bergson et l'inconscient."
90. Deleuze, *Le Bergsonisme*, 37.
91. Bergson, *Essais sur les données immédiates de la conscience*; Joussain, "Le sujet conscient et l'inconscient."
92. Hirth, "Thesen zu einer Lehre von den 'Merksystemen,'" 473. See also Hirth, *Energetische Epigenesis*.
93. See Janik and Toulmin, *Wittgenstein's Vienna*; Le Rider, *Modernité viennoise et crise de l'identité*.
94. Tuschling, "Subjektiver und objektiver Geist"; Bienenstock, "Qu'est-ce que l''esprit objectif' selon Hegel?"
95. Simmel, *Einleitung in die Moralwissenschaft*, 1:164–65; Köhnke, "Four Concepts of Social Science at Berlin University," 100–103 and 106n37. See also, more generally, Lepenies, *Between Literature and Science*.
96. Simmel, *The Philosophy of Money*, 477–8.
97. Simmel, 490. Italics added.
98. Simmel, 490.
99. Markowska, "Homo Libidinous," 489–97.
100. Simmel, "A Contribution to the Sociology of Religion," 105.
101. Simmel, 116.
102. Simmel, "On the Concept and Tragedy of Culture."
103. On the comparison between Simmel and Cassirer, and Cassirer's rejection of Simmel's pessimism by ignoring the economic aspect of modernity, see Skidelsky, "From Epistemology to Cultural Criticism."

104. Cassirer, *An Essay on Man*, 70; Bohr, "Die Kollektivität."
105. Cassirer, 71; Bohr, "Die Kollektivität."
106. Barash, ed., *The Symbolic Construction of Reality*.
107. Jung, "The Concept of Collective Unconscious," 42.
108. Bakhtin, *Speech Genres and Other Late Essays*, 144.
109. Kalmar, "The *Völkerpsychologie* of Lazarus and Steinthal."
110. Smith, *Politics and the Sciences of Culture in Germany*, 115. While his diagnosis of "deserted science" is certainly accurate, Woodruff Smith does not mention Lazarus and Steinthal, though they were in fact case studies for the failure of the liberal state. He credits the foundation to Theodor Waitz, Adolf Bastian, and Wilhelm Wundt, who never hid their indebtedness to Lazarus and Steinthal, and he mentions Georg Simmel only briefly. This is a stunning case of the erasure of the Jewish contribution to the science of culture.
111. Lazarus, "Einige synthetische Gedanken zur Völkerpsychologie," 4n.
112. Steinthal, *Philologie, Geschichte und Psychologie*, 29n. See also Trautmann-Waller, "La Zeitschrift für Völkerpsychologie"; Trautmann-Waller, *Aux origines d'une science allemande de la culture*.
113. Steinthal, *Philologie, Geschichte und Psychologie*, 51.
114. Horstmann, "'Erkenntnis des Erkannten,'" 66.
115. Boeckh, *Enzyklopädie und Methodologie der philologischen Wissenschaften*, 11.
116. Jennings, "From Philology to Existential Psychology"; Mead, "The Relations of Psychology and Philology."
117. Gadamer, *Truth and Method*, 186–92.
118. On the linguistic turn in the humanities, see Benes, *In Babel's Shadow*, 244–48.
119. Zunz, *Etwas über die rabbinische Literatur*.
120. Harpham, "Roots, Races, and the Return to Philology."
121. Renan, *L'avenir de la science*, 3:841. See also Bataillon, "Philologie et critique historique chez Renan jeune," 4–9; Benes, *In Babel's Shadow*, 1–5.
122. Chamberlain, *Foundations of the Nineteenth Century*, xcii; Leicht, *Lazarus*; Hartung, *Sprach-Kritik*, esp. the chapter on Moritz Lazarus on pages 61–86, containing an analysis of his paper "Geist und Sprache, eine psychologische Monographie."
123. "The form of the coexistence of humanity is precisely in its separation into peoples." Lazarus and Steinthal, "Einleitende Gedanken über Völkerpsychologie," 5.
124. Zimmerman, *Anthropology and Antihumanism in Imperial Germany*, 53–54.
125. Zimmerman, 55; Koepping, *Adolf Bastian*, 237.
126. Adolf Bastian claims that *Völkergedänke* (collective thought) harbors "elementary ideas." According to Joseph Campbell, Jung derived his archetypes from the concept of "elementary ideas." Campbell with Moyers, *The Power of Myth*, 60.
127. Klautke, "The Mind of the Nation."
128. Boas, "The History of Anthropology," 518. See also Kalmar, "The *Völkerpsychologie* of Lazarus and Steinthal," 673; Lesser, "Franz Boas"; Klautke, "*Völkerpsychologie* in Nineteenth-Century Germany."
129. Hermann Cohen's critique can be found in Cohen, *Jüdische Schriften*, 1–35.
130. Cohen, *Die Religion der Vernunft*, 36. See Wiedebach, *The National Element*.
131. See Köhnke, "Der Kulturbegriff von Moritz Lazarus," ix–xlii.
132. Nordau, *Der Sinn der Geschichte*, 141. This is an incorrect characterization in which the behavior of crowds has to do with, among other factors, magnetic

influences responsible for a "collective unconsciousness." It looks at crowds as group dynamics, prone to contagious excitability, laden with irrationality, and easy to manipulate—an influential read for twentieth-century fascist leaders. Lazarus and Steinthal's observations, which predate Gustave Le Bon's writings, detect psychological patterns and work in the *longue durée*. Ginneken, *Crowds, Psychology, and Politics*; Le Bon, *The Crowd*.

133. On Max Nordau, see Zudrell, *Der Schriftsteller und Kulturkritiker Max Nordau*, 36–39; Bechtel, Bourel, and Le Rider, eds., *Max Nordau*.
134. See the entry on Heymann Steinthal in Singer and Adler, eds., *The Jewish Encyclopedia*, 11:547.
135. Mosse, *Germans and Jews*, 77–115.
136. Zvi Yehuda Kook (1891–1982) praises Steinthal and his Völkerpsychologie as a source for particularism in *Li-Netivot Israel*. See Garb, "'Alien' Culture in the Thought of Rabbi Kook's Circle" [in Hebrew]; Mirsky, *Towards the Mystical Experience of Modernity*.
137. For instance, Thomas, "The Scope and Method of Folk-Psychology." See also Klautke, "The French Reception of *Völkerpsychologie*." See also D'Agostino, "Craniums, Criminals, and the 'Cursed Race'"; Pick, *Faces of Degeneration*; Boas, *Anthropology and Modern Life*, 122.
138. Paul, *Prinzipien der Sprachgeschichte*, 11.
139. The chair was once held by Georg Hegel. See Makkreel, *Dilthey*, and Makkreel, "Wilhelm Dilthey and the Neo-Kantians" (2009).
140. Anderson, "The Debate over the Geisteswissenschaften."
141. Dilthey, *Gesammelte Schriften*, 5:144.
142. Makkreel, *Dilthey*, 35–73.
143. Dilthey, *Introduction to the Human Sciences*, 92.
144. Danziger, "On the Threshold of the New Psychology"; Rieber, *Wilhelm Wundt*—Moritz Lazarus only gets one mention in the latter.
145. Wundt, introduction to *Elemente der Völkerpsychologie*, 2.
146. Wundt, *Völkerpsychologie*; Wundt, *Elemente der Völkerpsychologie*; Freitas Araujo, *Wundt*.
147. Wundt, "Über Ziele und Wege der Völkerpsychologie," 21–22.
148. Köhnke, "Four Concepts of Social Science at Berlin University."
149. See Damiron, *Essai sur l'histoire de la philosophie en France*, 67 and 271. A historian and professor of moral sciences, Jean-Philibert Damiron (1794–1862) held the chair of the history of philosophy at the Sorbonne from 1838. He founded the *Globe* newspaper in Paris with Pierre Leroux in 1824. Damiron was an early influence on Elia Benamozegh, who mentions Damiron's course on psychology in Bereshit 18b of *"Em-la-Miqra,"* his commentary on the Bible.
150. Wundt, *Ethik*, iii.
151. Lazarus, *Die Ethik des Judenthums*, vol. 1. See Baumgardt, "The Ethics of Lazarus and Steinthal"; Steinthal, *Allgemeine Ethik*, vi, where he calls his book "a child of pain."
152. Lazarus, *Das Leben der Seele*, 3:389.
153. Meschiari, "Lazarus and Georg Simmel."
154. Lazarus, "What Does National Mean?," 329.
155. Simmel, *Soziologie*, 685–91; Simmel, *On Individuality and Social Forms*, 143–50.
156. Makkreel, "The Emergence of the Human Sciences."

157. Koepping, *Adolf Bastian*; Trautmann-Waller, "L'ethnologie d'Adolf Bastian." See also Barth et al., *One Discipline, Four Ways*.
158. Mauthner, *Die Sprache*, 9. See also Mauthner, *Beiträge zu einer Kritik der Sprache*. On Fritz Mauthner, see Bredeck, *Metaphors of Knowledge*; Janik and Toulmin, *Wittgenstein's Vienna*, 126–27.

Chapter Seven

1. Weir, "The Riddles of Monism," 3.
2. Ira Robinson terms similar attempts "orthodox strategies of modernization" in "Kabbala and Science in *Sefer Ha-Berit*."
3. Heymann Steinthal, letter to Gustav Glogau, January 17, 1882, as quoted in Pénisson, "Steinthal," 58.
4. Dühring, *Kritische Geschichte*, 523–27. Eugen Dühring was a utopian socialist, a rabid anti-Semite, and a critic of higher education and the military. He is known for being the target of Friedrich Engels's *Anti-Dühring*, which attacked his base materialism. Dühring offered an "ethics of sympathy" to replace the dichotomy between proletariat and capitalist. His optimism stood in stark contrast to the Schopenhauerian ethos. Beiser, *Weltschmerz*, 87–121.
5. Quoted in Jensen, "The Rogue of All Rogues"; Weyembergh, *Nietzsche et E. von Hartmann*.
6. Nietzsche, *Nachgelassene Fragmente*, 262 (as translated in Nicholls and Liebscher, "Introduction," 1). Friedrich Nietzsche was hardly Hartmann's first staunch opponent. A whole generation fiercely opposed Hartmann's theories. As early as 1883, the future famous psychologist Hermann Ebbinghaus defended a dissertation in which he aimed to demolish them.
7. A translation of the book, "revised by the author," came out in France in 1877, and an English edition appeared in 1884. A bibliography of all the literature dedicated to the work of Eduard von Hartmann listed 750 items published between 1869 and 1880. See Plümacher, *Der Kampf um's Unbewusste*, 115–50.
8. For this more nuanced approach, see the examination of Friedrich Nietzsche's multiple references and recommendations in Jensen, "The Rogue of All Rogues."
9. Nietzsche, "On the Uses and Disadvantages of History for Life," § 9, in Nietzsche, *Untimely Meditations*, 109. See Jensen, "The Rogue of All Rogues," 59n37.
10. Jensen, "The Rogue of All Rogues," 53–55.
11. Jung, "The Psychology of the Child Archetype" (1940), 9:152.
12. Carus, *Zur Entwicklungsgeschichte der Seele*.
13. Béguin, *L'âme romantique et le rêve*, 129. A classic study of the dream in Romanticism, Albert Béguin's book offers a remarkably insightful study of Carl Gustav Carus's work.
14. Carus's notion of an all-encompassing unconscious found in the natural realm would also appear in his *Vergleichende Psychologie, oder Geschichte der Seele in der Reihenfolge der Thierwelt* [Comparative psychology, or History of the soul in its place in the sequence of the animal world, 1866]. See Bell, "Carl Gustav Carus and the Science of the Unconscious," 166–67.
15. The division between absolute and partial corresponds to the Jungian personal and impersonal/collective unconscious. As Yvon Brès has rightly noted, Carus's

1866 study expanded his understanding of the soul to nonhuman beings and established a continuum between species and between human beings and the world—hence his interest in animal life, to which Carus devoted half his book *Vergleichende Psychologie, oder Geschichte der Seele in der Reihenfolge der Tierwelt* [Comparative psychology, or History of the soul in the order of the animal realm]. See Brès, "Home, Carus, Hartmann."

16. "How far he has succeeded in his attempt and how much I have borrowed from him in my own work, I leave the judgment of the reader." Hartmann, *Philosophy of the Unconscious*, 1:38.
17. Gibian, "C. G. Carus' Psyche and Dostoevsky."
18. See Damoi, *The Unconscious and Eduard von Hartmann*.
19. Hartmann, *Das Judenthum in Gegenwart und Zukunft*; Poliakov, *The History of Anti-Semitism*, 4:7–8. See Bergmann, "Eduard von Hartmann." On the 1879–81 wave of anti-Semitism, see Meyer, "Great Debate on Antisemitism."
20. Weir, "The Riddles of Monism," 4. The term *monism* was coined by Gottfried Leibniz's disciple Christian Wolff in 1720. Wolff, *Vernünftige Gedanken*.
21. Freud, *Inhibitions, Symptoms, Anxiety* (1926), 20:95.
22. Hartmann, *Die Selbstzersetzung des Christenthums*, 99–121; Wolf, *Eduard von Hartmann*.
23. Weir, "The Riddles of Monism," 5 and 16.
24. Hartmann, *Das religiöse Bewusstsein*.
25. Haeckel, *Generelle Morphologie der Organismen*, 450.
26. Weir, *Secularism and Religion*, 67–70.
27. Ernst Haeckel was an advocate of scientific racism, natural selection, and the social Darwinism that was pivotal to Nazi ideology. The dubious argument to exculpate him from responsibility in the Holocaust is that in his racial hierarchy, he placed Jews at the top and readily acknowledged their contribution to German culture.
28. Hartmann, *Philosophy of the Unconscious*, 3:201. For other mentions of monism, see 3:191, 199–201, and 346.
29. Gardner, "Eduard von Hartmann's *Philosophy of the Unconscious*," 182.
30. Hartmann, *Philosophy of the Unconscious*, 2:235.
31. "In fact, if we view the objects of the senses as mere appearances, as is fitting, then we thereby admit at the very same time that a thing in itself underlies them, although we are not acquainted with this thing as it may be constituted in itself, but only with its appearance, i.e., with the way in which our senses are affected by this unknown something." Kant, *Prolegomena to Any Future Metaphysics*, 66.
32. Hartmann, *Philosophy of the Unconscious*, 2:236.
33. Hartmann, *Zur Geschichte und Begründung des Pessimismus*. On the meaning of his pessimism and its reception in the first part of the twentieth century, see Tsanoff, "Hartmann's Pessimism." On the pessimism controversy, see Beiser, *After Hegel*, 158–216, and also, on Hartmann, 45–48.
34. On Hartmann's defense, see Beiser, *Weltschmerz*, 261–62; Vial, *The Unconscious in Philosophy*, 24–25, 34, and 36.
35. Mann, *Essays*, 285.
36. Janet, *Principes de métaphysique et de psychologie*, 2:389–90. On the "cultural pessimism" of the German fin de siècle, see Stern, *The Politics of Cultural Despair*; Beiser, *Weltschmerz*.

37. Schlitt, "Die Idee als Ideal."
38. Beiser, *Weltschmerz*, 125–26.
39. Hartmann, *Philosophy of the Unconscious*, 1:28.
40. Hartmann, 2:332.
41. Hartmann, 2:336.
42. Hartmann, 1:18.
43. Hartmann, 1:19.
44. Bloch, *Geist der Utopie*, 262. My translations of *Geist der Utopie* are based on the 1918 edition. See Pelletier, "The Sources of Ernst Bloch's Philosophy of History," 267.
45. Hartmann, *Philosophy of the Unconscious*, 1:19.
46. Hartmann, *Gesammelte Studien*, 518; Hartmann, *Philosophy of the Unconscious*, 1:300.
47. Hartmann, 1:300.
48. Hartmann, 1:300.
49. Moritz Lazarus, letter to David Kaufmann, December 15, 1884, in Lazarus and Steinthal, "Einleitende Gedanken über Völkerpsychologie," 172. The criticism was of Hartmann's *Die Selbstzersetzung des Christenthums und die Religion der Zukunft* [Self-destruction of Christianity and the religion of the future]. Lazarus also decided to say nothing about Hartmann's anti-Jewish *Judenthum in Gegenwart und Zukunft* [Judaism in the present and the future]—reasoning that it would give Hartmann's writing a "significance that it does not possess."
50. Lazarus and Steinthal, "Einleitende Gedanken über Völkerpsychologie," 333 and 336.
51. Lazarus, *The Ethics of Judaism*, 1:89.
52. Nordau, *The Interpretation of History*, 130. See also Nordau, *Der Sinn der Geschichte*, 146; Klautke, *The Mind of the Nation*, 30, 52nn102–3.
53. Ribot, *La psychologie allemande contemporaine*, 52.
54. Ribot, 49. On Ribot's characterization of Lazarus and Steinthal, see 49–57. See Klautke, *The Mind of the Nation*, 39 and 55n150.
55. Hartmann, *Philosophy of the Unconscious*, 2:180.
56. Hartmann, 1:359.
57. Wolfson, *Venturing Beyond*, 5, 111–12, and 122.
58. Hartmann, *Philosophy of the Unconscious*, 1:359.
59. In *L'Automatisme psychologique*, Pierre Janet posits two contrasting forms of mental activity, automatism-the subconscious, and synthesis-consciousness.
60. "Theological journals rejoiced to see under the name 'unconscious' an allpowerful wisdom that seems closer to Christian theism than to the inflexible Hegelian Idea. They relished—as a providential manifestation—the triumph of a pessimism that, alongside Christianity, teaches the vanity and the emptiness of life." Nolen, "Introduction du traducteur," 1:viii.
61. See Laurant, "Le regard savant d'Adolphe Franck."
62. The idea of the unconscious as a material and mechanical protoconsciousness appears in an 1877 book by Ernst Kapp, *Elements of a Philosophy of Technology*. The book directly draws on Eduard von Hartmann and has proved essential in media theory.
63. Franck, "'Philosophie de l'inconscient,'" article 3, 601.
64. Franck, article 1, 433.

65. Papus uses Adolphe Franck's letter as an introduction to his treatise on occult science. Franck, "Lettre-préface," viii and ix.
66. On the significance of Gnosticism in the twentieth century, see Jonas, *The Gnostic Religion*; Lazier, *God Interrupted*.
67. Franck, "Philosophie de l'inconscient,'" article 2, 481.
68. Hartmann, *Philosophy of the Unconscious*, 2:118.
69. Franck, "'Philosophie de l'inconscient,'" article 2, 482.
70. Digeon, *La crise allemande de la pensée française*, 147, 362, and 393. One of the main figures of this optimism and the faith in a "new spirit" was the philosopher and politician Edgard Quinet. See Quinet, *L'esprit nouveau*.
71. Simon-Nahum, "Philosophie et science du judaïsme."
72. As Claude Digeon puts it in his magisterial study, *La crise allemande de la pensée française*, "The name of the German philosophers seems to be the symbol of the antagonistic tendencies that divide them," and so was the unconscious, as presented by Eduard von Hartmann (p. 340).
73. On this *franco-judaïsme*, see Simon-Nahum, *La cité investie*.
74. Digeon, *La crise allemande de la pensée française*, 340.
75. Laforgue, *Poésies complètes*, 11–12. See Grojnowski, *Jules Laforgue et l'"originalité"*, 27–39; Marchal, "Laforgue et Hartmann."
76. Barrès, *Le jardin de Bérénice*, 179–83. See Honoré, "Écritures de l'allégorie." Reviews at the time listed Hartmann among Barrès's influences. See Leymarie, "On the Antisemitism of Maurice Barrès."
77. Franck, "Philosophie de l'inconscient," article 2, 484.
78. Hartmann, *Philosophy of the Unconscious*, 2:22–23.
79. Scholem, "A Candid Word," 31–32.
80. Scholem, 32.
81. On Ernst Bloch's initial lack of exposure to the Jewish tradition, see his illuminating interview with Jean-Michel Palmier in Palmier, "La traversée du siècle d'Ernst Bloch (II)," 8: "I grew up without any relationship with Judaism. I learned about it later, when I met a Zionist student in Würzburg. She introduced me to Judaism, not through the writings of Buber, but through other sources, and all the while taking long strolls. It is I who later assimilated myself to Judaism. Later, I got interested in Kabbalah but also in the Gnosis, in philosophy, and in the German romantic tradition. Judaism was but an element among all of that—and perhaps unfortunately so."
82. This argument of the missing piece is made by Michael Löwy in "Jewish Messianism."
83. Geoghegan, *Ernst Bloch*; Hudson, *The Marxist Philosophy of Ernst Bloch*.
84. The influence of most of these thinkers would endure and be digested—and one finds evidence of it in Ernst Bloch's final work, *Experimentum mundi*, 113–44. Wilhelm Wundt, for instance, appears in "Über Heterogonie der Zwecke" [On the heterogeneity of purposes], 10:431–42.
85. Pelletier, "Ernst Bloch et les juifs"; Jung, "The Early Aesthetic Theories of Bloch and Lukács"; Bielik-Robson, "Dreams of Matter"; Münster, "*Experimentum mundi* et le problème des categories."
86. Bloch, *Traces*, 47.
87. Pelletier, "Ernst Bloch et les juifs."
88. Mosse, *Germans and Jews*, 77–115.

89. Principe and Weeks, "Jacob Boehme's Divine Substance *Salitter*"; Feuerbach, *Geschichte der neueren Philosophie*, 177.
90. Hudson, *The Marxist Philosophy of Ernst Bloch*, 22.
91. "One must realize that in Germany philosophy is so thoroughly imbued with Protestant spirit that Catholics who wish to philosophize must almost turn Protestant, while on the other hand Catholic thought has never emerged from the ivory tower of Thomism except in non-philosophical form. In this light, Bloch's philosophy (which incidentally interprets Christ very much in the spirit of the Old Testament, as a prophet of a kingdom of this world) assumes interesting functions of mediating between traditional Protestant philosophies." Habermas, "Ernst Bloch," 317.
92. Löwy, "Jewish Messianism," 109.
93. Landauer, "Der Anarchismus in Deutschland," 29. See also Lunn, *Prophet of Community*, 90–91.
94. Bloch, *Geist der Utopie*, 254.

Chapter Eight

1. Another instance of potential—but later—retrospective apologetics is Maimonides's treatise on asthma, written in Arabic for the son of King Saladin, which emphasizes the unconscious element in an ailment. Maimonides held that the symptom can be cured by language—thus subtly alluding to its psychosomatic nature. The book came to be known as *Sefer ha Mis'adim* [Treatise on diet] and was only published in Hebrew in 1940. It resurfaced at a moment of increased interest in psychology, and it was regarded as evidence that Maimonides was a precursor of Freud, as seen in the introduction and commentary by the historian of medicine Süssmann Munter. See Maimonides, *Rabbeinu Mosheh Ben Maimon, Sefer ha-Qazeret, o Sefer ha-Mis'adim* [Treatise on asthma, or Book of nourishments].
2. James, *The Varieties of Religious Experience*, 10–17.
3. Gershom Scholem, as quoted in Wasserstrom, *Religion after Religion*, 197. He was also inspired by what major historians of the *Annales* called "psychologie historique." See Ghica, "De quelques questions." Scholem described Sabbatai Zevi's own unconscious at work in the figure of his angelic mentor, called the Maggid (whose name means an itinerant Jewish preacher), who reveals the secrets of creation to Sabbatai Zevi. It is a "product of the unconscious levels of psyche," Scholem claimed. Even in this depiction of a singular character, this type of unconscious is not a personal, repressive type but constituted of its archetypal and collective dimension: he is "the living archetype of the paradox of the holy sinner" (*Major Trends in Jewish Mysticism*, 293). Although he denied using archetypes and being influenced by Jung, or by Freudianism in general, that approach might have been fueled by his encounters with Carl Jung at the Eranos seminars, where the Iranologist Henry Corbin and the historian of religion Mircea Eliade also met. Scholem, *Sabbatai Sevi*, 58. On his denials, see Scholem, *Of Jews and Judaism in Crisis*, 28–29. On the encounters, see Wasserstrom, *Religion after Religion*, 65 and 197.
4. See Zachhuber, "F. W. J. Schelling and the Rise of Historical Theology." Henry Corbin also uses the term *historiosophy*, as noted by Steven Wasserstrom. "By

contrast, that which certain Western philosophers, like Baader, and Schelling, have called 'Historiosophy' would not be able to do without a metaphysics, for if one ignores or excludes the hidden, esoteric sense of things, the living phenomena of this world are reduced to those of a cadaver." Corbin, "For the Concept of Irano-Islamic Philosophy," 121. See also Wasserstrom, *Religion after Religion*, 159–60.

5. Scholem, *Lamentations of Youth*, 212. This diary entry is dated March 14, 1918.
6. Guetta, *Philosophy and Kabbalah*.
7. Benamozegh, *Bibliothèque de l'hébraïsme*, 16, as quoted in Guetta, *Philosophy and Kabbalah*, 11–12.
8. Benamozegh, *Teologia dogmatica e apologetica*, 271.
9. Benamozegh, 271.
10. Benamozegh, *Bibliothèque de l'hébraïsme*, 16, as quoted in Guetta, *Philosophy and Kabbalah*, 11–12.
11. Aristotle, *De Anima*, bk. 3, chap. 5; Aristotle, *Metaphysics*, chap. 12; Maimonides, *The Guide of the Perplexed*, 1:68; Maimonides, *Yesodei ha-Torah*, 2:10.
12. Gioberti, *Della protologia di Vincenzo Gioberti*.
13. "Ognuno s'accorge come questa facoltà rivelatrice di Dio sia l'origine della umana perfettibilità = del progresso." Benamozegh, *Teologia dogmatica e apologetica*, 93 and 94. See Rothschild, *Economic Sentiments*. It paralleled a Christian self-definition, and in times of crisis it aimed at setting forth a base for Judaism that would enable crypto Jews to think of themselves as Jewish upon accepting those beliefs.
14. Renan, *L'avenir de la science*, xvi.
15. Benamozegh, "Israel et l'humanité," manuscript, 821.
16. Quinet, *La création*.
17. "The tendencies pitted against one another in the macrocosm (geniuses, characters, ideas, human interests) reveal themselves as elements constitutive of the microcosm, in the exact same way as the microcosms, pitted against one another, produce, through their struggle, the reality of the macrocosm." Benamozegh, *Israël et l'humanité*, 252.
18. Benamozegh, "Israel et l'humanité," manuscript, 821.
19. Consider the rest of the passage: "For myself, when it is a question of the moral and intellectual law that regulates humanity, and to speak of Revelation in the Jewish sense, we will see its supreme identity in the cosmic, universal law and it will be there for us an unhoped-for means of understanding the proposition in the Kabbalah which sees the same Logos, the same Word in the Creation and the Revelation, which is called Tiferet, the intelligible world under the name of Torah, seeing in the Hohma or wisdom, which, according to the Proverbs, presided at the creation of the world, nothing but the Law itself, the revealed Law, which is perfectly identical even to the literal meaning of the words of the prophets, as we will show, if it please God, in his place." Benamozegh, *Israël et l'humanité*, 252.
20. Benamozegh, 380. Elia Benamozegh was quoting from Hartmann's *Philosophy of the Unconscious* in its French edition: *La philosophie de l'inconscient*, 346.
21. Franck, *The Kabbalah*, 39.
22. Damiron, *Essai sur l'histoire de la philosophie en France*, 67 and 271.
23. The concept of deferred action or meaning came to play a significant role in Freudianism. See Freud, *A Case of Hysteria*. Sigmund Freud narrowed the

concept of deferred action to *nachträgliche Gehorsam*, deferred obedience, in *Totem and Taboo*, 178. See Brunner, *Freud and the Politics of Psychoanalysis*, 161. See also "latent content" in Laplanche and Pontalis, *The Language of Psychoanalysis*, 235.

24. Normandin and Wolfe, eds., *Vitalism and the Scientific Image*.
25. Tomlinson, *Head Masters*, 50–76; Esfeld, *Holism in Philosophy of Mind and Philosophy of Physics*.
26. Kosch, *Freedom and Reason in Kant, Schelling, and Kierkegaard*, 87–121.
27. Dov Katz, *Tenu'at ha-musar*, vols. 1 and 2. The two main monographs in English are centered on the figure of the founder. See Etkes, *Israel Salanter*; Goldberg, *Israel Salanter*; Fishman, "The Musar Movement"; Ross, "Ha-Megamah ha-anti-ratsionalit bi-tenu'at ha-musar"; Stone, "Musar Ethics."
28. I will use the term *Musar*, capitalized, to refer the movement and *musar*, lowercase, for the category of ethical writings that predates the movement. As a genre, *musar* dates back to the tenth-century treatise *Chovot ha Levavot* [The duties of the heart] by ibn Paquda and constitutes a rich tradition, including Moses Cordovero's *Tomer Devorah* [The palm tree of Deborah], Elijah de Vidas's *Reshit Hokhmah* [The beginning of wisdom], Isaiah Horowitz's *Shnei Luhot ha-Brit* [The two tablets of the alliance], and Moses Hayyim Luzzatto's *Messilat Yesharim* [The path of the just].
29. *Iggeret ha-musar* [The epistle on musar] was published by Rabbi Israel Salanter as an appendix to the 1858 edition of Moses Cordovero's work of kabbalistic musar, *Tomer Devorah*. On the opposition between musar and Kabbalah, see Brown, "'It Does Not Relate to Me'" [in Hebrew]; Pachter, "The Musar Movement and the Kabbalah"; Garb, *Yearnings of the Soul*, 22, 33, and 66; Koch, *Human Self-Perfection*, 1–45.
30. In a letter with a rare direct mention of Kabbalah, Israel Salanter wrote, "It has nothing to do with me: I do not involve myself in such things. Nor do I know if this is the right time for them." As quoted in Brown, "'It Does Not Relate to Me'" [in Hebrew], 426. The two main monographs on Salanter take opposite views. Immanuel Etkes's stance is that Salanter was opposed to Kabbalah. See Etkes, *Israel Salanter*, 93–95 and 120–21. Hillel Goldberg, on the other hand, contends that Salanter did study Kabbalah, in *Israel Salanter*, 209–19.
31. Whether Kabbalah was judged irrelevant for their purposes (according to Mordechai Pachter) or whether the kabbalistic teachings were reserved to an elite group (as Jonathan Garb argues), Musar scholars were initially disinclined to add Kabalistic materials. This changed with a second generation, most of whom were students of Salanter, such as Simhah Zissel Ziv (1824–1898). On this convergence, see Claussen, *Sharing the Burden*, 101–3; Ross, "Moral Philosophy in the Writings of Rabbi Salanter's Disciples." See also Solomon, "R. Eliyahu Eliezer Dessler."
32. Brown, *HaHazon Ish* [in Hebrew], 95; Glenn, *Israel Salanter*.
33. Israel Salanter's main writings can be found in sermons published in 1861 in a journal of ethics, *Tevunah*, founded in 1861–62, and in the *Eṣ Pri*, an 1881 pamphlet calling for support for Jewish education. On the various stages of his writings, see Goldberg, *Israel Salanter*, 6–13; Goldberg, "Israel Salanter's Suspended Conversation" (on *Tevunah*, see 38–39).

34. Salanter, *Eṣ Pri*, 13, par. 2.
35. The influence is attested by the fact that Mendel Lefin's book was reprinted at Salanter's request in 1845. Etkes, *Israel Salanter*, 126. Other possible influences include John Locke's *Essay concerning Human Understanding*, Étienne Bonnot de Condillac's *Traité des Sensations*, and David Hume's *A Treatise on Human Nature*. On the echoes of Benjamin Franklin's autobiography in Lefin's work, see Sinkoff, *Out of the Shtetl*, 139–41.
36. On the reception strategies of non-Jewish fields of knowledge, see Leiman, "Rabbinic Openness to General Culture."
37. Lefin lived for a few years in Berlin, and despite gravitating to Moses Mendelssohn's circle, he returned to Galicia with a vision for an eastern European Enlightenment not solely modeled on the Berlin Haskalah's program. See Sinkoff, *Out of the Shtetl*, 45.
38. Salanter, *Sefer Tevunah*, 38, col. 1.
39. Goodfriend, "Ethical Theory and Practice in the Hebrew Bible," 36.
40. The concept of *axis mundi* was borrowed from Mircea Eliade by Arthur Green, who defined it as a principle of the organization of sacred space. See Green, "The Zaddiq as Axis Mundi."
41. Etkes, "Rabbi Zalman of Lyady."
42. For an analysis of *yeṣer* and *yeṣarim*, see Rosen-Zvi, *The Evil Inclination*.
43. Salanter, *Sefer Tevunah* 38, col. 1. Translation in Goldberg, *Israel Salanter*, 106.
44. Jung, *Archetypes and the Collective Unconscious*, 17–18.
45. Salanter wrote the German words *ganz dunkel* in Hebrew characters. Salanter, *Eṣ Pri*, 13, par. 2. *Keheh* also means "faint" or "dim" (Lev. 13:28 and Isa. 42:3), and in its verbal form it denotes the action of fading away (Lev. 13:6 and 13:21). Hillel Goldberg has painstakingly identified "outer forces" (or faculties) as "mental acts done in self-awareness," and "inner forces" as absence of awareness or "conscious perception." Goldberg, *Israel Salanter*, 168.
46. Gellman, *Abraham! Abraham!*; Green, *Devotion and Commandment*.
47. On the *Yalkut Shimoni*, see Elbaum, "Yalkut Shimoni"; Börner-Klein, "Yalkut Shimoni *Numbers* on Proselytes" [in Hebrew]. On the interpretative tendencies of the *Yalkut Shimoni*, see Marx, "Kompilation oder Interpretation."
48. Genesis Rabbah 56:8, in which the two aspects are in the same text: "Abraham stretches out his hand to take the knife and tears fall from his eyes into the eyes of Isaac from the compassion of a father. Nevertheless, his heart rejoiced at doing the will of his creator."
49. Salanter, *Eṣ Pri*, 13–14, par. 5.
50. Maimonides, *The Guide of the Perplexed*, 1:39; Delitzsch, *A System of Biblical Psychology*.
51. Habermas, *The Philosophical Discourse of Modernity*, 6.
52. Goldberg, *Israel Salanter*, 161.
53. On *hitpa'alut*, see Goldberg, 139 and 284n190.
54. *Sefer Eṣ Pri*, 13–14, par. 5.
55. Jacobs, *Religion and the Individual*, 1–9.
56. On hylic intellect, see Kreisel, *Maimonides' Political Thought*, 65–66, 73, and 91. On the actualization of the active intellect, see Bakan, Merku, and Weiss, *Maimonides' Cure of Souls*, 11–12. The concept is found in Maimonides in *The Guide of the Perplexed*, 2:4.

57. The literature on Emmanuel Levinas and otherness is vast. On Levinas and the *aqedah* more specifically, see Levinas, *Noms propres*, 84–85; Stolle, "Levinas and the Akedah"; Katz, "The Voice of God"; Brezis, *Levinas et le tournant sacrificiel*, 271ff.
58. Goldberg, *Israel Salanter*, 160–61.
59. Goldberg, 159–60.
60. Goldberg, *The Fire Within*. This book is a subjective and personal account of Hillel Goldberg's experience of the Musar and companion to the more academic study of Salanter, aimed at a broader, popular audience. On the politics and purposes of ArtScroll, see Stolow, *Orthodox by Design*.
61. Eckman, *A History of the Musar Movement*, 167. In this his overview of the movement, Lester Samuel Eckman even compares Salanter's work with Viktor Frankl's best-selling *Man's Search for Meaning* (1946), which the Viennese therapist, a Holocaust survivor, wrote in order to make sense of the trauma and loss he had experienced.
62. Scholem, *Major Trends in Jewish Mysticism*, 340–41.
63. Scholem, 341.
64. Idel, *Kabbalah*, 150–53; Idel, *Hasidism*, 41, 45–47, 52, 134, 171–76, and 227–38; Schatz-Uffenheimer, *Hasidism as Mysticism*, 72, 179–83, and 204–14; Margolin, *Inner Religion* [in Hebrew], 273–83; Garb, *Yearnings of the Soul*, 47–65; Brill, *Thinking God*, 110–33.
65. Marcus, *Ahron Marcus*; Kitzis, "Aaron Marcus's 'Hasidism'" [in Hebrew]; Shanes, "Ahron Marcus."
66. Marcus, *Der Chassidismus*; Idel, "Transfers of Categories."
67. For a comprehensive yet rather weak overview, see Goldman, "Rabbinic Theology."
68. Marcus, *Hartmann's Inductive Philosophie*, 16.
69. The use of inductive argumentation also appeared in a Talmudic context. See Reichman, *Abduktives Denken und talmudische Argumentation*.
70. Bulgakov, *Unfading Light*.
71. Zalkin, "Scientific Thinking"; Feiner, *The Jewish Enlightenment*.
72. On Hayyim Selig Slonimski, an official government censor, editor of the Warsaw, Congress Poland–based newspaper *Hatzefirah*, and inspector of the rabbinical seminary in Zhitomir, see Robinson, "Hayyim Selig Slonimski."
73. Slonimski, *Mezti'ut ha-nefesh ve-kiyumah mi-hutz la-guf* [On the immortality of the soul].
74. Marcus, *Hartmann's Inductive Philosophie*, 75.
75. Marcus, *Der Chassidismus*, 220.
76. Darnton, *Mesmerism*, 29; Pattie, *Mesmer and Animal Magnetism*.
77. Margoliouth, "The Doctrine of the Ether in the Kabbalah."
78. On mesmerism, see Roussillon, *Du baquet de Mesmer*; Crabtree, *From Mesmer to Freud*.
79. Darnton, *Mesmerism*, 98. See also Armando, Belhoste, and Johnson, "Mesmerism"; Taves, *Fits, Trances, and Visions*, 140.
80. Darnton, *Mesmerism*, 127.
81. Darnton, 115.
82. Charles Deslon, quoted in Darnton, 115.
83. Hegel, *Philosophy of Mind*, § 379, p. 6.

84. Schopenhauer, *On Will in Nature*.
85. Podmore, *From Mesmer to Christian Science*. On mesmerism as hypnotism, see Chajes, "Entzauberung and Jewish Modernity," 196–200; Straus, "The Baal-Shem of Michelstadt."
86. Marcus, *Der Chassidismus*, 91.
87. On the *Idra*, see Hellner-Eshed, *Seekers of the Face*.
88. Marcus, *Der Chassidismus*, 67.
89. Du Prel, *Die Philosophie der Mystik*, 14.
90. In the 1914 edition of *Die Traumdeutung*, Freud called Du Prel a "gestreiche geistreiche Mystiker," a "witty mystic" (p. 48n). Weber, "Carl du Prel"; Braun, "Traumgeburten"; Josephson-Storm, *The Myth of Disenchantment*, 189–95. This attempt is best shown in Du Prel's *Die Entdeckung der Seele durch die Geheimwissenschaften* [The discovery of the soul through the occult sciences].
91. Carl du Prel, quoted in Keithley, "A Synopsis of Baron du Prel's 'Philosophie der Mystik,'" 13–14.
92. Du Prel, *Die Philosophie der Mystik*, 119.
93. Schelling, *On the History of Modern Philosophy*, 39.
94. In his October 12, 1916, entry, Gershom Scholem cites Ahron Marcus's recension of a monograph about Rabbi Nachman: "According to Duprel [sic] (as cited by Markus [sic] in Hartmann and Hasidism), 'mysticism is a person's magical relation to himself.'" Scholem, *Lamentations of Youth*, 144 and 147; Scholem, "Ahron Marcus and Hasidism." See also Marcus, review of *Rabbi Nachman von Brazlaw*.
95. On the Maggid of Mezeritch, see Scholem, *Devarim be go*, 351–60. On the role of the Besht, see Rosman, *Founder of Hasidism*, 6; Etkes, *The Besht*.
96. The Maggid left no writings of his own, but the *Liqqutei Amarim* and *Or ha-Emet* were collected by his students and published in 1780 and 1899, respectively.
97. Dov Baer, *Maggid Devarav le-Ya'aqov*, 19a.
98. Maggid of Mezeritch, *Or ha-Emet*, 15b–16a. For an analysis of this homily with respect to the nullification of human speech, see Schatz-Uffenheimer, *Hasidism as Mysticism*, 182.
99. Gershom Scholem's essay, "The Unconscious and the Concept of *Qadmut ha-Sekhel* in Hasidic Literature," first appeared in *Hagut* (a Hugo Bergmann Festschrift) in 1944. It was reprinted in Scholem, *The Latest Phase* [in Hebrew], 268–76. He is critical of the proponent of a thesis of the discovery of the unconscious by Hasidic masters penned by Ahron Marcus. See Marcus, *Hartmann's Inductive Philosophie*. Scholem never returned to these questions, but they were subsequently taken up by two Jewish students of Jung, Siegmund Hurwitz and Erich Neumann. See Hurwitz, "Psychological Aspects in Early Hasidic Literature"; Neumann, *The Roots of Jewish Consciousness*, vol. 2, *Hasidism*.
100. See Scholem, "The Unconscious and the Concept of *Qadmut ha-Sekhel*" [in Hebrew].
101. The Maggid of Mezeritch, quoted in Baer, *Torat ha-Maggid, Parshat Va-Yeṣe*.
102. The Maggid of Mezeritch, quoted in Baer, *Maggid Devarav le-Ya'aqov*, 19a.
103. Wolfson, *Through a Speculum that Shines*, 39.
104. Schatz-Uffenheimer, *Hasidism as Mysticism*, 182.
105. On the question of speech and language in the work of the Maggid, see Mayse, *Speaking Infinities*.

106. Assaf, "'A Heretic Who Has No Faith'"; Mayse, "'Or haHayyim.'" I use his translation of the *Or ha-Hayyim* as printed in the *Mikra'ot Gedolot*.
107. Ibn Attar, *Or ha-Hayim*, interpreted by Ahron Marcus; quoted in Mayse, "'Or haHayyim,'" 76.
108. Mayse, 76.
109. Mayse, 76. In *The Guide of the Perplexed*, 1:67, Maimonides wrote, "'Va-yinafash' means: 'That which He desired was accomplished; what He wished had come into existence.'" From there, Samson Raphael Hirsch, in *Commentary on Shemot* 31:7, deduces that "he withdrew into Himself"—as into his own essence. See also Hirsch, *The Hirsch Chumash*, 743; Hirsch, *The Nineteen Letters on Judaism*, 32.
110. Marcus quotes the passage in Hebrew (transliterated below) and highlights "the following play on words": "Weaudia lemitbonen bipnimiut haskalat bamuskal sche haskalat balliaskel taskil bahaskalot, ubehaskel bebaskalato jaskil schemuskal muschlal habaskel." Ibn Attar, *Or ha-Hayim* on Leviticus 16:1. More than a play on words, it is the alliteration process that he spells out quite literally for a potentially non-Hebrew-speaking audience, which sheds light on the audience he was targeting.
111. Marcus quotes ibn Attar in *Barsilai* (1905), xxii, where he immediately adduces Wilhelm Wundt, but also in *Hartmann's Inductive Philosophie*, 121.
112. Ibn Attar, *Or ha-Hayim*, 319.
113. Wundt, *Beiträge zur Theorie der Sinneswahrung*, 438.
114. The question mark is Ahron Marcus's addition.
115. The quote ends here, but Marcus fails to indicate it, so that it looks like the whole paragraph is Wundt's.
116. Marcus, *Barsilai* (1905), xxii.
117. See Gershom Scholem's letter to the historian of ancient religion Morton Smith, dated December 30, 1950, in Smith and Scholem, *Correspondence*, 52.
118. Hurwitz, "Archetypische Motive in der Chassidischen Mystik"; Hurwitz. *Lilith*.
119. Hurwitz, "Psychological Aspects in Early Hasidic Literature." Adding to Scholem's claim, it is true that the concept precedes the Maggid: it can be traced back to the Maharal of Prague. Elliot Wolfson traces the influence of the Maharal through his use of *qadmut ha-sekhel* in "Suffering Time," 21n50.
120. Abraham of Kosov, *Yesod Ha-Emunah*.
121. Abraham ben Dov Baer, *Hesed Le-Avraham*, 29.
122. On the thoughts and the practice for their elevation, see Mayse, *Speaking Infinities*, 219, 288, and 296; Mondshine, "Elevating the Attributes of the Alien Thought" [in Hebrew]; Margolin, *Inner Religion in Jewish Sources*, 118–21. On the *mahshavot zarot* in the work of other thinkers, see Brill, *Thinking God*.
123. Marcus, *Hartmann's Inductive Philosophie*, 75.
124. The Prague-born author Jiří Langer, in *Nine Gates to the Chasidic Mysteries*, the account of his departure from his assimilated family and his sojourn among Hasidic communities in 1913, uses only coded language to describe his erotic attraction to the rabbi of Belz. Ten years later, he launched into Freudian territory. See Langer, *Die Erotik der Kabbalah*.
125. Samuel Alexandrov's work tends to be discussed, in a very unusual articulation, in connection with the inception of religious Zionism and his proximity to Ahad Ha-Am, the father of cultural Zionism. See Slater, "A Forgotten Variety of Religious Zionism"; Schweid, *A History of Modern Jewish Religious Philosophy*,

3:319–26. For a more expansive study of Alexandrov's thought, see Luz, "Spiritualism and Religious Anarchism" [in Hebrew]; Slater, "'Those Who Yearn for the Divine'"; Slater, "To Purify Religion."

126. Alexandrov's metaphor of choice was the Tree of Knowledge, shared with Christianity and from which all can learn. See Alexandrov, "Takhlit Ma'aseh shamayim va-arez," 268.

127. *Sobernost* is often understood as ecumenism, as the integral community of the Eastern Orthodox churches, and as a defining feature of Russian identity. But it also pertains to the reuniting of the physical world and the divine, and to the idea of a kingdom of heaven on earth. On the dialogue between Vladimir Solovyov and Judaism, see Solovyov, *The Burning Bush*. See also Bar-Yosef, "The Jewish Reception of Vladimir Solov'ëv," 382–83. Schelling might have connected Samuel Alexandrov and Solovyov. On the proximity between Solovyov and the positive philosophy of the later Schelling, see Valliere, "Solov'ëv and Schelling's Philosophy of Revelation."

128. Alexandrov, *Mikhtevei Meḥqar u- Viqqoret* [Letters on research and criticism], 77; translation in Wolfson, *Suffering Time*, 413. Italics added.

129. The source for this might be the prolific author of the Haskalah, Salomon Rubin (1823–1910), famous for his Hebrew translation of Spinoza but also for his treatise *Yesod Mistere ha-'Akkum we-Sod Ḥokmat ha-Ḳabbalah*, published in German as "Paganism and Kabbalah": *Heidenthum und Kabbala*. Alexandrov corresponded with Rubin and disputed his dismissive stance on Kabbalah as superstition. Nonetheless, he may have adopted his views on its Neoplatonic, Essene, and Gnostic sources. On Rubin, see Kohler, *Kabbalah Research*, 257–58.

130. Alexandrov, *Mikhtevei Meḥqar u- Viqqoret*, 77.

131. See Samuel Alexandrov's manuscript letter to Eliezer Yitzhak Sheinboim, in Slater, "To Purify Religion," 233n200. I thank Isaac Slater for bringing these issues to my attention and for sharing the letter as well as the exchange with Salomon Rubin.

132. Slater, "God Has Wrapped Himself in a Cloak of Materialism."

133. Rav Kook and Alexandrov's correspondence seems to have ended in 1914, however. We do not have evidence of any letters exchanged after the Russian Revolution.

134. Scholem, *Major Trends in Jewish Mysticism*, 341.

135. Buber, preface to his doctoral dissertation, "Zur Geschichte des Individuationsproblems." See also Schmidt, *Martin Buber's Formative Years*, 34–44, esp. 35.

136. Buber, "Zur Geschichte des Individuationsproblems," 276.

137. Martin Buber, letter to Marcus Ehrenpreis, February 19, 1904; Martin Buber and Marcus Ehrenpreis Archive, National and University Library, Jerusalem, as quoted in Urban, *Aesthetics of Renewal*, 56. In this letter, Buber invited Ehrenpreis, a fellow member of the World Zionist Organization who sat on the editorial board of the *Jüdische Almanach*, to collaborate on an anthology—an invitation that was declined.

138. In *On Judaism* (1916), Buber refers to Moritz Lazarus as "a clever and amiable popular philosopher" when evoking Lazarus's posthumous *Renewal of Judaism* (1909). He acknowledged the impression this slim volume had made on him, especially in light of its injunction to revive the spirit of prophecy. See Luz, "Buber's Hermeneutics."

139. Buber, *Elemente des Zwischenmenschlichen* in *Werke*, 1:269. Paul Mendes-Flohr sees a gap between these early years and the 1923 magnum opus *I and Thou*, which, he observes, is an "ontology of the interhuman." See Mendes-Flohr, *From Mysticism to Dialogue*, 1, 31–47, and 131–32nn1, 8.
140. Mendes-Flohr and Susser, "'Alte und Neue Gemeinschaft.'"
141. Buber, *Die Geschichten des Rabbi Nachman*.
142. Buber, *Die Legende des Baal-Schem*, translated as *The Legend of the Baal Shem*; Silberstein, *Martin Buber's Social and Religious Thought*, 43–70; Hollander, "Buber, Cohen, Rosenzweig."
143. Buber, "The Revelation," 63–64.
144. *Ungrund* is indeed used for more peaceful descriptions, such as eternity, as in "Denn alles Leben der kommenden Welt ist zu schreiten von Heer zu Heer, nach oben und oben, bis in den Ungrund der Ewigkeit" (For all life of the world to come is to march from host to host, higher and higher, into the abyss of eternity). Buber, "Von Heer zu Heer," 197.
145. Mendes-Flohr, "Zarathustra as a Prophet of Jewish Renewal"; Kaufmann and Soll, eds., *Nietzsche, Heidegger, and Buber*. This is especially the case with Nietzschean Zionism; see Aschheim, *The Nietzsche Legacy in Germany*.
146. Buber, *Vom Geist des Judentums*, 55; Buber, *On Judaism* (1995 ed.), 82.
147. Buber, *Vom Geist des Judentums*, 82.
148. Buber, *The Legend of the Baal Shem*, 13. On the I-Thou, see Heard, "The Unconscious Functions."
149. Buber, *The Legend of the Baal Shem*, 26 and 39.
150. Jacobi, *Main Philosophical Writings and the Novel "Allwill*," 231.
151. Buber uses the word *revolution* in "Alte und Neue Gemeinschaft" (see note 140 above). See Mendes-Flohr, *From Mysticism to Dialogue*, 82; Franks, "Mythology, Essence, and Form," 73.
152. Buber, "Religion und modernes Denken." The text became the fifth chapter of his *Eclipse of God*, published the following year. See Buber, "Religion and Modern Thinking," 71; Buber, "Supplement: Reply to C. G. Jung," 113–17. On the controversy, see Buber Agassi, *Martin Buber on Psychology and Psychotherapy*, 34–71 and 201–24; Stephens, "The Martin Buber–Carl Jung Disputations."
153. This is also why Buber rejects the myths and calls the Hasidic stories "legends." On the legends as I and Thou, see Friedman, *Martin Buber's Life and Work*, 100–115.
154. Jung, "Religion und Psychologie," translated as "Religion and Psychology," 665. Italics in original.
155. Buber, "God and the Spirit of Man," 162; Buber, "Reply to C. G. Jung," 175.
156. Buber, "Mystik als religiöser Solipsismus."
157. Magid, "For the Sake of a Jewish Revival." See also Friedman, "Interpreting Hasidism."
158. Buber, *On Judaism* (1967 ed.), 8.
159. The editor of the volume, Ann Conrad Lammers, rightly makes this observation in her introduction to Neumann, *The Roots of Jewish Consciousness*, 2:xxviii. On Neumann, see Krüger, "After Eighty Years of Slumber."
160. Neumann, *The Roots of Jewish Consciousness*, 2:171.
161. Neumann, 2:171.
162. Neumann, 2:175.
163. Lacan, *The Four Fundamental Concepts of Psychoanalysis*, 25.

Coda

1. Shagar, *Faith Shattered and Restored*, 22; Valentini and Tourage, eds., *Esoteric Lacan*.
2. Auden, "In Memory of Sigmund Freud," 217.
3. "The repressed is the prototype of the unconscious for us." Freud, "The Ego and the Id" (1923), 19:15.
4. On this continuity, see Erwin, *The Freud Encyclopedia*, 311–20.
5. Derrida, *Positions*, 71.
6. Bois, "'A la recherche du temps perdu,'" 4.
7. Rose, *Jewish Philosophical Politics in Germany*, 1.
8. Emerson, "The Transcendentalist," 205.
9. Du Bois, *Dusk of Dawn*, 148. See Bruce, "W. E. B. Du Bois."
10. This sense of a split consciousness and the need for cultural pluralism was expressed notably by Horace Kallen and the *Menorah Journal* in the United States. Founded in 1915, the journal had grown out of the Menorah Society organized by a group of Jewish students at Harvard University in 1906. Among its contributors were Louis Brandeis—who would go on to be the first Jew to sit on the US Supreme Court the following year—and the sociologist Horace M. Kallen, best known for his critique of the "melting pot" and his advocacy of "cultural pluralism" in 1924. See Korelitz, "The Menorah Idea"; Greene, *The Jewish Origins of Cultural Pluralism*.
11. Thiem, "Transgender Quarrels."
12. On Freud's own double consciousness, see Scherer, *The Freudian Orient*. On Judaism and double consciousness, traced back to Abraham abandoning the religion of the father, see Boyarin, *Storm from Paradise*, 66.

Bibliography

Abraham of Kosov. *Yesod Ha-Emunah*. Josefow [Józefów, Poland]: Zetsr, 1883.
Abrams, M. H. *Natural Supernaturalism: Tradition and Revolution in Romantic Literature*. New York: W. W. Norton, 1973.
Achelis, Thomas. *Moritz Lazarus*. Hamburg: Richter, 1900.
Adler, Abraham. "Die Kabbala, oder Die Religionsphilosophie der Hebräer." *Jahrbuch für speculative Philosophie* 3 (1846): 183–98.
Adler, Hans. "Herder's Concept of *Humanität*." In *A Companion to the Works of Johann Gottfried Herder*, edited by Hans Adler and Wulf Köpke, 93–116. Rochester, NY: Camden House, 2009.
Alexandrov, Samuel. *Mikhtevei Meḥqar u- Viqqoret* [Letters on research and criticism]. Vilna [Vilnius, Lithuania]: Romm, 1907.
Alexandrov, Shmuel. "Takhlit Ma'aseh shamayim va-arez." *ha-Eshkol* 4 (1902): 265–70.
Amir, Yehoyada. "The Perplexity of Our Time: Rabbi Nachman Krochmal and Modern Jewish Existence." *Modern Judaism* 23, no. 3 (October 2003): 264–301.
Anderson, Benedict. *Imagined Communities: Reflections on the Origin and Spread of Nationalism*. New York: Verso, 1983.
Anderson, R. Lanier. "The Debate over the *Geisteswissenschaften* in German Philosophy, 1880–1910." In *The Cambridge History of Philosophy: 1870–1945*, edited by Thomas Baldwin, 221–34. Cambridge: Cambridge University Press, 2003.
Anidjar, Gil. *Semites: Race, Religion, Literature*. Stanford, CA: Stanford University Press, 2008.
Arens, Katherine. *Structures of Knowing: Psychologies of the Nineteenth Century*. Dordrecht: Kluwer, 1989.
Aristotle. *De Anima*. New York: Penguin Classics, 1987.
Aristotle. *Metaphysics*. Indianapolis: Hackett, 2016.
Armando, David, Bruno Belhoste, and Joan Johnson. "Mesmerism between the End of the Old Regime and the Revolution: Social Dynamics and Political Issues." *Annales historiques de la Révolution française* 391, no. 1 (2018): 3–26.
Asad, Talal. *Formations of the Secular: Christianity, Islam, Modernity*. Stanford, CA: Stanford University Press, 2003.
Ascher, Saul. *Die Germanomanie: Skizze zu einem Zeitgemälde*. Berlin: Achenwall, 1815.

Aschheim, Steven E. *The Nietzsche Legacy in Germany, 1890–1990*. Irvine: University of California Press, 1992.

Assaf, David. "'A Heretic Who Has No Faith in the Great Ones of the Age': The Clash over the Honor of the Or Ha-Hayyim." *Modern Judaism* 29, no. 2 (2009): 194–225.

Atlas, Dustin N. "Solomon Maimon's Philosophical Exegesis of Mystical Representations of Time and Temporal Consciousness." In *Time and Eternity in Jewish Mysticism: That Which Is Before and That Which Is After*, edited by Brian Ogren, 69–70. Leiden: Brill, 2015.

Attar, R. Hayyim ibn. *Or ha-Hayim*. Vol. 3 of *Mikra'ot Gedolot*. Jerusalem: Mekhon Ha-Maor, 1990.

Auden, W. H. "In Memory of Sigmund Freud." In *Collected Poems*, edited by Edward Mendelson, 215–18. New York: Random House, 1976.

Avineri, Shlomo. "The Fossil and Phoenix: Hegel and Krochmal on Jewish Volksgeist." In *History and System: Hegel's "Philosophy of History"*, edited by R. L. Perkins, 47–64. Albany: State University of New York Press, 1984.

Avineri, Shlomo. "Hegel and the Emergence of Zionism." *Bulletin of the Hegel Society of Great Britain*, no. 6 (Winter 1982): 12–18.

Bach, Hans. "Bernays und Schelling: Eine unbekannte Tagebuch-aufzeichnung." *Zeitschrift für Religions- und Geistesgeschichte* 25, no. 4 (1973): 336–40.

Bach, Hans. "Der Bibel'sche Orient und sein Verfasser." *Zeitschrift für die Geschichte der Juden in Deutschland* 7, no. 1 (1937): 14–45.

Baczko, Bronislaw. *Utopian Lights: The Social Evolution of the Idea of Progress*. New York: Paragon House, 1989.

Baer, Dov. *Maggid Devarav le-Ya'aqov*. Edited by Rivka Schatz-Uffenheimer. Jerusalem: Magnes, 1990.

Baer, Dov. *Torat ha-Maggid, Parshat Va-Yeṣe*. Tel Aviv: Pe'er ha-Sefer, 1969.

Bähr, Karl Christian Wilhelm Felix. *Symbolik des Mosaischen Cultus*. Heidelberg: J. C. B. Mohr, 1837.

Bakan, David. *Sigmund Freud and the Jewish Mystical Tradition*. Princeton, NJ: D. Van Nostrand, 1958.

Bakan, David, Dan Merku, and David S. Weiss. *Maimonides' Cure of Souls: Medieval Precursor of Psychoanalysis*. Albany: State University of New York Press, 2009.

Bakhtin, Mikhail. *Speech Genres, and Other Late Essays*. Austin: University of Texas Press, 1986.

Barash, Jeffrey Andrew, ed. *The Symbolic Construction of Reality: The Legacy of Ernst Cassirer*. Chicago: University of Chicago Press, 2008.

Barnard, Frederick M. *Herder on Nationality, Humanity, and History*. Montreal: McGill-Queen's University Press, 2003.

Baron, Salo. "Review of *Das Judentum und die geistigen Strömungen des 19. Jahrhunderts*, by Albert Lewkowitz." *Review of Religion* 2, no. 1 (November 1937): 80–83.

Barrès, Maurice. *Le jardin de Bérénice*. Paris: Perrin, 1891.

Barth, Fredrik, Andre Gingrich, Robert Parkin, and Sydel Silverman. *One Discipline, Four Ways: British, German, French, and American Anthropology*. Chicago: University of Chicago Press, 2005.

Bar-Yosef, Hamutal. "The Jewish Reception of Vladimir Solov'ëv." In *Vladimir Solov'ëv: Reconciler and Polemicist*, edited by Wil van den Bercken, Manon de Courten, and Ervert von Zweerde, 363–92. Leuven: Peters, 2000.

Bataillon, Marcel. "Philologie et critique historique chez Renan jeune." *Études renaniennes*, no. 31 (1977): 4–9.
Bauer, Bruno. *Die Judenfrage*. Braunschweig: F. Otto, 1853.
Baumgardt, David. "The Ethics of Lazarus and Steinthal." *The Leo Baeck Institute Year Book* 2, no. 1 (January 1957): 205–17.
Baur, Ferdinand Christian. *Die christliche Gnosis, oder Die christliche Religionsphilosophie in ihrer geschichtlichen Entwicklung*. Tübingen: C. F. Osiander, 1835.
Beach, Edward Allen. *The Potencies of God(s): Schelling's "Philosophy of Mythology."* Albany: State University of New York Press, 1994.
Bechtel, Delphine, Dominique Bourel, and Jacques Le Rider, eds. *Max Nordau (1849–1923): Critique de la dégénérescence, médiateur franco-allemand, père fondateur du sionisme*. Paris: Cerf, 1996.
Beer, Peter. *Geschichte, Lehren und Meinungen aller bestandenen und noch bestehenden religiösen Sekten der Juden und der Geheimlehre oder Cabbalah*. 2 vols. Brno, Austrian Empire: J. G. Trassler, 1822–23.
Béguin, Albert. *L'âme romantique et le rêve*. Paris: José Corti, 1939.
Beiser, Frederick. *After Hegel: German Philosophy, 1840–1900*. Princeton, NJ: Princeton University Press, 2014.
Beiser, Frederick. *The Berlin Antisemitism Controversy*. London: Routledge, 2024.
Beiser, Frederick. *Enlightenment, Revolution, and Romanticism: The Genesis of Modern German Political Thought, 1790–1800*. New York: Cambridge University Press, 1994.
Beiser, Frederick C. *Weltschmerz: Pessimism in German Philosophy 1860–1900*. Oxford: Oxford University Press, 2016.
Bell, Matthew. "Carl Gustav Carus and the Science of the Unconscious." In Nicholls and Liebscher, *Thinking the Unconscious*, 156–72.
Bell, Matthew. *The German Tradition of Psychology in Literature and Thought, 1700–1840*. New York: Cambridge University Press, 2005.
Benamozegh, Elia. *Bibliothèque de l'hébraïsme*. Livorno, Italy, 1897.
Benamozegh, Elia. *"Em la-Miqra": Il Pentateuco con commenti, ricerche e lunghe note di scienza, di critica e di filologia*. Leghorn [Livorno]: Benamozegh, 1862.
Benamozegh, Elia. *Israël et l'humanité*. Edited by Aimé Pallière. Paris: E. Leroux, 1914.
Benamozegh, Elia. "Israel et l'humanité." Manuscript. Archivo storico della Communità Ebraica di Livorno.
Benamozegh, Elia. *Teologia dogmatica e apologetica*. Leghorn [Livorno]: Vigo, 1877.
Bendavid, Lazarus. *Etwas zur Charackteristick der Juden*. Leipzig: J. Stahel, 1793.
Bendavid, Lazarus. "Über den Glauben der Juden an einen künftigen Messias (Nach Maimonides und den Kabbalisten)." *Zeitschrift für die Wissenschaft des Judenthums* 1 (1823): 197–230.
Benes, Tuska. *In Babel's Shadow: Language, Philology, and the Nation in Nineteenth-Century Germany*. Detroit: Wayne State University, 2008.
Benor, Ehud. *Ethical Monotheism: A Philosophy of Judaism*. New York: Routledge, 2017.
Ben-Pazi, Hanoch. "Moritz Lazarus and the Ethics of Judaism." [In Hebrew.] *Daat: A Journal of Jewish Philosophy and Kabbalah* 88 (2019): 91–104.
Benz, Ernst. *The Mystical Sources of German Romantic Philosophy*. New York: Wipf and Stock, 1983.

Berggren, Erik. "Anmerkungen zu Einem Eckhartstudium." In *Ex Orbe Religionum*, edited by C. J. Bleeker, S. G. F. Brandon, and M. Simon, 423–31. Leiden: Brill, 1972.

Bergmann, Hugo. "Eduard von Hartmann und die Judenfrage in Deutschland." *Yearbook of the Leo Baeck Institute* 5 (1960): 177–98.

Bergson, Henri. *Essais et conférences*. Paris: Alcan, 1919.

Bergson, Henri. *Essais sur les données immédiates de la conscience*. Paris: PUF, 2007.

Bergson, Henri. *Matière et mémoire: Essai sur la relation du corps à l'esprit*. Paris: Félix Alcan, 1896.

Berlin, Adele, and Maxine Grossman, eds. *The Oxford Dictionary of Jewish Religion*. New York: Oxford University Press, 2011.

Berlin, Isaiah. *Against the Current: Essays in the History of Ideas*. Princeton, NJ: Princeton University Press, 2013.

Berlin, Isaiah. *Three Critics of the Enlightenment*. Princeton, NJ: Princeton University Press, 2000.

Berman, Nathaniel. *Divine and Demonic in the Poetic Mythology of the "Zohar."* Leiden: Brill, 2018.

Bernardini, Paolo, and Diego Lucci. *The Jews, Instructions for Use: Four Eighteenth-Century Projects for the Emancipation of European Jews*. Boston: Academic Studies Press, 2012.

Bettelheim, Bruno. *Freud and Man's Soul: An Important Re-interpretation of Freudian Theory*. New York: Knopf, 1982.

Bhabha, Homi. "Of Mimicry and Man: The Ambivalence of Colonial Discourse." In "Discipleship: A Special Issue on Psychoanalysis," edited by Joan Copjec. Special issue, *October* 28 (Spring 1984): 125–33.

Biale, David. "Gershom Scholem and Anarchism as a Jewish Philosophy." *Judaism* 32, no. 1 (Winter 1983): 70–76.

Biale, David. *Gershom Scholem: Kabbalah and Counter-History*. Cambridge, MA: Harvard University Press, 1979.

Biale, David. "The Kabbala in Nachman Krochmal's Philosophy of History." *Journal of Jewish Studies* 32, no. 1 (1981): 85–97.

Bielik-Robson, Agata. "Dreams of Matter: Ernst Bloch on Religion as Organized Fantasy." *Revue internationale de philosophie* 289, no. 3 (2019): 333–60.

Bielik-Robson, Agata. "God of Luria, Hegel, Schelling: The Divine Contraction and the Modern Metaphysics of Finitude." In *Mystical Theology and Continental Philosophy*, edited by S. Podmore, 32–50. London: Routledge, 2017.

Bielik-Robson, Agata. "Introduction: An Unhistorical History of Tsimtsum; A Break with Neoplatonism?" In Bielik-Robson and Weiss, *Tsimtsum and Modernity*, 1–38.

Bielik-Robson, Agata. *Jewish Cryptotheologies of Late Modernity: Philosophical Marranos*. London: Routledge, 2014.

Bielik-Robson, Agata. "'The Story Continues . . .': Schelling and Rosenzweig on Narrative Philosophy." *International Journal of Philosophy and Theology* 80, no. 1–2 (2019): 127–42.

Bielik-Robson, Agata, and Daniel H. Weiss. *Tsimtsum and Modernity: Lurianic Heritage in Modern Philosophy and Theology*. Berlin: De Gruyter, 2020.

Bienenstock, Myriam. "Qu'est-ce que l'esprit objectif' selon Hegel?" *Revue germanique internationale* 15 (2001): 103–26.

Bishop, Jonathan. *Emerson on the Soul*. Cambridge, MA: Harvard University Press, 1964.
Bishop, Paul. "Jung's Red Book and Its Relation to Aspects of German Idealism." *Journal of Analytical Psychology* 57, no. 3 (June 2012): 335–63.
Bishop, Paul. "The Unconscious from the Storm and Stress to Weimar Classicism: The Dialectic of Time and Pleasure." In Nicholls and Liebscher, *Thinking the Unconscious*, 26–56.
Blackbourn, David. *The Long Nineteenth Century: A History of Germany, 1780–1918*. New York: Oxford University Press, 1997.
Blackwell, Richard J. "Christian Wolff's Doctrine of the Soul." *Journal of the History of Ideas* 22, no. 3 (1961): 339–54. Bloch, Ernst. "'Entfremdung, Verfremdung': Alienation, Estrangement." *Drama Review: TDR* 15, no. 1 (1970): 120–25.
Bloch, Ernst. *Experimentum mundi: Frage, Kategorien des Herausbringens, Praxis* [Experimentum mundi: Inquiry, categories of emergence, practice]. Frankfurt: Suhrkamp, 1975.
Bloch, Ernst. *Geist der Utopie*. Munich: Duncker und Humblot, 1918.
Bloch, Ernst. *Geist der Utopie*. Berlin: Paul Cassirer, 1923.
Bloch, Ernst. *Philosophische Aufsätze zur objektiven Phantasie* [Philosophical essays on objective fantasy]. In *Werkausgabe*, 16 vols., 10:431–42. Frankfurt am Main: Suhrkamp, 1969.
Bloch, Ernst. *"Symbole: Les juifs": Un chapitre "oublié" de "L'esprit de l'utopie"*. Paris: Editions de l'éclat, 2009.
Bloch, Ernst. *Traces*. Stanford, CA: Stanford University Press, 2006.
Bloom, Harold. *The American Religion*. 2nd ed. New York: Chu Hartley, 2006.
Bloom, Harold. "Emerson: The American Religion." In *Ralph Waldo Emerson*, edited by Harold Bloom, 33–62. New York: Chelsea House, 2006.
Bloom, Harold. *Essayists and Prophets*. Philadelphia: Chelsea House, 2005.
Bloom, Harold. "Introduction: The American Sublime." In *Emerson's Essays*, edited by Harold Bloom, 1–26. New York: Chelsea House, 2006.
Bloom, Harold. *Kabbalah and Criticism*. New York: Continuum, 1982.
Blumenberg, Hans. *The Legitimacy of the Modern Age*. Translated by Robert M. Wallace. Cambridge, MA: MIT Press, 1985.
Blumenberg, Hans. *Paradigms for a Metaphorology*. Translated by Robert Savage. Ithaca, NY: Cornell University Press, 2010.
Boas, Franz. *Anthropology and Modern Life*. New York: W. W. Norton, 1962.
Boas, Franz. "The History of Anthropology." *Science* 20 (1904): 513–24.
Boeckh, August. *Enzyklopädie und Methodologie der philologischen Wissenschaften*. Edited by Ernst Bratuscheck. Leipzig: Druck und Verlag, 1877.
Boehme, Jakob. *"Aurora" (Morgen Röte im auffgang, 1612) and "Fundamental Report" (Gründlicher Bericht, Mysterium Pansophicum, 1620)*. Translated by Andrew Weeks. Leiden: Brill, 2013.
Boehme, Jacob. *Forty Questions of the Soul*. New York: Kessinger, 1992.
Boehme, Jacob. *Six Theosophic Points*. Ann Arbor: University of Michigan Press, 1958.
Boehme, Jakob. *Von der Menschwerdung Jesu Christi* [The human genesis of Christ], pt. 4, pp. 120–21. In *Sämtliche Schriften* (11 vol.), vol. 2, pt. 1, p. 8. Stuttgart: Frommann-Holzboog, 1988.
Boehme, Jacob. *The Way to Christ*. Mahwah, NJ: Paulist Press, 1977.

Böhme, Jakob. *"The Forty Questions of the Soul" and "The Clavis"*. London: J. M. Watkins, 1911.
Bohr, Jörn. "Die Kollektivität der inneren Sprachform als kulturtheoretische Denkform—bei Ernst Cassirer, Moritz Lazarus u.a." *Naharaim* 4, no. 1 (2011): 120–32.
Bois, Elie-Joseph. "'A la recherche du temps perdu.'" *Le Temps* (Geneva), November 13, 1913.
Bollack, Jean. *Jacob Bernays: Un homme entre deux mondes*. Lille: Presses Universitaires du Septentrion, 1998.
Bollack, Jean. "Un homme d'un autre monde." In *Jacob Bernays: Un philologue juif*, edited by John Glucker and André Laks, 135–225. Villeneuve d'Ascq: Presses Universitaires du Septentrion, 1996.
Börner-Klein, Dagmar. "Yalkut Shimoni *Numbers* on Proselytes." In *"Let the Wise Listen and Add to Their Learning." Prov 1:5: Festschrift for Günter Stemberger on the Occasion of His Seventy-Fifth Birthday* [in Hebrew], edited by Constanza Cordoni and Gerhard Langer, 331–44. Berlin: De Gruyter, 2016.
Boulouque, Clémence. *Another Modernity: Elia Benamozegh's Jewish Universalism*. Stanford, CA: Stanford University Press, 2020.
Bourel, Dominique. "A l'origine du kantisme juif: Lazarus Bendavid." In *La philosophie allemande dans la pensée juive*, edited by Gérard Bensussan, 67–79. Paris: Presses Universitaires de France, 1997.
Bourel, Dominique. "Eine Generation später: Lazarus Bendavid (1762–1832)." In *Moses Mendelssohn und die Kreise seiner Wirksamkeit*, edited by Michael Albrecht, Eva J. Engel, and Norbert Hinske, 363–80. Tübingen: De Gruyter, 1994.
Bourel, Dominique. "Lazarus Bendavid et l'éducation des juifs à Berlin au début du XIXe siècle." In *Plurales Deutschland–Allemagne plurielle*, edited by Peter Schöttler, Patrice Veit, and Michael Werner, 118–26. Göttingen: Wallstein Verlag, 1999.
Bourel, Dominique. "Nostalgie et 'Wissenschaft': Note sur l'étude du judaïsme allemand." *Pardes* 5 (1987): 187–94.
Bourel, Dominique. "Trois lettres inédites de Lazarus Bendavid." *Revue des études juives* 149 (January–June 1990): 129–35.
Bowen, Francis. Review of Emerson. *Christian Examiner* 21 (January 1837): 377–78.
Bowie, Andrew. *Schelling and Modern European Philosophy: An Introduction*. London: Routledge, 2002.
Bowman, Brady. "Nature, Freedom, History: The World Soul in German Idealism." In Wilberding, *World Soul*, 258–83.
Boyarin, Jonathan. *Storm from Paradise: The Politics of Jewish Memory*. Minneapolis: University of Minnesota Press, 1992.
Braham, Lionel. "Emerson and Boehme: A Comparative Study in Mystical Ideas." *Modern Language Quarterly* 20 (1959): 31–35.
Brandist, Craig. "The Rise of Soviet Sociolinguistics from the Ashes of Völkerpsychologie." *Journal of the History of the Behavioral Sciences* 42, no. 3 (2006): 261–77.
Braun, Peter. "Traumgeburten: Über einige okkulte Motive bei Carl du Prel, Gyula Krùdy und Thomas Mann." *Kea: Zeitschrift für Kulturwissenschaften* 13 (2000): 167–86.

Breckman, Warren. "Eduard Gans and the Crisis of Hegelianism." *Journal of the History of Ideas* 62, no. 3 (July 2001): 543–64.
Bredeck, Elizabeth. *Metaphors of Knowledge: Language and Thought in Mauthner's Critique*. Detroit: Wayne State University Press, 1992.
Brenner, Michael. "Between Haskalah and Kabbalah: Peter Beer's History of Jewish Sects." In *Jewish History and Jewish Memory: Essays in Honor of Yosef Haim Yerushalmi*, edited by E. Carlebach, J. M. Efron, and David N. Myers, 389–404. Hanover, NH: Brandeis University Press, 1998.
Brenner, Michael. "Gnosis and History: Polemics of German-Jewish Identity from Graetz to Scholem." *New German Critique*, no. 77 (1999): 45–60.
Brès, Yvon. "Home, Carus, Hartmann (histoire de l'inconscient)." *Revue philosophique de la France et de l'étranger* 129, no. 2 (2004): 225–30.
Brezis, David. *Levinas et le tournant sacrificiel*. Paris: Hermann, 2012.
Brill, Alan. *Thinking God: The Mysticism of Rabbi Zadok of Lublin*. New York: Yeshiva University Press, 2002.
Brown, Benjamin. *HaHazon Ish: Halakhist, Believer and Leader*. [In Hebrew.] Jerusalem: Magnes, 2011.
Brown, Benjamin. "'It Does Not Relate to Me': Rabbi Israel Salanter and the Kabbalah." In *And This Is for Yehuda: Studies Presented to Our Friend, Professor Yehuda Liebes, on the Occasion of his Sixty-Fifth Birthday* [in Hebrew], edited by Maren R. Niehoff, Ronit Meroz, and Jonathan Garb, 420–39. Jerusalem: Mandel Institute of Jewish Studies and Bialik Institute, 2012.
Brown, Jeremy. "Glimmers of the World Soul in Kabbalah." In Wilberding, *World Soul*, 124–50.
Brown, Robert F. *The Later Philosophy of Schelling: The Influence of Boehme on the Works of 1809–1815*. Lewisburg, PA: Bucknell University Press, 1977.
Bruce, Dickson D. "W. E. B. Du Bois and the Idea of Double Consciousness." *American Literature* 64, no. 2 (1992): 299–309.
Brunner, Jose. *Freud and the Politics of Psychoanalysis*. Oxford: Blackwell, 1995.
Buber Agassi, Judith. *Martin Buber on Psychology and Psychotherapy*. New York: Syracuse University Press, 1999.
Buber, Martin. *Die Geschichten des Rabbi Nachman*. Frankfurt am Main: Rütten und Loening, 1906.
Buber, Martin. *Die Legende des Baal-Schem*. Frankfurt am Main: Literarische Ansalt / Rütten und Loening, 1920.
Buber, Martin. *Eclipse of God: Studies in the Relation between Religion and Philosophy*. Princeton, NJ: Princeton University Press, 2015.
Buber, Martin. *Elemente des Zwischenmenschlichen in Werke*. Vol. 1. Heidelberg: Verlag Lambert Schneider, 1962.
Buber, Martin. "God and the Spirit of Man." In *Eclipse of God*, 106–12.
Buber, Martin. *The Legend of the Baal Shem*. Translated by Maurice Friedman. Princeton, NJ: Princeton University Press, 1995.
Buber, Martin. *Martin Buber Werkausgabe*. Vol. 2.1, *Mythos und Mystik: Frühe religionswissenschaftliche Schriften*. Edited by David Groiser. Gütersloh: Gütersloher Verlagshaus, 2013.
Buber, Martin. "Mystik als religiöser Solipsismus." In *Martin Buber Werkausgabe*, 2.1:150–51.

Buber, Martin. *On Judaism*. Edited by Nahum N. Glatzer. New York: Schocken, 1967 and 1995.
Buber, Martin. "Religion and Modern Thinking." In *Eclipse of God*, 53–82.
Buber, Martin. "Religion und modernes Denken" [Religion and modern thinking]. *Merkur* 6, no. 2 (February 1952): 101–20.
Buber, Martin. "The Revelation." In *The Legend of the Baal Shem*, 62–72.
Buber, Martin. "Supplement: Reply to C. G. Jung." In *Eclipse of God*, 113–17.
Buber, Martin. *Vom Geist des Judentums: Reden und Geleitworte*. Munich: K. Wolff, 1921.
Buber, Martin. "Von Heer zu Heer." In *Die Legende des Baal-Schem*, 193–200.
Buber, Martin. "Zur Geschichte des Individuationsproblems: Nicolaus von Cues und Jakob Boehme" [1904]. In *Martin Buber Werkausgabe*, 2.1:75–101.
Buchheim, Thomas, and Friedrich Hermanni. *Alle Persönlichkeit ruht auf einem dunkeln Grunde: Schellings Philosophie der Personalität*. Berlin: De Gruyter, 2015.
Büchner, Ludwig. *Kraft und Stoff: Empirisch-naturphilosophische Studien, in allgemein-verständlicher Darstellung*. 5th ed. Frankfurt am Main: Meidinger Sohn, 1858.
Bulgakov, Sergius. *Unfading Light*. Grand Rapids, MI: B. Eerdmans, 2012.
Bumann, Waltraud. *Die Sprachtheorie Heymann Steinthals, dargestellt im Zusammenhang mit seiner Theorie der Geisteswissenschaft*. Meisenheim am Glan: Anton Hain, 1966.
Bunzl, Matti. "*Völkerpsychologie* and German-Jewish Emancipation." In *World Provincialism: German Anthropology in the Age of Empire*, edited by H. Glenn Penny and Matti Bunzl, 47–85. Ann Arbor: University of Michigan Press, 2003.
Burnham, John, ed. *After Freud Left: A Century of Psychoanalysis in America*. Chicago: University of Chicago Press, 2012.
Buxdorf, Johann. *Synagoga Judaica, Hoc est, Schola Judaeorum In Qua Nativitas, Institutio, Religio, Vita, Mors, Sepulturaque ipsorum e libris eorundem; A. M. Johanne Buxdorfio literarum Hebraearum in inclyta Academia Basiliensi Profess. graphice descripta est*. Frankfurt am Main: Stöckle Hanoviae Antonius, 1622.
Cabot, James Elliot. *A Memoir of Ralph Waldo Emerson*. Boston: Houghton Mifflin, 1888.
Cahnman, Werner Jacob. "Friedrich Wilhelm Schelling über die Judenemanzipation." *Zeitschrift für Bayerische Landesgeschichte* 37, no. 2 (1974): 614–25.
Cahnman, Werner Jacob. *German Jewry: Its History and Sociology; Selected Essays of Werner Cahnman*. Edited by Joseph B. Maier, Judith Marcus, and Zoltan Tarr. New Brunswick, NJ: Transaction, 1989.
Cahnman, Werner Jacob. "Schelling and the New Thinking of Judaism." *Proceedings of the American Academy for Jewish Research* 48 (1981): 1–56.
Cameron, Kenneth. *Young Emerson's Transcendental Visions*. New York: Transcendental Books, 1971.
Campbell, Jan. *Psychoanalysis and the Time of Life: Durations of the Unconscious Self*. New York: Routledge, 2007.
Campbell, Joseph, with Bill Moyers. *The Power of Myth*. Edited by Betty Sue Flowers. New York: Anchor Books, 1991.
Campos Moura, Patricia de. "Notes on an Ontology in Lacan: A Dialogue with Heidegger." *Psicologia USP* 28, no. 3 (2017): 451–56.

Cantoni, Carlo. *G. B. Vico: Studi critici e comparativi*. Turin: Civelli, 1867.
Carus, C. G. *Vergleichende Psychologie, oder Geschichte der Seele in der Reihenfolge der Thierwelt* [Comparative psychology, or History of the soul in its place in the sequence of the animal world]. Vienna: Wilhelm Braumüller, 1866.
Carus, C. G. *Zur Entwicklungsgeschichte der Seele*. Pforzheim: Flammer und Hoffmann, 1846.
Cassirer, Ernst. *An Essay on Man: An Introduction to the Philosophy of Human Culture*. New Haven, CT: Yale University Press, 1944.
Cassirer, Ernst. *An Essay on Myth*. New Haven, CT: Yale University Press, 1979.
Cassirer, Ernst. *The Logic of the Humanities*. New Haven, CT: Yale University Press, 1960.
Cassirer, Ernst. *Platonic Renaissance in England*. Edinburgh: Nelson, 1953.
Chajes, J. H. "Entzauberung and Jewish Modernity: On 'Magic,' Enlightenment, and Faith." *Jahrbuch des Simon Dubnow Instituts* 6 (2007): 191–200.
Chajes, J. H. "Romanticising Rashbi: Moses Kunitz's Ben Yoḥai." *Kabbalah: Journal for the Study of Jewish Mystical Texts* 40 (2018): 85–105.
Chamberlain, Houston. *Foundations of the Nineteenth Century*. New York: John Lane, 1912.
Christy, Arthur. *The Orient in American Transcendentalism: A Study of Emerson, Thoreau and Alcott*. New York: Columbia University Press, 1932.
Clark, Robert. *Herder: His Life and Thought*. Berkeley: University of California Press, 1955.
Claussen, Geoffrey D. *Sharing the Burden: Rabbi Simhah Zissel Ziv and the Path of Musar*. Albany: State University of New York Press, 2015.
Clayton, Philip. "Panentheisms East and West." *Sophia* 49, no. 2 (June 2010): 183–91.
Cohen, Hermann. *Die Religion der Vernunft aus den Quellen des Judentums*. Leipzig: Gustav Fock, 1919.
Cohen, Hermann. *Jüdische Schriften: Dritter Band Zur jüdischen Religionsphilosophie und ihrer Geschichte*. Berlin: C. A. Schwetschke, 1924.
Cohen, Philip. "David Einhorn: Biblical Theology as Response and Reform." PhD diss., Brandeis University, 1994.
Cohn, Bernhard N. "David Einhorn: Some Aspects of His Thinking." In *Essays in American Jewish History*, edited by Jacob Rader Marcus, 315–24. Cincinnati: American Jewish Archives, 1958.
Coleridge, Samuel. *Aids to Reflection*, edited by John B. Beer. Vol. 9 of *The Complete Works of Samuel Taylor Coleridge*. Princeton Legacy Library. Princeton, NJ: Princeton University Press, 2017.
Coleridge, Samuel. *Biographia Literaria*. Boston: Leavitt, Lord, 1834.
Condorcet. *Political Writings*. Edited by Steven Lukes and Nadia Urbinati. New York: Cambridge University Press, 2012.
Copleston, Frederick C. "Hegel and the Rationalisation of Mysticism." *Royal Institute of Philosophy Supplements* 2 (1968): 118–32.
Corbin, Henry. "For the Concept of Irano-Islamic Philosophy." *Philosophical Forum* 4 (1972): 114–23.
Cordovero, Moses. *Tomer Devorah* [The palm tree of Deborah]. Zitomir [Zhytomyr, Ukraine]: Shapira, 1864.
Coudert, Allison P. "Henry More, the Kabbalah, and the Quakers." In *Philosophy, Science, and Religion in England (1640–1700)*, edited by Richard Ashcraft,

Richard Kroll, and Perez Zagorin, 31–67. Cambridge: Cambridge University Press, 2008.
Coudert, Allison P. *Leibniz and Kabbalah*. Dordrecht: Kluwer Academic, 1995.
Courcelles, Dominique de. "Bergson et les grandes traditions religieuses et mystiques, au risque de l'histoire contemplée des religions." In *Bergson et la religion*, edited by Ghislain Waterlot, 331–52. Paris: PUF, 2008.
Cousin, Victor. *Elements of Psychology*. Hartford, CT: Cooke, 1834.
Cousin, Victor. *Fragments philosophiques*. Paris: Ladrange, 1833.
Cousin, Victor. *Introduction to the History of Modern Philosophy*. Boston: Hilliard, Gray, Little, and Wilkins, 1832.
Cowley, Malcolm. "A Note on the Selections." In Ralph Waldo Emerson, *The Portable Emerson*, edited by Carl Bode, xxxiii–xvi. Rev. ed. New York: Penguin, 1981.
Crabtree, Adam. *From Mesmer to Freud: Magnetic Sleep and the Roots of Psychological Healing*. New Haven, CT: Yale University Press, 1993.
Creuzer, Friedrich. *Symbolik und Mythologie der alten Völker, besonders der Griechen*. 4 vols. Leipzig: Leske, 1841.
D'Agostino, Peter. "Craniums, Criminals, and the 'Cursed Race': Italian Anthropology in American Racial Thought, 1861–1924." *Comparative Studies in Society and History* 44, no. 2 (2002): 319–43.
Damiron, Jean-Philibert. *Essai sur l'histoire de la philosophie en France*. Paris: Chubart et Heideloff, 1828.
Damoi, D. N. K. *The Unconscious and Eduard von Hartmann: A Historico-Critical Monograph*. The Hague: Martinus Nijhoff, 1967.
D'Anna, Giuseppe, Edoardo Massimilla, Francesco Piro, Manuela Sanna, and Francesco Toto, eds. *Morfologie del rapporto parti-tutto: Totalità e complessità nelle filosofie dell'età moderna*. Milan: Mimesis, 2019.
Danziger, Kurt. "On the Threshold of the New Psychology: Situating Wundt and James." In *Wundt Studies: A Centennial Collection*, edited by W. G. Bringmann and E. D. Tweney, 362–79. Toronto: Hogrefe, 1980.
Darnton, Robert. *Mesmerism and the End of the Enlightenment in France*. Cambridge, MA: Harvard University Press, 1968.
Davidson, Donald. "Paradoxes of Irrationality." In *Philosophical Essays on Freud*, edited by Richard Wollheim and James Hopkins, 289–304. Cambridge: Cambridge University Press.
Davies, Martin. "Karl Philipp Moritz's *Erfahrungsseelenkunde*: Its Social and Intellectual Origins." *Oxford German Studies* 16 (1985): 13–35.
Dayan, Maurice. "L'inconscient selon Bergson." *Revue de métaphysique et de morale* 70, no. 3 (1965): 287–324.
Deleuze, Gilles. *Le Bergsonisme*. Paris: PUF, 2011.
Deleuze, Gilles. *Logic of Sense*. London: Athlone Press, 1990.
Deleuze, Gilles. *Logique du sens*. Paris: Minuit, 1969.
Deleuze, Gilles, and Félix Guattari. *A Thousand Plateaus: Capitalism and Schizophrenia*. New York: Continuum, 2004.
Delitzsch, Franz. *A System of Biblical Psychology*. Translated by Robert E. Wallis. Eugene, OR: Wipf and Stock, 2003.
Der Bibel'sche Orient—eine Zeitschrift in zwanglosen Heften. Munich: E. A. Fleischmann, 1821.

Derrida, Jacques. *Dissemination*. Chicago: University of Chicago Press, 1981.
Derrida, Jacques. *Glas*. Lincoln: University of Nebraska Press, 1986.
Derrida, Jacques. *Positions*. Paris: Minuit, 1972.
Derrida, Jacques. "Qu'est-ce qu'une traduction 'relevante'?" In *Cahier Derrida*, edited by Marie-Louise Mallet and Ginette Michaud, 561–76. Paris: L'Herne, 2004.
Desmazières, Agnès. *Comment les Catholiques ont reçu la psychanalyse*. Paris: Payot, 2011.
Detweiler, Robert. "The Overrated Oversoul." *American Literature* 36, no. 1 (March 1964): 65–68.
Devereux, Georges. "Freud, Discoverer of the Principle of Complementarity (A Serious Inaccuracy of Translation in the Standard Edition)." *International Review of Psycho-Analysis* 7 (1980): 521.
Dews, Peter. *Schelling's Late Philosophy in Confrontation with Hegel*. New York: Oxford University Press, 2022.
Di Biase, Giuliana. "Henry More's Panentheism and the Kabbalah." *Archivio di filosofia* 89, no. 1 (2021): 89–98.
Diehl, Joanne Feit. "Emerson, Dickinson, and the Abyss." *English Literary History* 44, no. 4 (December 1977): 683–700.
Dietrich, Peter, and Uta Lohmann. "'Daß die Kinder aller Confessionen sich kennen, ertragen und lieben lernen': Die jüdische Freischule in Berlin zwischen 1778 und 1825." In *Dialog zwischen den Kulturen: Erziehungshistorische und religionspädagogische Gesichtspunkte interkultureller Bildung*, edited by Ingrid Lohmann and Wolfram Weiße, 37–47. Munich: Waxmann, 1994.
Digeon, Claude. *La crise allemande de la pensée française*. Paris: PUF, 1992.
Dilthey, Wilhelm. *Gesammelte Schriften*. Vol. 5, *Die geistige Welt: Einleitung in die Philosophie des Lebens; Erste Hälfte*. Leipzig: B. G. Teubner, 1924.
Dilthey, Wilhelm. *Introduction to the Human Sciences: An Attempt to Lay a Foundation for the Study of Society and History*. Translated by Ramon Betanzos. Detroit: Wayne State University Press, 1988.
Dilthey, Wilhelm. *Selected Works*. Vol. 1. Edited by Frithjof Rodi. Princeton, NJ: Princeton University Press, 1989.
Dobie, Robert. "Meister Eckhart's 'Ontological Philosophy of Religion.'" *Journal of Religion* 82, no. 4 (2002): 563–85.
Dohm, Christian Wilhelm von. *Über die bürgerliche Verbesserung der Juden*. Berlin: Nicolai, 1781.
Dov Baer, Abraham ben. *Hesed Le-Avraham*. Jerusalem: Machon Siftei Tsadikim, 2013.
Dowden, Stephen D., and Meike G. Werner, eds. *German Literature, Jewish Critics: The Brandeis Symposium*. Suffolk, UK: Camden House, 2002.
Drecoll, Volker Henning. "Ferdinand Christian Baur's View of Christian Gnosis, and of the Philosophy of Religion in His Own Day." In *Ferdinand Christian Baur and the History of Early Christianity*, edited by Martin Bauspiess, Christof Landmesser, and David Lincicu, 116–46. Oxford: Oxford University Press, 2017.
Du Bois, W. E. B. *Dusk of Dawn*. New York: Oxford University Press, 2014.
Duckesz, Eduard. "Zur Biographie des Chacham Isaak Bernays." *Jahrbuch der Jüdisch-Literarischen Gesellschaft* 5 (1907): 297–320.
Dufour, Dany-Robert. *Lacan et le miroir sophianique de Boehme*. Paris: Unebévue, 1998.

Dühring, Eugen. *Kritische Geschichte der Philosophie von ihren Anfängen bis zur Gegenwart*. 3rd ed. Leipzig: Fues, 1878.
Dupré, Louis. *Religion and the Rise of Modern Culture*. South Bend, IN: University of Notre Dame Press, 2008.
Dupré, Louis. "The Role of Mythology in Schelling's Late Philosophy." *Journal of Religion* 87, no. 1 (2007): 1–20.
Du Prel, Carl. *Die Entdeckung der Seele durch die Geheimwissenschaften* [The discovery of the soul through the occult sciences]. 2 vols. Leipzig: Max Altmann, 1894–95.
Du Prel, Carl. *Die Philosophie der Mystik*. Leipzig: E. Günther, 1885.
Dweck, Yaakob. *The Scandal of Kabbalah: Leon Modena, Jewish Mysticism, Early Modern Venice*. Princeton, NJ: Princeton University Press, 2011.
Eckardt, Georg, ed. *Völkerpsychologie—Versuch einer Neuentdeckung: Texte von Lazarus, Steinthal und Wundt*. Weinheim: Psychologie Verlags Union, 1997.
Eckhart, Meister. *Meister Eckharts Predigten*. Vol. 1 of *Die Deutschen Werke*, edited by Josef Quint. Stuttgart: Kohlhammer, 1958.
Eckman, Lester Samuel. *A History of the Musar Movement (1840–1945)*. New York: Shenngold, 1975.
Eckmeyer, Jost. "Johann Angelius Werdenhagen (1581–1652) und seine 'Psychologia Vera J[acobi] B[öhmii] T[eutonici]' (1632)." In *Offenbarung und Episteme: Zur europäischen Wirkung Jakob Böhmes im 17. und 18. Jahrhundert*, edited by Wilhelm Kühlmann and Friedrich Vollart, 67–92. Berlin: De Gruyter, 2012.
Einhorn, David. "Abschiedspredigt, gehalten am 13. Dezember 1851 in der Synagoge zu Schwerin." *Sinai* I/6 (July 1856); II/5 (June 1857); VII/12 (January 1863). As cited in Greenberg, "Mendelssohn in America," 286n27.
Einhorn, David. *Ausgewählte Predigten und Reden*. In Kohler, ed., *David Einhorn*, 1–399.
Einhorn, David. *Das Prinzip des Mosaismus und dessen Verhältnis zum Heidenthum und Rabbinischen Judenthum*. Leipzig: C. L. Fritzsche, 1854.
Einhorn, David. *Olat Tamid: Gebetbuch für Israelitische Reform-Gemeinden*. Baltimore, 1858.
Elbaum, Jacob. "Yalkut Shimoni." In *Encyclopaedia Judaica*, edited by Michael Berenbaum and Fred Skolnik, 22 vols., 21:275–76. 2nd ed. Detroit: Macmillan, 2007.
Ellenberger, Hans. *The Discovery of the Unconscious*. New York: Basic Books, 1970.
El Shakry, Omnia S. *The Arabic Freud: Psychoanalysis and Islam in Modern Egypt*. Princeton, NJ: Princeton University Press, 2017.
Emden, Jacob. *Megilat Sefer: The Autobiography of Rabbi Jacob Emden (1697–1776)*. Baltimore: Shaftek Enterprises, 2011.
Emerson, Ralph Waldo. "The American Scholar." In *Essays and Lectures*, 51–72.
Emerson, Ralph Waldo. "Brahma." In *Collected Poems and Translations*, edited by Harold Bloom and Paul Kane, 159. New York: Library of America, 1994.
Emerson, Ralph Waldo. "Compensation." In *Essays and Lectures*, 283–302.
Emerson, Ralph Waldo. *English Traits*. New and rev. ed. New York: Houghton Mifflin, 1896.
Emerson, Ralph Waldo. *Essays and Lectures*. Edited by Joel Porte. New York: Library of America, 1983.
Emerson, Ralph Waldo. "History." In *Essays and Lectures*, 235–56.

Emerson, Ralph Waldo. *Journals.* Edited by Edward Waldo Emerson and Waldo Emerson Forbes. 10 vols. Boston: Houghton Mifflin, 1909–14.
Emerson, Ralph Waldo. *The Journals and Miscellaneous Notebooks of Ralph Waldo Emerson.* Edited by William Gilman, Alfred Ferguson, George Clark, and Merrell Davis. 16 vols. Cambridge, MA: Harvard University Press, 1960–82.
Emerson, Ralph Waldo. *The Letters of Ralph Waldo Emerson.* Edited by Ralph L. Rusk. 10 vols. New York: Columbia University Press, 1939.
Emerson, Ralph Waldo. "The Method of Nature." In *Essays and Lectures,* 113–32.
Emerson, Ralph Waldo. "Monadnoc." In *Ralph Waldo Emerson: The Major Poetry,* edited by Albert J. Von Frank, 51–63. Cambridge, MA: Harvard University Press, 2015.
Emerson, Ralph Waldo. "Natural History of Intellect." In *The Complete Works of Ralph Waldo Emerson,* edited by Edward Waldo Emerson, 12:1–110. Boston: Houghton Mifflin, 1904.
Emerson, Ralph Waldo. "The Over-Soul." In *Essays and Lectures,* 383–400.
Emerson, Ralph Waldo. "The Philosophy of History." In *The Early Lectures of Ralph Waldo Emerson,* edited by Stephen E. Whicher, Robert E. Spiller, and Wallace E. Williams, 3 vols., 2:1–190. Cambridge, MA: Harvard University Press, 1964–72.
Emerson, Ralph Waldo. "The Poet." In *Essays and Lectures,* 445–68.
Emerson, Ralph Waldo. "Plato: New Readings." In *Essays and Lectures,* 655–60.
Emerson, Ralph Waldo. "Self-Reliance." In *Essays and Lectures,* 257–82.
Emerson, Ralph Waldo. "The Transcendentalist." In *Essays and Lectures,* 191–210.
Emerson, Ralph Waldo. "The World Soul." In *Collected Poems and Translations,* edited by Harold Bloom and Paul Kane, 17–20. New York: Library of America, 1994.
Erwin, Edward. *The Freud Encyclopedia: Theory, Therapy, and Culture.* London: Routledge, 2002.
Esfeld, Michael. *Holism in Philosophy of Mind and Philosophy of Physics.* Dordrecht: Kluwer, 2001.
Espagne, Michel, Nora Lafi, and Pascale Rabault-Feuerhahn, eds. *Silvestre de Sacy: Le projet européen d'une science orientaliste.* Paris: Editions du Cerf, 2016.
Etkes, Immanuel. *The Besht: Magician, Mystic, and Leader.* Waltham, MA: Brandeis University Press, 2005.
Etkes, Immanuel. *Israel Salanter and the Musar Movement.* Philadelphia: Jewish Publication Society, 1993.
Etkes, Immanuel. "Rabbi Zalman of Lyady as an Educator." In *Continuity and Change: A Festschrift in Honor of Irving Greenberg's Seventy-Fifth Birthday,* edited by Steven T. Katz and Steven Bayme, 81–104. New York: University Press of America, 2012.
Fackenheim, Emil. "Hirsch and Hegel: A Study of Hirsch's *Religionsphilosophie der Juden* (1842)." In *Studies in Nineteenth-Century Jewish Intellectual History,* edited by Alexander Altmann, 171–201. Cambridge, MA: Harvard University Press, 2013.
Fackenheim, Emil. *The Religious Dimension in Hegel's Thought.* Chicago: University of Chicago Press, 1982.
Fackenheim, Emil. "Schelling's Conception of Positive Philosophy." *Review of Metaphysics* 7, no. 4 (1954): 563–82.
Fahn, Reuven. *Pirke Haskalah: Kitvei Reuven Fahn* [Chapters of the Enlightenment: Selected writings of Reuven Fahn]. Vol. 2. Stanisławów [now Ivano-Frankivsk, Ukraine], Poland: Grafika Press, 1937.

Faivre, Antoine. "La critique boehmienne de Franz von Baader." In *Jacob Boehme ou l'obscure lumière de la connaissance mystique: Hommage à Jacob Boehme dans le cadre du Centre d'études et de recherches interdisciplinaires de Chantilly*, edited by Heinz Schmitz, P. Deghaye, J.-L. Vieillard-Baron, et al., 135–54. Paris: Vrin, 1979.
Fechner, Gustav Theodor. *Elemente der Psychophysik*. 2 vols. Leipzig: Breitkopf und Härtel, 1860.
Feiner, Shmuel. *The Jewish Enlightenment*. Philadelphia: Pennsylvania University Press, 2003.
Feldman, Burton, and Robert Richardson. *The Rise of Modern Mythology, 1680–1860*. Bloomington: Indiana University Press, 1972.
Fenichel, Teresa. *Schelling, Freud, and the Philosophical Foundations of Psychoanalysis*. New York: Routledge, 2019.
Fenton, Paul. "Qabbalah and Academia: The Critical Study of Jewish Mysticism in France." *Shofar* 18, no. 2 (2000): 45–69.
Fenton, Paul. "Salomon Munk and the Franco-Jewish Discovery of Orientalism." In *Modern Jewish Scholarship on Islam in Context: Rationality, European Borders, and the Search for Belonging*, edited by Ottfried Fraisse, 267–90. Berlin: De Gruyter, 2019.
Feuerbach, Ludwig. *Essence of Christianity*. Translated from the 2nd German ed. by Marian Evans. New York: Calvin Blanchard, 1855.
Feuerbach, Ludwig. *Geschichte der neueren Philosophie von Bacon von Verulam bis Benedikt Spinoza*. Vol. 3 of *Ludwig Feuerbach: Sämtliche Werke*, edited by Wilhelm Bolin and Friedrich Jodl. Stuttgart: Fr. Frommans Verlag (E. Hauff), 1903–11.
Feuerbach, Ludwig. *Thoughts on Death and Immortality*. Berkeley: University of California, 1980.
Ffytche, Matt. *The Foundations of the Unconscious: Schelling, Freud, and the Birth of the Modern Psyche*. New York: Cambridge University Press, 2012.
Fichte, J. G. "A State within a State (1793)." In *The Jew in the Modern World: A Documentary History*, edited by Paul Mendes-Flohr and Jehuda Reinharz, 309. 2nd ed. New York: Oxford University Press, 1995.
Finkelstein, Gabriel. *Emil du Bois-Reymond: Neuroscience, Self, and Society in Nineteenth-Century Germany*. Cambridge, MA: MIT Press, 1993.
Fischbach, Franck. "Transformations du concept d'aliénation: Hegel, Feuerbach, Marx." *Revue germanique internationale* 8 (2008): 93–112.
Fishman, David E. "The Musar Movement in Interwar Poland." In *The Jews of Poland between Two World Wars*, edited by Yisrael Gutman, Ezra Mendelsohn, Jehuda Reinharz, and Chone Shmeruk, 247–71. Hanover, NH: Brandeis University Press, 1989.
Foucault, Michel. *Introduction à l'anthropologie de Kant*. Paris: Vrin, 2008.
Foucault, Michel. *The Order of Things: An Archaeology of the Human Sciences*. New York: Pantheon, 1970.
Fox, Russell Arben. "J. G. Herder on Language and the Metaphysics of National Community." *Review of Politics* 65, no. 2 (2003): 237–62.
Franck, Adolphe. *The Kabbalah: The Religious Philosophy of the Hebrews*. New York: Forgotten Books, 2008.
Franck, Adolphe. "Lettre-préface." In Papus, *Traité méthodique de science occulte*, v–x. Paris: Georges Carré, 1891.

Franck, Adolphe. "'Philosophie de l'inconscient,' par Édouard de Hartmann (Deuxième article)." *Journal des Savants* (August 1877): 474–86.

Franck, Adolphe. "'Philosophie de l'inconscient,' par Édouard de Hartmann (Première article)." *Journal des Savants* (July 1877): 432–47.

Franck, Adolphe. "'Philosophie de l'inconscient,' par Édouard de Hartmann (Troisième article)." *Journal des Savants* (October 1877): 589–602.

Franks, Paul. "From World-Soul to Universal Organism: Maimon's Hypothesis and Schelling's Physicalization of a Platonic-Kabbalistic Concept." In *Schelling's Philosophy: Freedom, Nature, and Systematicity*, edited by G. Anthony Bruno, 71–92. Oxford: Oxford University Press, 2020.

Franks, Paul. "Inner Anti-Semitism or Kabbalistic Legacy? German Idealism's Relationship to Judaism." In *Yearbook of German Idealism*, vol. 7, *Faith and Reason*, edited by F. Rush, J. Stolzenberg, and P. Franks, 269–75. Berlin: De Gruyter, 2010.

Franks, Paul. "The Midrashic Background of the Doctrine of Divine Contraction: Against Gershom Scholem on *Tsimtsum*." In Bielik-Robson and Weiss, *Tsimtsum and Modernity*, 39–60.

Franks, Paul. "Mythology, Essence, and Form: Schelling's Jewish Reception in the Nineteenth Century." *International Journal of Philosophy and Theology* 80 (2019): 71–89.

Franks, Paul. "'Nothing Comes from Nothing': Judaism, the Orient and the Kabbalah in Hegel's Reception of Spinoza." In *The Oxford Handbook of Spinoza*, edited by Michael Della Rocca, 512–39. Oxford: Oxford University Press, 2017.

Franks, Paul. "Peirce's 'Schelling-Fashioned Idealism' and 'The Monstrous Mysticism of the East.'" *British Journal for the History of Philosophy* 23, no. 4 (2015): 732–55.

Franks, Paul. "Rabbinic Idealism and Kabbalistic Realism: Jewish Dimensions of Idealism and Idealist Dimensions of Judaism." In *The Impact of Idealism*, vol. 4, *Religion*, edited by Nicholas Adams, Nicholas Boyle, and Liz Disley, 219–45. Cambridge: Cambridge University Press, 2013.

Freeman, Linda. *Emily Dickinson and the Religious Imagination*. New York: Cambridge University Press, 2011.

Freitas Araujo, Saulo de. *Wundt and the Philosophical Foundations of Psychology: A Reappraisal*. New York: Springer, 2016.

Freud, Sigmund. *The Antithetical Meaning of Primal Words* (1910). In *The Standard Edition of the Complete Works*, 11:153–62.

Freud, Sigmund. *A Case of Hysteria*. New York: Vintage, 2001.

Freud, Sigmund. *Die Traumdeutung*. Leipzig: Franz Deuticke, 1914.

Freud, Sigmund. "The Ego and the Id" (1923). In *The Standard Edition of the Complete Works*, 19:1–66.

Freud, Sigmund. *Inhibitions, Symptoms, Anxiety* (1926). In *The Standard Edition of the Complete Works*, 20:75–176.

Freud, Sigmund. *The Interpretation of Dreams*. New York: Basic Books, 2010.

Freud, Sigmund. *A Life for Our Times*. New York: Oxford University Press, 1988.

Freud, Sigmund. *New Introductory Lectures on Psycho-Analysis* (1933). In *The Standard Edition of the Complete Works*, 22:7–184.

Freud, Sigmund. "A Note on the Prehistory of the Technique of Analysis" (1920). In *The Standard Edition of the Complete Works*, 18:263–65.

Freud, Sigmund. "On Dreams" (1901). In *The Standard Edition of the Complete Works*, 5:629–714.
Freud, Sigmund. *The Standard Edition of the Complete Works of Sigmund Freud*. Edited by James Strachey. 24 vols. London: Hogarth Press, 1953–74.
Freud, Sigmund. *Totem and Taboo*. New York: Norton, 1990.
Freud, Sigmund. *Vorlesungen zur Einführung in die Psychoanalyse*. Leipzig: Internationaler Psychoanalytischer Verlag, 1920.
Freud, Sigmund, and Sándor Ferenczi. *The Correspondence of Sigmund Freud and Sándor Ferenczi*. Vol. 2, *1914–1919*, edited by Eva Brabant, Ernst Falzeder, and Patricia Giampieri-Deutsch. Cambridge, MA: Harvard University Press, 1996.
Friedman, Maurice. "Interpreting Hasidism: The Buber-Scholem Controversy." *The Leo Baeck Institute Year Book* 33, no. 1 (January 1988): 449–67.
Friedman, Maurice. *Martin Buber's Life and Work*. Detroit: Wayne State University Press, 1988.
Fromm, Harold. "Overcoming the Over-Soul: Emerson's Evolutionary Existentialism." *Hudson Review* 57, no. 1 (Spring 2004): 71–95.
Fuhrer, Urs. *Cultivating Minds: Identity as Meaning-Making Practice*. London: Routledge, 2004.
Funkenstein, Amos. *Perceptions of Jewish History*. Berkeley: University of California Press, 1993.
Fürst, Julius. "Vorläufiger Bericht über mein Studium der Münchner hebräischen Handschriften." *Literaturblatt des Orients* 21 (May 21, 1845): 321–27.
Gadamer, Hans-Georg. *Truth and Method*. New York: Continuum, 2004.
Gans, Eduard. "Vorwort zur ersten Ausgabe der Vorlesungen über die Philosophie der Geschichte." In Georg Wilhelm Friedrich Hegel, *Sämtliche Werke*, edited by Hermann Glockner, 11:5–6. Stuttgart: Frommann, 1957.
Garb, Jonathan. "'Alien' Culture in the Thought of Rabbi Kook's Circle." In *Study and Knowledge in Jewish Thought* [in Hebrew], edited by Howard Kreisel, 23–64. Beer Sheva, Israel: Ben-Gurion University of the Negev, 2006.
Garb, Jonathan. *A History of Kabbalah: From the Early Modern Period to the Present Day*. New York: Cambridge University Press, 2022.
Garb, Jonathan. *Yearnings of the Soul: Psychological Thought in Modern Kabbalah*. Chicago: University of Chicago Press, 2015.
Gardner, Sebastien. "Eduard von Hartmann's *Philosophy of the Unconscious*." In Nicholls and Liebscher, *Thinking the Unconscious*, 182.
Gay, Peter. *Freud for Historians*. New York: Oxford University Press, 1985.
Gearhart, Suzanne. "The Remnants of Philosophy: Psychoanalysis after *Glas*." In *Hegel after Derrida*, edited by Stuart Barnett, 147–70. London: Taylor and Francis, 1998.
Geiger, Abraham. Review of M. H. Landauer, *Jehova und Elohim*. *Wissenschaftliche Zeitschrift für Jüdische Theologie* 3 (1837): 402–13.
Gellman, Jerome. *Abraham! Abraham! Kierkegaard and the Hasidim on the Binding of Isaac*. Aldershot, UK: Ashgate, 2003.
Gellner, Ernest. "Holism versus Individualism." In *Readings in the Philosophy of the Social Sciences*, edited by May Brodbeck, 254–68. Cambridge, MA: MIT Press, 1968.
Genna, Caterina. *Carlo Cantoni tra spiritualismo e criticismo*. Milan: Franco Angeli, 2005.

Geoghegan, Vincent. *Ernst Bloch*. London: Routledge, 1996.
Geuss, Raymond. *The Idea of a Critical Theory: Habermas and the Frankfurt School*. Cambridge: Cambridge University Press, 1981.
Geuss, Raymond. "Kultur, Bildung, Geist." *History and Theory* 35, no. 2 (1996): 151–64.
Ghica, Felicia. "De quelques questions que psychologie historique d'Ignace Meyerson actualise en psychologie." *Lato Sensu: Revue de la Société de philosophie des sciences* 5, no. 1 (2017): 61–68.
Gibian, George. "C. G. Carus' Psyche and Dostoevsky." *American Slavic and East European Review* 14, no. 3 (1955): 371–82.
Ginneken, Jaap van. *Crowds, Psychology, and Politics, 1871–1899*. Cambridge: Cambridge University Press, 1992.
Ginzburg, Carlo. "Selfhood as Otherness: Constructing English Identity in the Elizabethan Age." *Historein* 2 (2001): 31–46.
Gioberti, Vincenzo. *Della protologia di Vincenzo Gioberti pubblicata per cura Giuseppe Massari*. 3 vols. Turin: Presso gli editori Eredi Botta, 1857.
Glasenapp, Gabriele von, and Hans Otto Horch. *Ghettoliteratur: Eine Dokumentation zur deutsch-jüdischen Literaturgeschichte des 19. und frühen 20. Jahrhunderts*. Berlin: Max Niemeyer Verlag, 2011.
Glatzer, Nahum N. "The Beginnings of Modern Jewish Studies." In *Studies in Nineteenth-Century Jewish Intellectual History*, edited by Alexander Altmann, 27–45. Cambridge, MA: Harvard University Press, 1964.
Glenn, Menachem. *Israel Salanter—Religious-Ethical Thinker: The Story of a Religious-Ethical Current in Nineteenth-Century Judaism*. New York: Bloch/Dropsie, 1953.
Göcke, Benedikt. *The Panentheism of Karl Christian Friedrich Krause (1781–1832): From Transcendental Philosophy to Metaphysics*. New York: Peter Lang, 2018.
Gödde, Günter. *Traditionslinien des Unbewussten: Schopenhauer, Nietzsche, Freud*. Tübingen: Diskord, 1999.
Goethe, Johann Wolfgang von. *The Autobiography of Goethe: "Poetry and Truth"; "From My Own Life."* Vol. 2, *Books XIV–XX, Together with His Annals; or, Day and Year Papers*. London: George Bell, 1882.
Goethe, Johann Wolfgang von. *Conversations with Eckermann: Being Appreciations and Criticisms on Many Subjects of Goethe by Johann Peter Eckermann*. New York: M. Walter Dunne, 1901.
Goethe, Johann Wolfgang von. "Elegy from Marienbad" ("Elegie von Marienbad"). In *103 Great Poems: A Dual-Language Book*, translated and edited by Stanley Appelbaum, 207–9. Mineola, NY: Dover, 1999.
Goethe, Johann Wolfgang von. "Mighty Surprise." In *Poems of Goethe: A Sequel to Goethe, the Lyrist*, translated and edited by Edwin H. Zeydel, 70. Chapel Hill: University of North Carolina Press, 1957.
Goetschel, Roland. "Peter Beers Blick auf die Kabbala." In Goodman-Thau, Mattenklott, and Schulte, *Kabbala und Romantik*, 293–306.
Goldberg, Hillel. *The Fire Within: A Living Heritage of the Musar*. New York: ArtScroll, 1987.
Goldberg, Hillel. *Israel Salanter: Text, Structure, Idea*. New York: KTAV, 1982.
Goldberg, Hillel. "Israel Salanter's Suspended Conversation." *Tradition: A Journal of Orthodox Jewish Thought* 22, no. 3 (1986): 31–43.

Goldman, Norman Saul. "Rabbinic Theology and the Unconscious." *Journal of Religion and Health* 17, no. 2 (April 1978): 144–50.
Gombrich, E. H. "The Symbol of the Veil: Psychological Reflections on Schiller's Poetry." In *Freud and the Humanities*, edited by Peregrine Horden, 75–109. London: St. Martin's Press, 1985.
Goodfriend, Elaine Adler. "Ethical Theory and Practice in the Hebrew Bible." In *The Oxford Handbook of Jewish Ethics and Morality*, edited by Elliot N. Dorff and Jonathan N. Crane, 35–50. Oxford: Oxford University Press, 2013.
Goodman-Thau, Eveline. "Meyer Heinrich Hirsch Landauer: Bible Scholar and Kabbalist." In *Mysticism, Magic and Kabbalah in Ashkenazi Judaism*, edited by Karl Erich Grözinger and Joseph Dan, 275–94. Berlin: De Gruyter, 2012.
Goodman-Thau, Eveline. "Meyer Heinrich Hirsch Landauer—eine Brücke zwischen Kabbala und aufgeklärtem Judentum." In Goodman-Thau, Mattenklott, and Schulte, *Kabbala und Romantik*, 249–78.
Goodman-Thau, Eveline, Gert Mattenklott, and Christoph Schulte, eds. *Kabbala und Romantik: Die jüdische Mystik in der romantischen Geistesgeschichte*. Berlin: De Gruyter, 2011.
Gordin, Jacob. "La pensée juive du XIXe siècle (A propos d'un ouvrage récent)." *Revue des études juives*, 100 bis, no. 199–200 (January–June 1936): 74–86.
Gordin, Jacob. "Moritz Lazarus." In *Encyclopaedia Judaica*, edited by Jakob Klatzkin and Ismar Elbogen, 10 vols., 10:708–9. Berlin: Eschkol, 1934.
Gorog, Jean-Jacques. "L'identité est 'de l'autre.'" *Champs lacaniens* 1, no. 6 (2008): 59–65.
Görres, Joseph von. *Die christliche Mystik* [On Christian mysticism]. 4 vols. Regensburg: Verlag von Joseph Manz, Krull'sche Universitätsbuchhandlung, 1836–42.
Görres, Joseph von. *Mythengeschichte der asiatischen Welt*. Heidelberg, 1810.
Gotzmann, Andreas. "Reconsidering Judaism as a Religion: The Religious Emancipation Period." *Jewish Studies Quarterly* 7, no. 4 (2000): 352–66.
Graetz, Heinrich. *Frank und die Frankisten: Eine Sekten Geschichte aus der letzten Hälfte des vorigen Jahrhunderts*. Breslau, Germany, 1868.
Graetz, Heinrich. *History of the Jews*. 6 vols. New York: Jewish Publication Society, 1892.
Graetz, Michael. *The Jews in Nineteenth-Century France: From the French Revolution to the Alliance Israélite Universelle*. Stanford, CA: Stanford University Press, 1996.
Graevenitz, Gerhart von. "'Verdichtung' das Kulturmodell der Zeitschrift für Völkerpsychologie und Sprachwissenschaft." *KEA—Zeitschrift für Kulturwissenschaften* 12 (1999): 19–57.
Grassi, Ernesto. "Vico versus Freud: Creativity and the Unconscious." In *Vico: Past and Present*, edited by Giorgio Tagliacozzo, 144–61. Atlantic Highlands, NJ: Humanities Press, 1981.
Green, André. *Narcissisme de vie, narcissisme de mort*. Paris: Minuit, 1983.
Green, Arthur. *Devotion and Commandment: The Faith of Abraham in the Hasidic Imagination*. Pittsburgh: University of Pittsburgh Press and Hebrew Union College Press, 1989.
Green, Arthur. "The Zaddiq as Axis Mundi in Later Judaism." *Journal of the American Academy of Religion* 45, no. 3 (1977): 327–47.

Green, Harold M. "Adolf Stoecker: Portrait of a Demagogue." *Politics and Policy* 31, no. 1 (2003): 106–29.
Greenberg, Gershon. "Mendelssohn in America: David Einhorn's Radical Reform Judaism." *Leo Baeck Institute Year Book* 27 (1982): 281–93.
Greenberg, Gershon. "Religionswissenschaft and Early Reform Jewish Thought." In *Modern Judaism and Historical Consciousness: Identities, Encounters, Perspectives*, edited by Andreas Gotzmann and Christian Wiese, 110–44. Leiden: Brill, 2007.
Greenberg, Gershon. "The Significance of America in David Einhorn's Conception of History." *American Jewish Historical Quarterly* 63 (1973): 160–84.
Greene, Daniel. *The Jewish Origins of Cultural Pluralism: The Menorah Association and American Diversity*. Bloomington: Indiana University Press, 2011.
Greenham, David. "'Altars to the Beautiful Necessity': The Significance of F. W. J. Schelling's 'Philosophical Inquiries in the Nature of Human Freedom' in the Development of Ralph Waldo Emerson's Concept of Fate." *Journal of the History of Ideas* 76, no. 1 (2015): 115–37.
Greenham, David. *Emerson's Transatlantic Romanticism*. New York: Palgrave, 2012.
Gregory, Bradley C., and Admiel Kosman. "Ḥesed." In *Encyclopedia of the Bible and Its Reception Online*, edited by Constance M. Furey, Peter Gemeinhardt, Joel Marcus LeMon, Thomas Chr. Römer, Jens Schröter, Barry Dov Walfish, and Eric Ziolkowski, n.p. Berlin: De Gruyter, 2015.
Grojnowski, Daniel. *Jules Laforgue et l'"originalité"*. Neuchâtel: La Baconnière, 1988.
Grollman, Earl A. *Judaism in Sigmund Freud's World*. New York: Appleton-Century-Crofts, 1965.
Grossert, Werner. *"Sulamith," die Friedliebende aus Dessau 1806–1848: Die erste jüdische Zeitschrift in deutscher Sprache und deutscher Schrift*. Dessau: Moses-Mendelssohn-Gesellschaft e.V., 2001.
Groves, Jason. *The Geological Unconscious: German Literature and the Mineral Imaginary*. New York: Fordham University Press, 2020.
Guetta, Alessandro. *Philosophy and Kabbalah: Elijah Benamozegh and the Reconciliation of Western Thought and Jewish Esotericism*. Albany: State University of New York Press, 2009.
Guttmann, Jacob. "Lazarus Bendavid: Seine Stellung zum Judentum und seine literarische Wirksamkeit." *Monatsschrift für Geschichte und Wissenschaft des Judentums* 61, no. 21 (1917): 26–50, 176–211.
Habermas, Jürgen. "Ernst Bloch: A Marxist Romantic." *Salmagundi*, no. 10–11 (1969): 311–25.
Habermas, Jürgen. *The Philosophical Discourse of Modernity*. Cambridge, MA: MIT Press, 1987.
Habermas, Jürgen. *Philosophical-Political Profiles: The German Idealism of Jewish Philosophers*. Cambridge, MA: MIT Press, 1985.
Hackel, Christiane, and Sabine Seifert. *August Boeckh: Philologie, Hermeneutik und Wissenschaftspolitik*. Berlin: BWV, 2014.
Hacohen, Malachi Haim. *Jacob and Esau: Jewish European History between Nation and Empire*. Cambridge: Cambridge University Press, 2019.
Hadot, Pierre. *The Veil of Isis: An Essay on the History and the Idea of Nature*. Cambridge, MA: Belknap Press of Harvard University Press, 2006.
Haeckel, Ernst. *Generelle Morphologie der Organismen*. Berlin: Reimer, 1866.

Hale, Nathan G., Jr. *The Rise and Crisis of Psychoanalysis: Freud and the Americans, 1917–1985*. New York: Oxford University Press, 1995.

Hampton, Alexander. *Romanticism and the Re-invention of Modern Religion: The Reconciliation of German Idealism and Platonic Realism*. Cambridge: Cambridge University Press, 2019.

Hanegraaff, Wouter. *Esotericism and the Academy: Rejected Knowledge in Western Culture*. Cambridge: Cambridge University Press, 2012.

Harpham, Geoffrey Galt. "Roots, Races, and the Return to Philology." *Representations* 106, no. 1 (2009): 34–62.

Harris, Jay M. *Nachman Krochmal: Guiding the Perplexed of the Modern Age*. New York: New York University Press, 1991.

Harris, W. T. "Emerson's Orientalism." In *The Genius and Character of Emerson*, edited by F. B. Sanborn and John Osgood, 372–85. Boston: James R. Osgood, 1884.

Hart, Onno van der, and Rütger Horst. "The Dissociation Theory of Pierre Janet." *Journal of Traumatic Stress* 2, no. 4 (1989): 397–412.

Hart, Ray L. *God Being Nothing: Toward a Theogony*. Chicago: University of Chicago Press, 2016.

Hartmann, Eduard von. *Das Judenthum in Gegenwart und Zukunft*. Leipzig: Friedrich, 1884.

Hartmann, Eduard von. *Das religiöse Bewusstsein der Menschheit im Stufengang seiner Entwickelung*. Berlin: Duncker, 1882.

Hartmann, Eduard von. *Die Selbstzersetzung des Christenthums und die Religion der Zukunft*. Berlin: Duncker, 1874.

Hartmann, Eduard von. *Gesammelte Studien und Aufsätze gemeinverständlichen Inhalts*. Berlin: Duncker, 1876.

Hartmann, Eduard von. *La philosophie de l'inconscient*. Paris: Baillière, 1877.

Hartmann, Eduard von. *Philosophy of the Unconscious: Speculative Results according to the Inductive Method of Physical Science*. 3 vols. London: Routledge, 2014. Orig. pub. 1869.

Hartmann, Eduard von. *Zur Geschichte und Begründung des Pessimismus*. Berlin: Duncker, 1880.

Hartston, Barnet Pertz. *Sensationalizing the Jewish Question: Anti-Semitic Trials and the Press in the Early German Empire*. Leiden: Brill, 2005.

Hartung, Gerald. *Sprach-Kritik: Sprach und kulturtheoretische Reflexionen im deutsch-jüdischen Kontext*. Weilerswist, Germany: Velbruck Wissenschaft, 2012.

Haskell, Ellen. *Mystical Resistance: Uncovering the "Zohar's" Conversations with Christianity*. New York: Oxford University Press, 2016.

Heard, W. G. "The Unconscious Functions of the I-It and I-Thou Realms." *Humanistic Psychologist* 23, no. 2 (1995): 239–58.

Hecht, Dieter. "Self-Assertion in the Public Sphere: The Jewish Press on the Eve of Legal Emancipation." *Religions* 7, no. 8 (2016): 109–19.

Hecht, Louise. *Ein jüdischer Aufklärer in Böhmen: Der Pädagoge und Reformer Peter Beer (1758–1838)*. Cologne: Böhlau Verlag, 2008.

Hedge, Frederick Henry. "Coleridge's Literary Character." *Christian Examiner* 14, no. 1 (March 1833): 108–29.

Hegel, G. W. F. *Lectures on the Philosophy of Religion*. Irvine: University of California Press, 1988.

Hegel, G. W. F. *Lectures on the Philosophy of World History: Introduction*. Translated by Hugh Barr Nisbet. Cambridge: Cambridge University Press, 1980.
Hegel, G. W. F. *The Phenomenology of Mind*. Translated by J. B. Baillic. 2nd ed. London: Dover, 2003.
Hegel, G. W. F. *The Phenomenology of Spirit*. New York: Oxford University Press. 1977.
Hegel, G. W. F. *The Philosophy of History*. New York: Dover, 1956.
Hegel, G. W. F. *Philosophy of Mind*. New York: Oxford University Press, 2010.
Hegel, G. W. F. *The Spirit of Christianity and Its Fate*. In *On Christianity: Early Theological Writings*, translated by T. M. Knox and Richard Kroner. New York: Harper, 1961.
Heinemann, Isaac. "The Relationship between Samson Raphael Hirsch and His Teacher Isaac Bernays." *Zion* 16 (1951): 69–77.
Heinze, Andrew. *Jews and the American Soul: Human Nature in the Twentieth Century*. Princeton, NJ: Princeton University Press, 2004.
Heinze, Andrew. "*Peace of Mind* (1946): Judaism and the Therapeutic Polemics of Postwar America." *Religion and American Culture* 12, no. 1 (Winter 2002): 31–58.
Hellner-Eshed, Melila. *Seekers of the Face: Secrets of the "Idra Rabba" (The Great Assembly) of the "Zohar."* Stanford, CA: Stanford University Press, 2021.
Hemecker, William. *Vor Freud: Philosophiegeschichte Voraussetzungen der Psychoanalyse*. Munich: Philosophia Verlag, 1991.
Henry, Michel. *Généalogies de la psychanalyse: Le commencement perdu*. Paris: Presses Universitaires de France, 1985.
Herbart, Johann Friedrich. *Psychologie als Wissenschaft: Neu gegründet auf Erfahrung, Metaphysik und Mathematik*. Königsberg [now Kaliningrad, Russia]: Unzer, 1824.
Herder, Johann Gottfried. *God: Some Conversations*. Indianapolis: Bobbs-Merrill, 1940.
Herder, Johann Gottfried. *Ideen zur Philosophie der Geschichte der Menschheit*. New York: Bergman, 1966.
Herder, Johann Gottfried. "Letters for the Advancement of Humanity (1793–97)." In Herder, *Philosophical Writings*, translated and edited by Michael Forster, 374–79. Cambridge: Cambridge University Press, 2002.
Herder, Johann Gottfried. *Shakespeare*. Translated and edited by Gregory Martin Moore. Princeton, NJ: Princeton University Press, 2008.
Herder, Johann Gottfried. *The Spirit of Hebrew Poetry*. Translated by James Marsh. 2 vols. Burlington, VT: Edward Smith, 1833.
Herzog, Dagmar. *Cold War Freud: Psychoanalysis in an Age of Catastrophes*. Cambridge: Cambridge University Press, 2016.
Heschel, Susannah. *Abraham Geiger and the Jewish Jesus*. Chicago: University of Chicago Press, 1998.
Heschel, Susannah. "Revolt of the Colonized: Abraham Geiger's *Wissenschaft des Judentums* as a Challenge to Christian Hegemony in the Academy." *New German Critique* 77 (1999): 61–85.
Hess, Jonathan. *Germans, Jews, and the Claims of Modernity*. Princeton, NJ: Princeton University Press, 2002.
Hessayon, Ariel, and Sarah Apetrei, eds. *An Introduction to Jacob Boehme: Four Centuries of Thought and Reception*. London: Routledge, 2014.

Hillman, James. *Archetypal Psychology*. Putnam, CT: Spring Publications, 1983.
Hillman, James. *Loose Ends*. Putnam, CT: Spring Publications, 1975.
Hillman, James. *Plotinus, Ficino and Vico as Precursors of Archetypal Psychology*. Rome: Instituto della Enciclopedia Italiana, 1973.
Hillman, James. *Re-visioning Psychology*. New York: Harper, 1975.
Hirsch, Emil G. "David Einhorn: A Memorial Oration Preached before the Central Conference of American Rabbis on the Centenary of Einhorn's Birth, Nov. 10, 1909, at Temple Beth-El, New York." In Kohler, ed., *David Einhorn*, 457–82.
Hirsch, Eric Donald. *Wordsworth and Schelling: A Typological Study of Romanticism*. New Haven, CT: Yale University Press, 1960.
Hirsch, Samson Raphael. *Der Pentateuch übersetzt und erläutert*. 4 vols. Frankfurt am Main: Kaufmann, 1867–78.
Hirsch, Samson Raphael. *The Hirsch Chumash: Shemot*. New York: Feldheim, 2008.
Hirsch, Samson Raphael. *The Nineteen Letters on Judaism*. New York: Feldheim, 1969.
Hirsch, Samson Raphael. "Wie gewinnen wir das Leben für unsere Wissenschaft?" *Jeschurun* 8 (1862): 73–91.
Hirsch, Samuel. "Jewish Mystics: An Appreciation." *Jewish Quarterly Review* 20, no. 1 (October 1907): 50–73.
Hirth, Georg. *Energetische Epigenesis und epigenetische Energieformen insbesondere Merksysteme und plastische Spiegelungen*. Munich, 1898.
Hirth, Georg. "Thesen zu einer Lehre von den 'Merksystemen.'" In *Dritter Internationaler Congress für Psychologie in München vom 4. Bis 7. August 1896*, 458–73. Munich: J. F. Lehmann, 1897.
Hobsbawm, Eric. *The Age of Revolution, 1789–1848*. London: Weidenfeld and Nicolson, 1962.
Hoeschen, Andreas. "Die 'Zirkulation der Ideen' bei Lazarus/Steinthal: Von öffentlicher Kunstproduktion zu sozial-normativer 'Wilhelm Meister'-Rezeption." In *Gedächtnis und Zirkulation*, edited by Harald Schmidt and Marcus Sandl, 207–34. Göttingen: Vandenhoeck and Ruprecht, 2002.
Hoeschen, Andreas, and Lothar Schneider. "Herbartianismus im 19. Jahrhundert: Umriß einer intellektuellen Konfiguration." In *Ideen als gesellschaftliche Gestaltungskraft im Europa der Neuzeit: Beiträge für eine erneuerte Geistesgeschichte*, edited by Raphael Lutz, 447–77. Munich: Oldenbourg, 2006.
Hollander, Dana. "Buber, Cohen, Rosenzweig, and the Politics of Cultural Affirmation." *Jewish Studies Quarterly* 13, no. 1 (2006): 87–103.
Holub, Robert C. "From the Pedestal to the Couch: Goethe, Freud and Jewish Assimilation." In *Goethe in German-Jewish Culture*, edited by Klaus Berghahn and Jost Hermand, 104–20. Rochester, NY: Camden House, 2001.
Holub, Robert C. *Nietzsche's Jewish Problem: Between Anti-Semitism and Anti-Judaism*. Princeton, NJ: Princeton University Press, 2016.
Home, Henry, Lord Kames. *Essays on the Principles of Morality and Natural Religion*. 2nd ed. London: C. Hitch et al., 1758.
Honoré, Juliette. "Écritures de l'allégorie avant et après Freud: *Le jardin de Bérénice* de Maurice Barrès et *La victime* de Pierre Jean Jouve." In *Déclins de l'allégorie?*, edited by Bernard Vouilloux, 123–38. Pessac: Presses Universitaires de Bordeaux, 2006.
Horowitz, Isaiah. *Shnei Luḥot ha-Brit* [The two tablets of the alliance]. Lemberg [Lviv, Ukraine]: Segal, 1860.

Horstmann, Axel. "'Erkenntnis des Erkannten': Philologie und Philosophie bei August Boeckh (1785-1867)." *Zeitschrift für Germanistik* 20, no. 1 (2010): 64-78.
Horwitz, Rivka. "From Hegelianism to a Revolutionary Understanding of Judaism: Franz Rosenzweig's Attitude toward Kabbala and Myth." *Modern Judaism* 26, no. 1 (2006): 31-54.
Horwitz, Rivka. "On Kabbala and Myth in Nineteenth-Century Germany: Isaac Bernays." *Proceedings of the American Academy for Jewish Research* 59 (1993): 137-83.
Hudson, Wayne. *The Marxist Philosophy of Ernst Bloch*. New York: St. Martin's Press, 1982.
Hühn, Lore. *Kierkegaard und der deutsche Idealismus: Konstellationen des Übergangs*. Tübingen: Mohr Siebeck, 2009.
Humboldt, Wilhelm von. *Briefe an Friedrich August Wolf*. Edited by Philip Mattson. Berlin: De Gruyter, 1990.
Humboldt, Wilhelm von. *Gesammelte Schriften*. 17 vols. Berlin: Behr, 1903.
Humboldt, Wilhelm von. *On Language: The Diversity of Human Language Structure and Its Influence on the Mental Development of Mankind*. Cambridge: Cambridge University Press, 1988.
Hurwitz, Siegmund. "Archetypische Motive in der Chassidischen Mystik." *Studien aus dem C. G. Jung Institut* 3 (1952): 121-212.
Hurwitz, Siegmund. *Lilith—the First Eve: Historical and Psychological Aspects of the Dark Feminine*. Einsiedeln, Switzerland: Daimon, 2009.
Hurwitz, Siegmund. "Psychological Aspects in Early Hasidic Literature." In *Timeless Documents of the Soul*, by Helmuth Jacobsohn, Marie-Louise von Franz, and Siegmund Hurwitz, 149-239. Evanston, IL: Northwestern University Press, 1968.
Huss, Boaz. "Admiration and Disgust: The Ambivalent Re-Canonization of the Zohar in the Modern Period." In *Study and Knowledge in Jewish Thought* [in Hebrew], edited by Howard Kreisel, 2 vols., 1:203-37. Beer Sheva, Israel: Ben-Gurion University of the Negev Press, 2006.
Huss, Boaz. "All You Need Is LAV: Madonna and Postmodern Kabbalah." *Jewish Quarterly Review* 95, no. 4 (2005): 611-24.
Huss, Boaz. *The Question about the Existence of Jewish Mysticism: The Genealogy of Jewish Mysticism and the Theologies of Kabbalah Research*. [In Hebrew.] Jerusalem: Van Leer Institute Press and Hakkibutz Hameuchad, 2016.
Huss, Boaz. "The Theologies of Kabbalah Research." *Modern Judaism* 34, no. 1 (February 2014): 3-26.
Huss, Boaz, Marco Pasi, and Kocku von Stuckrad, eds. *Kabbalah and Modernity: Interpretations, Transformations, Adaptations*. Leiden: Brill, 2010.
Idel, Moshe. "Conceptualizations of Tzimtzum in Baroque Italian Kabbalah." In *The Value of the Particular: Lessons from Judaism and the Modern Jewish Experience; Festschrift for Steven T. Katz on the Occasion of His Seventieth Birthday*, edited by Michael Zank and Ingrid Anderson, 28-54. Leiden: Brill, 2015.
Idel, Moshe. *Hasidism: Between Ecstasy and Magic*. New York: State University of New York Press, 1995.
Idel, Moshe. "Italy in Safed, Safed in Italy: Toward an Interactive History of Sixteenth-Century Kabbalah." In *Cultural Intermediaries: Jewish Intellectuals in Early Modern Italy*, edited by David B. Ruderman and Giuseppe Veltri, 254-56. Philadelphia: University of Pennsylvania Press, 2004.

Idel, Moshe. *Kabbalah: New Perspectives*. New Haven, CT: Yale University Press, 1988.

Idel, Moshe. "Major Currents in Italian Kabbalah between 1560 and 1660." In *Essential Papers on Jewish Culture in Renaissance and Baroque Italy*, edited by David Ruderman, 345–72. New York: New York University Press, 1992.

Idel, Moshe. "Transfers of Categories: The German-Jewish Experience and Beyond." In *The German-Jewish Experience and Beyond*, edited by Steven E. Aschheim and Vivian Liska, 15–44. Berlin: De Gruyter, 2015.

Jacobi, Friedrich Heinrich. *Main Philosophical Writings and the Novel "Allwill"*. Edited and translated by George Di Giovanni. Montreal: McGill-Queen's University Press, 2009.

Jacobs, Louis. *Religion and the Individual: A Jewish Perspective*. New York: Cambridge University Press, 1992.

Jacobson, Eric. "The Future of the Kabbalah: On the Dislocation of Past Primacy, the Problem of Evil and the Future of Illusions." In *Kabbalah and Modernity: Interpretations, Transformations, Adaptations*, edited by Boaz Huss, Marco Pasi, and Kocku von Stuckrad, 53. Leiden: Brill, 2010.

Jahoda, Gustav. *A History of Social Psychology from the Eighteenth-Century Enlightenment to the End of the Second World War*. Cambridge: Cambridge University Press, 2007.

Jakobson, Roman. *Studies on Child Language and Aphasia*. Berlin: De Gruyter, 2018.

James, William. *The Varieties of Religious Experience: A Study in Human Nature*. New York: Penguin, 1982.

Janet, Paul. *Principes de métaphysique et de psychologie*. 2 vols. Paris: Delagrave, 1897.

Janet, Pierre. *L'automatisme psychologique: Essai de psychologie expérimentale sur les formes inférieures de l'activité humaine*. Paris: Alcan, 1889.

Janik, Allan, and Stephen Toulmin. *Wittgenstein's Vienna*. Chicago: Ivan R. Dee, 1996.

Jankélévitch, Vladimir. *L'odyssée de la conscience dans la dernière philosophie de Schelling*. Paris: Alcan, 1933.

Jaspers, Karl. *Schelling: Größe und Verhängnis*. Munich: Piper, 1986.

Jean Paul. *Choix de rêves*. Paris: Corti, 1964.

Jean Paul. *Dämmerungschmetterlinge oder Sphinxe* [Dusk butterfly or sphinx]. In *Jean Pauls Sämtliche Werke*, vol. 34, *Siebente Lieferung: Vierter Band; Frieden-Predigt an Deutschland*. Berlin: De Gruyter, 2018.

Jennings, Jerry L. "From Philology to Existential Psychology: The Significance of Nietzsche's Early Work." *Journal of Mind and Behavior* 9, no. 1 (1988): 57–76.

Jensen, Anthony K. "The Rogue of All Rogues: Nietzsche's Presentation of Eduard von Hartmann's *Philosophie des Unbewussten* and Hartmann's Response to Nietzsche." *Journal of Nietzsche Studies*, no. 32 (2006): 41–61.

Joel, David. *Die Religionsphilosophie des Sohar und ihr Verhältnis zur allgemeinen jüdischen Theologie: Zugleich eine kritische Beleuchtung der Franck'schen "Abbala"*. Leipzig: O. L. Fritzsche, 1849.

Johach, Helmut. "Dilthey, Freud und die humanistische Psychologie." In *Dilthey-Jahrbuch für Philosophie und Geschichte der Geisteswissenschaften*, edited by Frithjof Rodi, 32–65. Göttingen: Vandenhoeck und Ruprecht, 1995.

Johnston, Adrian. "Ghosts of Substance Past: Schelling, Lacan and the Denaturalization of Nature." In *Lacan: The Silent Partners*, edited by Slavoj Žižek, 34–55. New York: Verso, 2006.

Jonas, Hans. *The Gnostic Religion: The Message of the Alien God and the Beginnings of Christianity*. 3rd ed. Boston: Beacon Press, 2001.

Jones, Ernest. *The Life and Work of Sigmund Freud*. 3 vols. New York: Basic Books.

Jonte-Pace, Diane, and William B. Parson. *Religion and Psychology: Mapping the Terrain*. New York: Routledge, 2001.

Josephson, Joseph A. "Specters of Reason: Kantian Things and the Fragile Terrors of Philosophy." *Journal of Nineteenth-Century Americanists* 3, no. 3 (2015): 204–11.

Josephson-Storm, Jason Ananda. *The Myth of Disenchantment: Magic, Modernity, and the Birth of the Human Sciences*. Chicago: University of Chicago Press, 2017.

Joussain, André. "Le sujet conscient et l'inconscient dans leur rapport avec la durée pure chez Bergson." *Archives de philosophie* 22, no. 1 (1959): 5–23.

Jung, C. G. *Archetypes and the Collective Unconscious* (1959). In *Collected Works*, vol. 9. Princeton, NJ: Princeton University Press, 1969.

Jung, C. G. *C. G. Jung Speaking: Interviews and Encounters*. Edited by William McGuire and R. F. C. Hull. Princeton, NJ: Princeton University Press, 2020.

Jung, C. G. *Collected Works*. Edited by Herbert Read, Michael Fordham, and Gerhard Adler. 20 vols. Princeton, NJ: Princeton University Press, 1954–73.

Jung, C. G. "The Concept of Collective Unconscious" (1936). In *Collected Works*, 9.1:42–53.

Jung, C. G. *Memories, Dreams, Reflections*. New York: Pantheon Books, 1963.

Jung, C. G. "The Psychology of the Child Archetype" (1940). In *Collected Works*, 9.1:151–81.

Jung, C. G. "Religion and Psychology: A Reply to Martin Buber" (1952). In *Collected Works*, 18:663–70.

Jung, C. G. "Religion und Psychologie." *Merkur* [Stuttgart] 6, no. 5 (May 1952): 467–73.

Jung, Werner. "The Early Aesthetic Theories of Bloch and Lukács." *New German Critique*, no. 45 (1988): 41–54.

Kagan, Henry Enoch. "God and the Psychiatrist in Psychotherapy." *Journal of Religion and Health* 7, no. 1 (1968): 79–90.

Kahn, Laurence. "Car à présent tout est processus." *Libres cahiers pour la psychanalyse*, no. 14 (2006): 157–79.

Kalmar, Ivan. "The *Völkerpsychologie* of Lazarus and Steinthal and the Modern Concept of Culture." *Journal of the History of Ideas* 48, no. 4 (1987): 671–90.

Kant, Immanuel. *Anthropology from a Pragmatic Point of View*. Translated and edited by Robert Louden. New York: Cambridge University Press, 2006.

Kant, Immanuel. *Prolegomena to Any Future Metaphysics*. New York: Cambridge, 2004.

Kant, Immanuel. *Theoretical Philosophy, 1755–1770*. Cambridge: Cambridge University Press, 1992.

Kaplan, Lawrence. "Yehezkel Kaufmann, R. Nachman Krochmal, and the 'Anxiety of Influence.'" In *Yehezkel Kaufmann and the Reinvention of Jewish Biblical Exegesis*, edited by Benjamin D. Sommer, Thomas Staubli, and Job Y. Jindo, 122–46. Fribourg, Switzerland: Academic Press, 2017.

Kapp, Ernst. *Elements of a Philosophy of Technology*. Minneapolis: University of Minnesota Press, 2018. Orig. pub. 1877.
Katsh, Abraham I. "Nachman Krochmal and the German Idealists." *Jewish Social Studies* 8, no. 2 (1946): 87–102.
Katz, Claire Elise. "The Voice of God and the Face of the Other: Levinas, Kierkegaard, and Abraham." *Journal of Textual Reasoning* 10 (2001): 58–80.
Katz, Dov. *Tenu'at ha-musar*. Vols. 1 and 2. Tel Aviv: Orly Press, 1975.
Katzoff, Charlotte. "Salomon Maimon's Critique of Kant's Theory of Consciousness." *Zeitschrift für philosophische Forschung* 35, no. 2 (April–June 1981): 185–95.
Kaufmann, Walter, and Inge Soll, eds. *Nietzsche, Heidegger, and Buber: Discovering the Mind*. London: Routledge, 1992.
Keating, Ann Louise. "Renaming the Dark: Emerson's Optimism and the Abyss." *Atq* 4, no. 4 (1990): 305–25.
Keithley, Bertram. "A Synopsis of Baron du Prel's 'Philosophie der Mystik.'" *Theosophical Siftings* 1 (1888): 13–14.
Kern, Udo. *Der Gang der Vernunft bei Meister Eckhart*. Münster: LIT Verlag, 2012.
Kerslake, Christian. *Deleuze and the Unconscious*. New York: Continuum, 2007.
Kilcher, Andreas B. *Die "Kabbala denudata": Text und Kontext; Akten der 15. Tagung der Christian Knorr von Rosenroth-Gesellschaft*. Bern: Peter Lang, 2006.
King, Anthony. *The Structure of Social Theory*. New York: Routledge, 2012.
Kinzig, Wolfram. *Harnack, Marcion und das Judentum: Nebst einer kommentierten Edition des Briefwechsels Adolf von Harnacks mit Houston Stewart Chamberlain*. Leipzig: Evangelische Verlagsanstalt, 2004.
Kitzis, Gershon. "Aaron Marcus's 'Hasidism.'" [In Hebrew.] *HaMa'ayan* 21 (1981): 64–88.
Klages, Ludwig. *Goethe als Seelenforscher*. Leipzig: Johann Ambrosius Bart, 1932.
Klautke, Egbert. "The French Reception of *Völkerpsychologie* and the Origins of the Social Sciences." *Modern Intellectual History* (August 2013): 293–316.
Klautke, Egbert. "The Mind of the Nation: The Debate about *Völkerpsychologie*, 1851–1900." *Central Europe* 8, no. 1 (2010): 1–19.
Klautke, Egbert. *The Mind of the Nation: Völkerpsychologie in Germany, 1851–1955*. New York: Berghahn, 2013.
Klautke, Egbert. "*Völkerpsychologie* in Nineteenth-Century Germany: Lazarus, Steinthal, Wundt." In *Doing Humanities in Nineteenth-Century Germany*, edited by Efraim Podoksik, 243–63. Leiden: Brill, 2019.
Kléber Monod, Paul. *Solomon's Secret Arts: The Occult in the Age of Enlightenment*. New Haven, CT: Yale University Press, 2013.
Klein, Dennis B. *The Jewish Origins of the Psychoanalytic Movement*. Chicago: University of Chicago Press, 1985.
Kluge, Friedrich. *Etymological Dictionary of the German Language*. London, 1891.
Koch, Katharina. *Franz Joseph Molitor und die jüdische Tradition: Studien zu den kabbalistischen Quellen der Philosophie der Geschichte*. Berlin: De Gruyter, 2006.
Koch, Patrick B. *Human Self-Perfection: A Re-assessment of Kabbalistic Musar-Literature of Sixteenth-Century Safed*. Los Angeles: Cherub Press, 2015.
Koch, Patrick B. "'Universalist Particularism': (Jewish) Ethics in the Thought of Moritz Lazarus and Felix Adler." In *Zwischen Universalismus und partikularem Anspruch: Das Prinzip Aufklärung*, edited by Kristina-Monika Hinneburg and Grazyna Jurewicz, 49–62. Munich: Wilhelm Fink Verlag, 2014.

Kochan, Lionel. *The Jew and His History*. New York: Schocken, 1977.
Koepping, Klaus-Peter. *Adolf Bastian and the Psychic Unity of Mankind: The Foundations of Anthropology in Nineteenth-Century Germany*. Münster: Lit. Verlag, 2005.
Kohler, George Y. "Judaism Buried or Revitalised? *Wissenschaft des Judentums* in Nineteenth-Century Germany: Impact, Actuality, and Applicability Today." In *Jewish Thought and Jewish Belief*, edited by Daniel J. Lasker, 27–63. Beer Sheva, Israel: Ben-Gurion University of the Negev Press, 2012.
Kohler, George Y. *Kabbalah Research in the Wissenschaft des Judentums (1820–1880): The Foundation of an Academic Discipline*. Berlin: De Gruyter, 2019.
Kohler, George Y. *Reading Maimonides' Philosophy in Nineteenth-Century Germany: The Guide to Religious Reform*. Dordrecht: Springer, 2012.
Kohler, Kauffman. "Biographical Essay." In *David Einhorn*, 403–56.
Kohler, Kaufmann, ed. *David Einhorn: Memorial Volume; Selected Sermons and Addresses*. New York: Bloch, 1911.
Kohn, Hans. "The Eve of German Nationalism (1789–1812)." *Journal of the History of Ideas* 12, no. 2 (1951): 256–84.
Kohn, Hans. "The Paradox of Fichte's Nationalism." *Journal of the History of Ideas* 10, no. 3 (1949): 319–43.
Köhnke, Klaus Christian. "Der Kulturbegriff von Moritz Lazarus." In Moritz Lazarus, *Grundzüge der Völkerpsychologie und Kulturwissenschaft*, edited by Klaus Christian Köhnke, ix–xlii. Hamburg: Meiner, 2003.
Köhnke, Klaus Christian. "Einleitung." In Moritz Lazarus, *Grundzüge der Völkerpsychologie und Kulturwissenschaft*, edited by Klaus Christian Köhnke, ix–xxxvii. Hamburg: Meiner, 2003.
Köhnke, Klaus Christian. "Four Concepts of Social Science at Berlin University: Dilthey, Lazarus, Schmoller and Simmel." In *Georg Simmel and Contemporary Sociology*, edited by Michael Kaern, 99–108. Dordrecht: Kluwer Academic Publishers, 1990.
Kolakowski, Leszek. *La philosophie positiviste: Science et philosophie*. Paris: Denoël/Gonthier, 1976.
Koltun-Fromm, Naomi. "Imagining the Temple in Rabbinic Stone: The Evolution of the 'Even Shetiyah." *AJS Review* 43, no. 2 (2019): 355–77.
Kook, Zvi Yehuda. *Li-Netivot Israel*. Jerusalem, 1967.
Korelitz, Seth. "The Menorah Idea: From Religion to Culture, from Race to Ethnicity." *American Jewish History* 85, no. 1 (1997): 75–100.
Kosch, Michelle. *Freedom and Reason in Kant, Schelling, and Kierkegaard*. New York: Oxford University Press, 2006.
Koslowski, Peter, ed. *Die Philosophie, Theologie und Gnosis Franz von Baaders: Spekulatives Denken zwischen Aufklärung, Restauration und Romantik*. Vienna: Passagen, 1993.
Koyré, Alexandre. *La philosophie de Jacob Boehme*. Paris: Vrin, 1979.
Krause, Karl Friedrich. *Vorlesungen über das System der Philosophie*. Göttingen: Dieterich, 1828.
Krauss, Chiara Russo, and Edoardo Massimilla. "La lettura steinthaliana di Humboldt tra Hegel e Kant." In *Wilhelm von Humboldt, duecentocinquant'anni dopo*, edited by Antonio Carrano, Edoardo Massimilla, and Fulvio Tessitore, 333–61. Naples: Liguori Editore, 2017.

Kreisel, Howard. *Maimonides' Political Thought: Studies in Ethics, Law, and the Human Ideal.* Albany: State University of New York Press, 1999.

Krell, David Farrell. *The Tragic Absolute: German Idealism and the Languishing of God.* Bloomington: Indiana University Press, 2005.

Krieger, Karsten. *Der Berliner Antisemitismusstreit 1879–1881: Eine Kontroverse um die Zugehörigkeit der deutschen Juden zur Nation; Quellenedition, Kommentierte.* 2 vols. Munich: De Gruyter Saur, 2004.

Kristianpoller, Alexander. *Les rêves et leur interprétation dans le Talmud.* Lagrasse: Verdier, 2017.

Krochmal, Nachman. *Moreh Nevukhe ha-Zeman.* In *Kitvei Nachman Krochmal* [The writings of Nachman Krochmal], edited by S. Rawidowicz, chap. 4. London: Ararat, 1961.

Krone, Kerstine von der. *Wissenschaft in Öffentlichkeit: Die Wissenschaft des Judentums und ihre Zeitschriften.* Amsterdam: De Gruyter, 2011.

Krüger, Reuven. "After Eighty Years of Slumber: The Rediscovery of Erich Neumann's Jewish Corpus." *Modern Judaism* 41, no. 3 (October 2021): 339–59.

Kuklick, Bruce. *A History of Philosophy in America: 1720–2000.* Oxford: Clarendon Press, 2001.

Kunitz, Moses. *Sefer Ben Yohai.* Vienna: Georg Holzinger, 1815.

Lacan, Jacques. *Écrits.* Paris: Seuil, 1966.

Lacan, Jacques. *The Four Fundamental Concepts of Psychoanalysis.* New York: Norton, 1973.

Lacan, Jacques. *Le moi dans la théorie freudienne et dans le discours psychanalytique.* Paris: Seuil, 1978.

Lacan, Jacques. *Le séminaire.* 19 vols. Paris: Seuil, 1973–2024.

Laforgue, Jules. *Poésies complètes.* Paris: Jules Vanier, 1894.

Lammers, Ann Conrad. "Introduction to Volume Two." In Erich Neumann, *The Roots of Jewish Consciousness,* edited and translated by Ann Conrad Lammers, 2 vols., 2:xxvi–xxx. New York: Routledge, 2019.

Landau, Judah Leo. *Nachman Krochmal: Ein Hegelianer.* Berlin: S. Calvary, 1904.

Landauer, Gustav. "Der Anarchismus in Deutschland." *Die Zukunft* 10 (1895): 29–34.

Landauer, Meyer. "Interim Report on My Study" (posthumous installments). *Literaturblatt des Orients,* no. 34 (August 20, 1845): 542–44.

Landauer, Meyer. *Jehova und Elohim, oder Die althebräische Gotteslehre als Grundlage der Geschichte, der Symbolik und der Gesetzgebung der Bücher Mosis.* Stuttgart: Cotta, 1836.

Landauer, Meyer. *Wesen und Form des Pentateuchs.* Stuttgart: Cotta, 1838.

Lange, Horst. "Goethe and Spinoza: A Reconsideration." *Goethe Yearbook* 18 (2011): 11–33.

Langer, Georg. *Die Erotik der Kabbalah.* Prague: Verlag Josef Flesch, 1923.

Langer, Jiří. *Nine Gates to the Chasidic Mysteries.* Northvale, NJ: Jason Aronson, 1993. Orig. pub. 1937.

Laplanche, Jean, and Jean-Bertrand Pontalis. *The Language of Psychoanalysis.* London: Hogarth Press and Institute of Psycho-Analysis, 1973.

Latura, George. "Plato's Visible God: The Cosmic Soul Reflected in the Heavens." *Religions* 3, no. 3 (2012): 880–86.

Lauer, Quentin. *A Reading of Hegel's "Phenomenology of the Spirit."* New York: Fordham University Press, 1993.

Laurant, Jean-Pierre. "Le regard savant d'Adolphe Franck sur le martinisme et les sciences occultes." In Rothschild and Grondeux, *Adolphe Franck*, 173–81.

Lazarus, Moritz. *Das Leben der Seele*. 3 vols. Berlin: Dümmler, 1876–78. Orig. pub. 1855–57.

Lazarus, Moritz. *Die Erneuerung des Judentums, ein Aufruf von Moritz Lazarus*. Edited by Nahida Ruth Lazarus. Berlin: G. Reimer, 1909.

Lazarus, Moritz. *Die Ethik des Judentums*. 2 vols. Frankfurt am Main: J. Kauffmann, 1898 (vol. 1) and 1911 (vol. 2).

Lazarus, Moritz. *Die sittliche Berechtigung Preussens in Deutschland*. Berlin: Carl Schultze, 1850.

Lazarus, Moritz. "Eine kleine Gemeinde/Elternhaus und Jugend." In *Jüdische Memoiren aus drei Jahrhunderten*, edited by Hans Bach, 165–203. Berlin: Schocken, 1936.

Lazarus, Moritz. "Einige synthetische Gedanken zur Völkerpsychologie." *Zeitschrift für Völkerpsychologie und Sprachwissenschaft* 3 (1865): 1–94.

Lazarus, Moritz. *The Ethics of Judaism: In Four Parts*. 4 vols. Philadelphia: Jewish Publication Society of America, 1900.

Lazarus, Moritz. *Ideale Fragen in Reden und Vorträgen*. Berlin: A. Hofmann, 1879.

Lazarus, Moritz. *Moritz Lazarus' Lebenserinnerungen*. Edited by Nahida Lazarus and Alfred Leicht. Berlin: Druck und Verlag von Georg Reimer, 1906.

Lazarus, Moritz. *Treu und Frei: Gesammelte Reden und Vorträge über Juden und Judenthum*. Leipzig: Winter'sche Verlagshandlung, 1887.

Lazarus, Moritz. "Über den Begriff und die Möglichkeit einer Völkerpsychologie." *Deutsches Museum: Zeitschrift für Literatur, Kunst und öffentliches Leben* 1 (July 1851): 112–26.

Lazarus, Moritz. *Über den Ursprung der Sitten: Antrittsvorlesung gehalten am 23 März 1860 in der Aula der Hochschule zu Bern*. Berlin: Fred Dummlers Verlagsbuchhandlung, 1860.

Lazarus, Moritz. *Über die Ideen in der Geschichte: Berner Rectoratsrede*. Berlin, 1865.

Lazarus, Moritz. "Verdichtung des Denkens in der Geschichte." *Zeitschrift für Völkerpsychologie und Sprachwissenschaft* 2 (1862): 54–62.

Lazarus, Moritz. *Was heißt national?* Berlin: Dümmler, 1880.

Lazarus, Moritz. "What Does National Mean? A Lecture." In Marcel Stötzler, *The State, the Nation and the Jews: Liberalism and the Anti-Semitism Dispute in Bismarck's Germany*, appendix 2, 317–59. Lincoln: University of Nebraska Press, 2009.

Lazarus, Moritz, and Heymann Steinthal. "Einleitende Gedanken über Völkerpsychologie, als Einladung zu einer Zeitschrift für Völkerpsychologie und Sprachwissenschaft." *Zeitschrift für Völkerpsychologie und Sprachwissenschaft* 1 (1860): 1–73.

Lazarus, Moritz, and Heymann Steinthal. "Einleitende Gedanken über Völkerpsychologie, als Einladung zu einer Zeitschrift für Völkerpsychologie und Sprachwissenschaft." In Heymann Steinthal, *Kleine sprachtheoretische Schriften*, edited by Waltraud Bumann, 307–79. Hildesheim: Olms, 1970.

Lazarus, Nahida Ruth. "Wie Steinthal und Lazarus Bruder wurden." In *Jahrbuch für jüdische Geschichte und Literatur* (1900): 149–66.

Lazier, Benjamin. *God Interrupted: Heresy and the European Imagination between the World Wars*. Princeton, NJ: Princeton University Press, 2012.

Leary, David E. *Metaphors in the History of Psychology*. Cambridge: Cambridge University Press, 1990.

Le Bon, Gustave. *The Crowd: A Study of the Popular Mind*. New York: Macmillan, 1896.

Leibniz, Gottfried Wilhelm. *New Essays on Human Understanding*. Edited by Peter Remnant and Jonathan Bennett. Cambridge: Cambridge University Press, 1996.

Leibniz, Gottfried Wilhelm. *Principes de la philosophie ou Monadologie* (1714). In *Principes de la nature et de la grâce: Monadologie*, edited by André Robinet. Paris: PUF, 1954.

Leibniz, Gottfried Wilhelm. *Principles of Nature and Grace*. In *Philosophical Essays*, edited by Roger Ariew and Daniel Garber. Indianapolis: Hackett, 1989.

Leicht, Alfred. *Lazarus, der Begründer der Völkerpsychologie*. Leipzig: Dürr'sche Buchhandlung, 1904.

Leiman, Shnayer Z. "Rabbinic Openness to General Culture in the Early Modern Period in Western and Central Europe." In *Judaism's Encounter with Other Cultures: Rejection or Integration?*, edited by Jacob J. Schacter, 180–201. Northvale, NJ: Jason Aronson, 1997.

Leland, Patrick R. "Unconscious Representations in Kant's Early Writings." *Kantian Review* 23, no. 2 (2018): 257–84.

Lepenies, Wolf. *Between Literature and Science: The Rise of Sociology*. Cambridge: Cambridge University Press, 1998.

Le Rider, Jacques. *Modernité viennoise et crise de l'identité*. Paris: PUF, 1990.

Lesser, Alexander. "Franz Boas and the Modernization of Anthropology (1981)." In *History, Evolution, and the Concept of Culture: Selected Papers by Alexander Lesser*, edited by Sidney W. Mintz, 15–33. Cambridge: Cambridge University Press, 1985.

Letham, Jeremy. "Newborn Bards of the Holy Ghost: The Seven Seniors and Emerson's 'Divinity School Address.'" *New England Quarterly* 86, no. 4 (2013): 593–624.

Levinas, Emmanuel. *Difficult Freedom*. Baltimore: Johns Hopkins University Press, 1997.

Levinas, Emmanuel. *Noms propres*. Montpellier: Fata Morgana, 1976.

Levinas, Emmanuel. *Totality and Infinity*. Pittsburgh: Duquesne University Press, 1969.

Levinas, Emmanuel. "The Trace of the Other." Translated by Alphonso Lingis. In *Deconstruction in Context: Literature and Philosophy*, edited by Mark C. Taylor, 345–59. Chicago: University of Chicago Press, 1986.

Lewkowitz, Albert. *Das Judentum und die geistigen Strömungen des 19. Jahrhunderts*. Breslau: M. and H. Marcus, 1935.

Leymarie, Michel. "On the Antisemitism of Maurice Barrès: From Childhood to the Eve of the Dreyfus Affair." *Archives juives* 52, no. 1 (2019): 125–43.

Liebman, Joshua Loth. *Peace of Mind*. London: William Heinemann, 1946.

Lincoln, Bruce. *Theorizing Myth: Narrative, Ideology, and Scholarship*. Chicago: University of Chicago Press, 1999.

Linker, Damon. "The Reluctant Pluralism of J. G. Herder." *Review of Politics* 62, no. 2 (2000): 267–93.

Lipps, Theodor. "Der Begriff des Unbewussten in der Psychologie." In *Dritter Internationaler Congress für Psychologie in München vom 4. bis 7. August 1896*, 146–64. Munich: J. F. Lehmann, 1897.

Lipps, Theodor. *Grundtatsachen des Seelenlebens*. Bonn: Max Cohen und Sohn, 1883.
Lissa, Giuseppe. "Deux modèles philosophiques de l'antijudaïsme: Hegel et Nietzsche." *Pardes* (2005): 139–50.
Livingstone, David N. *Adam's Ancestors: Race, Religion, and the Politics of Human Origins*. Baltimore: Johns Hopkins University Press, 2008.
Livneh-Freudenthal, Rachel. "Jewish Studies: The Paradigm and Initial Patrons." [In Hebrew.] In *Historiography and the Science of Judaism* [in Hebrew], edited by M. F. Mach and Y. Jacobson, 187–214. Tel Aviv: University of Tel Aviv, 2005.
Locke, John. *An Essay concerning Human Understanding*. New York: Penguin, 1997.
Lord, Beth. "Herder and Spinozistic Naturalism." In *Kant and Spinozism: Renewing Philosophy*. London: Palgrave Macmillan, 2011.
Löwengard, Hirsch Maier. *Auch einige Worte über das neue Gebetbuch im Hamburger Tempel*. Tübingen: Fues, 1842.
Löwengard, Hirsch Maier [Juda Leon, pseud.]. *Beiträge zur Kritik der Reformbestrebungen in der Synagoge*. Stuttgart, 1841.
Löwengard, Hirsch Maier. *Jehova, nicht Moloch, war der Gott der alten Hebräer: Entgegnung auf [Friedrich Wilhelm] Ghillany's Werk; "Die Menschenopfer der alten Hebräer"*. Berlin: Schultze, 1843.
Löwy, Michael. "Jewish Messianism and Libertarian Utopia in Central Europe (1900–1933)." In "Special Issue 2: Germans and Jews," *New German Critique*, no. 20 (Spring–Summer 1980): 105–15.
Lukács, Georg. *The Destruction of Reason*. New York: Verso, 2021. Orig. pub. 1954.
Lukács, Georg. "Schellings Irrationalismus." *Deutsche Zeitschrift für Philosophie* 1, issue JG (1953): 53–102.
Lunn, Eugene. *Prophet of Community: The Romantic Socialism of Gustav Landauer*. Berkeley: University of California Press, 1973.
Luther, Martin. *Dr. Martin Luthers Sämmtliche Werke*. Edited by Ernst Ludwig Enders. 67 vols. Frankfurt am Main: Erlangen, 1828–70.
Luz, Ehud. "Buber's Hermeneutics: The Road to the Revival of the Collective Memory and Religious Faith." *Modern Judaism* 15, no. 1 (1995): 69–93.
Luz, Ehud. "Spiritualism and Religious Anarchism in the Teaching of Shmuel Alexandrov." [In Hebrew.] *Daat* 7 (1981): 121–38.
Luzzatto, Moses Ḥayyim. *Messilat Yesharim* [The path of the just]. New York: Mesorah Publications, 2014.
Luzzatto, Samuel David. *Vikkuah al Hokhmat ha Kabbalah* [Disputation on the wisdom of Kabbalah]. Gorizia, Italy: I. B. Seitz, 1852.
Mack, Michael. *German Idealism and the Jew: The Inner Anti-Semitism of German Philosophy and Some Jewish Responses*. Chicago: University of Chicago Press, 2003.
Madden, Kathryn Wood. "Images of the Abyss." *Journal of Religion and Health* 42, no. 2 (2003): 117–31.
Magee, Glenn Alexander. *Hegel and the Hermetic Tradition*. Ithaca, NY: Cornell University Press, 2001; Cornell Paperbacks edition, 2008.
Magee, Glenn Alexander. *The Hegel Dictionary*. New York: Continuum, 2011.
Magee, Glenn Alexander. "Hegel's Reception of Jacob Boehme." In *An Introduction to Jacob Boehme: Four Centuries of Thought and Reception*, edited by Ariel Hessayon and Sarah Apetrei, 224–43. London: Routledge, 2014.
Maggid of Mezeritch. *Liqqutei Amarim*. Jerusalem: Mosdot Shuvi Nafshi, n.d.

Maggid of Mezeritch. *Or ha-Emet*. Zhitomir, Russia, 1900.

Magid, Shaul. "For the Sake of a Jewish Revival: Gershom Scholem on Hasidism and Its Relationship to Martin Buber." In *Scholar and Kabbalist: The Life and Work of Gershom Scholem*, edited by Mirjam Zadoff and Noam Zadoff, 39–75. Leiden: Brill, 2018.

Magid, Shaul. "Origin and Overcoming the Beginning: Zimzum as a Trope of Reading in Post-Lurianic Kabbala." In *Beginning/Again: Toward a Hermeneutics of Jewish Texts*, edited by Aryeh Cohen and Shaul Magid, 164–65. New York: Seven Bridges Press, 2002.

Maier, Joseph. "Vico and Critical Theory." *Social Research* 43, no. 4 (1976): 845–56.

Maimon, Salomon. *An Autobiography*. Translated by J. Clark Murray. Urbana: University of Illinois Press, 2001.

Maimonide, Moïse [Moses Maimonides]. *Le guide des égarés*. Edited by Salomon Munk. 3 vols. Paris: Maisonneuve and Larose, 1981. Orig. pub. 1856–70.

Maimonides, Moses. *The Guide of the Perplexed*. Translated by Shlomo Pines. 2 vols. Chicago: University of Chicago Press, 1963.

Maimonides, Moses. *Rabbeinu Mosheh Ben Maimon, "Sefer ha-Qazeret, o Sefer ha-Mis'adim"* [Treatise on asthma, or Book of nourishments]. In *Be-Targumo ha-Ivri shel ha-Rofe R. Shmuel Benveniste*, edited by Süssmann Munter. Jerusalem: Rubin Mass, 1940.

Maimonides, Moses. *Yesodei ha-Torah*. New York: Moznaim, 1989.

Makkreel, Rudolf A. *Dilthey, Philosopher of the Human Studies*. Princeton, NJ: Princeton University Press, 1975.

Makkreel, Rudolf A. "The Emergence of the Human Sciences from the Moral Sciences." In *Cambridge History of Philosophy in the Nineteenth Century (1790–1870)*, edited by Allen W. Wood and Songsuk Susan Hahn, 293–322. New York: Cambridge University Press, 2013.

Makkreel, Rudolph A. "Wilhelm Dilthey and the Neo-Kantians: The Distinction of the Geisteswissenschaften and the Kulturwissenschaften." *Journal of the History of Philosophy* 7, no. 4 (October 1969): 423–40.

Makkreel, Rudolf A. "Wilhelm Dilthey and the Neo-Kantians: On the Conceptual Distinction between Geisteswissenschaft and Kulturwissenschaft." In *Neo-Kantianism in Contemporary Philosophy*, edited by Rudolf A. Makkreel and Sebastian Luft, 253–71. Bloomington: Indiana University Press, 2009.

Mann, Thomas. *Essays by Thomas Mann*. New York: Vintage, 1957.

Marchal, Bertrand. "Laforgue et Hartmann: Quelques remarques sur les 'Vers Philo.'" *Revue d'histoire littéraire de la France* 117, no. 2 (2017): 283–98.

Marcus, Ahron. *Barsilai*. Krakow: A. Marcus, 1908.

Marcus, Ahron. *Barsilai: Sprache als Schrift der Psyche; Hebräisches Wurzel-Wörterbuch*. Berlin: Louis Lamm, 1905.

Marcus, Ahron. *Der Chassidismus: Eine Kulturgeschichtliche Studie*. Pleschen [Pleszew, Poland]: Verlag des Jeschurun, 1901.

Marcus, Ahron. *Hartmann's Inductive Philosophie im Chassidismus*. Lemberg [Lviv, Ukraine]: Verlag von Michael Wolf, 1889.

Marcus, Ahron. Review of *Rabbi Nachman von Brazlaw: Beitrag zur Geschichte der jüdischen Mystik*, by S. A. Horodezky. *Monatsschrift für Geschichte und Wissenschaft des Judentums* 54, no. 18 (1910): 749–55.

Marcus, Markus. *Ahron Marcus: Die Lebensgeschichte eines Chossid.* Montreux: D. Marcus, 1966.
Margolin, Ron. *Inner Religion.* [In Hebrew.] Ramat Gan, Israel: Bar-Ilan University Press, 2011.
Margolin, Ron. *Inner Religion in Jewish Sources.* Brighton, UK: Academic Studies Press, 2021.
Margoliouth, George. "The Doctrine of the Ether in the Kabbalah." *Jewish Quarterly Review* 20, no. 4 (July 1908): 825–61.
Markowska, Barbara. "Homo Libidinous and the Economy of Desire: Rereading Simmel's *The Philosophy of Money* after Freud." *Polish Sociological Review,* no. 204 (2018): 485–98.
Marquet, Jean-François. "Schelling: Du processus naturel au processus mythologique." In *Philosophies de la nature,* edited by Olivier Bloch, 227–36. Paris: Éditions de la Sorbonne, 2000.
Marr, Wilhelm. *Der Weg zum Siege des Germanenthums über das Judenthum.* Berlin: Hentze, 1880.
Marsh, James. "Preliminary Essay to Coleridge's *Aids to Reflection.*" In *Selected Writings of the American Transcendentalists,* edited by Martha F. Davis, 105–12. New Haven, CT: Yale University Press, 2004.
Martensen, Hans Lassen. *Jacob Boehme: His Life and Teaching or Studies in Theosophy.* London: Hodder and Stoughton, 1885.
Marx, Farina. "Kompilation oder Interpretation: Der Yalkut Shimoni zu Habakuk." In *Jenseits der Tradition? Tradition und Traditionskritik in Judentum, Christentum und Islam,* edited by Regina Grundmann and Assaad Elias Kattan, 74–88. Berlin: De Gruyter, 2015.
Mauthner, Fritz. *Beiträge zu einer Kritik der Sprache.* 3 vols. Stuttgart, 1901–2.
Mauthner, Fritz. *Die Sprache.* Frankfurt am Main, 1906.
Mayer, Paola. *Jena Romanticism and Its Appropriation of Jakob Böhme: Theosophy—Hagiography—Literature.* Montreal: McGill-Queen's University Press, 1999.
Mayse, Ariel. "'Or haHayyim': Creativity, Tradition, and Mysticism in the Torah Commentary of R. Hayyim ibn Attar." *Conversations* 13 (2012): 68–89.
Mayse, Ariel. *Speaking Infinities: God and Language in the Teachings of Rabbi Dov Ber of Mezritsh.* Philadelphia: University of Pennsylvania Press, 2020.
McGinn, Bernard. *The Harvest of Mysticism in Medieval Germany (1300–1500).* New York: Herder and Herder, 2005.
McGinn, Bernard. "Lost in the Abyss: The Function of Abyss Language in Medieval Mysticism." *Franciscan Studies* 72 (2014): 433–52.
McGrath, Sean J. *The Dark Ground of Spirit: Schelling and the Unconscious.* New York: Routledge, 2012.
McGrath, Sean J. "The Psychology of Productive Dissociation, or What Would Schellingian Psychotherapy Look Like?" *Comparative and Continental Philosophy* 6, no. 1 (2014): 35–48.
McGrath, Sean J. "Schelling and the History of the Dissociative Self." *Symposium: Canadian Journal of Continental Philosophy* 19, no. 1 (2015): 52–66.
McGrath, Sean J. "Schelling and the Unconscious." *Research in Phenomenology* 40 (2010): 72–91.
Mead, George H. "The Relations of Psychology and Philology." *Psychological Bulletin* 1 (1904): 375–91.

Meir, Jonatan. "Haskalah and Esotericism in Galicia: The Unpublished Writings of Elyakim Gezel Hamilzahgi." [In Hebrew.] *Kabbalah: Journal for the Study of Jewish Mystical Texts* 33 (2015): 273–313.

Meir, Jonatan. "Haskalah and Esotericism: The Strange Case of Elyakim Getzel Hamilzahgi (1780–1854)." *Aries* 18 (2018): 153–87.

Meir, Jonatan. "Haskalah, Kabbalah and Mesmerism: The Case of Isaac Baer Levinsohn." In *Finden und Erfinden: Die Romantik und ihre Religionen 1790–1820*, edited by Daniel Cyranka, Diana Matut, and Christian Soboth, 205–27. Würzburg: Verlag Königshausen und Neumann, 2020.

Meir, Jonatan. "The Origins of Hevrat Mekize Nirdamim in Eastern Europe." In *From the Depths of the Archive to the Bookshelf: 150th Anniversary of Mekitzei Nirdamim Publishers*, edited by Shulamit Elitzur. *Zutot* 20 (2013): 33–47.

Melamed, Yitzhak. "Salomon Maimon and the Rise of Spinozism in German Idealism." *Journal of the History of Philosophy* 42, no. 1 (2004): 79–80.

Melamed, Yitzhak. "Salomon Maimon et l'échec de la philosophie juive moderne." *Revue germanique internationale* 9 (2009): 175–87.

Menand, Louis. *The Metaphysical Club: A Story of Ideas in America*. New York: Farrar, Straus and Giroux, 2001.

Mendes-Flohr, Paul. *Divided Passions: Jewish Intellectuals and the Experience of Modernity*. Detroit: Wayne State University Press, 1991.

Mendes-Flohr, Paul. *From Mysticism to Dialogue: Martin Buber's Transformation of German Social Thought*. Detroit: Wayne State University Press, 1989.

Mendes-Flohr, Paul. "Zarathustra as a Prophet of Jewish Renewal: Nietzsche and the Young Martin Buber." *Revista Portuguesa de Filosofia* 57, no. 1 (2001): 103–11.

Mendes-Flohr, Paul, and Bernard Susser. "'Alte und Neue Gemeinschaft': An Unpublished Buber Manuscript." *AJS Review* 1 (1976): 41–56.

Merleau-Ponty, Maurice. *La structure du comportement*. Paris: Presses Universitaires de France, 1942.

Meroz, Ronit. "Faithful Transmission versus Innovation: Luria and His Disciples." In *Gershom Scholem's "Major Trends in Jewish Mysticism": 50 Years After*, edited by Peter Schäfer and Joseph Dan, 257–75. Tübingen: Mohr Siebeck, 1993.

Meroz, Ronit. "The School of Sarug: A New History." [In Hebrew.] *Shalem* 7 (2002): 149–93.

Mertens, Bram. "'This Still Remarkable Book': Franz Joseph Molitor's Judaeo-Christian Synthesis." *Journal of Modern Jewish Studies* 1, no. 2 (2002): 167–81.

Mertens, Bram. "'The True Words of the Mystic': Gershom Scholem and Franz Joseph Molitor." *Australian Journal of Jewish Studies* 17 (2003): 131–51.

Meschiari, Alberto. "Lazarus and Georg Simmel." *Simmel-Newsletter* 2 (1997): 11–16.

Meschiari, Alberto. "Per una storia del concetto di 'condensazione' (Verdichtung)." *Giornale critico della filosofia italiana* 70, no. 3 (1998): 293–306.

Meyer, Michael A. "Abraham Geiger's Historical Judaism." In *New Perspectives on Geiger*, edited by Jakob Petuchowski, 3–16. New York: Hebrew Union College Press/KTAV, 1975.

Meyer, Michael A. "America: The Reform Movement's Land of Promise." In *The American Jewish Experience*, edited by Jonathan Sarna, 60–81. New York: Holmes and Meier, 1986.

Meyer, Michael A. "The Emergence of Modern Jewish Historiography: Motives and Motifs." *History and Theory* 27 (1988): 160–75.

Meyer, Michael A. "Great Debate on Antisemitism: Jewish Reaction to New Hostility in Germany, 1879–1881." *Yearbook of the Leo Baeck Institute* 11 (1966): 136–70.
Meyer, Michael A. *Ideas of Jewish History*. New York: Behrman House, 1974.
Meyer, Michael A. *The Origins of the Modern Jew: Jewish Identity and European Culture in Germany, 1749–1824*. Detroit: Wayne State University Press, 1967.
Meyer, Michael A. "Religious Reform and Political Revolution in Mid-Nineteenth Century Germany: The Case of Abraham Jakob Adler." In *German-Jewish Thought between Religion and Politics: Festschrift in Honor of Paul Mendes-Flohr on the Occasion of His Seventieth Birthday*, edited by Christian Wiese and Martina Urban, 59–82. Berlin: De Gruyter, 2012.
Meyer, Michael A. *Response to Modernity: A History of the Reform Movement in Judaism*. Detroit: Wayne State University Press, 1995.
Meyer, Michael A. "Two Persistent Tensions within *Wissenschaft des Judentums*." In *Modern Judaism and Historical Consciousness: Identities, Encounters, Perspectives*, edited by Andreas Gotzmann and Christian Wiese, 73–90. Leiden: Brill, 2007.
Midrash Tanhuma. Vilna [Vilnius, Lithuania]: Solomon Buber, 1885.
Mieses, Fabius. *Geschichte der neuern Philosophie*. Leipzig: Moritz Schäfer, 1887.
Mieses, Fabius. "Korot ha-Philosophia ha-Hadashah." *Hatsefira* (Warsaw), June 18, 1878.
Mieses, Isaac. *Darstellung und kritische Beleuchtung der jüdischen Geheimlehre*. Krakow: Budweiser, 1863.
Miletto, Gianfranco. "Leopold Zunz and the Hebraists." *European Journal of Jewish Studies* 15 (2004): 50–60.
Mill, John Stuart. *System of Logic, Ratiocinative and Inductive*. 2 vols. London: Parker, 1843.
Miller, Lucius Hopkins. "The Religious Implicates of Bergson's Doctrine regarding Intuition and the Primacy of Spirit." *Journal of Philosophy, Psychology and Scientific Methods* 12, no. 23 (November 11, 1915): 617–32.
Mills, Jon, ed. *Rereading Freud: Psychoanalysis through Philosophy*. Albany: State University of New York Press, 2004.
Mills, Jon. *The Unconscious Abyss: Hegel's Anticipation of Psychoanalysis*. Albany: State University of New York Press, 2002.
Mine, Hideki. *Ungrund und Mitwissenschaft: Das Problem der Freiheit in der Spätphilosophie Schellings*. New York: Peter Lang, 1983.
Mirsky, Yehudah. *Towards the Mystical Experience of Modernity: The Making of Rav Kook*. Boston: Academic Studies Press, 2021.
Mohr, Richard. "The World-Soul in the Platonic Cosmology." *Illinois Classical Studies* 7 (1982): 41–48.
Molitor, Franz Joseph. *Philosophie der Geschichte, oder Über die Tradition*. 4 vols. Frankfurt am Main: Hermann, 1827.
Mondshine, Yehoshua. "Elevating the Attributes of the Alien Thought." [In Hebrew.] *Pardes Chabad* 1 (1997): 77–115.
Monroe, J. W. "Evidence of Things Not Seen: Spiritism, Occultism and the Search for a Modern Faith in France, 1853–1925." PhD diss., Yale University, 2002.
Moore, A. W. *Noble in Reason, Infinite in Faculty: Themes and Variations in Kant's Moral and Religious Philosophy*. London: Routledge, 2003.

Moore, John Brooks. "Emerson on Wordsworth." *PMLA* 41, no. 1 (1926): 179–92.
Morais, H. S. *Eminent Israelites of the Nineteenth Century*. Philadelphia, 1880.
More, Henry. *A Platonick Song of the Soul*. Lewisburg, PA: Bucknell University Press, 1998.
Mosse, George L. *Germans and Jews: The Right, the Left, and the Search for a "Third Force" in Pre-Nazi Germany*. New York: Fertig, 1970.
Münster, Arno. "*Experimentum mundi* et le problème des catégories." In *Ernst Bloch: Messianisme et utopie; Introduction à une phénoménologie de la conscience anticipante*, edited by Arno Münster, 192–218. Paris: Presses Universitaires de France, 1989.
Muratori, Cecilia. *The First German Philosopher*. New York: Springer, 2016.
Myers, David. "Philosophy and Kabbalah in Wissenschaft des Judentums: Rethinking the Narrative of Neglect." *Studia Judaica* 16 (2008): 56–71.
Myers, David. *Re-inventing the Jewish Past: European Jewish Intellectuals and the Zionist Return to History*. New York: Oxford University Press, 1995.
Myers, David. *Resisting History: Historicism and Its Discontents in German-Jewish Thought*. Princeton, NJ: Princeton University Press, 2003.
Myers, Jody. "Kabbalah as a Tool of Orthodox Outreach." In Ogren, *Kabbalah in America*, 343–57.
Nahme, Paul E. "Ghosted: Jewishness and the Haunted Hegemony of Racial Modernity." *Journal of Religion* 102, no. 2 (April 2022): 204–36.
Nakdami, M. V. *The Bhagavad Gita for the Modern Reader: History, Interpretation, Philosophy*. New York: Taylor and Francis, 2019.
Nassar, Dalia. *The Romantic Absolute: Being and Knowing in Early German Romantic Philosophy, 1795–1804*. Chicago: University of Chicago Press, 2014.
Nathan of Gaza. *Derush ha Taninim*. In Gershom Scholem, *Be-Ikevot Mashi'aḥ* [In the footsteps of the Messiah]. Jerusalem: Sifre Tarshish, 1944.
Nathan of Gaza. *Sefer Haberiya* [The book of creation]. Jerusalem: L. Holzer, 2019.
Naugle, David. *Worldview: The History of a Concept*. Grand Rapids, MI: Eerdmans, 2002.
Naumann, Barbara. *Philosophie und Poetik des Symbols: Cassirer und Goethe*. Munich: Wilhelm Fink, 1998.
Necker, Gerold. "'Out of Himself, to Himself': The Kabbalah of Jacob Böhme." In *Jacob Böhme and His World*, edited by Bo Andersson, Lucinda Martin, Leigh Penman, and Andrew Weeks, 197–220. Leiden: Brill, 2019.
Neumann, Erich. *The Roots of Jewish Consciousness*. Edited and translated by Ann Conrad Lammers. 2 vols. New York: Routledge, 2019.
Nicholls, Angus. "The Philosophical Concept of the Daemonic in Goethe's 'Mächtiges Überraschen.'" *Goethe Yearbook* (2007): 147–70.
Nicholls, Angus. "The Scientific Unconscious: Goethe's Post-Kantian Epistemology." In Nicholls and Liebscher, *Thinking the Unconscious*, 87–120.
Nicholls, Angus, and Martin Liebscher. "Introduction: Thinking the Unconscious." In Nicholls and Liebscher, *Thinking the Unconscious*, 1–25.
Nicholls, Angus, and Martin Liebscher, eds. *Thinking the Unconscious: Nineteenth-Century German Thought*. New York: Oxford University Press, 2006.
Nicolas, Serge, and Laurent Fedi. *Un débat autour de l'inconscient: La réception de Eduard von Hartmann chez les psychologues et philosophes français*. Paris: L'Harmattan, 2008.

Nietzsche, Friedrich. *Nachgelassene Fragmente Sommer 1872 bis Ende 1874*. Berlin: De Gruyter, 1978.
Nietzsche, Friedrich. *Untimely Meditations*. Edited by Daniel Breazeale. Cambridge: Cambridge University Press, 1997.
Nolen, Désiré. "Introduction du traducteur." In Eduard von Hartmann, *Philosophie de l'inconscient*, translated by Désiré Nolen, 2 vols., 1:v–lxxi. Paris: Baillière, 1877.
Noll, Richard. "Multiple Personality and the Complex Theory: A Correction and Rejection of C. G. Jung's 'Collective Unconscious.'" *Journal of Analytic Psychology* 38 (1993): 321–23.
Nordau, Max. *The Interpretation of History*. New York: Wiley, 1911.
Nordau, Max. *Der Sinn der Geschichte*. Berlin: Carl Duncker, 1909.
Norman, Judith, and Alistair Welchman, eds. *The New Schelling*. New York: Bloomsbury, 2004.
Normandin, Sebastian, and Charles T. Wolfe, eds. *Vitalism and the Scientific Image in Post-Enlightenment Life Science, 1800–2010*. London: Springer, 2013.
Novak, David. *The Theology of Nahmanides Systematically Presented*. Providence, RI: Brown Judaic Studies, 2020.
Noyes, John K. "The Voice of History: Sigmund Freud/E. T. A. Hoffmann/G. H. Schubert." *Journal of Literary Studies* 6, nos. 1–2 (1990): 36–61.
Nussbaum, Max. "Nachman Krochmal: The Philosopher of Israel's Eternity." *American Jewish Year Book* 44 (1942): 81–92.
Ogren, Brian, ed. *Kabbalah in America: Ancient Lore in the New World*. Studies in Jewish History and Culture, 64. Leiden: Brill, 2020.
Ogren, Brian. *Kabbalah and the Founding of America: The Early Influence of Jewish Thought in the New World*. New York: New York University Press, 2021.
Olender, Maurice. *The Languages of Paradise: Race, Religion, and Philology in the Nineteenth Century*. Translated by Arthur Goldhammer. Cambridge, MA: Harvard University Press, 2009.
Ollman, Bertell. *Alienation: Marx's Concept of Man in Capitalist Society*. Cambridge: Cambridge University Press, 1976.
O'Regan, Cyril. *Gnostic Apocalypse*. Albany: State University of New York Press, 2002.
O'Regan, Cyril. *Gnostic Return in Modernity*. Albany: State University of New York Press, 2001.
Ormiston, Alice. "'The Spirit of Christianity and Its Fate': Towards a Reconsideration of the Role of Love in Hegel." *Canadian Journal of Political Science/Revue Canadienne de Science Politique* 35, no. 3 (2002): 499–525.
Owen, Alex. *The Place of Enchantment: British Occultism and the Culture of the Modern*. Chicago: University of Chicago Press, 2004.
Pachter, Mordechai. "The Musar Movement and the Kabbalah." In *Let the Old Make Way for the New*, edited by D. Assaf and A. Rapoport-Albert, 2 vols., 1:223–50. Jerusalem: Zalman Shazar Center for Jewish History, 2009.
Palmier, Jean-Michel. "La traversée du siècle d'Ernst Bloch (II): L'après-guerre de Marcuse à Sartre." *Les nouvelles littéraires* 54, no. 2531 (1976): 8.
Paquda, Bahya ibn. *Chovot ha Levavot* [The duties of the heart]. Translated by Yaakov Feldman. New York: J. Aronson, 1996.
Parson, William B. *The Enigma of the Oceanic Feeling: Revisioning the Psychoanalytic Theory of Mysticism*. New York: Oxford University Press, 1999.

Paslick, Robert H. "From Nothingness to Nothingness: The Nature and Destiny of the Self in Boehme and Nishitani." *Eastern Buddhist* 30, no. 1 (1997): 13–31.
Pattie, Frank A. *Mesmer and Animal Magnetism: A Chapter in the History of Medicine*. Hamilton, NY: Edmonston, 1994.
Paul, Hermann. *Prinzipien der Sprachgeschichte*. Berlin: De Gruyter, 2010.
Peirce, Charles. "The Law of Mind." In *Essential Peirce*, 2 vols., 1:312–33. Bloomington: Indiana University Press, 1992.
Pektaş, Virginie. *Mystique et philosophie: Grunt, abgrunt et Ungrund chez Maître Eckhart et Jacob Böhme*. Amsterdam: B. R. Grüner, 2006.
Pelletier, Lucien. "Ernst Bloch et les juifs: Autour d'une traduction récente." *Philosophiques* 37, no. 1 (2010): 219–36.
Pelletier, Lucien. "The Sources of Ernst Bloch's Philosophy of History." *Revue internationale de philosophie* 3 (2019): 261–77.
Penhoën, Baron Barchou de. *Histoire de la philosophie allemande*. 2 vols. Paris: Charpentier, 1836.
Pénisson, Pierre. "Heymann Steinthal et la psychologie linguistique des peuples." *Revue germanique internationale* 10 (1998): 41–50.
Pénisson, Pierre. "Steinthal: La linguistique entre l'allemand et l'hébreu." *Revue germanique internationale* 17 (2002): 55–63.
Perkins, Robert L. "Hegel and the Secularisation of Religion." *International Journal for Philosophy of Religion* 1, no. 3 (1970): 130–46.
Perl, Joseph. *Joseph Perl's "Revealer of Secrets": The First Hebrew Novel*. Translated by Dov Taylor. Boulder, CO: Westview, 1997.
Peters, Uwe. "Goethe und Freud." *Goethe-Jahrbuch* 103 (1986): 86–105.
Petkas, Virgine. *Mystique et philosophie: Grunt, abgrunt et Ungrund chez Maître Eckhart et Jacob Böhme*. Amsterdam: B. R. Grüner, 2006.
Pick, Daniel. *Faces of Degeneration: A European Disorder, c. 1848–c. 1918*. New York: Cambridge University Press, 1989.
Pinchard, Bruno. "Diis Manibus, ou Vico chez les morts." *Archives de philosophie* 56, no. 4 (October–December 1993): 549–60.
Platner, Ernst. *Philosophische Aphorismen ebst einigen Anleitungen zur philosophischen Geschichte*. Leipzig: Im Schwickertschen Verlage, 1776.
Plümacher, Olga. *Der Kampf um's Unbewusste*. Berlin: Duncker, 1881.
Podmore, Frank. *From Mesmer to Christian Science: A Short History of Mental Healing*. New York: University Books, 1963.
Podmore, Simon. "'Abyss Calls unto Abyss': *Tsimtsum* and Kenosis in the Rupture of God-Forsakenness." In Bielik-Robson and Weiss, *Tsimtsum and Modernity*, 311–38.
Poliakov, Leon. *The History of Anti-Semitism*. Vol. 4, *Suicidal Europe*. Philadelphia: University of Pennsylvania Press, 200.
Prickett, Stephen. *Origins of Narrative: The Romantic Appropriation of the Bible*. New York: Oxford University Press, 1996.
Principe, Lawrence M., and Andrew Weeks. "Jacob Boehme's Divine Substance *Salitter*: Its Nature, Origin, and Relationship to Seventeenth Century Scientific Theories." *British Journal for the History of Science* 22, no. 1 (March 1989): 53–61.
Quinet, Edgar. *L'esprit nouveau*. Paris: Dentu, 1875.
Quinet, Edgar. *La création*. Paris: Librairie Internationale, 1870.

Rahden, Till van. "Germans of the Jewish Stamm: Visions of Community between Nationalism and Particularism, 1850 to 1933." In *German History from the Margins, 1800 to the Present*, edited by Mark Roseman, Nils Roemer, and Neil Gregor, 27–48. Bloomington: Indiana University Press, 2006.

Rahden, Till van. "Jews and the Ambivalences of Civil Society in Germany, 1800–1933: Assessment and Reassessment." *Journal of Modern History* 77, no. 4 (2005): 1024–47.

Rasmussen, Joel David Stormo. "Schelling and the New England Mind." *International Journal of Philosophy and Theology* 80, no. 1–2 (2019): 101–14.

Rawidowicz, Simon. "Nachman Krochmal als Historiker." In *Festschrift zu Simon Dubnows siebzigstem Geburtstag*, edited by Ismar Elbogen, Josef Meisl, and Mark Wischnitzer, 58–75. Berlin: Jüdischer Verlag, 1930.

Rawidowicz, Simon. *Nachman Krochmals Werke (Kitvei Rabbi Nachman Krochmal)*. London: Ararat Publishing Society, 1961.

Reform Rabbinical Conference at Frankfurt (1845). "Hebrew as a Language of Prayer." In *The Jew in the Modern World: A Documentary History*, edited by Paul Mendes-Flohr and Jehuda Reinharz, 181–82. 2nd ed. New York: Oxford University Press, 1995.

Reichman, Ronen. *Abduktives Denken und talmudische Argumentation: Eine rechtstheoretische Annäherung an eine zentrale Interpretationsfigur im babylonischen Talmud*. Tübingen: Mohr Siebeck, 2006.

Renan, Ernest. *L'avenir de la science*. Paris: Calmann Levy, 1890.

Ribot, Théodule. *La psychologie allemande contemporaine (école expérimentale)*. Paris: Alcan, 1885.

Richards, Robert J. "Christian Wolff's Prolegomena to Empirical and Rational Psychology: Translation and Commentary." *Proceedings of the American Philosophical Society* 124, no. 3 (June 30, 1980): 227–39.

Richardson, Robert D., Jr. *Emerson: The Mind on Fire*. Berkeley: University of California Press, 1995.

Ricœur, Paul. *Freud and Philosophy: An Essay on Interpretation*. New Haven, CT: Yale University Press, 1970.

Ricœur, Paul. *Hermeneutics and the Human Sciences*. New York: Cambridge University Press, 1991.

Rieber, Robert. *Wilhelm Wundt and the Making of a Scientific Psychology*. New York: Springer, 2003.

Rieff, Philip. *The Triumph of the Therapeutic: Uses of Faith after Freud*. Chicago: University of Chicago Press, 1987.

Riepe, Dale. "Emerson and Indian Philosophy." *Journal of the History of Ideas* 28, no. 1 (1967): 115–22.

Ripalda, José. "Philosophie als Dichtung und Verdichtung." *Deutsche Zeitschrift für Philosophie* 39, no. 1–6 (1991): 421–36.

Robinson, Ira. "Hayyim Selig Slonimski and the Diffusion of Science among Jewry in the Nineteenth Century." In *Interaction of Scientific and Jewish Cultures in Modern Times*, edited by Yakov M. Rabkin and Ira Robinson, 49–65. New York: E. Mellen Press, 1983.

Robinson, Ira. "Kabbala and Science in *Sefer ha-Berit*: A Modernization Strategy for Orthodox Jews." *Modern Judaism: A Journal of Jewish Ideas and Experience* 9, no. 3 (October 1989): 275–88.

Rodgers, Daniel T. *Atlantic Crossings: Social Politics in the Progressive Era.* Cambridge, MA: Harvard University Press, 1998.

Roelcke, Volker. "Jewish Mysticism in Romantic Medicine? Indirect Incorporation of Kabbalistic Elements in the Work of Gotthilf Heinrich Schubert." *History and Philosophy of the Life Sciences* 16, no. 1 (1994): 117–40.

Rorty, Richard. "The Historiography of Philosophy: Four Genres." In *Philosophy in History*, edited by Richard Rorty, J. B. Schneewind, and Quentin Skinner, 49–76. Cambridge: Cambridge University Press, 1984.

Rose, Paul Lawrence. *German Question/Jewish Question: Revolutionary Antisemitism in Germany from Kant to Wagner.* Princeton, NJ: Princeton University Press, 2014.

Rose, Sven-Erik. *Jewish Philosophical Politics in Germany.* Waltham, MA: Brandeis University Press, 2014.

Rose, Sven-Erik. "Lazarus Bendavid's and J. G. Fichte's Kantian Fantasies of Jewish Decapitation in 1793." *Jewish Social Studies* 13, no. 3 (Spring–Summer 2007): 73–102.

Rosenkranz, Karl. *Georg Wilhelm Friedrich Hegels Leben.* Berlin: Duncker und Humblot, 1844.

Rosen-Zvi, Ishay. *The Evil Inclination in Early Judaism and Christianity.* Cambridge: Cambridge University Press, 2021.

Rosenzweig, Franz. *Gesammelte Schriften.* Vol. 1, *Briefe und Tagebücher*, edited by Rachel Rosenzweig, Edith Rosenzweig-Scheinmann, and Bernhard Casper. The Hague: Nijhoff, 1979.

Rosenzweig, Franz. "'Urzelle' to the *Star of Redemption.*" In *Philosophical and Theological Writings*, edited by Paul W. Franks and Michael L. Morgan, 48–72. Indianapolis: Hackett, 2000.

Rosman, Moshe. *Founder of Hasidism: A Quest for the Historical Ba'al Shem Tov.* Berkeley: University of California Press, 1996.

Ross, Tamar. "Ha-Megamah ha-anti-ratsionalit bi-tenu'at ha-musar." In *'Ale shefer: Meḥkarim be-sifrut ha-hagut ha-yehudit*, edited by Mosheh Ḥalamish, 145–62. Ramat Gan, Israel: Bar-Ilan University Press, 1990.

Ross, Tamar. "Moral Philosophy in the Writings of Rabbi Salanter's Disciples in the Musar Movement." [In Hebrew.] PhD diss., Hebrew University, 1986.

Rotenstreich, Nathan. "Hegel's Image of Judaism." *Jewish Social Studies* 15, no. 1 (1953): 33–52.

Rotenstreich, Nathan. "On Cyclical Patterns and Their Interpretation: The Interpretations of Judaism in the Wake of Vico and Hegel." *Hegel-Studien* 11 (1976): 181–203.

Roth, Joseph. *On the End of the World.* New York: Pushkin Press, 2019.

Rothschild, Emma. *Economic Sentiments: Adam Smith, Condorcet, and the Enlightenment.* Cambridge, MA: Harvard University Press, 2001.

Rothschild, Jean-Pierre, and Jérôme Grondeux, eds. *Adolphe Franck: Philosophe juif spiritualiste et libéral dans la France du XIXe siècle; Actes du colloque tenu à l'Institut de France le 31 mai 2010.* Turnhout, Belgium: Brepols, 2013.

Roudinesco, Elisabeth. "The Mirror Stage: An Obliterated Archive." In *The Cambridge Companion to Lacan*, edited by Jean-Michel Rabaté, 25–34. Cambridge: Cambridge University Press, 2003.

Roussillon, René. *Du baquet de Mesmer au "baquet" de S. Freud: Une archéologie du cadre et de la pratique psychanalytiques*. Paris: PUF, 1992.
Rubin, Salomon. *Heidenthum und Kabbala*. Vienna: Hermann und Altmann, 1893.
Rubin, Salomon. *Yesod Mistere ha-'Akkum we-Sod Ḥokmat ha-Ḳabbalah*. Vienna: Adolf Fanto, 1888.
Ruderman, David B. *A Best-Selling Hebrew Book of the Modern Era: "The Book of the Covenant" of Pinchas Hurwitz and Its Remarkable Legacy*. Seattle: University of Washington Press, 2014.
Said, Edward. *Orientalism*. London: Penguin, 1979.
Saint Girons, Baldine. "Vico, Freud et Lacan: De la science des universaux fantastiques à celle de l'inconscient." In "La scienza nuova de Vico: Quelle science? Le conflit des interprétations," edited by André Tosel. Special issue, *Noésis* (August 2005): 257–82.
Salanter, Israel. *Eṣ Pri*. Vilna [Vilnius, Lithuania]: Yehuda Leib Lipmann, 1881.
Salanter, Israel. *Iggeret ha-musar* [The epistle on Musar]. Königsberg [now Kaliningrad, Russia], 1858.
Salanter, Israel. *Sefer Tevunah*. Koenigsberg [now Kaliningrad, Russia], 1861.
Sayers, Sean. *Marx and Alienation: Essays on Hegelian Themes*. London: Palgrave Macmillan, 2011.
Schacter, J. J., ed., *Judaism's Encounter with Other Cultures: Rejection or Integration?* Northvale, NJ: Maggid, 1997.
Schäfer, Peter. "'Adversus cabbalam,' oder Heinrich Graetz und die jüdische Mystik." In *Reuchlin und seine Erben: Forscher, Denker, Ideologen und Spinner*, edited by Peter Schäfer and Irina Wandrey, 189–211. Ostfildern: Thorbecke, 2005.
Schatz-Uffenheimer, Rivka. *Hasidism as Mysticism: Quietistic Elements in Eighteenth-Century Hasidic Thought*. Princeton, NJ: Princeton University Press, 1993.
Schelling, F. W. J. *The Ages of the World (1811)*. Albany: State University of New York Press, 2019.
Schelling, F. W. J. *The Ages of the World: (Fragment) from the Handwritten Remains, Third Version (c. 1815)*. Albany: State University of New York Press, 2000.
Schelling, F. W. J. *Die Weltalter: Bruchstück* (ca. 1815). In *Friedrich Wilhelm Joseph von Schellings Sämmtliche Werke*, 8:195–344.
Schelling, F. W. J. *Friedrich Wilhelm Joseph von Schellings Sämmtliche Werke*. Edited by K. F. A. Schelling. 14 vols. Stuttgart: J. G. Cotta, 1856–61.
Schelling, F. W. J. *The Grounding of Positive Philosophy: The Berlin Lectures*. Translated by Bruce Matthews. Albany: State University of New York Press, 2007.
Schelling, F. W. J. *Historical-Critical Introduction to the Philosophy of Mythology*. Albany: State University of New York Press, 2007.
Schelling, F. W. J. *Idealism and the Endgame of Theory*. Edited by Thomas Pfau. Albany: State University of New York Press, 1994.
Schelling, F. W. J. *On the History of Modern Philosophy*. New York: Cambridge University Press, 2002.
Schelling, F. W. J. *Philosophical Investigations into the Essence of Human Freedom*. Translated by Jeff Love and Johannes Schmidt. Albany: State University of New York Press, 2006.

Schelling, F. W. J. "Philosophischen Untersuchungen über das Wesen der menschlichen Freiheit und die damit zusammenhängenden Gegenstände" (1809). In *Friedrich Wilhelm Joseph von Schellings Sämmtliche Werke*, 7:331–416.

Schelling, F. W. J. *Philosophy and Religion*. Putnam, CT: Spring Publications, 2010.

Schelling, F. W. J. *"Philosophy of Revelation" (1841–42) and Related Texts*. Putnam, CT: Spring Publications, 2020.

Schelling, F. W. J. *The Schelling Reader*. Edited by Benjamin Berger and Daniel Whistler. New York: Bloomsbury, 2020.

Schelling, F. W. J. "Stuttgarter Privatvorlesungen" (1810). In *Friedrich Wilhelm Joseph von Schellings Sämmtliche Werke*, 7.1:417–86.

Schelling, F. W. J. *System des transcendentalen Idealismus* (1800). In *Friedrich Wilhelm Joseph von Schellings Sämmtliche Werke*, 3:381.

Schelling, F. W. J. *System of Transcendental Idealism* (1800). Translated by Peter Heath. Charlottesville: University Press of Virginia, 1993.

Schelling, F. W. J. *Über die Gottheiten von Samothrake* (1815). In *Friedrich Wilhelm Joseph von Schellings Sämmtliche Werke*, 8:417–18n113.

Scherer, Frank F. *The Freudian Orient: Early Psychoanalysis, Anti-Semitic Challenge, and the Vicissitudes of Orientalist Discourse*. New York: Karnak Books, 2015.

Schiller, Friedrich. *Das verschleierte Bild zu Sais*. Tübingen: Cotta, 1795.

Schlitt, Dale M. "Die Idee als Ideal: Trias und Triplizität bei Hegel." *Review of Metaphysics* 41, no. 4 (1998): 822–24.

Schmidt, Gilya Gerda. *Martin Buber's Formative Years: From German Culture to Jewish Renewal, 1897–1909*. Tuscaloosa: University of Alabama Press, 1995.

Schmidt, Royal J. "Cultural Nationalism in Herder." *Journal of the History of Ideas* 17, no. 3 (June 1956): 407–17.

Schmidt-Biggemann, Wilhelm. "Jakob Böhme und die Kabbala." In *Geschichte der christlichen Kabbala*. 3 vols. Stuttgart: Frommann-Holzboog, 2013.

Schneersohn, Dov Ber. *Torat Hayyim: Bereshit*. New York: Kehot, 1993.

Scholem, Gershom. "Ahron Marcus and Hasidism." [In Hebrew.] *Behinot* 7 (1954): 3–8.

Scholem, Gershom. *Bibliographica Kabbalistica*. Leipzig, 1927.

Scholem, Gershom. *Briefe I: 1914–1947*. Edited by Itta Shedletzky. Munich: Beck, 1994.

Scholem, Gershom. "A Candid Word about the True Motives of My Kabbalistic Studies." In David Biale, *Gershom Scholem: Kabbalah and Counter-History*, 31–32. Cambridge, MA: Harvard University Press, 1979.

Scholem, Gershom. *Devarim be go*. Tel Aviv: Am Oved, 1976.

Scholem, Gershom. *Judaica*. 6 vols. Frankfurt am Main: Suhrkamp, 1963–84.

Scholem, Gershom. "Juden und Deutsche" (1966). In Scholem, *Judaica*, 1970, 2:20–46.

Scholem, Gershom. *Lamentations of Youth: The Diaries of Gershom Scholem, 1913–1919*. Cambridge, MA: Harvard University Press, 2007.

Scholem, Gershom. *Major Trends in Jewish Mysticism*. New York: Schocken Books, 1941.

Scholem, Gershom. *The Messianic Idea in Judaism, and Other Essays on Jewish Spirituality*. New York: Schocken Books, 1971; with a foreword by Arthur Hertzberg, 1995.

Scholem, Gershom. "Noch einmal: Das deutsch-jüdisch Gespräch" (1965). In Scholem, *Judaica*, 2:12–19.

Scholem, Gershom. *Of Jews and Judaism in Crisis: Selected Essays*. Philadelphia: Paul Dry Books, 2012.
Scholem, Gershom. *On Jews and Judaism in Crisis: Selected Essays*. New York: Schocken, 1976.
Scholem, Gershom. *On the Possibility of Jewish Mysticism in Our Time, and Other Essays*. Edited by Avraham Shapira. Philadelphia: Jewish Publication Society, 1997.
Scholem, Gershom. "Redemption through Sin." Translated by Hillel Halkin. In Scholem, *The Messianic Idea in Judaism*, 78–141.
Scholem, Gershom. *Sabbatai Sevi: The Mystical Messiah, 1626–1676*. Princeton, NJ: Princeton University Press, 2016.
Scholem, Gershom. "The Unconscious and the Concept of *Qadmut ha-Sekhel* in Hasidic Literature." In *The Latest Phase: Essays on Hasidism by Gershom Scholem* [in Hebrew], edited by David Assaf and Esther Liebes, 268–76. Jerusalem: Magnes, 2008.
Scholem, Gershom. *Walter Benjamin: Geschichte einer Freundschaft*. Frankfurt am Main: Suhrkamp, 1975.
Scholem, Gershom. "Wider den Mythos vom deutsch-jüdischen Gespräch" (1964). In Scholem, *Judaica*, 2:7–11.
Scholem, Gershom. ""Zur Literatur der letzten Kabbalisten in Deutschland" (1962). In Scholem, *Judaica*, 1973, 3:218–46.
Scholem, Gershom. "Zur Neuauflage des 'Stern der Erlösung'" (1931). In Scholem, *Judaica*, 1:226–34.
Schopenhauer, Arthur. *On Will in Nature*. In *"On the Fourfold Root of the Principle of Sufficient Reason," and Other Writings*, translated by David E. Cartwright, Edward E. Erdmann, and Christopher Janaway, 303–460. Cambridge: Cambridge University Press, 2012.
Schorsch, Ismar. "Breakthrough into the Past: The Verein für Cultur und Wissenschaft der Juden." *Yearbook of the Leo Baeck Institute* 33 (1988): 3–28.
Schorsch, Ismar. *From Text to Context: The Turn to History in Modern Judaism*. Waltham, MA: Brandeis University Press, 1994.
Schubert, Gotthilf Heinrich von. *Die Geschichte der Seele*. Stuttgart: J. G. Cotta, 1833.
Schulte, Christoph. "'Die Buchstaben haben ... ihre Wurzeln oben': Scholem und Molitor." In Goodman-Thau, Mattenklott, and Schulte, *Kabbala und Romantik*, 143–64.
Schulte, Christoph. "Die Wissenschaft des Judentums." In *Handbuch zur Geschichte der Juden in Europa*, edited by Julius H. Schoeps and Hiltrud Wallenborn, 2 vols., 2:268–84. Darmstadt: Primus Verlag, 2001.
Schulte, Christoph. *Zimzum: Gott und Weltursprung*. Frankfurt am Main: Suhrkamp, 2014.
Schulze, Wilhelm. "Zum Verständnis der Stuttgarter Privatvorlesungen Schellings." *Zeitschrift für Philosophische Forschung* 11, no. 4 (1957): 575–93.
Schwarzschild, Steven S. "An Agenda for Jewish Philosophy in the 1980s." In *Studies in Jewish Philosophy: Collected Essays of the Academy for Jewish Philosophy 1980–1985*, edited by Norbert Samuelson, 101–25. Lanham, MD: University Press of America, 1987.
Schweid, Eliezer. *A History of Jewish Thought in Modern Times*. [In Hebrew.] Jerusalem: Keter, 1977.

Schweid, Eliezer. *A History of Modern Jewish Religious Philosophy*. Translated by Leonard Levin. 5 vols. Leiden: Brill, 2011–24.

Seidman, Naomi. *Faithful Renderings: Jewish-Christian Difference and the Politics of Translation*. Chicago: University of Chicago Press, 2006.

Shagar, Rabbi. *Faith Shattered and Restored: Judaism in the Postmodern Age*. New York: Magid Modern Classics, 2017.

Shalev, Eran. *American Zion: The Old Testament as a Political Text from the Revolution to the Civil War*. New Haven, CT: Yale, 2014.

Shanes, Joshua. "Ahron Marcus: Portrait of a Zionist Hasid." *Jewish Social Studies* 16, no. 3 (2010): 116–60.

Sharp, Lynn Louise. "Rational Religion, Irrational Science: Men, Women, and Belief in French Spiritism, 1853–1914." PhD diss., University of California, Irvine, 1996.

Sharvit, Gilad. "Luria, Schelling, and Freud: From Zimzum to the Oedipus Complex." *Journal of Jewish Thought and Philosophy* 29, no. 2 (2021): 231–61.

Sherry, Jay. *The Jungian Strand in Transatlantic Modernism*. New York: Palgrave, 2018.

Shnayer, Z. Leiman. "Rabbinic Openness to General Culture in the Early Modern Period in Western and Central Europe." In *Judaism's Encounter with Other Cultures: Rejection or Integration?*, edited by Jacob J. Schacter, 146–216. Northvale, NJ: Jason Aronson, 1997.

Sieg, Ulrich. "Der Preis des Bildungsstrebens: Jüdische Geisteswissenschaftler im Kaiserreich." In *Juden, Bürger, Deutsche: Zur Geschichte von Vielfalt und Differenz 1800–1933*, edited by Andreas Gotzmann, Rainer Liedtke, and Till van Rahden, 67–95. Tübingen: Mohr Siebeck, 2001.

Silberstein, Laurence. *Martin Buber's Social and Religious Thought: Alienation and the Quest for Meaning*. New York: New York University Press, 1989.

Simmel, Georg. "A Contribution to the Sociology of Religion." In *Essays on Religion*, 101–20. New Haven, CT: Yale University Press, 1997.

Simmel, Georg. *Einleitung in die Moralwissenschaft: Eine Kritik der ethischen Grundbegriffe*. 2 vols. Berlin: Hertz, 1892–93.

Simmel, Georg. "On the Concept and Tragedy of Culture" (1911). In *The Conflict in Modern Culture, and Other Essays*, translated by K. Peter Etzkorn, 27–46. New York: Teachers College Press, 1968.

Simmel, Georg. *On Individuality and Social Forms*. Chicago: University of Chicago Press, 1971.

Simmel, Georg. *The Philosophy of Money*. New York: Routledge, 2011. Orig. pub. 1900.

Simmel, Georg. *Soziologie: Untersuchungen über die Formen der Vergesellschaftung*. Leipzig: Duncker und Humblot, 1908.

Simon-Nahum, Perrine. *La cité investie: La "Science du Judaïsme" français et la République*. Paris: Le Cerf, 1992.

Simon-Nahum, Perrine. "Philosophie et science du judaïsme: La place d'Adolphe Franck dans le paysage intellectuel français du XIXe siècle." In Rothschild and Grondeux, *Adolphe Franck*, 185–95.

Singer, Isidore, and Cyrus Adler, eds. *The Jewish Encyclopedia*. New York: Funk and Wagnalls, 1905.

Sinkoff, Nancy. *Out of the Shtetl: Making Jews Modern in the Polish Borderlands*. Providence, RI: Brown Judaic Studies, 2004.

Sitbon-Peillon, Brigitte. "Bergson et l'inconscient: Entre métaphysique et psychanalyse." In *Bergson et Freud*, edited by Brigitte Sitbon-Peillon, 181–95. Paris: Presses Universitaires de France, 2014.

Skidelsky, Edward. "From Epistemology to Cultural Criticism: Georg Simmel and Ernst Cassirer." *History of European Ideas* 29, no. 3 (2003): 365–81.

Skolnik, Jonathan. *Jewish Pasts, German Fictions: History, Memory, and Minority Culture in Germany, 1824–1955.* Stanford, CA: Stanford University Press, 2020.

Slater, Isaac. "A Forgotten Variety of Religious Zionism: The Thought of Shmuel Alexandrov." *Journal of Jewish Studies* 74 (2023): 140–63.

Slater, Isaac. "God Has Wrapped Himself in a Cloak of Materialism: Marxism and Jewish Religious Thought in the Early Soviet Union." *Religions* 14, no. 5 (2023): 673.

Slater, Isaac. "'Those Who Yearn for the Divine': Rabbi Shmuel Alexandrov and the Russian Religious Philosophical Renaissance." *Judaica Petropolitana* 5 (2016): 55–68.

Slater, Isaac. "To Purify Religion: Nationalism, Individualism, and Mysticism in the Thought of Shmuel Alexandrov." PhD diss., Ben-Gurion University of the Negev, 2020.

Slonimski, H. S. *Mezti'ut ha-nefesh ve-kiyumah mi-hutz la-guf* [On the immortality of the soul]. Warsaw, 1880.

Smith, Morton, and Gershom Scholem. *Correspondence 1945–1982.* Leiden: Brill, 2008.

Smith, Woodruff. *Politics and the Sciences of Culture in Germany, 1840–1920.* New York: Oxford University Press, 1991.

Snedeker, George. "The Politics of Epistemology: Georg Lukács and the Critique of Irrationalism." *Science and Society* 49, no. 4 (1985): 437–50.

Snow, Dale. "The Role of the Unconscious in Schelling's System of Transcendental Idealism." *Idealistic Studies* 19 (1989): 231–50.

Solomon, Esther. "R. Eliyahu Eliezer Dessler: Not Quite the Mussar Traditionalist." *Da'at* 82 (2016): cvi–cvii.

Solomon, Norman. *Torah from Heaven: The Reconstruction of Faith.* Portland, OR: Littman Library of Jewish Civilization, 2012.

Solovyov, Vladimir. *The Burning Bush: Writings on Jews and Judaism.* Edited and translated by Gregory Yuri Glazov. South Bend, IN: University of Notre Dame Press, 2006.

Sossnitz, Joseph Judah Löb. *Aken Yesh Adonai* [Yes, there is a God]. Vilna [Vilnius, Lithuania]: Bi-defus Y. L. Mets, 1875.

Steele, Jeffrey. *Unfolding the Mind: The Unconscious in American Romanticism and Literary Theory.* London: Routledge, 2018. Orig. pub. 1987.

Steigerwald, Joan. "Rethinking Organic Vitality in Germany at the Turn of the Nineteenth Century." In Normandin and Wolfe, *Vitalism and the Scientific Image in Post-Enlightenment Life Science*, 51–75.

Steinmetz, George. *The Politics of Method in Human Sciences: Positivism and Its Epistemological Others.* Durham, NC: Duke University Press, 2005.

Steinthal, Heymann. *Abriss der Sprachwissenschaft: Einleitung in die Psychologie und Sprachwissenschaft.* 2 vols. Berlin: Dümmler, 1881–93.

Steinthal, Heymann. *Allgemeine Ethik.* Berlin: Georg Reimer, 1885.

Steinthal, Heymann. "Assimilation und Attraction, psychologisch beleuchtet." *Zeitschrift für Völkerpsychologie und Sprachwissenschaft* 1 (1860): 93–179.

Steinthal, Heymann. *Die Arten und Formen der Interpretation, in Kleine sprachtheoretische Schriften.* Hildesheim: G. Olms Verlag, 1970.

Steinthal, Heymann. *Der Ursprung der Sprache im Zusammenhange mit den letzten Fragen alles Wissens: Eine Darstellung, Kritik und Fortentwickelung der vorzüglichsten Ansichten.* Berlin: Ferdinand Dümmler, 1851.

Steinthal, Heymann. *Die Sprachphilosophischen Werke Wilhelm's von Humboldt.* Berlin: Dümmler, 1884.

Steinthal, Heymann. *Einleitung in die Psychologie und Sprachwissenschaft.* Berlin, 1881.

Steinthal, Heymann. *Grammatik, Logik, Psychologie: Ihre Prinzipien und ihre Verhältnis zu Einander.* Berlin: Dümmler, 1855.

Steinthal, Heymann. *Kleine sprachtheoretische Schriften.* Edited by Waltraud Bumann. Hildesheim: Olms, 1970.

Steinthal, Heymann. *Philologie, Geschichte und Psychologie in ihren Gegenseitigen Beziehungen.* Berlin, 1864.

Steinthal, Heymann. *Über Juden und Judentum.* Berlin: Gesellschaft zur Förderung der Wissenschaft des Judentums, Poppelauer, 1906.

Steinthal, Heymann. *Zu Bibel und Religionsphilosophie.* Berlin: Reimer, 1890.

Steinthal, Heymann. "Zur Religionsphilosophie." *Zeitschrift für Völkerpsychologie und Sprachwissenschaft* 9 (1877): 257–99.

Stephens, B. D. "The Martin Buber–Carl Jung Disputations: Protecting the Sacred in the Battle for the Boundaries of Analytical Psychology." *Journal of Analytical Psychology* 46, no. 3 (July 2001): 455–91.

Stern, Eliyahu. *Jewish Materialism: The Intellectual Revolution of the 1870s.* New Haven, CT: Yale University Press, 2018.

Stern, Eliyahu. "Pragmatic Kabbalah: J. L. Sossnitz, Mordecai Kaplan and the Reconstruction of Mysticism and Peoplehood in Early Twentieth-Century America." In Ogren, *Kabbalah in America*, 147–58.

Stern, Fritz. *The Politics of Cultural Despair: A Study in the Rise of the Germanic Ideology.* Berkeley: University of California Press, 1974.

Stern, Ignaz. "Versuch einer umständlichen Analyse des Sohar." *Ben-Chananja* 6 (1858): 266–69.

Sternhell, Zeev. *The Anti-Enlightenment Tradition.* New Haven, CT: Yale University Press, 2009.

Stoecker, Adolf. "Our Demands on Modern Jewry." In *Antisemitism: A Historical Encyclopedia of Prejudice and Persecution*, ed. Richard S. Levy. 2 vols., 1:525–26. Santa Barbara, CA: ABC-Clio Press, 2005.

Stolle, Jeffrey. "Levinas and the Akedah: An Alternative to Kierkegaard." *Philosophy Today* 45, no. 2 (2001): 132–43.

Stolow, Jeremy. *Orthodox by Design: Judaism, Print Politics, and the ArtScroll Revolution.* Irvine: University of California Press, 2010.

Stolz, Joseph. "Bernhard Felsenthal." *Publications of the American Jewish Historical Society* 17 (1909): 218–22.

Stolzenberg, Daniel. "What Was Oriental Studies in Early Modern Europe? 'Oriental Languages' and the Making of a Discipline." In *The Allure of the Ancient: Receptions of the Ancient Middle East, ca. 1600–1800*, edited by Margaret Geoga and John Steele, 343–74. Leiden: Brill, 2022.

Stone, Ira F. "Musar Ethics and Other Nineteenth-Century Jewish Ethical Theories." In *The Oxford Handbook of Jewish Ethics and Morality*, edited by Elliot N. Dorff and Jonathan K. Crane, 118–33. Oxford: Oxford University Press, 2013.

Straus, Raphael. "The Baal-Shem of Michelstadt: Mesmerism and Cabbala." *Historica Judaica* 8, no. 2 (1946): 135–48.

Szafran, Willy. "Aspects socio-culturels judaïques de la pensée de Freud." *Evolution psychiatrique* 36, no. 1 (1971): 89–107.

Szymkowiak, Mildred Galland. "La symbolique de Friedrich Creuzer: Philologie, mythologie, philosophie." *Revue germanique internationale* 14 (2011): 91–112.

Tanner, Jakob. "Unfassbare Gefühle: Emotionen in der Geschichtswissenschaft vom Fin de siècle bis in die Zwischenkriegszeit." In *Rationalisierung des Gefühls: Zum Verhältnis von Wissenschaft und Emotionen, 1880–1930*, edited by Uffa Jensen and Daniel Morat, 35–59. Munich: Fink, 2008.

Tardits, Annie. "La mélancolie du hiatus, un sonnet inaugural de Lacan." *Le genre humain*, no. 48 (2009): 159–82.

Tauler, Johannes. *Die Predigten Taulers*. Zürich: Weiman, 1968.

Taves, Ann. *Fits, Trances, and Visions: Experiencing Religion and Explaining Experience from Wesley to James*. Princeton, NJ: Princeton University Press, 1999.

Taylor, Charles C. *Sources of the Self: The Making of Modern Identity*. Cambridge, MA: Harvard University Press, 1989.

Taylor, Mark. *Last Works: Lessons in Leaving*. New Haven, CT: Yale University Press, 2018.

Thiem, Yannik. "Transgender Quarrels and the Unspeakable Whiteness of Psychoanalysis." In *Psychoanalysis, Gender and Sexualities: From Feminism to Trans*, edited by Patricia Gherovici and Manya Steinkoler, 287–324. New York: Routledge, 2022.

Thomas, William Isaac. "The Scope and Method of Folk-Psychology." *American Journal of Sociology* 1 (1896): 434–45.

Thumiger, Chiara, ed. *Holism in Ancient Medicine and Its Reception*. Leiden: Brill, 2020.

Tillich, Paul. *Mysticism and Guilt-Consciousness in Schelling's Philosophical Development*. Translated by Victor Nuovo. Lewisburg, PA: Bucknell University Press, 1974. Orig. pub. 1912.

Tomlinson, Stephen. *Head Masters: Phrenology, Secular Education, and Nineteenth-Century Social Thought*. Tuscaloosa: University of Alabama Press, 2005.

Toury, Jacob. "German Jewry in Mid-nineteenth Century, as Background to Jacob Bernays' Life." In *Jacob Bernays, un philologue juif*, edited by John Glucker and André Laks, 3–16. Villeneuve d'Ascq, France: Presses Universitaires du Septentrion, 1996.

Trautmann-Waller, Céline. *Aux origines d'une science allemande de la culture: Linguistique et psychologie des peuples chez Heymann Steinthal*. Paris: CNRS, 2006.

Trautmann-Waller, Céline. "La Zeitschrift für Völkerpsychologie und Sprachwissenschaft (1859–1890): Entre Volksgeist et Gesamtgeist." In *Quand Berlin pensait les peuples: Anthropologie, ethnologie et psychologie (1850–1890)*, edited by Trautmann-Waller, 105–19. Paris: CNRS Éditions, 2004.

Trautmann-Waller, Céline. "L'ethnologie d'Adolf Bastian entre mélancolie de la déperdition, comparatisme débridé et universalité inductive." *Revue germanique internationale* 21 (2004): 197–212.

Treitschke, Heinrich von. "Unsere Aussichten" [Our prospects]. *Preußische Jahrbücher* 44, no. 5 (November 1879): 559–76.

Trilling, Lionel. *The Liberal Imagination: Essays on Literature and Society*. New York: Harcourt, 1979.

Trueblood, D. Elton. "The Influence of Emerson's Divinity Address." *Harvard Theological Review* 32, no. 1 (1939): 41–56.

Tsanoff, Radoslav A. "Hartmann's Pessimism." *Philosophical Review* 38, no. 4 (1929): 350–71.

Tuschling, Burkhard. "Subjektiver und objektiver Geist, oder Die Deduktion des Rechts aus dem Begriff des Geistes." In *Hegels enzyklopädisches System der Philosophie: Von der "Wissenschaft der Logik" zur Philosophie des absoluten Geistes*, edited by Hans-Christian Lucas, Burkhard Tuschling, and Ulrich Vogel, 269–355. Stuttgart: Fromman-Holzboog, 2004.

Tyler, Peter. *The Pursuit of the Soul: Psychoanalysis, Soul-Making and the Christian Tradition*. London: Bloomsbury, 2016.

Ulanov, Ann Belford. "Jung and Religion: The Opposing Self." In *The Cambridge Companion to Jung*, edited by Polly Young-Eisendrath and Terence Dawson, 296–313. Cambridge: Cambridge University Press, 1997.

Urban, Martina. *Aesthetics of Renewal: Martin Buber's Early Representation of Hasidism as Kulturkritik*. Chicago: University of Chicago Press, 2008.

Valentini, Philipp, and Mahdi Tourage, eds. *Esoteric Lacan*. London: Rowman and Littlefield, 2019.

Valliere, Paul. "Solov'ëv and Schelling's Philosophy of Revelation." In *Vladimir Solov'ëv: Reconciler and Polemicist*, edited by Wil van den Bercken, Manon de Courten, and Ervert von Zweerde, 119–29. Leuven: Peters, 2000.

Vassányi, Miklós. *Anima Mundi: The Rise of the World Soul Theory in Modern German Philosophy*. Dordrecht: Springer, 2011.

Versluis, Arthur. *American Transcendentalism and Asian Religions*. New York: Oxford University Press, 1993.

Vial, Fernand. *The Unconscious in Philosophy, and French and European Literature: Nineteenth and Early Twentieth Century*. Amsterdam: Rodopi, 2009.

Vico, Giambattista. *Grundzüge einer neuen Wissenschaft über die gemeinsame Natur der Völker*. Leipzig: Brockhaus, 1822.

Vico, Giambattista. *New Science*. Translated by Dave Marsh. New York: Penguin Classics, 2000.

Vidas, Elijah de. *Reshit Ḥokhmah* [The beginning of wisdom]. Amsterdam, 1737.

Vieillard-Baron, Jean-Louis. *Le spiritualisme français*. Paris: Le Cerf, 2021.

Vieillard-Baron, Jean-Louis. "Schelling et Jacob Böhme: Les *Recherches* de 1809 et la lecture de la *Lettre pastorale*." In "L'idéalisme allemand entre gnose et religion chrétienne," special issue, *Les études philosophiques*, no. 2 (April–June 1999): 223–42.

Vital, Hayyim ben Joseph. *The "Tree of Life": Chayyim Vital's Introduction to the Kabbalah of Isaac Luria; The Palace of Adam Kadmon*. Northvale, NJ: Jason Aronson, 1999.

Völmicke, Elke. *Das Unbewusste im Deutschen Idealismus*. Würzburg: Königshaufen und Neumann, 2005.

Wagner, Richard. *Mein Leben: Zweiter Teil, 1842–1850*. Munich: Paul List, 1994.

Walls, Laura Dassow. "The World Soul in American Transcendentalism." In Wilberding, *World Soul*, 290–313.

Wasserstrom, Steven M. *Religion after Religion: Gershom Scholem, Mircea Eliade, and Henry Corbin at Eranos*. Princeton, NJ: Princeton University Press.

Weber, Thomas. "Carl du Prel (1839–1899): Explorer of Dreams, the Soul, and the Cosmos." *Studies in the History and Philosophy of Science* 38, no. 3 (2007): 593–60.

Weeks, Andrew. *Boehme: An Intellectual Biography of the Seventeenth-Century Philosopher and Mystic*. Albany: State University of New York Press, 1991.

Weinstein, Roni. *Kabbalah and Jewish Modernity*. Portland, OR: Littman Library of Jewish Civilization, 2013.

Weir, Todd H. "The Riddles of Monism: An Introductory Essay." In *Monism: Science, Philosophy, Religion and the History of a Worldview*, edited by Todd H. Weir, 1–44. New York: Palgrave Macmillan, 2012.

Weir, Todd H. *Secularism and Religion in Nineteenth Century Germany: The Rise of the Fourth Confession*. Cambridge: Cambridge University Press, 2014.

Weiss, Daniel H. "*Tsimtsum* between the Bible and Philosophy: Levinas, Luria, and Genesis 1." In Bielik-Robson and Weiss, *Tsimtsum and Modernity*, 61–82.

Wellek, René. *Confrontations: Studies in the Intellectual and Literary Relations between Germany, England, and the United States during the Nineteenth Century*. Princeton, NJ: Princeton University Press, 1965.

Wellek, René. "Emerson and German Philosophy." *New England Quarterly* 16, no. 1 (March 1943): 41–62.

Weyembergh, Maurice. *Nietzsche et E. von Hartmann*. Brussels: Vrije Universiteit, 1977.

Whyte, Lancelot Law. *The Unconscious before Freud: A History of the Evolution of Human Awareness*. New York: Basic Books, 1960. 2nd ed., London: Julian Friedmann, 1978.

Wiedebach, Hartwig. *The National Element in Hermann Cohen's Philosophy and Religion*. Leiden: Brill, 2012.

Wiedebach, Hartwig, and Annette Winkelmann, eds. *Chajim H. Steinthal: Sprachwissenschaftler und Philosoph im 19. Jahrhundert*. Leiden: Brill, 2002.

Wiese, Christian. "Samuel Holdheim's 'Most Powerful Comrade in Conviction': David Einhorn and the Debate concerning Jewish Universalism in the Radical Reform Movement." In *Re-defining Judaism in an Age of Emancipation: Comparative Perspectives on Samuel Holdheim*, edited by Christian Wiese, 306–73. Leiden: Brill, 2006.

Wiese, Christian. *Wissenschaft des Judentums und protestantische Theologie in wilhelminischen Deutschland: Ein Schrei ins Leere?* Tübingen: Mohr Siebeck, 1999.

Wilberding, James, ed. *World Soul: A History*. Oxford: Oxford University Press, 2021.

Wolf, Immanuel. "On the Concept of a Science of Judaism." Translated by L. Kochan. *The Leo Baeck Institute Year Book* 2, no. 1 (January 1957): 194–204.

Wolf, Jean-Claude. *Eduard von Hartmann: Ein Philosoph der Gründerzeit.* Würzburg: Königshaufen and Neumann, 2006.

Wolff, Christian. *Psychologia Empirica.* Frankfurt, 1732.

Wolff, Christian. *Vernünftige Gedanken von Gott, der Welt und der Seele des Menschen.* Halle Renger Halle, Saale Universitäts- und Landesbibliothek Sachsen-Anhalt Halle, Saale, 1720.

Wolfson, Elliot. "Achronic Time, Messianic Expectation, and the Secret of the Leap in Habad." In *Habad Hasidism: History, Thought, Image,* edited by J. Meir and G. Sagiv, 45–86. Jerusalem: Zalman Shazar Center, 2016.

Wolfson, Elliot. *Alef, Mem, Tau: Kabbalistic Musings on Time, Truth, and Death.* Berkeley: University of California Press, 2006.

Wolfson, Elliot. "By Way of Truth: Aspects of Naḥmanides' Kabbalistic Hermeneutic." *AJS Review* 14, no. 2 (1989): 103–78.

Wolfson, Elliot. *A Dream Interpreted within a Dream: Oneiropoiesis and the Prism of Imagination.* New York: Zone Books, 2012.

Wolfson, Elliot. *Heidegger and Kabbalah: Hidden Gnosis and the Path of Poiēsis.* Bloomington: Indiana University Press, 2019.

Wolfson, Elliot. "The Holy Cabala of Changes: Jacob Böhme and Jewish Esotericism." *Aries* 18 (2018): 21–53.

Wolfson, Elliot. "Imagination and the Theolatrous Impulse: Configuring God in Modern Jewish Thought." In *The Cambridge Companion of Modern Jewish Philosophy: The Modern Era,* edited by Michael L. Morgan and Peter Eli Gordon, 663–703. Cambridge: Cambridge University Press, 2012.

Wolfson, Elliot. *Language, Eros, Being: Kabbalistic Hermeneutics and Poetic Imagination.* New York: Fordham University Press, 2005.

Wolfson, Elliot. "Secrecy, Modesty, and the Feminine: Kabbalistic Traces in the Thought of Levinas." *Journal of Jewish Thought and Philosophy* 14, no. 1–2 (2006): 193–224.

Wolfson, Elliot. "Suffering Time: Maharal's Influence on Hasidic Perspectives on Temporality." *Kabbalah* 44 (2019): 7–71.

Wolfson, Elliot. *Suffering Time: Philosophical, Kabbalistic, and Ḥasidic Reflections on Temporality.* Leiden: Brill, 2021.

Wolfson, Elliot. "Theosemiosis through a Peircean Lens." In *Signs of Salvation: A Festschrift for Peter Ochs,* edited by Mark Randall James and Randi Rashkover, 163–86. Eugene, OR: Cascade Books, 2021.

Wolfson, Elliot. *Through a Speculum that Shines: Vision and Imagination in Medieval Jewish Mysticism.* Princeton, NJ: Princeton University Press, 1994.

Wolfson, Elliot. "Tsimtsum, Lichtung, and the Leap of Bestowing Refusal: Kabbalistic and Heideggerian Metaontology in Dialogue." In Bielik-Robson and Weiss, *Tsimtsum and Modernity,* 141–90.

Wolfson, Elliot. *Venturing Beyond: Law and Morality in Kabbalistic Mysticism.* Oxford: Oxford University Press, 2006.

Wordsworth, William. *The Prelude, or Growth of a Poet's Mind: An Autobiographical Poem.* London: Edward Moxon, 1850.

Wundt, Wilhelm. *Beiträge zur Theorie der Sinneswahrnehmung.* Leipzig: Winter, 1862.

Wundt, Wilhelm. *Elemente der Völkerpsychologie: Grundlinien einer psychologischen Entwicklungsgeschichte der Menschheit.* Leipzig: A. Kröner, 1912.

Wundt, Wilhelm. *Ethik: Eine Untersuchung der Thatsachen und Gesetze*. Stuttgart: Ferdinand Enke, 1892.
Wundt, Wilhelm. "Über Ziele und Wege der Völkerpsychologie." *Philosophische Studien* 4 (1888): 21–22.
Wundt, Wilhelm. *Völkerpsychologie: Eine Untersuchung der Entwicklungsgesetze von Sprache, Mythus und Sitte*. 3 vols. Leipzig: Engelmann, 1905–9.
Yerushalmi, Yosef. *Zakhor*. Seattle: University of Washington Press, 2006.
Yovel, Yirmiyahu. *Dark Riddle: Hegel, Nietzsche and the Jews*. Philadelphia: Penn State University Press, 1996.
Yovel, Yirmiyahu. "Sublimity and Ressentiment: Hegel, Nietzsche, and the Jews." *Jewish Social Studies* 3, no. 3 (1997): 1–25.
Zachhuber, Johannes. "F. W. J. Schelling and the Rise of Historical Theology." *International Journal of Philosophy and Theology* 80, no. 1–2 (2019): 23–38.
Zachhuber, Johannes. "World Soul and Celestial Heat: Platonic and Aristotelian Ideas in the History of Natural Philosophy." In *World Soul—Anima Mundi: On the Origins and Fortunes of a Fundamental Idea*, edited by Christof Helmig, 335–53. Berlin: De Gruyter, 2019.
Zachhuber, Johannes. "The World Soul in Early Christian Thought." In *Platonism and Christianity in Late Ancient Cosmology: God, Soul, Matter*, edited by Ana Schiavoni-Palanciuc and Johannes Zachhuber, 46–73. Leiden: Brill, 2022.
Zalkin, Mordechai. "Scientific Thinking and Cultural Transformation in Nineteenth-Century East European Jewish Society." *Aleph* 5 (2005): 249–71.
Zimmerman, Andrew. *Anthropology and Antihumanism in Imperial Germany*. Chicago: University of Chicago Press, 2001.
Žižek, Slavoj, and F. W. J. Schelling. *The Abyss of Freedom/Ages of the World: An Essay by Slavoj Žižek with the Text of Schelling's "Die Weltalter"*. Ann Arbor: University of Michigan Press, 1997.
Zudrell, Petra. *Der Schriftsteller und Kulturkritiker Max Nordau: Zwischen Zionismus, Deutschtum und Judentum*. Würzburg: Königshaufen und Neumann, 2003.
Zunz, Leopold. *Etwas über die rabbinische Literatur*. Berlin: Maurer, 1818.
Zunz, Leopold. *Zur Geschichte und Literatur*. Berlin: Veit und Comp, 1845.
Zwiep, Irene. "Scholarship of Literature and Life: Leopold Zunz: Verlag Veit und Comp and the Invention of Jewish Culture." In *How the West Was Won: Essays on Literary Imagination, the Canon and the Christian Middle Ages for Burcht Pranger*, edited by Willemien Otten, Arjo Vanderjagt, and Hent de Vries, 165–73. Leiden: Brill, 2010.

Index

abolitionism, 100
Abrams, M. H., 223n6
Absolute, the, 19, 29–31, 50–51, 53, 207n15. *See also* Kabbalah
Abulafia, Abraham, 51, 78, 215n56, 221n71
abyss: and creation, 57–62, 90, 99; creation of, 12, 61; depictions of, 25, 53–54, 57, 210n30, 224n16; and God's will, 29; relationship with humans, 190–96; and self, 88–89; and wrath, 57–58, 160. *See also* unconscious; Ungrund
Adler, Abraham, 80
Adler, Nathan, 38
affirmative apologetics, 6, 82–85, 165, 205n26
Alexandrov, Samuel, 187–89
alienation, 67, 113–18, 131, 165, 192
American religion, 87–88, 97, 99. *See also* Emerson, Ralph Waldo; United States
anarchism, 162–63
animal magnetism, 179–80
anthropology, 23, 30, 101, 106, 136–38, 142
antinomianism, 38, 49–50, 69, 74, 166, 187
antirationalist movements, 66
anti-Semitism, 8, 14, 66, 105–7, 120–22, 148, 188, 220n42, 232n21. *See also* Judaism
Antisemitismusstreit, 106–7

apperception, 127
archetypes, 44, 96, 99, 110, 188, 193, 242n3
Aristotle, 94, 125, 168, 170, 209
art nouveau, 133
Ascher, Saul, 66
assimilation, 5–9, 65, 69, 148, 205n22. *See also* dissimilation
atomism, 170–71
Auden, W. H., 197
authorship, 40–41

Baader, Franz Xaver von, 32, 48, 171, 242n4
Baal Shem Tov, 180, 182, 191
Bacharach, Naftali, 56
Baeck, Leo, 122
Bahya ibn Paquda, 155, 244n28
Bakhtin, Mikhail, 105, 136, 142, 228n1
Baron, Salo, 204n16
Barrès, Maurice, 159, 241n76
Bastian, Adolf, 138, 142, 236n110
Bauer, Bruno, 43
Beer, Peter, 76–77, 82, 221n67
Béguin, Albert, 147
Benamozegh, Elia, 15, 64, 107, 165, 167–79, 204n8, 214n39, 237n149
Bendavid, Lazarus, 70–73
ben Eliezer, Israel, 180, 191
Benjamin, Walter, 48, 162
Bergson, Henri, 10–11, 33, 96–97, 132, 189
Berlin, Adele, 205n26
Berlin, Isaiah, 110

Bernays, Isaac, 37–42, 177, 184
berur, 58, 216n87
Bhabha, Homi, 85
Bhagavad Gita, 94
Biale, David, 219n23
Bing, Abraham, 38
Bloch, Ernst, 14–15, 48, 107, 153–54, 160–61, 163, 241n81, 242n91
Bloom, Harold, 5, 13, 97, 99
Blumenberg, Hans, 205n25, 207n49
Boas, Franz, 138, 142, 229n5 (chap. 4)
Boeckh, August, 80, 120, 137
Boehme, Jacob, 12, 21, 25–36, 49, 54, 61–62, 89, 98, 161–62, 190–91, 211n63
Bois-Reymond, Emil du, 52
borer, 58, 216n87
Börne, Ludwig, 66–67, 218n18
Bowen, Francis, 223n10
Brahmanic tradition, 47
Brandeis, Louis, 251n10
Brès, Yvon, 238n15
British empiricism, 95–96
Buber, Martin, 15, 59, 107, 139, 160, 165, 187, 190–96, 241n81, 249n138
Büchner, Ludwig, 52
Bulgakov, Sergei, 178
Buxdorf, Johann, 85

Cabot, James, 90–91
Cahnman, Werner, 37
Campbell, Joseph, 138
Cantoni, Carlo, 231n2
capitalism, 159
Cartesianism, 21
Carus, Carl Gustav, 3, 146–47, 238n15
Cassirer, Ernst, 135, 235n103
Chamberlain, Houston, 112–13, 138
Chicago school of sociology, 140
Christianity, 14; coexistence with Judaism, 48, 85, 114, 167; conversion to, 219n33; perceptions of, 101, 150; and the soul, 93, 95; universalism of, 40. *See also* religion
Christian Kabbalah, 27, 54–55, 57, 93, 99
Cohen, Hermann, 122, 139
Coleridge, Samuel Taylor, 90–91, 99, 224n22, 227n71

collective unconscious, 8, 13–14, 44–45, 95–96, 105, 109–11, 120–21, 128–33, 135–36, 140–42, 156, 167, 198, 228n1. *See also* ethnopsychology; national identity; oversoul
condensation, 10, 45, 58, 106, 128–33, 142. *See also* dreamwork; *Geist*
Condorcet, 168
Congregationalism, 223n4
Congress of Psychology, 133–34
Corbin, Henry, 242nn3–4
Cordovero, Moses, 55, 244nn28–29
cosmogony, 7, 18. *See also* creation
Cousin, Victor, 90, 93–96
creation, 28–29, 37, 51–52, 57–62, 87, 90, 168, 184. *See also* cosmogony
Creuzer, Friedrich, 46–47, 214n34
Cudworth, Ralph, 94
Cuvier, Frédéric, 171

daemonic, the, 23–24, 163, 208n17
Damiron, Jean-Philibert, 170, 237n149
Darwinism, 50, 215n58, 239n27
Deleuze, Gilles, 11, 56, 58, 97, 132, 207n48
De Quincey, Thomas, 224n22
Derrida, Jacques, 59, 113, 198, 230n24
Deslon, Charles, 179
Detweiler, Robert, 92
diaspora, 60, 81
Dickinson, Emily, 224n16
Diehl, Joanne Feit, 224n16
Dilthey, Wilhelm, 65, 83, 140, 190
dissimilation, 5, 205n22. *See also* assimilation
dissociation, 4, 7–8, 31, 33, 50–51, 53, 60–61, 90, 97, 210n30, 212n68, 227n68
Dohm, Christian, 71
Dostoevsky, Fyodor, 148
double consciousness, 198, 251n12
dreams, 49, 147, 206n44, 209n21
dreamwork, 1, 10, 132. *See also* condensation; Freud, Sigmund
Du Bois, W. E. B., 198–99
du Bois-Reymond, Emil, 52
Dühring, Eugen, 146, 238n4
du Prel, Carl, 181

Eckhart, Meister, 25–26, 210n28
education, 6
Eger, Akiva, 120
Egyptian theology, 39, 76
Eibeschütz, Jonathan, 50, 214n46
Einhorn, David, 38, 45–48, 61, 99–100, 102, 120
electrophysiology, 215n58
Eliade, Mircea, 242n3, 245n40
Emden, Jacob, 74, 80, 214n46
Emerson, Ralph Waldo, 13, 44, 87, 89–98, 190, 198, 223n10, 224n16, 225n40, 226n46, 226n55. *See also* American religion
empiricism, 22–23, 110, 126
energeia, 125
Engels, Friedrich, 211n60, 238n4
Enlightenment, 18, 39, 49, 66–68, 76, 110, 158, 204n16, 229n12
esoteric psychology, 21
ethical monotheism, 75
ethics, 9, 14, 40, 59, 101–2, 120–24, 141–43, 151–52, 155, 165, 170–73, 191
ethnopsychology, 105, 119, 124, 136. *See also* collective unconscious; psychology
exile, 7, 55, 60
Exodus, 57
exoteric esotericism, 48–49

Fackenheim, Emil, 122
Fechner, Gustav Theodor, 3
Feuerbach, Ludwig, 18, 25, 30, 90, 116, 161, 171
Fichte, Johann Gottlieb, 24, 30, 41, 45, 69
First World War, 10–11, 203n5
Foucault, Michel, 23, 83
Fourier, Charles, 159
Franck, Adolphe, 14, 64, 79–80, 84, 107, 152, 156, 158–59, 169, 221n77
Franco-Judaism, 158
Frank, Jacob, 219n33
Frankist movement, 69
Franks, Paul, 37, 49
Franz Joseph II, Emperor, 76
French revolutionary values, 79–80, 105, 158–59
Freud, Sigmund, 1, 33; early work of, 41–42; influence of, 10–11, 33, 49, 131, 149; and irrationalism, 209n21; Jewish identity, 203n3; legacy of, 1, 9, 132, 196; and literature, 111; reception of, 87, 106, 128, 199; and science, 204n11; and *Völkerpsychologie*, 136–37. *See also* dreamwork; psychoanalysis
Friedrich, Caspar David, 146
Funkenstein, Amos, 75, 84, 118
Fürst, Julius, 77

Gadamer, Georg, 137, 140
Gall, Franz Josef, 171
Galvani, Luigi, 179
Gans, Eduard, 67, 111
Garb, Jonathan, 203n4, 206n41
Geiger, Abraham, 44, 69, 80, 122
Geist, 14, 102, 111, 113–18, 138–39, 152, 154, 204n11. *See also* condensation; soul; *Völkerpsychologie*
Geisteswissenschaft, 65–66, 82–85, 140, 222n95
Gemeinschaft, 136, 191, 193
Genesis, 28, 53, 57–58, 114, 184
German idealism, 73, 94–96
German identity, 5, 40–41, 109, 111, 137
Gioberti, Vincenzo, 168
Globe (newspaper), 237n149
Gnosticism, 26, 56–57, 60, 96–97, 157, 188, 196, 210n32
Gnothi Sauton, oder Magazin zur Erfahrungsseelenkunde, 70
God: and the Absolute, 50–51, 53; communication with, 102; depictions of, 54–56, 72, 168, 178, 194–95; dwelling place of, 54; and Gnosticism, 26, 58, 60; and human nature, 30, 33; and the leap, 50–53, 215n56; limitlessness of, 17–18, 28, 192; names of, 78; and panentheism, 55; and progressive revelation, 170, 183; and self-consciousness, 59–60; and self-restriction, 97; and unknowability, 114. *See also* Holy of Holies; religion; *tsimtsum*
Gödde, Günter, 21
Goethe, Johann Wolfgang von, 23, 30, 146, 208nn16–17
Goldberg, Hillel, 176, 246n60

Gordin, Jacob, 205n16, 205n26
Görres, Joseph von, 46–47
Graetz, Heinrich, 40–41, 60, 69, 219n27, 221n67
grammar, 68–69. *See also* language
Greek philosophy, 204n16
Grossman, Maxine, 205n26
Guattari, Félix, 207n48

Habad, 50–51
Habermas, Jürgen, 4, 162, 242n91
Hadot, Pierre, 18
Haeckel, Ernst, 149–50, 215n58
Hagut, 247n99
Hamagid, 188
Hamilzahgi, Elyakim, 64, 81–82
Hare, Julius Charles, 224n22
Hartmann, Eduard von, 3, 9–15, 24, 82–83, 105–7, 136, 145–48, 151–52, 156–59, 161, 168–70, 177–78
Hasidism, 6, 9–10, 15, 50–52, 68–69, 117, 166, 171–73, 176–91, 194. *See also* Judaism
Haskalah, 64, 81–82, 118, 172, 249n129
Hatsefira, 214n49
Heath, John, 96
Hebrew, 17, 53, 64, 68
Hegel, Georg Wilhelm Friedrich, 14, 24, 31–33, 64, 71–72, 74, 109, 113–17, 124, 133, 149, 180
Heine, Heinrich, 67, 71
"Hep" riots, 66–67
Heraclitus, 18
Herbart, Johann Friedrich, 119, 124, 126–27, 129–31, 133, 154–55
Herder, Johann Gottfried von, 14, 23, 39, 109, 111–13, 119, 124, 171, 214n34, 229n12
Herrera, Abraham Cohen de, 56
Heschel, Abraham, 122
Heyse, Karl, 119
Hilaire, Auguste Théodore, 90, 225n23
Hillman, James, 110
Hinduism, 221n74
Hirsch, Emil, 100–101, 103
Hirsch, Samson Raphael, 42, 184, 248n109

Hirsch, Samuel Abraham, 45, 82, 215n27
Hirth, Georg, 133
historical psychology, 166
historiosophy, 166, 242n4
Hobsbawm, Eric, 203n5
Hoffmann, E. T. A., 49
Holy of Holies, 54, 58. *See also* God
Home, Henry, 203n2
human nature, 24, 30, 33, 40, 101
Humboldt, Alexander von, 128
Humboldt, Wilhelm von, 119, 124–26, 179
Hurwitz, Pinchas, 52–53
Hurwitz, Siegmund, 186
Husserl, Edmund, 153
hylic intellect, 175, 186

ibn Attar, Haim, 184
Idea, the, 31, 147, 152, 240n60
Idra Rabba, 180–81
individuality, 158, 193, 209n19. *See also* self
irrationality, 6, 12, 49, 63–65, 75, 151, 209n21. *See also* reason
Isaiah, book of, 216n77

Jacobi, Friedrich Heinrich, 193
Jakobson, Roman, 131
James, William, 166, 199
Janet, Paul, 3, 151
Janet, Pierre, 97, 156, 240n59
Jankélévitch, Vladimir, 53
Jaspers, Karl, 33
Jean Paul, 128–29, 234n63
Jellinek, Adolf, 64, 80–81
Jewish Enlightenment, 64, 81–82, 118, 172, 249n129
Jewish law, 38, 40, 57, 82, 103, 115
Jewish mysticism: appreciation of, 68; continuing influence of, 45; influence of, 19; and Oedipus complex, 203n3; and psychology, 65–66; scholarly attention to, 6–7, 13, 77–78; and the unconscious, 1–4. *See also* Kabbalah; mysticism; unconscious
Jewish Reform movement, 13, 41, 44–45, 88, 99–104

Jewish thought: development of, 37–38; and German philosophy, 73–74; reception in United States, 13; and universal truths, 2, 4, 12, 166
Jewish Times, 100
Jewish universalism, 13, 45–48, 82, 99–106
Joel, David, 75, 81, 221n77
Josephson-Storm, Jason, 205n25
Jost, Isaak Marcus, 221n67
Judaism: ambitions of, 168–69; coexistence with Christianity, 48, 85, 114, 167; and community, 107, 175–76; defense of, 2, 49, 145, 197–98; and Hinduism, 221n74; and magnetism, 179–80; and national identity, 5–6, 109; perceptions of, 20, 41, 43, 46, 66, 114–16, 121, 166; and progress, 41; and reason, 49, 60, 63; relevance of, 47–48, 70–71, 160, 165–66, 187–88; shared values of, 68–69; symbolism of, 35; theological centrality of the Temple in, 102–3. *See also* anti-Semitism; Hasidism; religion; *Wissenschaft des Judentums* (WdJ)
Jüdische Freischule, 70
Jugend (magazine), 133
Jung, Carl Gustav, 9, 11, 47, 49, 95–97, 99, 110, 135–36, 138, 146–47, 152, 173, 186, 190, 193–96, 242n3, 247n99
Junges Deutschland (group), 66

Kabbalah: and cosmogony, 18, 29; critics of, 34, 62, 68, 73–75; defense of, 72, 167, 182; depictions of, 33–34, 81; and exile, 55; familiarity with, 27–28; influence of, 4, 20, 34–35, 37, 54–55, 59–60, 89; interpretations of, 13, 27–28, 30, 75; and myth, 42; organization of, 78–79, 183; origins of, 76–77; and paganism, 39; perceptions of, 52–53, 189, 244n31; promotion of, 48, 54–55, 59–60, 65–66, 74, 79–81, 160–61, 169–70, 180–81; and reparation, 104; scholarly attention to, 6–7, 35, 37, 44, 63, 65–66, 70, 77–78, 82–85, 196, 206n41, 218n10; and spiritual development, 80; universal aspects of, 156–57; and the unknown, 52. *See also* Absolute, the; Jewish mysticism; mysticism; *tsimtsum*; *Wissenschaft des Judentums* (WdJ); Zohar
Kabbalah Centre, 104
Kalb, H. A., 212n5
Kallen, Horace, 251n10
Kant, Immanuel, 14, 21–24, 30, 41, 45, 67, 70–72, 91, 104, 115, 126, 146, 149–51, 153, 157, 170, 172, 181, 193
Kantianism, 65, 70–73, 181, 220n38
Kaplan, Mordecai, 50
Keith, George, 223n4
Kierkegaard, Søren, 211n60, 215n59, 224n14
Klages, Ludwig, 23
Kohler, Kauffman, 41, 46–47, 100
Kook, Rav Zvi Yehuda, 139, 188
Koyré, Alexandre, 210n30
Krause, Karl Friedrich, 215n70
Kristianpoller, Alexander, 206n44
Krochmal, Nachman, 14, 64, 73–75, 106, 111, 115–18, 188
Kunitz, Moses, 35

Lacan, Jacques, 8–9, 51, 61–62, 131–32, 196–97, 210n30
Lachelier, Jules, 96
Laforgue, Jules, 159
Lamennais, Félicité, 32, 211n63
Landauer, Gustav, 162–63
Landauer, Meyer, 38, 44, 51, 64, 77–79, 221n71
Lange, Friedrich Albert, 128
language, 110–12, 119, 123–25, 127–28, 131, 136–37, 142, 154, 160, 185, 192–93, 234n59, 248n110. *See also* grammar
Laplanche, Jean, 132
Lazarus, Moritz, 9–10, 14, 105–7, 113, 119–23, 127, 130, 136, 138, 140, 142, 145, 153–55, 190, 231n2, 236n110, 249n138
Le Bon, Gustave, 139
Lefin, Mendel, 172–73, 245n35
Left Hegelians, 72

Leibniz, Gottfried Wilhelm, 21–23, 94, 126–27, 153, 179, 203n2, 208n3
Leon, Juda. *See* Löwengard, Hirsch Maier
Leroux, Pierre, 237n149
Levinas, Emmanuel, 7, 170, 206n33, 217n94, 246n57
Lewkowitz, Albert, 204n16
Liebman, Joshua Loth, 11, 207n46
Lipps, Theodor, 4, 131, 161
literalism, 35
Locke, John, 21–22, 95–96, 126, 208n3
Lombroso, Cesare, 140
Löwengard, Hirsch Maier, 37–38, 42–44, 213n13
Löwy, Michael, 162
Ludwig I, King, 41
Lukács, Georg, 24, 44, 209n20
Luria, Isaac, 7, 27–28, 54–55
Lurianic Kabbalah, 53–56, 58–60, 104, 211n44
Luther, Martin, 121, 232n18
Luzzatto, Samuel David, 64, 221n77

Mach, Ernst, 161
Maggid of Mezeritch, 177, 182–87, 242n3
Maimon, Salomon, 30, 34, 67–68, 70
Maimonides, 74, 81, 116, 168, 175, 242n1
Maistre, Joseph de, 32, 211n63
Mann, Thomas, 151
Marcionism, 56–57, 216n78
Marcion of Sinope, 56
Marcus, Ahron, 15, 42, 64, 165, 177, 180–87, 190
Marr, Wilhelm, 122, 232n21
Marsh, James, 91
Marx, Karl, 116
Marxism, 24, 160–62, 189, 209n20
materialism, 49–50, 134–35, 138, 156, 166, 189
Mather, Increase, 223n4
Mauthner, Fritz, 143
Max II (king), 42
McGrath, Sean, 212n68
Mendelssohn, Moses, 67–68, 71, 103
Menorah Journal, 251n10
Merleau-Ponty, Maurice, 11

Mesmer, Anton, 179–80
messianism, 14, 58, 72–73, 160–62, 189
metaphysics, 3, 7, 9, 11–12, 30–31, 110, 118, 150, 153
Meyer, Michael, 221n67
Mieses, Fabius, 50
Mieses, Isaac, 50, 75
Mill, John Stuart, 222n95, 229n3 (chap. 4)
mimicry, 85
Mirandola, Pico della, 54
Mitnaggedim, 50
Mitteler Rebbe, 51
modernity, 2, 4, 6, 14, 17, 20, 60, 65, 71, 84, 96–97, 138, 163, 169
Molitor, Franz Joseph, 48–49
Monis, Judah, 223n4
monism, 14, 92, 145, 149–50, 152–53, 155, 157, 163, 188–89, 215n58
monotheism, 35–36, 47–48, 65, 100
Montesquieu, 109
Morais, Sabato, 231n3
More, Henry, 35, 94
Munk, Salomon, 80–81
Musar movement, 171–72, 176, 201, 244nn28–29, 246n60
mysticism: and ethics, 151–52; influence of, 198; perceptions of, 45, 65–66, 98, 155–57, 176–77; and philosophy, 31–32; and reason, 60, 68, 71–74; and self-knowledge, 29; and sexual content, 78–79; and solipsism, 194; and the soul, 49; and the unconscious, 1–2, 6. *See also* Jewish mysticism; Kabbalah
myth, 37–44, 109, 207n15

Nachträglichkeit, 52, 170, 243n23
Nahmanides, 102, 228n86
Nathan of Gaza, 57–59
national identity, 2, 105, 111–14, 120–21, 125, 137, 232n19, 249n127. *See also* collective unconscious
nature, 18, 24, 52, 101, 161
Nazism, 24, 43, 239n27
Neoplatonism, 39, 54–55, 93, 118, 206n33, 249n129

Neumann, Erich, 190, 195–96
New Age spirituality, 104
Nietzsche, Friedrich, 24, 56, 71, 137, 146, 149, 161, 192, 220n42, 238nn6–7
Nordau, Max, 139, 155, 236n132
not-I, 30–31, 59, 199. *See also* self

objectification, 134–35
Oedipus complex, 203n3
Ogren, Brian, 223n4
ontology, 88, 95–99, 158, 162, 250n139
Orientalism, 39, 73, 94, 195
Orthodoxy, 100, 104, 145, 176–77, 182
otherness, 7–8, 12–13, 53–57, 59–62, 113, 142, 199, 210n30
oversoul, 88–89, 92–95, 99, 226n46. *See also* collective unconscious; soul; world soul

paganism, 39, 43
panentheism, 55, 215n70
pantheism, 157, 163, 229n12
Papus, 157
Paul, Hermann, 140
Peirce, Charles Sanders, 89
Pentateuch, 44, 68, 78, 212n75
Perl, Joseph, 68, 77
pessimism, 150–52, 158–59, 169
petites perceptions, 22, 153–54, 179, 203n2. *See also* unconscious
phenomenology, 153, 194
philology, 137–38
philosophy: and becoming, 98–99; dominant traditions of, 99, 162; and language, 192–93; perceptions of, 1, 54, 67–68; perspectives of, 30, 79–80; and psychology, 3; and religion, 115–16
phrenology, 170–71
physics, 52, 126
Plato, 94
Plotinus, 89, 206n33
poetic universals, 14, 109–11, 129, 188
polytheism, 35–36, 39
Pontalis, Jean-Bertrand, 132
positivism, 3
pragmatism, 89
progressive revelation, 130, 170, 204n8

Proudhon, Pierre-Joseph, 159
Proust, Marcel, 198
Psalms, 25, 101
psychoanalysis, 3, 9, 33, 61–62, 128, 186, 206n38, 206n41, 228n1. *See also* Freud, Sigmund
psychology, 3, 30, 51, 65–66, 70, 84, 95–99, 110–11, 122–23, 126–27, 136–37, 140–43, 197. *See also* ethnopsychology

Quakers, 223n4
Qualität, 26
Quinet, Edgar, 168

racism, 101, 106, 137–38, 239n27
Ranke, Leopold von, 120
Ravaisson, Félix, 96
reason: binaries of, 32, 49, 64–65; broadening of, 104; and intuition, 29; and mysticism, 60, 63, 68, 71–74; and revelation, 102; and shared humanity, 12; value of, 158–59, 218n11. *See also* irrationality
Reconstructionist movement, 50, 214n50
Reform Judaism, 69, 99–104
religion: and consciousness, 19, 43–44; critics of, 11; defense of, 6, 9; and dogma, 42, 135; goals of, 115; intimate knowledge of, 39; and myth, 35, 37–38; and polytheism, 35–36; and science, 5, 15; and the state, 71–72, 148; and symbolism, 100, 102, 193. *See also* Christianity; God; Judaism
Renaissance, 204n16
Renan, Ernest, 121, 138, 168
repression, 33, 87, 127, 198. *See also* unconscious
retrospective unconscious, 9–10, 15, 107, 165–67, 176, 198, 206n42. *See also* unconscious
Reuchlin, Johannes, 27
Ribot, Théodule, 155
Richter, Jean-Paul. *See* Jean Paul
Ricœur, Paul, 4, 62
Rieff, Philip, 99

Rodgers, Daniel T., 224n14
Romanticism, 17–18, 21, 39, 94, 147, 161, 229n12
Rorty, Richard, 206n42
Rosenberg, Shimon Gershon, 197
Rosenkranz, Karl, 114
Rosenroth, Christian Knorr von, 56
Rosenzweig, Franz, 5, 33, 59, 177
Roth, Joseph, 43
Rubin, Salomon, 249n129
Russian Revolution of 1917, 178

Sabbatean movement, 69
Sacy, Antoine-Isaac Silvestre de, 73
Said, Edward, 73
Saint Martin, Louis Claude de, 211n63
Saladin, King, 242n1
Salanter, Israel, 165, 172–74, 176, 244nn29–30, 244n33
Sarug, Israel, 27–28, 54–56, 59
Schatz-Uffenheimer, Rivka, 183
Schelling, Friedrich Wilhelm Joseph von: critics of, 24, 56; and Hasidism, 51–52; influence of, 1, 3, 9, 11, 37–38, 44–45, 48, 50–51, 61–62, 99–100, 182; and irrationalism, 209n21; and Jewish emancipation, 213n13; legacy of, 4–5, 21, 88–90, 152, 166, 177, 188; and metaphysics, 30; mystical turn of, 31–35; and myth, 207n15; philosophy of creation, 52–53; reception of, 13, 42–44, 53–54, 61, 76, 93, 170; reliance on Jewish thought, 5
Scheuer, Abraham Naftali Hertz, 38
Schiller, Friedrich, 17
Schlegel, Friedrich, 111
Schneuri, Dovbaer, 51
Schneur Zalman of Liadi, 50
Scholem, Gershom, 6–7, 27, 48, 53–56, 59–63, 122, 160–62, 166, 176–77, 182–85, 189, 195, 215n56, 242n3, 247n99
Schopenhauer, Arthur, 22, 24, 148, 150–52, 157, 159, 180, 238n4
Schubert, Gotthilf Heinrich von, 49
Schulte, Christoph, 210n43
Science du Judaïsme, 158. See also *Wissenschaft des Judentums* (WdJ)
Second World War, 11, 196

self, 4–5, 29–30, 37, 59, 87–88, 101, 117, 152, 158, 210n30. See also individuality; not-I
self-knowledge, 29, 59
sexual drives, 24
Shagar, Rav, 197
Sharvit, Gilad, 203n3
Simmel, Georg, 14, 133–34, 142, 190, 235n103, 236n110
Sinai (journal), 100
Skolnik, Jonathan, 205n22
Slonimski, Hayyim Selig, 178, 246n72
Smith, Woodruff, 136, 236n110
socialism, 159
Society for the Culture and Science of Judaism, 67
solipsism, 194
Solovyov, Vladimir, 188, 249n127
somnambulism, 181
sophiology, 178, 188
Sossnitz, Joseph Judah Löb, 38, 50, 52
soul, 18, 25, 29–30, 49, 91, 101–2, 126–27, 179–80, 184, 204n11. See also *Geist*; oversoul; world soul
Soviet Union, 189
Spinoza, Baruch, 23–24, 188, 229n12
Sprung, 50–52, 214n49
Steinschneider, Moritz, 63–64, 73, 217n4
Steinthal, Heymann, 9–10, 14, 105–6, 113, 119–20, 123–24, 127, 131, 136–38, 140, 145, 153–55, 190, 229n3 (chap. 4), 231n2, 236n110
Stiles, Ezra, 223n4
Stoecker, Alfred, 121
subconscious, 3, 156, 240n59. See also unconscious
sublime, 18, 92, 114–15
Sulamith (journal), 76, 220–21
Swedenborg, Emanuel, 98
Szold, Henrietta, 122

tabula rasa, 208n3
Talmud, 40, 77, 85, 100, 120, 172, 178, 206n44
Targum Neofiti, 54
Tauler, Johannes, 25
Taylor, Charles C., 205n25
Taylor, Mark, 224n14

tehiru, 57–59
Tevunah, 173, 244n33
transcendence, 37
transcendentalism, 93, 224n14
Treitschke, Heinrich von, 106–7, 121
Trilling, Lionel, 111, 128
tsimtsum, 5, 7–8, 27–28, 48–49, 53–60, 128, 197. See also God; Kabbalah

unconscious: and the Absolute, 31, 34; and artistic production, 208n16; boundaries of, 22, 175; and condensation, 128–29; and creation, 51–52, 59, 183; and the daemonic, 23–24; foreshadowing of, 165; and otherness, 80; and pessimism, 151–52; and politics, 156, 198; popularization of term, 30, 88, 91, 203n2; pre-Freudian development of, 1–3, 10–11, 17–18, 161, 172; scholarly attention to, 82–85, 197; structure of, 132, 134, 147–48. See also abyss; Jewish mysticism; *petites perceptions*; repression; retrospective unconscious; subconscious
Ungrund, 5, 12, 25–27, 29–30, 34, 37, 191–92, 250n144. See also abyss
United States, 13, 45, 100, 138, 199. See also American religion
universal imagination, 109
universalism, 4, 40, 45–48, 70–73, 82, 99–106, 119, 122–23, 130, 137, 139, 145, 166, 188
universals, 14, 71, 109–11, 118–19, 129, 188
unknowability, 17–18, 33, 114
Ursprung, 51

Vedic tradition, 93–94
Verdichtung, 128–32, 235n82
Verein für Kultur und Wissenschaft der Juden, 67, 218n19
Vico, Giovanni Battista, 14, 109–11, 118–19, 124, 128, 188–89, 231n2
Vienna Secession, 133
Vital, Haim, 27, 54
vitalism, 23
Völkerpsychologie, 14, 106–7, 119–43, 145, 153–54, 191, 231n2. See also *Geist*

Volksgeist, 106, 118
Volozhin Yeshiva, 188
Voltaire, 109

Waitz, Theodor, 236n110
Walter, Balthasar, 27
Weil, Gotthold, 217n4
Weir, Todd, 145
Wellek, René, 224n22
Whyte, Lancelot, 203n2
Wilkins, Charles, 94
William, Augustus, 224n22
Windelband, Wilhelm, 161
Wise, Isaac, 100
Wissenschaft des Judentums (WdJ), 13, 60–61, 63–82, 137, 160, 186–87, 195, 217n4. See also Judaism; Kabbalah; *Science du Judaïsme*
Wittgenstein, Ludwig, 143
Wolf, Immanuel, 63, 67, 76
Wolff, Christian, 21–22, 172
Wolfson, Elliot, 30, 58–59, 202
world soul, 44, 93–94, 114, 226n51. See also oversoul; soul
World War I, 10–11, 203n5
World War II, 11, 196
wrath, 56–58
Wundt, Wilhelm, 83, 140–41, 161, 185, 236n110

Yochai, Shimon bar, 212nn75–76
Young Germany, 66
Young Hegelians, 72

Zeitschrift für Völkerpsychologie und Sprachwissenschaft (*Journal of Ethnopsychology and Linguistics*), 119, 124, 139
Zevi, Sabbatai, 50, 57, 74, 166, 219n33, 242n3
Zionism, 7, 122, 139, 248n125
Žižek, Slavoj, 61
Zohar, 35, 57–58, 68, 74–75, 78–79, 180–81, 212nn75–76, 219n27, 221n71, 221n77. See also Kabbalah
Zunz, Leopold, 63, 65, 73, 80, 85, 116, 137, 219n23

www.ingramcontent.com/pod-product-compliance
Lightning Source LLC
Chambersburg PA
CBHW022035290426
44109CB00014B/868